Hedge Funds

Wiley Finance Series

Hedge Funds

Quantitative Insights

François-Serge Lhabitant

John Wiley & Sons, Ltd

Other Wiley Editorial Offices

John Wiley & Sons Inc., 111 River Street, Hoboken, NJ 07030, USA

Jossey-Bass, 989 Market Street, San Francisco, CA 94103-1741, USA

Wiley-VCH Verlag GmbH, Boschstr. 12, D-69469 Weinheim, Germany

John Wiley & Sons Australia Ltd, 33 Park Road, Milton, Queensland 4064, Australia

John Wiley & Sons (Asia) Pte Ltd, 2 Clementi Loop #02-01, Jin Xing Distripark, Singapore 129809

John Wiley & Sons Canada Ltd, 22 Worcester Road, Etobicoke, Ontario, Canada M9W 1L1

Wiley also publishes its books in a variety of electronic formats. Some content that appears
in print may not be available in electronic books.

Library of Congress Cataloging-in-Publication Data

Lhabitant, François-Serge.
Hedge funds : quantitative insights / by François-Serge Lhabitant.
    p.   cm.
Includes bibliographical references and index.
ISBN 0-470-85667-X (alk. paper)
1. Hedge funds.   I. Title.
HG4530.L472   2004
332.64′5–dc22   2004002909

British Library Cataloguing in Publication Data

A catalogue record for this book is available from the British Library

ISBN 13: 978-0-470-85667-3 (H/B)

Typeset in 10/12pt Times by TechBooks, New Delhi, India
Printed and bound in Great Britain by Antony Rowe Ltd, Chippenham, Wiltshire
This book is printed on acid-free paper responsibly manufactured from sustainable forestry
in which at least two trees are planted for each one used for paper production.

Contents

Foreword by Mark Anson[1]

When writing a book on hedge funds, the inevitable questions are: "Where to begin?" and "What to include?" It's not an easy task, yet François-Serge manages to accomplish the difficult, even the near-impossible. Writing a book that provides an in-depth quantitative approach to hedge funds that is simultaneously accessible to the practitioner and robust enough for the academic, is a balancing act rarely achieved.

As both an investor in hedge funds as well as a sometimes researcher of their empirical impact on portfolio management, I fall someplace in between the practitioner and the academic. Therefore, it is a relief to me to have a textbook that can bridge both worlds of hedge fund management. This book is both suitable as an introduction to the risks and benefits of hedge fund investing as well as a reference book for the empirical analysis of those risks and benefits.

Each chapter holds value to the end user, but allow me to select a few chapters that have particular importance to the investor. Chapter 5, Databases, Indices and Benchmarks; Chapter 8, Asset Pricing Models; and Chapter 11, Strategic Asset Allocation are critical to the key decision of how much of an investment portfolio to allocate to hedge funds. It is important for investors to note that there is no complete database of the hedge fund universe. The composition of hedge fund indices varies greatly. Furthermore, hedge fund benchmarks are rife with data biases. Consequently, the asset allocation decision can vary greatly based on the simple choice of the hedge fund benchmark. Chapter 5 provides an excellent dissertation of the problems of hedge fund index construction as well as a great overview of the various hedge fund indices available to investors.

Chapter 8 provides a comprehensive review with respect to an ongoing quest for academics and investors alike: trying to quantify the returns from hedge fund managers into an asset pricing model. Many researchers have approached this topic from many different directions. The author provides a complete review of both linear and non-linear models as well as single and multi-factor models. The science of hedge fund asset pricing is still developing, but François-Serge's summary is state of the art.

Chapters 5 and 8 then dovetail nicely with Chapter 11 on asset allocation. Every investor in hedge funds must sooner or later face the question of: "How much to invest?" Most investors use a mean–variance approach to asset allocation. However, as demonstrated in Chapter 8, hedge fund returns can be distinctly non-normal. Therefore, in Chapter 11, the author provides

[1] Mark Anson, Ph.D., CFA, CPA, Esq., is the Chief Investment Officer of the California Public Employees' Retirement System (CalPERS). The views expressed in this foreword reflect those of Mark Anson and not those of his employer, the California Public Employees' Retirement System.

alternative methods to the mean–variance approach for determining the optimal allocation to hedge funds.

Throughout the book, François-Serge provides numerous examples to highlight his points. Nothing is left to guesswork by the reader – every critical equation is spelled out and demonstrated by an example. While the book is sometimes quantitative, the math is not burdensome. Further, the numerous examples help to alleviate this burden. I enjoyed reading this book, and I look forward to using a copy of it as a handy reference to chart my way through the hedge fund universe.

Introduction

About two years ago, when I finished writing my first book *Hedge Funds: Myths and Limits*, most of my university and research acquaintances as well as my colleagues at Union Bancaire Privée were actually quite surprised. How could a quantitative person like me write a descriptive primer to the world of hedge funds, with no equations, no models and no technical jargon? Just about everything they ever wanted to know about hedge funds but were afraid to ask ... The numerous positive reactions, congratulations and thanks that I received subsequently confirmed my initial perception that there was a major need for this type of primer. Thanks to this first book, knowledge and understanding of hedge funds are no longer the key barriers to their accessibility.

The present book, contrary to some expectations, is not a revised edition of *Hedge Funds: Myths and Limits*. This time, as its title suggests, the focus is on a topic that I briefly introduced in the first book, namely quantitative analysis of hedge funds. Both topics are my areas of expertise, although that is a word I hesitate to use. Indeed, I sometimes really wonder how some people can dare call themselves "experts". The more I delve into hedge funds the more I realize that there is so much to learn, vindicating the claim that expertise is a relative concept. But that is another story.

Coming back to the subject of this book, I have to admit that the task of writing it turned out to be much more challenging than I had anticipated.

QUANTITATIVE INABILITY

My first aim was to make this book accessible and understandable, the prerequisite material being simply ... my previous book. This was obviously a challenge, due to the self-perceived inability of many people to work with numbers – the so-called "quantitative inability". Of course, this belief must somehow be overcome if the power offered by quantitative tools is to be exploited.

Unlike most "quants", I strongly believe that quantitative techniques that lack an intuitive explanation should not be used. People using quantitative techniques should understand what they are doing, perhaps not in the deepest mathematical detail, but at least in a general sense and sufficiently well to be able to analyze the results. In a sense, the situation is very similar to that of a person's attitude towards a car. Most people are unable to build a car from scratch or to repair one, but they know how to use it and, more importantly, how not to use it.[1] To reach that point, they had to study and practice a little bit. The same applies to quantitative techniques. To take advantage of the power they offer, you will have to read and practice a little. For that purpose this book will, I hope, be a useful guide.

If you still feel the need for encouragement, remember that quantitative analysis is really not the same as mathematics – although ability in formal mathematics is, of course, a form of quantitative literacy. Quantitative analysis is simply the ability to see meaning in numbers. Great care has been taken in this book to illustrate theoretical concepts with simple examples. You should thus be able to reproduce these examples in order to check your understanding of the methodology applied.

QUANTITATIVE VERSUS QUALITATIVE

The second challenge I faced in writing this book was more cultural. In the hedge fund industry, most people see an opposition between quantitative research and qualitative research, and are of course more supportive of the latter. The two are indeed by nature very different. Quantitative research is usually perceived as being synonymous with statistical techniques, an area that most of us love to hate and that we dropped as soon as we had the chance at school. Centered on deductive reasoning, it is by definition objective, seeks explanatory laws, and measures what it assumes to be a static reality in the hope of developing new universal laws. It is frequently associated with logical positivism, a philosophical doctrine according to which scientific knowledge is the only kind of factual knowledge. Qualitative research, on the other hand, has a long tradition going back to Aristotelian epistemology based on the development of descriptive categories, on inductive reasoning and on the explanation of objects by intentions, aims and purposes. It is subjective by nature, aims at in-depth description, and explores what is assumed to be a dynamic reality without any claim to universality.

It is not surprising, therefore, that most people feel more at ease with qualitative topics than with quantitative ones. However, the consequences are often dramatic. Many investors and financial intermediaries have set up a Great Wall of China between quantitative and qualitative analysts. The former group act as objective observers who neither participate in nor influence the investments or the strategy, while the second group can learn the most about a situation by participating and/or being immersed in it, e.g. visiting and talking to managers. This exemplifies what philosophers call an "either/or dichotomy". Research must be either quantitative or qualitative. There are no other possibilities, despite the fact that there are several kinds of quantitative research and several divisions of qualitative research.

For many years, this attitude was perfectly in tune with an investment process that was essentially a subjective, qualitative, bottom-up, fund-picking process rather than an objective, quantitative, top-down, asset allocation one. Consequently, the popular conception of quantitative analysis has often been one of screening funds based on any number of statistical criteria, including annual return, volatility, Sharpe ratio, etc., and producing flashy marketing graphics and presentations. In a sense, a façade that is only there to give an impression that something is being done and whose only purpose is to draw investor capital.

Needless to say, I strongly disagree with this view. From both experience and philosophical training, I have learned to be wary of such dualistic thought. I believe quantitative research and qualitative research are at the opposite ends of a continuum of research techniques, all of which

---

[1] Obviously, given the way an increasing number of reckless drivers behave on the roads these days, we may have to reconsider this example in any future edition of this book. We sincerely hope the contagion will not spread to quantitative analysts in the future.

are appropriate depending on the research objective. Relying exclusively either on qualitative judgment or on quantitative models for hedge fund investing is a dangerous proposition. Both approaches need to be used in combination: qualitative research can provide the answer to certain kinds of questions in certain conditions, and quantitative can do so for others. For example, placing confidence in a manager without ever meeting him face to face and visiting his operations is almost unthinkable. So is building up a portfolio without a quantitative model to control risk. Therefore, instead of ignoring, defending or justifying qualitative or quantitative research, effort should focus on understanding why and when to use one or the other, or both. I sincerely hope that this book will help to propagate this line of thought.

ACADEMICS VERSUS PRACTITIONERS

The third difficulty I faced in writing this book sprang from the strong opposition that exists between academics and practitioners. Predictably, neither side really understands or even tries to understand the purpose or motivation of the other. At the root of the conflict, there is a fundamental difference: practitioners look to the future and forecast. They want to know what to do now that will provide an acceptable result tomorrow. Consequently, practitioners' models rely entirely on intuition, are not validated by any type of established theory and are frequently changed in line with the reality of the market. Academics, in contrast, seek to understand how and why things work, and the only way to explain how things work is often to look back. Consequently, academics' models may be very good at explaining but they are usually very poor at forecasting, with the result that little value is attached to them by practitioners.[2]

Once again, I strongly disagree with this attitude. Being both a practitioner and an academic, I believe that, when intelligently thought out, academic approaches may be of value to practitioners. The academic approach helps in understanding how a system works. Understanding the why, where and how is always better than blindly applying a rule of thumb. In most cases, the rule of thumb does not exist, or will end up failing dismally. Hence, it is only once the academic world has developed an understanding of a system that practical heuristic decision techniques should follow. Some information, knowledgeably interpreted, is better than no information, and we cannot invest prudently without some guideposts from the past. But we cannot intelligently assess the reliability of these guideposts unless we have the current and ongoing personal knowledge of the hedge fund manager that only a practitioner will have. This shows once again that the existing dichotomies between qualitative and quantitative, practice and academia have no raison d'être.

Practitioners and academics have to learn to understand and work with one another. The academic is almost always looking backward, seeking to understand and explain. The practitioner looks forward, seeking to forecast. If the two would listen to one another, the result would be an understanding of the complete picture, both forward and backward. Unfortunately, in the complex and secretive world of hedge funds, academic research was for long quite limited due to the lack of data; it remained confined to universities and was communicated by word of mouth. With the proliferation of hedge fund databases and websites, quantitative information on hedge funds has now become more readily available. And the development of specialized journals (e.g. *Journal of Alternative Investments*) and research centers has finally allowed academics and practitioners to collaborate. I sincerely hope that this book will also help to propagate

---

[2] We are amazed when we hear practitioners claim that history and statistics are worthless, and that past performance tells us nothing about how a hedge fund will perform in the future. Surprisingly or not, the same people usually select the funds that had the best historical returns, regardless of their strategy.

this line of thought and fill the gap between the academic theories of the last 50 years and the practicalities of hedge fund investing in the twenty-first century.

OBJECTIVE, TARGET AUDIENCE AND CONTENT

This book was written primarily for practitioners, including portfolio managers, qualitative and quantitative analysts, consultants, marketers and investors – both institutional and private. It could also prove useful to final-year undergraduates and MBA students who want to get a better view of what is going on in the hedge fund world and extend their knowledge beyond the confines of "improving the efficient frontier".

The book is largely self-contained, and is divided into three parts. The first part deals with the measurement of risk-adjusted returns for hedge funds. The focus is not on determining whether hedge funds outperform or underperform traditional markets. It is rather on understanding the real meaning of performance statistics used by hedge fund managers and quantitative analysts. Chapter 1 summarizes the current state of the hedge fund industry as well as the essential qualitative characteristics of its major investment strategies. Chapter 2 describes the particular problems encountered during the collection of net asset values and the calculation of simple return statistics. Chapter 3 gives an overview of performance statistics, with a particular focus on those that are of concern to practitioners but are rarely treated in finance or statistics textbooks (drawdown, downside deviation, skewness, kurtosis, shortfall probability, upside and downside participation, gain–loss ratios, etc.). Chapter 4 presents a series of risk-adjusted performance measures and compares their strengths and weaknesses. Finally, Chapter 5 deals with the problems associated with the use of historical data in the case of hedge funds, particular attention being devoted to hedge fund databases, hedge fund indices and benchmarks.

The second part of this book leaves the field of descriptive statistics to discover the challenges of understanding the risk exposures of hedge funds, and subsequently, their return drivers. This field has effectively become a rather important and fertile area of academic research, but a lot still remains to be explored and discovered. Hence, we provide an overview of existing research and tools, and suggest several directions for future work. Chapter 6 reviews the essentials of correlation and covariance. Chapter 7 surveys simple and multiple linear regressions as well as alternative regression approaches (non-linear, stepwise and non-parametric). It also examines in detail the dangers of misspecification when using regression analysis. Chapter 8 examines the asset pricing models commonly applied to hedge funds, ranging from traditional linear models to new and promising approaches that basically consider hedge funds as option portfolios on traditional asset classes. The latter technique allows dealing simultaneously with non-linear instruments and non-normal return distributions. Finally, Chapter 9 covers style analysis, a technique that captures the non-linearity inherent in hedge fund returns by including hedge fund indices as regressors.

The third and last part of this book enters the field of portfolio construction and asset allocation. Chapter 10 revisits the benefits of hedge fund investing. Chapter 11 discusses asset allocation and the various ways investors should rationally consider to include hedge funds in their portfolios. Finally, Chapter 12 extensively discusses risk measurement and management, using techniques such as value at risk, Monte Carlo simulation, extreme value theory and the analysis of marginal and component risks.

There are no proprietary information or secret insights buried in this book. Just what it takes to be a serious investor in the world of hedge funds today.

Acknowledgments

I would naturally like to thank all the individuals who helped me with this book, and in particular the invaluable editorial assistance of Ian Hamilton, whose reviews and comments have helped me to clarify and define my thoughts in plain English. I also benefited from the comments and insights of Pascal Botteron, Shelley Collum, Andrew Green, Joseph Hanein, Nicolas Laporte, Michelle Learned de Piante Vicin, Esther May-Rodrigo, Jill Monney and Cédric Perret Gentil.

Writing a book and simultaneously holding a challenging job requires the unstinting support of the book's publisher. I wish to thank the staff at John Wiley & Sons, particularly Samantha Whittaker, Patrica Morrison and Carole Millett, for their patience for missed deadlines and enthusiasm in bringing this project to a successful conclusion.

Finally, I owe the biggest debt of gratitude to my family, whose forbearance I have tried. Once again, this book was written using time that was literally stolen from them. In particular, thanks to my wife who has tolerated what this book has done to my schedule, my dark and somber disposition as well as my temper for more than a year.

Naturally, I must stress that the opinions expressed in this book represent solely my viewpoint and may not reflect the opinions or activities of any organization with which I am associated. All errors and omissions remain my own responsibility.

It goes without saying that this book should not be taken as an investment recommendation or as a solicitation. In particular, the hedge funds whose names are mentioned explicitly in this book were taken as representative examples, but are not positively or negatively recommended in a given portfolio. Anyone interested in investing in hedge funds should first seek professional *and independent* advice.

Please address any comments or suggestions to me at f@lhabitant.net

Part I
Measuring Return and Risk

1
Characteristics of Hedge Funds

I don't play the game by a particular set of rules; I look for changes in the rules of the game.
A global macro manager

While their mainstream popularity seems to be a new phenomenon, hedge funds have been around for more than 50 years. Indeed, Alfred Winslow Jones, journalist, sociologist and fund manager, is credited with establishing the first hedge fund as a general partnership in 1949.[1] He operated in complete secrecy until 1966. Then, an article penned by Carol J. Loomis in the April edition of *Fortune Magazine*, entitled "The Jones that Nobody Keeps Up With", exposed to the public his unique and highly successful strategy ("speculative instruments for conservative purposes"), along with his truly astounding return rates. Since then, the number of hedge funds and the size of their assets have soared, particularly since the early 1990s. Estimates suggest there are now over 6000 active hedge funds managing around $600 billion in assets, compared with the 68 funds that existed in 1984.

Several factors may explain the extraordinary development of hedge funds over recent years. First of all, there was the unprecedented wealth creation that occurred during the equity bull market of the 1990s. That significantly expanded the base of "sophisticated" investors, especially high net worth private investors, and fundamentally altered the way people in the workaday world viewed their money and finances.

In addition, there was an unprecedented generational shift of wealth through inheritance, as the parents of baby boomers progressively left their assets to their children. These new investors were typically more sophisticated and had a higher tolerance for risk than the previous generation, but were also more demanding in terms of investment performance. This boded well for hedge funds and other alternative investments, which generally targeted higher absolute returns thanks to their flexibility and lack of constraints.

It was also at this time that the first institutional investors started showing a greater interest in hedge funds. In particular, in September 1999, the pension fund CalPERS raised the ceiling on its alternative investments allocation to $11.0 billion, that is, 6% of its total assets. This amount included about $1.0 billion specifically allocated to hedge funds.

After March 2000, the growth of the hedge fund industry continued. However, the motives for investing had changed dramatically: investors were then looking for an effective means of diversification to protect their capital from falling equity markets and depressed bond yields. In addition, sub-par performance in traditional asset categories started luring institutional investors toward absolute return strategies, and more specifically hedge funds. Until then, alternative investments had primarily focused on private equity and real estate.

The needs of these new investors – quite different from those of the wealthy private clients – triggered a process that led to several changes in the hedge fund industry. Many hedge funds

---

[1] Ziemba (2003) also traces early unofficial hedge funds, such as Keynes Chest Fund, etc., that existed in the 1920s to 1940s.

became more mature, and put in place stable investment processes, lower leverage, improved transparency and effective risk management to satisfy the high standards and rigorous selection processes of large institutions. In addition, many traditional financial institutions began to develop funds of hedge funds as part of their global product range, and offered them to their retail and affluent clients.

The total assets now managed by hedge funds may still seem small with respect to the $3.8 trillion allocated to more traditional strategies by institutional investors alone, or the $6.3 trillion of assets under management in the mutual fund industry. But the double-digit growth in asset size and the increasing popularity of hedge funds have also brought about a change in the attitude of regulators, who now regularly scrutinize the secretive world of alternative investments on both sides of the Atlantic Ocean. Nevertheless, the increased market volatility, the corporate activity and the extreme valuations (both on the upside and on the downside) continue to offer unrivaled opportunities for talented portfolio managers to exploit anomalies in the markets. As a consequence, the number of hedge funds should keep growing, and their strategies become more prominent and more popular in the near future.

1.1 WHAT ARE HEDGE FUNDS?

Originally, hedge funds were so named because their investment strategy aimed at systematically reducing risk with respect to the direction of the market by pooling investments in a mix of short and long market positions. However, in today's world, many "hedge funds" are not actually hedged, and the term has become a misnomer.

Surprisingly, though, there is no commonly accepted definition of what exactly a hedge fund is. To confuse matters further, the term "hedge fund" has different meanings on each side of the Atlantic. In Europe, a "hedge fund" denotes any offshore investment vehicle whose strategy goes beyond buying and holding stocks or bonds and that has an absolute (i.e. non-benchmark-related) performance goal. In the United States, a hedge fund is typically a domestic limited partnership that is not registered with the Securities and Exchange Commission (SEC) and whose manager is rewarded by an incentive fee and has a broad array of securities and investment strategies at his disposal.

In this book, we have adopted the following pragmatic definition as a starting point:

Hedge funds are privately organized, loosely regulated and
professionally managed pools of capital not widely available to the public

The private nature of hedge funds is the key issue in this definition, and we believe that most of the other characteristics of hedge funds follow directly from it. Indeed, as long as the general public has no access to a private pool,[2] regulators do not consider the pool as a traditional investment vehicle (e.g. a SICAV, an OPCVM, a mutual fund, etc.) and conclude that there is no need to regulate it or require regular specific disclosure. This makes sense, because the pool only caters to high net worth individuals and institutions through private placements, and these investors are likely to be educated enough to assess the risk of their own investments.

---

[2] What constitutes the "general public" varies from one country to another. For instance, in the United States, the Securities Act of 1933 allows securities to be offered to "accredited investors". The term "accredited investor" includes individuals with a minimum of $200 000 in annual income or $300 000 in annual income with their spouses, or a minimum of $1 000 000 in net assets. It also includes most organized entities with over $5 000 000 in assets, including registered investment companies.

Consequently:

- The pool is not subject to the requirements imposed on registered investment companies and, therefore, its manager may pursue any type of investment strategy. In particular, he may concentrate its portfolio in a handful of investments, use leverage, short selling and/or derivatives, and even invest in illiquid or non-listed securities. This is in total contrast to mutual funds, which are highly regulated and do not have the same breadth of investment instruments at their disposal.
- The pool manager has the primary goal of achieving a target rate of return, whatever happens on the market. This is what is meant by "absolute return". Falling markets are no more an excuse for poor performance, as the manager has the latitude to go short if he wants to.
- To attract the most skilled managers in the industry, the pool offers some performance fees (typically 20% or more of the hedge fund's annual profits) rather than asset-based fees (typically 1% or 2% of the assets). Assuming a 5% net trading profit for a hedge fund, the total fee would be equal to 200 basis points (1% management fee, plus 20% of the 5% performance) per annum. This would amount to more than five times the fees for most traditional, active equity products. But high fees will also attract managers with poorly established and executed strategies, potentially resulting in grim surprises for their investors. Hence, most hedge funds request their manager to invest a large fraction of his personal wealth in the fund alongside other investors. In addition, a hurdle rate of return must usually be achieved or any previous losses recouped before the performance fee is paid.
- To allow managers to focus on investments and performance rather than on cash management, the pool may impose long-term commitments and a minimum notice time for any redemption by its investors. This feature also provides the hedge funds with the flexibility to invest in securities that are relatively illiquid from the long-term point of view.
- Finally, as it is almost unregulated, the pool does not have to report and disclose its holdings and positions.[3] This feature contributed significantly to the mystery that surrounded hedge funds, a trait that attracted individual investors while at the same time keeping institutional investors away. However, institutional investors are gaining ground in obtaining greater transparency and thus are getting increasingly involved in hedge fund investing.

1.2 INVESTMENT STYLES

Although the term "hedge funds" is often used generically, in reality hedge funds are not all alike. In fact, there exist a plethora of investment styles with very different approaches and objectives, and the returns, volatilities and risk vary enormously according to the fund managers, the target markets and the investment strategies. Some hedge funds may be non-directional and less volatile than traditional bond or equity markets, while others may very well be completely directional and display a much higher volatility. Many managers even pretend to have their own, unique investment styles. Therefore, "one size fits all" does not apply in the evaluation process or in the arena of risk management.

As it is critical to have a basic understanding of the underlying hedge fund strategies and their differences in order to develop a coherent plan to exploit the opportunity offered by hedge

---

[3] Of course, if a hedge fund holds large public equity positions, the fund manager, like any other large institutional manager, has to publicly disclose those positions. The disclosure, however, does not necessarily provide significant insight into any particular hedge fund's portfolio or strategy, because the manager is permitted to aggregate all clients' holdings into one report. In addition, separate disclosure is not required for short and debt positions.

funds, consultants, investors and managers alike often segregate the hedge fund market into a range of investment styles. Unfortunately, there is no accepted norm to classify the different hedge fund strategies, and each consultant, investor, manager or hedge fund data provider may use his own classification. In the following, for the sake of simplicity, we have classified hedge funds into four main strategies: tactical trading, equity long/short, event-driven and relative value arbitrage. A fifth category comprises funds that follow more than one strategy as well as funds of funds. We do not claim that this classification is better than existing ones. It is just a working tool that is compatible with most existing classifications.

1.2.1   The tactical trading investment style

The tactical trading investment style refers to strategies that speculate on the direction of market prices of currencies, commodities, equities and/or bonds on a systematic or discretionary basis. Global macro investing and commodity trading advisors (CTAs) are the predominant styles in this category.

Global macro managers tend to make leveraged, directional, opportunistic investments in global currency, equity, bond and commodity markets on a discretionary basis. They usually rely on a top-down global approach and base their trading views on fundamental economic, political and market factors. Their portfolios are large in size but concentrated, relying heavily on derivatives (options, futures and swaps). Global macro managers are by no means homogenous in the specific strategies they employ, but their goal tends to be high returns with a more liberal attitude toward risk than other hedge fund categories. Due to their discretionary approach, the quality of the manager is the sole key to a fund's success.

Commodity trading advisors and *managed futures managers* primarily trade listed commodity and financial futures contracts on behalf of their clients. As with global macro managers, CTAs are by no means homogenous, but are usually split into two groups: systematic traders and discretionary traders. Systematic traders believe that future price movements in all markets may be more accurately anticipated by analyzing historical price movements within a quantitative framework. Hence, they rely heavily on computer-generated trading signals to maintain a systematic and disciplined approach, and often use multiple systems in order to reduce volatility and produce more stable returns. In contrast, discretionary traders base their trading decisions on fundamental and technical market analysis, as well as on their experience and trading skills developed over the years (Figure 1.1).

1.2.2   The equity long/short style

As their title indicates, long/short equity managers invest in equities, and combine long investments with short sales to reduce but not eliminate market exposure. Indeed, long/short strategies are not automatically market neutral. Most funds tend to have a net long exposure (more long gross exposure than short gross exposure), which implies that they can have significant correlation with traditional markets, and therefore experience large downturns at exactly the same times as major market downturns. However, a few funds also aggressively use their ability to be net short.

The long/short equity style can be divided into several sub-strategies:

- Regionally or industry focused managers specialize in a region (e.g. Asia, Europe), a country (e.g. the United States) or a specific industry (e.g. technology), while global managers can invest worldwide.

Compare to Ansem p. 35

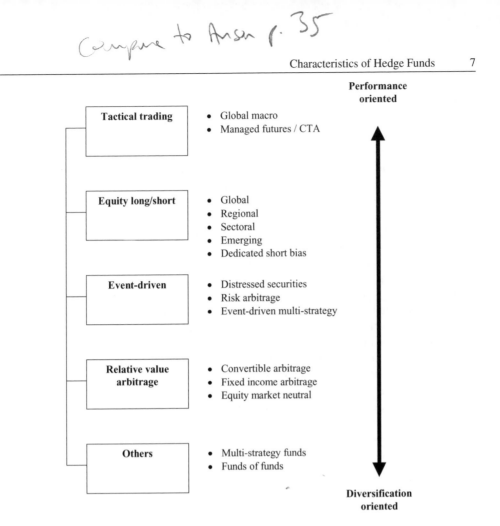

Figure 1.1   The various hedge fund strategies

- Dedicated short managers only use short positions. In a sense, they are the mirrors of traditional long-only managers. They suffered greatly during the bull market of the 1990s but put up a better overall performance during the bear market of the 2000s.
- Emerging market funds invest in all types of securities in emerging countries, including equities, bonds and sovereign debt. While many investors avoid investing in regions where information is scant, accounting standards are weak, political and economic turmoil is prevalent and experienced management is scarce, others see these as opportunities that can result in undetected, undervalued and under-researched securities. Emerging market hedge funds typically tend to be more volatile than developed market long/short equity funds. Because many emerging markets neither allow short selling nor offer viable futures or other derivative products with which to hedge, these funds often employ a long-biased strategy.
- Market timers vary their long/short exposure in response to market factors within a short period of time.

1.2.3   The event-driven style

Event-driven strategies focus on debt, equity or trade claims from companies that are in a particular stage of their life cycle, such as spin-offs, mergers and acquisitions, bankruptcy reorganizations, re-capitalization and share buybacks. Distressed securities and risk arbitrage are the predominant styles in this category.

Distressed securities funds focus on debt or equity of companies that are, or are expected to be, in financial or operational difficulty. This may involve reorganizations, bankruptcies, distressed sales and other corporate restructurings. The securities of such companies generally trade at substantial discounts, because of regulatory issues (many investors are unable to hold below investment grade securities), lack of analysts' coverage, low market liquidity and irrational fears of private investors. Distressed security specialists analyze and buy these securities when they perceive a turnaround. They take on credit and liquidity risk, and wait for these securities to appreciate in value after a restructuring is complete. Some managers may hedge with put options on the underlying market; others may even take a strategic holding in the firm and become actively involved in the restructuring. Hence, the distressed securities funds are long term in nature and have long redemption periods.

Merger arbitrage, also referred to as *risk arbitrage*, involves investments in event-driven situations that include a merger or acquisition, including leveraged buyouts, mergers and hostile takeovers. A typical trade within this style is to buy stock of the company being acquired while shorting the stock of the acquirer. Even though the transaction may be publicly announced, there is still a spread to be made following regulatory acceptance, etc. Hence, the most important risk to this style is deal breakage after the announcement.

Event-driven multi-strategy funds draw upon multiple themes, including risk arbitrage, distressed securities and occasionally other themes such as investments in micro and small capitalization public companies that are raising money in private capital markets (regulation D). Fund managers often shift assets between strategies in response to market opportunities.

1.2.4   The relative value arbitrage style

Relative value arbitrage strategies attempt to capitalize on relative pricing discrepancies between related instruments, including equities, debt, options and futures. The general theme among these strategies is a bet that two securities or market prices will converge over time.

Arbitrage is usually a two-sided strategy involving the simultaneous purchase and sale of related securities that are mispriced compared to each other. Managers using this strategy may utilize mathematical, fundamental or technical analysis to determine misvaluations. Over time the instrument's mispricing is expected to return to its theoretical or fair value.

Managers following the *convertible arbitrage* style seek to exploit pricing anomalies between convertible bonds and their underlying equity. As embedded options in convertible bonds are often undervalued with respect to their theoretical value, a typical investment is to be long the convertible bond and to hedge a portion of the equity risk by selling short the underlying common stock. The positions are designed to generate profit from the fixed income security as well as from the short sale of the stock, while protecting capital from market moves. Most managers employ some degree of leverage, ranging from zero to 6:1. That is, for every $1 of investor capital, $6 is invested in securities using a margin account. Risk factors, some of which can be hedged, include interest rate, credit,[4] liquidity and corporate event risk.

The *fixed income arbitrage* style encompasses a wide spectrum of strategies that seek to exploit pricing anomalies within and across global fixed income markets. These pricing anomalies

---

[4] However, the inherent default risk of the bond is partially mitigated, as the hedge is in place through the shorting of the underlying common stock.

are typically due to factors such as investor preferences, exogenous shocks to supply or demand, or structural features of the fixed income market. Typical strategies are yield curve arbitrage, sovereign debt arbitrage, corporate versus Treasury yield spreads, municipal bond versus Treasury yield spreads, cash versus futures (basis trading) and mortgage-backed securities arbitrage. Value may also be added by exploiting tax loopholes, yield curve anomalies and volatility differences. Fixed income arbitrage managers often neutralize interest rate risk in their portfolios and use a large amount of leverage to enhance returns.

The *equity market neutral style* (also referred to as *statistical arbitrage*) is a quantitative portfolio construction technique that seeks to exploit pricing inefficiencies between related equity securities while at the same time exactly neutralizing exposure to market risk. The neutrality is achieved by exactly offsetting long positions in undervalued equities and short positions in overvalued equities, usually on an equal dollar or zero beta basis. The strategy's profit objective is to exploit mispricings in as risk-free a manner as possible. Returns often come from mean reversion (the undervalued security that has been bought, moving up in price or the overvalued security that has been sold short, declining in price), or from sector/country bets. Pair trading, which involves highly correlated stock pairs that have deviated from their historical pricing relationship, is a popular example of this strategy. Note that market neutral funds should not be confused with long/short investment strategies. The key features of market neutral funds are the low correlation between their returns and those of traditional assets.

Other relative value arbitrage strategies include:

- The index arbitrage style, which exploits the relative mispricings of index and index-derivative securities. Usually, this strategy is implemented through long positions in the stocks that underlie an index and short positions in an index-derivative security.
- The mortgage-backed securities arbitrage style, which seeks to profit from the pricing difference between a mortgage instrument with uncertain prepayment and credit quality characteristics, and a non-prepayable Treasury security.

1.2.5   Funds of funds and multi-strategy funds

The different investment styles mentioned so far usually have very different risk–return parameters. Therefore, instead of selecting a single hedge fund manager following a single strategy, it can be more attractive to combine several individual hedge funds in a portfolio. Through diversification, this yields a more efficient portfolio – that is, a portfolio with less risk for potentially more return. The combination of hedge funds minimizes the potential impact of poor performance on the part of any individual manager and provides a more stable long-term investment return than any of the individual funds, much like what happens within traditional diversified portfolios. This idea has given birth to *funds of hedge funds* (referred to below as funds of funds) that allow investors to access a variety of managers and gain diversification through a single investment. A fund of funds manager may allocate his capital to several managers within a single strategy (style-specific fund of funds), or to several managers in multiple strategies (multi-strategy fund of funds).

Attracted by the free lunch, several individual hedge funds have also joined the diversification game and started combining several strategies within the same organization. These funds usually fall under the general heading of *multi-strategy funds*. Most of them claim to implement some sort of dynamic strategy allocation as market conditions change.

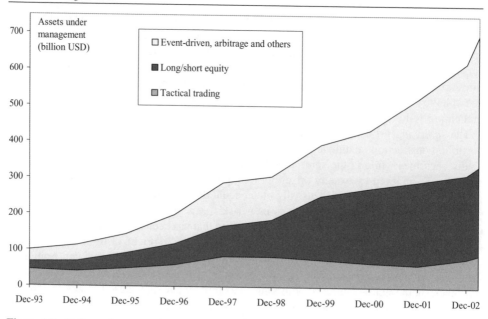

Figure 1.2   Estimated assets under management

1.3   THE CURRENT STATE OF THE HEDGE FUND INDUSTRY

It is relatively difficult to obtain statistics on the overall hedge fund industry, as advertising and reporting of hedge fund information is restricted by the Securities and Exchange Commission in the USA, by the Financial Services Authority in the UK, by the Central Bank in Ireland and more generally, by regulatory authorities in most countries. Consequently, most available hedge fund information is either voluntarily submitted or incomplete and therefore may be subject to many biases that we will discuss later. Hence, the conclusions drawn from these statistics should be treated with caution.

As mentioned previously, the number of hedge funds worldwide is estimated to be over 7000, managing total assets of around $800 billion. Further, it is important to keep in mind that this amount only represents the capital account balances of investors and not the actual number of dollars deployed in the markets. Hence, the amount of money invested by hedge funds in the market, given some of the leveraged strategies employed, could be as large as $1 trillion.

The average hedge fund has $135 million in assets under management, but 50% of funds have assets under management of less than $38 million, while the largest hedge fund in the world, Caxton Associates, now manages more than $10 billion. An astounding number of new hedge funds have been created in the past few years to meet investors' demands, and they are now literally starving for assets to manage (Figure 1.2).

Most of the funds are effectively managed[5] from the United States (New York), although around 70% are administered and registered in offshore locations. Europe (London) and Asia (Hong Kong and Singapore) are experiencing strong growth, but remain far behind the USA in terms of assets under management and number of hedge funds.

---

[5] To be politically correct, we should say that they are "advised" by a US-based advisor.

The majority of the assets under management by hedge funds come from wealthy private individuals. Indeed, high net worth individuals (HNWIs) – individuals with assets in excess of $1 million – account for a large part of the wealth invested in hedge funds, and there are numerous signs that hedge funds are becoming a standard component of HNWI portfolios. In Switzerland, anecdotal evidence suggests that private banks now recommend investing up to 30% of assets in alternative investments. Recent research by Bernstein Research concluded that approximately 5% of high net worth individuals invest through hedge funds, but that approximately 70% of high net worth individuals who invest in hedge funds have done so for at least three years and their average allocation is above 30% of their financial assets. This segment still represents a significant potential source of growth for hedge funds over the coming years.

Institutional investors (e.g. endowments, foundations, pension funds and insurance companies) still come well down the scale in terms of hedge fund investments, but they are showing increasing interest and now seem to view alternative investments as a necessary part of portfolio management. Participants at the SEC's roundtable forum on hedge funds confirm that around $175 billion invested in hedge funds comes from institutions, up from $52 billion in 1998. According to another report by industry researchers Greenwich Associates, titled *Asset Allocation: US Portfolios Adjust to Difficult Markets*, in 2002 nearly 60% of endowments and foundations invested in hedge funds, up from 50% in 2001, and 20% of pensions also allocated to the asset class, up from 15% in 2001. And according to a survey by Goldman Sachs and Frank Russell, the average US plan sponsor anticipates that its strategic allocation to alternative investments will rise to 8% over the next three years. If the forecast proves true, this should constitute a major source of inflows in the near future (Figure 1.3).

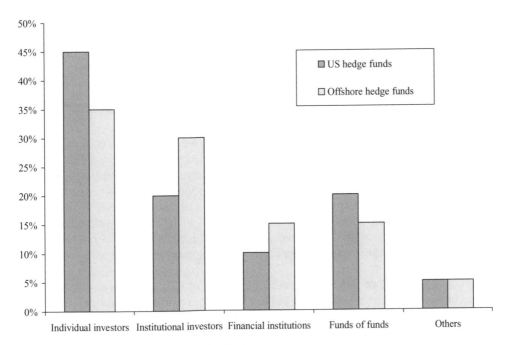

Figure 1.3 Estimated breakdown of hedge fund investors

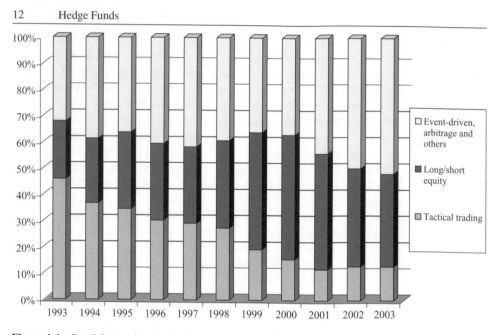

Figure 1.4 Breakdown of hedge fund assets by investment strategy

Figure 1.4 illustrates the breakdown of hedge fund assets by investment strategy. It appears very clearly that long/short equity is now the dominant strategy. This is a direct consequence of the bear market of the early 2000s that resulted in several long-only managers closing their traditional funds to open a new hedge fund in order to be able to sell short and capture performance fees. However, as we shall see, long/short equity is an easy strategy to understand, but picking its best managers is a daunting task.

An interesting statistic to monitor is the amount of money that has flowed into hedge funds. TASS Research – the information and research unit of Tremont Advisers Inc. – provides this information on a quarterly basis for a universe comprising a broad base of 3775 funds located and managed in the United States and overseas.[6] The flow of global capital to hedge funds has risen dramatically over the last decade, and not surprisingly, money seems to chase performance.

Today, the hedge fund industry bears a strong resemblance to the mutual fund industry of 25 years ago. Tremendous inflows of capital combined with reinvestment have fed the growth in assets, but have also resulted in little or no industry structure. Standalone funds each present themselves to investors using different investment styles, benchmarks and performance measures. High fees have attracted managers with poorly established and executed strategies, resulting in potentially grim surprises for the unwary. And while some sophisticated investors have the time, resources and intellect to evaluate and select hedge funds, the lack of transparency and disclosure deprive the average investor of access to comprehensive information about hedge fund performance.

Fortunately, in the near future, the increasing interest of institutional investors for hedge funds combined with the sophistication and rigor of their investment process should serve as an important catalyst for refining standards of practice. More regulation, more transparency

---

[6] The full research report also includes a commentary on strategies and information on quarterly asset flows.

and more risk control should shift the emphasis from the high absolute returns sought by high net worth individuals to the risk-adjusted returns needed by institutions. Considering the size of the capital pool theoretically available for investment and the present allocation to hedge funds,[7] the industry has plenty of room to increase its market share, either through an increase in the number of funds or through an increase in the average size of hedge funds. In both cases, we expect fund selection and portfolio construction methods to come under greater scrutiny. A better understanding of these issues is needed, and we hope that this book will contribute to this understanding.

---

[7] Currently only 1.2% of global high net worth and institutional assets are invested in hedge funds, according to Putnam Lovell (2002).

2
Measuring Return

A stock that fell by 90 percent is a stock that fell by 80 percent and then halved.

The two basic factors to be weighted in investing, risk and return, are obviously the opposite sides of the same coin. Each must be measured to assess and understand past performance, and convince investors that their money is in the right hands. Both must also be predicted in order to make intelligent investment decisions for the future. Of course, we all know that the future is uncertain and that history may not repeat itself, but understanding what happened in the past is likely to be a guide in formulating expectations about what may happen in the future.

Measuring the *ex post* return and risk of an investment may sound somewhat trivial. However, the number of hedge fund managers claiming that their fund has superior risk-adjusted returns often amazes me, particularly when we simultaneously hear the dissatisfaction of investors and the tentative explanations of consultants. The reason for this discordance is simply the lack of standards on how to measure risk and return, the multidimensionality of hedge fund returns in terms of descriptive statistics, and the lack of agreement on what constitutes an appropriate benchmark. Today, the hedge fund industry is so diverse that it is impossible to define a small number of sectors that are homogenous enough to ensure apples-with-apples comparisons.

In the traditional investment world, formal standards of performance measurement were drawn up and adopted in the early 1990s, under the influence of the Association of Investment Management and Research (AIMR). Compliance with the AIMR Portfolio Presentation Standards (AIMR-PPS) and the more recent Global Investment Performance Standards (GIPS) ensures full and fair disclosure of investment results to clients and prospective clients, and guarantees that all managers act on the same level playing field. Unfortunately, we do not have the equivalent yet for hedge funds and alternative investments.

As long as clearly-defined standards are lacking, performance measurement will have much in common with religion: it means something different to everyone, it results in veneration by some, and it is often the source of disputes and conflict. To make matters worse, smart swindlers take advantage of the lack of consensus by propagating hedge fund statistics that claim to be of value to investors, but which are in reality based on misconceptions, misinterpretations and flawed assumptions.

This situation is of some concern, particularly when we recall that risk and return – the two keys of performance – play an essential role in comparing different funds as well as in evaluating the compensation of hedge fund managers. It also raises serious doubts about the possibility of evaluating hedge funds from an *ex ante* perspective. If we cannot agree about what happened in the past, how can we attach any value to our forecasts for the future?

In order to interpret correctly the statistics of hedge fund performance and separate the wheat from the chaff, the reader must first understand the basic quantitative concepts and know what is hidden behind the notions of "risk" and "return". In this chapter, we attempt to demystify both the statistical analysis of hedge fund returns and result interpretation, in an effort to enhance our future decision-making process. Although we have made every effort to offer a clear and intuitive explanation of the associated issues, we could not avoid a few equations, some of them probably intimidating. But do not worry: the material is covered in the text and in examples, so that most equations do not need to be fully understood in order to clearly grasp the concepts involved.

You may be tempted at this point to skip this chapter and go straight to the next one. This would not be a judicious move, however, because the rest of the book builds upon what is learnt in this chapter. When the wind blows, a house with no foundations will not resist for long. The same applies to the hedge fund investor without a clear understanding of the material that follows. Without a thorough understanding of risk and return, it would be an uphill task to carry out the necessary quantitative analysis.

2.1   THE DIFFICULTIES OF OBTAINING INFORMATION

Investors accustomed to high levels of control and transparency in traditional investments often find the variations in what hedge funds disclose discouraging. In some cases, even the phone number of the hedge fund manager seems to be proprietary information.

Transparency is obviously a touchy subject for hedge fund managers. After Alfred Winslow Jones had formed the first hedge fund in 1949, he managed to operate his fund in complete secrecy for 17 years. Almost 50 years later, the hedge fund Long Term Capital Management (LTCM) was considered as being the very paragon of modern financial engineering, with two Nobel Prize winners among its partners and Wall Street's most celebrated trader as its CEO. It shrouded its operations in secrecy, denying lenders and their regulators any data about its positions or its liabilities to other lenders. "Do you want us to refund your money?" was the usual question to LTCM partners that were too inquisitive about the fund's activities.

These two examples, although not recent, are quite representative of the reputation of operating under a cloak of secrecy that most hedge fund managers have today. They still tend to avoid disclosing the securities they hold, their views on the market, the extent to which they are leveraged, or even in some cases their past performance figures. This attitude has often been perceived as hubris and arrogance. The true picture is somewhat different. In reality, there are at least three reasons that may help justify the relative secrecy surrounding hedge fund operations.

First, one should remember that, unlike mutual funds, onshore hedge funds are privately organized investment vehicles subject to minimal oversight from regulatory bodies. The numerous funds incorporated offshore for tax purposes are even less regulated. As long as smaller, unsophisticated investors do not join the band, regulators do not bother with the situation. Consequently, hedge funds are not required to disclose holdings, returns or even their existence beyond what is spelled out in the contract with their investors. And many hedge fund managers are very happy to remain boutiques catering primarily to high net worth individuals. They do not really care about attracting new investors. Hence, the lack of transparency to non-investors is not surprising!

Second, most regulators do not allow hedge funds to advertise or solicit money from the general public. Onshore hedge funds are only allowed to target limited groups of accredited investors, and offshore hedge funds are legally debarred from making domestic public offerings. Releasing information about past performance could easily be regarded as advertising, particularly if the figures are good and attract the attention of potential investors. Hedge fund managers will not take that risk and prefer to remain in the shade.

Third, many hedge fund managers shy away from disclosure, particularly those active in illiquid markets (e.g. distressed securities or merger arbitrage), or who frequently engage in heavy short selling or highly leveraged positions (e.g. fixed income arbitrage or global macro, for example). These managers believe that allowing competitors to see their trades is tantamount to revealing the underpinnings of their strategies and exposing them to disastrous short squeezes and numerous competitive risks. Arbitrage is often based on being the first to find rare market inefficiencies before anyone else has the chance to squeeze profit out of the trade, which effectively irons out the inefficiency. The more secretive you stay, the higher the profit. Furthermore, the market could easily trade against a hedge fund manager once its positions are revealed.[1]

For these reasons, among others, it is common practice for hedge fund managers to structure their funds so as not to trigger reporting requirements imposed by regulators[2] and to supply minimal information to their existing investors. This typically includes an estimate of the monthly return, a few statistics such as volatility and correlation, and possibly a quarterly letter from the manager himself. In a sense, the situation could be described as relatively opaque.

It was only after 1998 and the bail-out of Long Term Capital Management that regulators, investors and prime brokers started requiring greater disclosure, particularly in relation to the risk side. The demand for more transparency strengthened with the interest of institutional investors such as pension funds and insurance companies, which had, and still have, limited exposure in this market, but constitute a large potential source of demand for hedge fund products in the future. Under pressure from these new investors and fearing regulatory controls, the hedge fund industry is progressively institutionalizing itself. Many hedge funds have evolved from the start-up structure of a one-man trading company to a global financial institution, with written policies and procedures, separation of front, middle and back office, succession planning, disaster recovery, independent risk management, etc. This seems to be the new pattern of evolution for hedge funds.

In parallel, transparency has swept across markets, and while some hedge fund managers may not like it, they will have to live with it. An increasing number of managers are now willing to discuss portfolio information openly and directly with investors, at least on a monthly basis. Many investors are quite satisfied with this approach, as they have confidence in the manager. But some request more information, ranging from the dollar exposure by trader or portfolio manager, asset class, sector/industry, currency, strategy or style, to the leverage, the performance attribution and the complete value at risk analysis. In a few cases, the request concerns the individual position details on a weekly or even daily basis. For the time being, the majority of experienced hedge fund managers are still unwilling to offer this level of transparency, except perhaps through a managed account that they run in parallel with their fund.[3] But things could change very rapidly, as the demand for increased transparency is still around.

---

[1] The case of Long Term Capital Management in 1998 is a prime example of the market trading against a manager once the company was in distress and positions were revealed to the market.

[2] The only exception occurs if a hedge fund holds large public equity positions. In this case, the manager, like any other large institutional manager, must disclose these positions to the local market supervisor, e.g. the SEC in the United States.

[3] Note that despite facilitating complete transparency, a managed accounts platform is associated with several additional costs such as opportunity costs (some managers are not willing to provide managed accounts), large infrastructure requirements, investments in competent staff and systems, etc. Many investors consider that the costs associated with full transparency are not compensated by the additional benefits.

The question of determining the level of detail beyond net asset values that constitutes adequate or appropriate portfolio transparency still fuels an ongoing debate.[4] A few hedge funds have agreed to provide full transparency by allowing investors to gather position data from prime brokers. But most investors lack the skills and resources to interpret position-level information, so that complete transparency actually makes the job of analyzing risk and return more complicated. The emergence of risk transparency rather than position transparency seems to offer a good compromise, at least for the time being, and provides investors with a meaningful snapshot of a hedge fund's risks. It addresses investor concerns while avoiding position detail that may be difficult to obtain and overwhelming to receive.

The next step of risk transparency is the standardization of risk factors, so that the risk exposures can be aggregated across an investor's portfolio of hedge funds. Riskmetrics™ and other market leaders in the field of risk management are now offering solutions in order to fulfill this task. Value at risk (VaR) in particular has been used by both investors and managers in analyzing their portfolios and provided a common language for risk communication. But this is another topic, which we shall come to later.

2.2   EQUALIZATION, CRYSTALLIZATION AND MULTIPLE SHARE CLASSES

Obtaining a time series of historical net asset values for a given hedge fund may be difficult. Unfortunately, it is only the first part of the story. Unlike traditional mutual funds that have a clean way of calculating their net asset values, the world of hedge funds is a real jungle with its particularities and conventions. Hence, several adjustments must usually be made to historical data before performance can be measured. Among these, the most frequent are equalization calculations and crystallizations.

Equalization calculations are a series of accounting methods used to ensure that incentive fees are charged in a fair and equitable way to all investors in a hedge fund. Conceptually, determining the incentive fee at the fund level should be a fairly straightforward exercise. Incentive fees are typically calculated as a percentage of the annual or semi-annual increase in the gross asset value of the fund, either as a straight percentage of the appreciation or as a percentage of the increase over a certain threshold (hurdle rate). However, computational complications arise when investors are allowed to buy into the fund at different times during the year and, therefore, at different net asset values per share. Indeed, purchases at different times result in differing percentages of appreciation relative to other investors at the end of each measurement period. This raises several potential problems.

2.2.1   The inequitable allocation of incentive fees

In the absence of any adjustment, when the fund performance is positive, an investor who buys into the fund in the middle of the measurement period may be charged a full incentive fee, although he has only participated in a part of the performance. In a sense, he will be subsidizing another shareholder.

---

[4] It is interesting to note that investors and fund managers have very different perceptions of the transparency situation. As an illustration, consider the results of a recent survey conducted by Capital Market Risk Advisors Inc. (CMRA) at the request of the Alternative Investment Management Association (AIMA). On the one hand, only 7% of funds of funds and 4% of individual hedge funds reported cases of potential investors declining to invest because of the lack of transparency. On the other hand, 64% of investors claimed they had declined to invest in a fund for the same motive. And 86% of investors indicated that transparency is an issue when selecting hedge funds and funds of funds.

As an illustration, consider a hedge fund launched on 1 January at a share price of $100. To keep things simple, say the fund charges no management fee. Its incentive fee is equal to 20% of the performance, charged semi-annually without any hurdle rate. On 1 January, investor A subscribes for $1 000 000 to the fund, that is, 10 000 shares. The situation is as follows:

1 January	
Gross asset value per share	$100
Net asset value per share	$100

At the end of the first quarter, say the fund displays a positive performance of +10%. The gross asset value per share increases to $110. The hedge fund publishes a net asset value of $108, net of $2 incentive fee accrual. The $2 amount is still included in the gross asset value, but has not yet been paid to the fund manager. The situation is now as follows:

31 March		
Gross asset value per share	$110	
Incentive fee per share (accrual)	$2	(20% of performance)
Net asset value per share	$108	

Investor B then steps in and subscribes 10 000 shares at a price equal to the published net asset value of the fund ($108).

Three months later, say the gross asset value per share of the fund is now $120. The semi-annual profit of $320 000 should be split between investor A ($20 per share) and investor B ($12 per share). However, if the fund charges its semi-annual incentive fee at the fund level based on the gross asset value, the corresponding fee would be 20% of $320 000, that is, $64 000 in total, or $3.2 per share. The final net asset value published by the fund would therefore be $116.8 per share ($120 − $3.2). The situation would be as follows:

30 June		
Gross asset value per share	$120	
Incentive fee per share (accrual)	$3.20	(20% of performance)
Net asset value per share	$116.80	

Consequently, investor A would have paid $3.2 for an effective profit of $20, which equals 16.4%. Investor B would have paid the same $3.2, but for an effective profit of $12, which represents 26.66%. This allocation of incentive fees is clearly inequitable. The problem lies in the calculation of the fee using the gross asset value, which is the same for both investors and includes the incentive fee accrual, while investor B only benefited from a portion of the upside.

2.2.2 The free ride syndrome

Another type of problem may occur with incentive fees when a hedge fund has lost money and recoups its losses. In such a case, a shareholder who buys into the fund in the middle of the measurement period (at a price lower than the previous highest net asset value) may avoid part of the incentive fee until the fund has recovered, although in reality this investor enjoys an effective appreciation on his investment. This is called the free ride syndrome.

As an illustration, consider again a hedge fund launched on 1 January at a share price of $100. As before, the fund charges no management fee, but a performance fee equal to 20% of its performance, charged semi-annually. A high water mark clause in the offering memorandum states that the 20% incentive fee can be charged only if the fund manager makes money and has recovered from all previous losses. On 1 January, investor A subscribes for $1 000 000 to the fund, that is, 10 000 shares. The situation is as follows:

1 January	
Gross asset value per share	$100
Net asset value per share	$100

At the end of the first quarter, say the fund displays a negative performance of −10%. The gross asset value per share decreases to $90. The hedge fund publishes a net asset value of $90. There is no incentive fee accrual, because the fund manager did not perform well. The situation is now as follows:

31 March	
Gross asset value per share	$90
Incentive fee per share (accrual)	$0
Net asset value per share	$90

Investor B then steps in and subscribes 10 000 shares at a price equal to the published net asset value of the fund ($90).

Three months later, say the gross asset value per share of the fund is now back at $100. The total quarterly profit is $200 000. To be fair, it should be split equally between investors A and B ($10 per share). Only investor B who gained 11.11% should pay the incentive fee, because investor A just recovered his previous loss and simply broke even. However, if the fund charges its semi-annual incentive fee at the fund level based on the gross asset value evolution, there is no incentive fee because the performance is considered as being flat. The final net asset value published by the fund will therefore be $100 per share:

30 June	
Gross asset value per share	$100
Incentive fee per share (accrual)	$0
Net asset value per share	$100

Now, if investor B decides to realize his 11.11% return and redeem his shares, he will pay no performance fee, since the fund manager did not make any money according to the semi-annual high water mark. This gives investor B a free ride on his profits. This once again implies an inequitable allocation of incentive fees, as the manager did not receive his incentive fee although some investors obtained gains since they entered the fund later than the others.

2.2.3   Onshore versus offshore funds

The inequitable allocation of incentive fees and the free ride syndrome do not occur with onshore hedge funds that are structured as limited partnerships. There are two reasons for this. First, most limited partnerships are closed structures, so that no new investor may come in after the fund has been launched. Second, the partnership agreement may allocate portions of gains and losses in an individual way, if this is stated in the bylaws.

However, the two problems are present in offshore funds, which are often "open-ended". They allow investors to make capital contributions on a regular basis, therefore creating the potential for inequity between new investors and the original ones. The difficulty stems from the fact that all investors are usually offered a single class of shares, of which a fixed number has to be issued each time a new investor invests, and which is traditionally used also as a measure of the fund's performance. As soon as investors subscribe at different net asset value levels, calculating incentive fees may become quite complex. At the end of any measurement period, each investor may have a differing percentage appreciation or depreciation for his shares relative to other investors. Hence, the calculation of the incentive fee applicable to any appreciation in fund shares must be adjusted accordingly, in order to treat each investor equitably.

2.2.4 The multiple share approach

A straightforward solution to avoid the above-mentioned problems consists in considering each shareholding individually and issuing multiple series of shares. The first series of shares at the fund's creation is called the "lead series", and another series is created each time there is a new subscription. Then, each group of investors entering the fund at the same date and at the same net asset value will hold the same series of shares and will pay the same incentive fee based on the performance effectively earned.

By way of example, consider the case of a new hedge fund that has just started operations. We assume that the fund has a monthly subscription policy and has adopted the multiple share approach. The fund manager charges a 20% incentive fee on a quarterly basis, conditional on a 1% quarterly high water mark. Say the performance for the first three months is as follows: +7% in January, +5% in February and −4% in March.

On 1 January, investor A buys 1000 Series I shares of the fund at $1000 per share. This series of shares will constitute the lead series. At the end of January, the gross NAV of the lead series of shares has increased to $1070 per share (+7%) and the published NAV is $1056, net of $14 incentive fee accrual (20% of the $70 increase). A new series of 1000 shares called Series II is created, with a net asset value per share of $1000. Investor B then buys all Series II shares for $1 million.

At the end of February, the gross NAV of the fund's shares is now $1123.50 for the lead series (+5%) and $1050 for Series II shares (+5%). The hedge fund publishes a net asset value of $1098.80 (net of $24.70 incentive fee accrual) for the lead series and a net asset value of $1040 (net of $10 incentive fee accrual) for Series II. A new series of 1000 shares called Series III is created, with a net asset value per share of $1000. Investor C then buys all Series III shares for $1 million.

At the end of March, the gross net asset value of the fund's shares is now $1078.56 for the lead series, $1008 for Series II shares and $960 for Series III shares. The lead series and Series II shares pay their incentive fee ($15.71 and $1.60 per share, respectively). Series III shares are not profitable and do not pay any incentive fee. Table 2.1 summarizes the overall process.

The major advantage of this procedure is its simplicity. Each series of shares is valued independently of the others and has its own incentive fee accrual. There is no more free rider syndrome and no problem of incentive fee allocation. The drawback is that things can easily become cumbersome as the number of series rises. The coexistence of multiple series of shares implies tracking and reporting multiple net asset values (one for each series), which is quite confusing for an investor holding shares in several series. Furthermore, the independence of

Table 2.1   Evolution of gross and published net asset values in the case of multiple series of shares

	1 Jan	31 Jan	28 Feb	31 Mar	1 Apr
Performance		+7%	+5%	−4%	
Series I (lead series)					
Gross NAV	$1000	$1070	$1123.50	$1078.56	$1062.85
Net NAV (published)	$1000	$1056	$1098.80	$1062.85	$1062.85
Accrual of incentive fee	$0	$14	$24.70	$15.71	$0
Series II					
Gross NAV		$1000	$1050	$1008.00	$1006.40
Net NAV (published)		$1000	$1040	$1006.40	$1006.40
Accrual of incentive fee		$0	$10	$1.60	$0
Series III					
Gross NAV			$1000	$960	$960
Net NAV (published)			$1000	$960	$960
Accrual of incentive fee			$0	$0	$0

each series implies that the listing requirements and fees (for instance on the Irish Stock Exchange) must be applied to each series!

Funds that adopt multiple series regularly attempt to consolidate series of shares with the lead series in order to reduce the number of series outstanding. The necessary conditions to implement such a consolidation are (i) that the end of an accounting period for the lead series and another series coincide and (ii) that an incentive fee has been paid for both of them. In our previous example, Series II shares could be merged with the lead series on 1 April, just after the payment of the incentive fee. Investor B would have to exchange his 1000 shares, which are worth $1006.40 per share, against 946.89 shares of the lead series, which are worth $1062.85 per share. This reduces the number of outstanding series but introduces holdings of fractional shares, which is not necessarily much better. Moreover, an external observer monitoring only the net asset value of the shares held by investor B would conclude that the share appreciated from $1006.40 to $1062.85, which is wrong. It is precisely to avoid such situations that alternative methodologies have been suggested.

2.2.5   The equalization factor/depreciation deposit approach

If the fund manager wants to publish only one net asset value, another way to overcome the above-mentioned problems is to use the equalization factor approach. The latter is a correction mechanism that uses depreciation deposits and equalization factors as compensation for the inequitable allocation of incentive fees.

Consider for instance the case of a hedge fund that charges its incentive fee annually but allows monthly subscriptions and redemptions. Under the equalization factor approach, any subscription of shares that takes place within the year (that is, between the payment dates of the incentive fee) is made at the *net asset value* on the date of the purchase, plus an equalization factor if the net asset value has increased since the base net asset value.[5] Depending on the level of the net asset value at the end of the year, all or part of the equalization factor may

---

[5] The base net asset value refers to the highest net asset value the fund has reached at the end of any fiscal year. At the inception of the fund, the base net asset value equals the initial subscription amount. If the fund appreciates during its first year, the base net asset value becomes the net asset value at the end of its first year. If the fund depreciates, the base net asset value remains the initial net asset value. The base net asset value is essentially equal to the high water mark of the shares issued upon initial subscription.

be refunded to the investor, usually by granting him some "free" shares for the corresponding amount. Similarly, if the net asset value at the purchase date is lower than the base net asset value, the investor will receive a depreciation deposit. At the end of the year, all or part of the depreciation deposit is either paid to the investment manager by redeeming shares (if the fund's net asset value has gone up) or kept on deposit for the benefit of the investor and used in future years (if the fund's net asset value has gone down).

As an illustration, let us reconsider our previous example. Our first hedge fund started as follows:

1 January (inception)

Gross asset value per share	$100
Net asset value per share	$100

with investor A owning 10 000 shares. After a quarterly increase of 10%, the situation is as follows:

31 March (before subscriptions)

Gross asset value per share	$110	
Incentive fee per share (accrual)	$2	(20% of performance)
Net asset value per share	$108	
Allocation to A	10 000 shares	$1 080 000

We assume that the fund uses an equalization factor approach. When investor B steps in and subscribes 10 000 shares, the price is equal to the published net asset value of the fund ($108), plus the incentive fee ($2). Thus, investor B pays $1 100 000 and receives 10 000 shares, plus an equalization credit equal to the current performance fee (10 000 times $2 = $20 000). This equalization credit is accounted for as a liability of the fund. It is at risk in the fund and will therefore fluctuate with the performance of the fund subsequent to the investment. However, the value of the equalization credit will never increase above the performance fee at the time the investment was made ($20 000).

31 March (after subscriptions)

Allocation to A	10 000 shares	$1 080 000
Allocation to B	10 000 shares	$1 080 000
	Equal. credit	$20 000

Three months later, say the gross asset value per share of the fund is now down to $105. We have the following situation:

30 June

Gross asset value per share	$105	
Incentive fee per share (accrual)	$1	(20% of performance)
Net asset value per share	$104	
Allocation to A	10 000 shares	$1 040 000
Allocation to B	10 000 shares	$1 040 000
	Equal. credit	$10 000

Note that the equalization credit of investor B has been reduced to $10 000, which corresponds to the 10 000 shares times the $1 incentive fee.

In the next quarter, say the gross asset value per share of the fund is down again to $95. The performance fee disappears, since it is calculated with respect to the base net asset value of $100 at the beginning of the year. The equalization credit of investor B is therefore marked at a value of zero:

30 September (before subscriptions)

Gross asset value per share	$95	
Incentive fee per share (accrual)	$0	
Net asset value per share	$95	
Allocation to A	10 000 shares	$950 000
Allocation to B	10 000 shares	$950 000
	Equal. credit	$0

Investor C then steps in and subscribes 10 000 shares at a price equal to the published net asset value of the fund ($95). He pays $950 000 and receives 10 000 shares plus a depreciation deposit of −$10 000 on his account, which corresponds to the fee due on the performance of the 10 000 shares from $95 (the NAV at which he invested) to $100 (the previous high NAV per share). This depreciation deposit is at risk in the hedge fund and will therefore fluctuate with the performance of the fund subsequent to the investment. However, the value of the equalization debit (in absolute value) will never increase above $10 000:

30 September (after subscriptions)

Allocation to A	10 000 shares	$950 000
Allocation to B	10 000 shares	$950 000
	Equal. credit	$0
Allocation to C	10 000 shares	$950 000
	Equal. debit	−$10 000

For the sake of illustration, say the fund goes up during the next month, so that the gross asset value per share of the fund is $140 at the end of October:

31 October (before subscriptions)

Gross asset value per share	$140	
Incentive fee per share (accrual)	$8	(20% of performance)
Net asset value per share	$132	
Allocation to A	10 000 shares	$1 320 000
Allocation to B	10 000 shares	$1 320 000
	Equal. credit	$20 000
Allocation to C	10 000 shares	$1 320 000
	Equal. debit	−$10 000

Investor D then steps in and subscribes 10 000 shares at a price equal to the published net asset value of the fund ($132), plus the incentive fee ($8). He pays $1 400 000 and receives 10 000 shares, plus an equalization credit equal to the current performance fee (10 000 times

$8 = \$80\,000$). Similarly to B, this equalization credit is at risk in the hedge fund and will therefore fluctuate with the performance of the fund subsequent to the investment. However, the value of the equalization credit will never increase above the performance fee at the time the investment was made ($\$80\,000$):

31 October (after subscriptions)

Allocation to A	10 000 shares	$1 320 000
Allocation to B	10 000 shares	$1 320 000
	Equal. credit	$20 000
Allocation to C	10 000 shares	$1 320 000
	Equal. debit	−$10 000
Allocation to D	10 000 shares	$1 320 000
	Equal. credit	$80 000

Finally, at year-end, say the gross asset value per share of the fund is now down to $125. The situation is as follows:

31 December

Gross asset value per share	$125	
Incentive fee per share (accrual)	$5	(20% of performance)
Net asset value per share	$120	
Allocation to A	10 000 shares	$1 200 000
Allocation to B	10 000 shares	$1 200 000
	Equal. credit	$20 000
Allocation to C	10 000 shares	$1 200 000
	Equal. debit	−$10 000
Allocation to D	10 000 shares	$1 200 000
	Equal. credit	$80 000

As we are at the end of the year, the new net asset value becomes the new offering price and a new high water mark needs to be determined for the next year. This operation is often referred to as *crystallization*. The investment manager is due his incentive fee and a new calculation is made of any remaining equalization factor attributable to shareholders.

- Investor A invested at a gross asset value equal to $100, so he has to pay the full performance fee from $100 to $125, that is, $5 per share. This corresponds to what the fund charges, so there is no particular need for adjustment. Investor A therefore starts the next year with 10 000 shares having a net asset value of $120 per share.
- Investor B invested at a gross asset value equal to $110, so he only has to pay the performance fee from $110 to $125, that is, $3 per share. As the fund charges a total incentive fee of $5 per share, investor B is owed back $2 – the incentive fee from the gross asset value of $100 to the gross asset value of $110. This amount corresponds to the $20 000 of equalization credit. Hence, 166.6667 new shares representing this value will be issued and granted to investor B. The equalization credit disappears, and investor B therefore starts the next year with 10 166.6667 shares having a net asset value of $120 per share.
- Investor C invested at a gross asset value equal to $95, so he has to pay the performance fee from $95 to $125, that is, $6 per share. As the fund charges a total incentive fee of $5 per share, investor B still has to pay $1, that is, the incentive fee from the gross asset value

of $95 to the gross asset value of $100. This amount due corresponds to the $-$\$10000$ of equalization debit. Hence, 83.3333 shares representing this value at the year-end net asset value will be redeemed from the account of investor C. The equalization debit disappears, and investor C therefore starts the next year with 9916.6667 shares having a net asset value of $120 per share.

- Investor D invested at a gross asset value equal to $140, so he should not be charged anything. He is the only investor below his high water mark. As the fund charges a total incentive fee of $5 per share, investor D is owed back $50000 – the incentive fee from the gross asset value of $100 to the gross asset value of $125. Hence, 416.6667 new shares representing this value will be issued and granted to investor D. The equalization credit is reduced by $50000, and the remaining $30000 equalization credit is carried over to the next year if the investor stays in the fund.[6] Investor D therefore starts the next year with 10416.6667 shares having a net asset value of $120 per share and an equalization credit of $30000:

1 January (following year)		
Gross asset value per share	$120	
Incentive fee per share (accrual)	$0	
Net asset value per share	$120	
Allocation to A	10 000 shares	$1 200 000
Allocation to B	10 166.6667 shares	$1 220 000
Allocation to C	9916.6667 shares	$1 190 000
Allocation to D	10 416.6667 shares	$1 250 000
	Equal. credit	$30 000

The new high water mark for all investors is $120 for the next year, except for investor D, who has a high water mark of $140. The $30000 equalization credit guarantees that investor D will be compensated for the fees taken at the fund level below the $140 threshold. In a sense, the equalization factor is only a memorandum account showing each shareholder's previous high water mark.

2.2.6 Simple equalization

An alternative approach that is also sometimes implemented by hedge funds is "simple equalization". It consists in calculating the fair performance fee for each investor based on the latter's effective entry level and allocating it investor by investor. Investors who came into the fund at different levels will end up with different net asset values, similarly to the example of multiple series of shares. However, in order to arrive at a common net asset value for all shares in the fund, the lowest of all the net asset values calculated at the end of the year is selected to become the new net asset value of the fund for all investors. Shareholders with a higher individual net asset value per share will be exactly compensated by the distribution of a fractional number of new shares. The procedure is relatively simple, and there is only one net asset value for each fund. However, the historical net asset values no longer accurately reflect the fund's performance, and the distribution of free equalization shares to investors is rather confusing.

---

[6] Note that some funds will simply cancel out the remaining equalization factor if investor D leaves the fund in December. Their argument is that the fund has lost 37.5% of its year's gains (15 out of 40) since investor D subscribed, so that investor D loses a similar proportion of his equalization factor ($30 000 out of $80 000). As usual, the details are in the fine print.

2.2.7   Consequences for performance calculation

Whatever the final choice, any equalization accounting methodology obviously imposes an additional burden on the administrator of the hedge fund and needs to be clearly explained to investors, who generally have great difficulty in understanding that nothing underhand is going on. Nevertheless, its application effectively ensures that all investors are fairly rewarded or penalized when buying into the fund at different times and different net asset values. Furthermore, it allows the net asset value to be uniform and common to all shareholders. This explains why it is often employed by offshore funds. However, it is worth noting that in such a case, the net asset values published by the fund – and obtained on a subscribing database system – no longer reflect the effective performance, unless the investor has been in the fund since its inception. Surprisingly, very few academic papers so far have taken into account accurately the potential biases that are likely to result from this.

2.3   MEASURING RETURNS

While much of the early work on quantitative analysis involved the statistical behavior of asset prices (e.g. the random walk of asset prices), much of the recent work in financial econometrics has involved time series of returns rather than net asset values or prices. The major reason for this paradigm shift is that returns standardize the evolution of a price by considering price *per unit of investment*. In addition, returns often have more attractive statistical properties than prices. In the following section, we will therefore convert our net asset values into return figures.

2.3.1   The holding period return

Let us denote by NAV_t the net asset value at time t of a given hedge fund, with the index t representing any point in time. We assume that the net asset value has already been adjusted to take into account all realized and non-realized capital gains, accrued dividends and interest income, capital distributions, splits and all the impacts of equalization and crystallization. We therefore ignore these aspects henceforth.

The *simple net return* R_{T_1,T_2} on the fund between any time T_1 and $T_2 \geq T_1$ is defined as:

$$R_{T_1,T_2} = \frac{\text{NAV}_{T_2} - \text{NAV}_{T_1}}{\text{NAV}_{T_1}} \tag{2.1}$$

It measures the relative change in the fund's net asset value over the considered time period and is sometimes called the *holding period return* or percent return. The simple net return can be used to express the future net asset value as a function of the present net asset value:

$$\text{NAV}_{T_2} = (1 + R_{T_1,T_2}) \times \text{NAV}_{T_1} \tag{2.2}$$

The term $(1 + R_{T_1,T_2})$ is often called the *simple gross return*.

As an illustration, Table 2.2 shows the calculation of several holding period returns over different holding horizons. The series of end-month net asset values provided in the second column and equation (2.1) are the only inputs needed to calculate these holding period returns.

Although the net asset value is only measured at a monthly frequency, it is possible to calculate holding period returns over more than one month. To do so, one may use the standard definition provided by equation (2.1) and use the final and initial net asset values. Alternatively,

Table 2.2 Calculation of a series of holding period returns from a series of end-month net asset values

Time	Date	End-month NAV ($)	Monthly return	Quarterly returns	Annual returns
0	Dec-01	134.64			
1	Jan-02	135.81	$R_{0,1} = 0.87\%$		
2	Feb-02	135.95	$R_{1,2} = 0.10\%$		
3	Mar-02	136.73	$R_{2,3} = 0.57\%$	$R_{0,3} = 1.55\%$	
4	Apr-02	137.49	$R_{3,4} = 0.56\%$		
5	May-02	137.80	$R_{4,5} = 0.23\%$		
6	Jun-02	135.15	$R_{5,6} = -1.92\%$	$R_{3,6} = -1.16\%$	
7	Jul-02	132.47	$R_{6,7} = -1.98\%$		
8	Aug-02	132.88	$R_{7,8} = 0.31\%$		
9	Sep-02	133.03	$R_{8,9} = 0.11\%$	$R_{6,9} = -1.57\%$	
10	Oct-02	133.24	$R_{9,10} = 0.16\%$		
11	Nov-02	135.40	$R_{10,11} = 1.62\%$		
12	Dec-02	137.04	$R_{11,12} = 1.21\%$	$R_{9,12} = 3.01\%$	$R_{0,12} = 1.78\%$

the holding period return may also be calculated by compounding the impact of several consecutive returns. Obviously, the cost of carrying money from time T_1 to time $T_3 \geq T_1$ is the same as the cost of carrying money from T_1 to $T_2 \geq T_1$, and then from T_2 to $T_3 \geq T_2$, since

$$\begin{aligned}
\text{NAV}_{T_3} &= (1 + R_{T_1,T_3}) \times \text{NAV}_{T_1} \\
&= (1 + R_{T_1,T_2}) \times (1 + R_{T_2,T_3}) \times \text{NAV}_{T_1}
\end{aligned} \tag{2.3}$$

More generally, we can have as many intermediary periods as we want, so that the simple gross return over N periods can be expressed as the product of the N simple gross returns of each shorter period:[7]

$$(1 + R_{T_1,T_N}) = (1 + R_{T_1,T_2}) \times (1 + R_{T_2,T_3}) \times \cdots \times (1 + R_{T_{N-1},T_N}) \tag{2.4}$$

Algebraically, this is denoted as follows:

$$1 + R_{T_1,T_N} = \prod_{i=1}^{i=N-1} (1 + R_{T_i,T_{i+1}}) \tag{2.5}$$

The process of multiplying several gross returns is called *compounding*.[8] As an illustration, the first quarterly return of Table 2.2 can be obtained by using equation (2.1), that is, $R_{0,3} = (136.73 - 134.64)/134.64 = 1.55\%$, or by compounding the three monthly returns $R_{0,1} = 0.87\%$, $R_{1,2} = 0.10\%$ and $R_{2,3} = 0.57\%$. Both approaches yield exactly the same result. However, one should not compare any monthly return with the 1.55% figure, which is expressed on a quarterly basis.

An essential question with respect to holding period returns is whether they are calculated before the deduction of management fees and other expenses (gross returns) or after (net returns). Both figures are useful, since gross returns reflect a manager's raw investment performance,

---

[7] Note that this property applies even if the N periods considered have different lengths.

[8] We will often loosely say that we compound simple returns. In reality, we will use the corresponding gross returns in the calculation.

while net returns reflect actual investor results. Similarly, it is also important to know the net asset value calculation methodology used by administrators, in particular:

- The type of prices used to determine the net asset value. A recent survey by Capital Market Risk Advisors on valuation practices evidenced no consistent market practice across hedge funds when several quotes were available. About 50% of hedge fund respondents used an average quote, 36% made a subjective judgment, 7% used the median quote, and 7% dropped the high and low values and then averaged the remaining quotes. In addition, 60% of hedge funds indicated that they marked their long positions to the mid-point of the market versus the more conservative approach of using the bid side, and 75% of hedge funds marked their shorts to the mid-point rather than the more conservative approach of using the offered side. All these choices may be justified in specific situations, but in any case it is important to be aware of their existence.
- The adjustments made to the "market" prices received from the valuation sources. The above-mentioned survey also evidenced that about 22% of hedge fund respondents adjusted the prices used to calculate the net asset value of their fund, mostly for liquidity and time zone differences. Although the adjustments represented less than 2% of the final net asset value in the majority of cases, they represented up to 30% of the net asset value in a few cases.
- The valuation methodology and the source of information for infrequently traded or non-marketable assets, such as non-listed stocks, real estate, private placements and distressed securities. Those who believe that valuation does not matter should remember that several hedge funds (e.g. Granite Partners, Lipper Convertible Arbitrage) collapsed when investors evaluated their holdings at market value rather than at the manager's estimated value!
- The use of cash versus accrual accounting. In cash accounting, income is recorded only when received and expenses are recorded only when paid. Accrual accounting is based on the fundamental rule that all income earned for a period must be matched with the expenses that are assignable to that period. The industry recommended standard is accrual accounting, as required under Generally Accepted Accounting Principles (GAAP), but some hedge funds prefer the simplicity of cash accounting.
- The use of trade date versus settlement date. Trade date is the day on which an order is executed, while settlement date is the date on which an executed order must be settled (e.g. for purchases, the cash for the purchase must be paid; for sales, the proceeds of the sale are placed in a cash account). The industry recommended standard is trade date. The current settlement period is usually two to three business days after the trade date for stocks and mutual funds, and one business day after the trade date for options trades. It can be considerably longer in emerging markets.
- The manager's choice of return adjustment methodology for intermediate withdrawals and contributions, if any.

All these elements are likely to affect net asset values considerably and should be explicitly disclosed by managers in the prospectus of their funds.

2.3.2 Annualizing

We mentioned earlier that a monthly return should not be compared with a quarterly figure, or more generally with a figure calculated over a different time horizon. Although holding period returns are scale-free (with respect to the size of the investment), they are not unit-less, as they are calculated with respect to some holding period. A return per month is ob-viously not expressed in the same units as a return per year. As a consequence, stating the value of a holding period return without mentioning the time interval considered is not very informative.

Among practitioners and in the financial press, there seems to be an implicit convention, particularly for comparison purposes: all rates of return should be expressed on a yearly basis.[9] Hence, investors frequently need to transform a holding period return into an annual figure, which they call the compound annual growth rate or CAGR. This process is called "annualizing". Most of the time, returns calculated on a period shorter than one year (e.g. year-to-date, last month, first quarter) are not annualized, except for predictive purposes.

When the holding period is more than a year, annualizing means figuring out the constant annual return necessary to achieve the observed holding period return once compounding effects are taken into account. When the holding period is less than a year, annualizing means taking the return made over a short period and calculating what the annual return would have been if the investment had continued to gain at the same rate for a full year.

A quick estimate of the annualized return is obtained by simply comparing the length of the holding period with one year, and adjusting linearly the holding period return. For instance, a six-month return of 5% would give a 10% annual return (as a six-month period represents one half, or 6/12 of a year), while an 18-month return of 15% would also result in a 10% annual return (12/18 of the original value). Although useful, this rough-and-ready approach is flawed because it does not take into account the compounding effects. The correct way of annualizing the holding period return (HPR) is:

$$\text{Annualized return} = (1 + \text{HPR})^{\text{number of holding periods in one year}} - 1 \qquad (2.6)$$

where the number of holding periods in one year must be expressed as a ratio with re-spect to one year. As an illustration, if a six-month holding period return is equal to 5%, the equivalent annualized return would be $(1 + 5\%)^{2/1} - 1 = (1.05)^{2/1} - 1 \approx 10.25\%$. Simi-larly, an 18-month return of 15% would result in an annual return of $(1 + 15\%)^{(12/18)} - 1 = (1.15)^{(12/18)} - 1 \approx 9.77\%$. We see from this that the number of holding periods in one year does not necessarily have to be a whole number.

2.3.3 Multiple hedge fund aggregation

Frequently, we also need to calculate the performance of a portfolio of funds or the average performance of a sample of funds over a common time period. How should we proceed?

Let N be the number of funds. First, we need to compute the holding period return for each hedge fund over the common period. Let us denote the holding period return of fund number i by R_i, with $i = 1, \ldots, N$. Ideally, these returns should be measured over exactly the same period and according to the same calculation rules. In practice, they are often based on the monthly variation of the net asset value provided by each manager.

Next, we need to assign a weight w_i to each fund at the beginning of the considered period. Three major weighting schemes are used in the industry: the equal weighting approach, the asset weighting approach and the arbitrary weight approach.

---

[9] There are some exceptions, such as the current monthly performance or year-to-date figures, which are usually not annualized.

Table 2.3   Calculation of a monthly performance index

Fund name	Return in 2002	Assets in January 2002	Equal weights	Asset-based weights	Arbitrary chosen weights
Fund 1	2.61%	$4.5 billion	1/3	81.80%	20%
Fund 2	17.43%	$851 million	1/3	15.47%	20%
Fund 3	−10.42%	$150 million	1/3	2.73%	60%
		$5.501 billion			

- In the *equal weighting* approach, each hedge fund return has an equal weight in the average. If there are N funds in a sample, each of these has a weight $w_i = 1/N$. The corresponding average can then be perceived as the "average fund behavior", irrespective of the assets under management. If each fund in the sample has its dedicated manager, the equal weighted average will then also capture the average manager behavior.
- In the *asset weighting* approach, each hedge fund return has a specific weight w_i in the average. This weight is based on the fund's assets under management in proportion to the total assets managed by all hedge funds considered. If fund number i has assets A_i (with $i = 1, \ldots, N$), the weight of fund i in the average is $w_i = A_i/\Sigma A_i$. The resulting average figure can therefore be perceived as the "average dollar invested" behavior.
- In the *arbitrary weight* approach, each hedge fund return has a specific weight w_i in the average. This weight is arbitrarily chosen, and may change over time. The only requirement is that the sum of all the weights should equal 100%.

Once the return (R_i) and the weight (w_i) for each hedge fund have been determined, the performance index is simply computed as a weighted average of the individual returns:

$$R_{\text{Index}} = \sum_{i=1}^{N} w_i \cdot R_i \tag{2.7}$$

As an illustration, consider the performance of the three funds listed in Table 2.3. All these funds were active in the same sector, namely, global long/short equity. With the equal weighting approach, the performance of the group would be equal to 3.21%, while it would jump to 4.55% using the asset weighting approach. Finally, with the arbitrarily chosen weights of Table 2.3, the performance would become negative at −2.24%. All these differences in final returns arise only because of the difference in weights used to calculate the average.

Note that in the case of multiple fund aggregation, several consultants prefer reporting the median return rather than the average return. The *median fund return* can be defined by stating that half of the funds have a higher return than the median and half of the funds have a lower return. When the data set contains an odd number of funds, the middle value is the median value and corresponds to the median fund for the period considered. When the data set contains an even number of funds, the middle two numbers are added, the sum is divided by two and the resulting value is the median.[10] The fact that outliers are automatically excluded from the calculation makes the median more robust than the average.

---

[10] In a sense, the median return is a very particular weighted average, where only one return (odd-size sample) or two returns (even-size sample) have a weight different from zero.

Table 2.4 Calculation of a series of simple and continuously compounded holding period returns from a series of end-month net asset values

Month	End-month NAV	Simple compounding			Continuous compounding		
		Monthly return	Quarterly return	Annual return	Monthly return	Quarterly return	Annual return
Dec-01	134.64						
Jan-02	135.81	0.869%			0.865%		
Feb-02	135.95	0.103%			0.103%		
Mar-02	136.73	0.574%	1.552%		0.572%	1.540%	
Apr-02	137.49	0.556%			0.554%		
May-02	137.80	0.225%			0.225%		
Jun-02	135.15	−1.923%	−1.156%		−1.942%	−1.162%	
Jul-02	132.47	−1.983%			−2.003%		
Aug-02	132.88	0.310%			0.309%		
Sep-02	133.03	0.113%	−1.569%		0.113%	−1.581%	
Oct-02	133.24	0.158%			0.158%		
Nov-02	135.40	1.621%			1.608%		
Dec-02	137.04	1.211%	3.014%	1.783%	1.204%	2.970%	1.767%

2.3.4   Continuous compounding

It is relatively easy to calculate simple net and simple gross returns over a single holding period return. However, it is tiresome to take into account compounding effects using multiplications and powers as soon as we have more than one period – see for instance equations (2.5) and (2.6). Things would be much simpler if we could just add and subtract simple returns rather than multiply and divide simple gross returns.

This has motivated an alternative approach to measuring returns, which produces *continuously compounded returns* or *log returns*. The continuously compounded return r_{T_1,T_2} on a fund between any time T_1 and $T_2 \geq T_1$ is defined as the natural logarithm of its simple gross return:[11]

$$r_{T_1,T_2} = \ln(1 + R_{T_1,T_2}) \tag{2.8}$$

As an illustration, Table 2.4 shows the calculation of a series of continuously compounded returns from a series of monthly net asset values. We intentionally express the result with three decimals to show that simple returns and continuously compounded returns are in fact slightly different.

The fact that continuous returns are close to simple returns is confusing. Many people believe that continuously compounded returns are just an approximation of simple returns. This is not true. In a sense, simple returns and continuously compounded returns are parallel worlds, much like miles versus kilometers to measure distances. Do you feel more comfortable using miles or kilometers? The answer probably depends on which type of country you are from. Are miles more accurate than kilometers, or is it the opposite? Well, both measures are accurate as long as you do not mix elements from each world together in the same calculation. The same answers apply to simple returns and continuously compounded returns. Some people prefer continuously compounded returns (e.g. statisticians, or people dealing with option

---

[11] Note the use of a lowercase letter to emphasize the use of continuously compounded returns as opposed to the simple return.

pricing in continuous time), while others stick to simple returns. In all cases, using simple returns would be correct; likewise, using continuously compounded returns would also be correct.

The advantage of using continuously compounded returns is purely computational. Using logarithms converts a multiplication to an addition and a division to a subtraction, which simplifies some calculations greatly.

For instance, the one-period continuously compounded return is just the change in the log price:

$$r_{T_1,T_2} = \ln(1 + R_{T_1,T_2}) = \ln\left(\frac{\text{NAV}_{T_2}}{\text{NAV}_{T_1}}\right) = \ln(\text{NAV}_{T_2}) - \ln(\text{NAV}_{T_1}) \tag{2.9}$$

Also, multi-period log returns are simply the sum of the single-period log returns over the period:

$$
\begin{aligned}
r_{T_1,T_3} &= \ln(\text{NAV}_{T_3}) - \ln(\text{NAV}_{T_1}) \\
&= \ln(\text{NAV}_{T_3}) - \ln(\text{NAV}_{T_2}) + \ln(\text{NAV}_{T_2}) - \ln(\text{NAV}_{T_1}) \\
&= r_{T_1,T_2} + r_{T_2,T_3}
\end{aligned}
\tag{2.10}
$$

Hence, annualizing or compounding is a straightforward operation using continuously compounded returns. As an illustration, the annual continuously compounded return of 1.767% in Table 2.4 is simply obtained by summing the 12 monthly continuously compounded returns, or the four quarterly continuously compounded returns. Similarly, annualizing a monthly continuously compounded return is equivalent to multiplying it by 12.

In addition, as we will see shortly, continuously compounded returns offer the advantage of being easier to model. The reason is simply that it is much simpler to derive the properties of an additive process rather than the properties of a multiplicative process, particularly when using time series of returns. Thus, in the financial literature, it is common to see the use of continuously compounded returns when modeling the properties of time series of returns.[12]

Note, however, that the result of a calculation involving continuously compounded returns is itself a continuously compounded return. To obtain a simple return, it is therefore necessary to use an exponential, which is the inverse function of the logarithm. This gives:

$$R_{T_1,T_2} = \exp(r_{T_1,T_2}) - 1 \tag{2.11}$$

Hence, equations (2.8) and (2.11) define our conversion functions between the world of continuously compounded returns and that of simple returns. In the following discussion, to keep things simple, we will stick as much as possible to simple returns, unless otherwise explicitly stated.

---

[12] The disadvantage of using continuously compounded returns is, however, that the continuously compounded return of a portfolio is no longer a weighted average of the continuously compounded returns of its components. The reason is simply that the sum of a log is not equal to the log of a sum. In practice, this problem is usually minor, and most people use the weighted average of the continuously compounded returns as an approximation for the portfolio's log return.

3

Return and Risk Statistics

Kids are for people that cannot afford a dog.

François-Serge Lhabitant, former quant & philosopher

Despite the deep-seated belief of many people that human beings are the most intelligent and complex animals on earth, we have to temper this belief about our intellectual superiority with a measure of humility. The average human brain fails miserably when dealing with more than 10 to 15 numbers. By comparison, the simplest computer is many times more powerful and more capable because it can perform calculations thousands of times faster, work out logical computations without error and store memory at incredible speeds with flawless accuracy.

3.1 CALCULATING RETURN STATISTICS

When the number of returns increases significantly beyond the threshold of 10 to 15, the human brain needs statistics to summarize and understand the information. As we will see, dimension reduction is a leitmotif of statistics.

As an illustration, consider Table 3.1, which shows a series of simple monthly returns for a hedge fund since its inception. In total, there are 203 numbers, far too many for our brain to be able to identify any pattern or trend. To be interpretable, this collection of returns must be organized in some sort of logical way.

One of the easiest ways to reorganize a return series and make it more intelligible is to plot it in some sort of graphical form. The graph preferred by marketers is the historical evolution of $100 invested in the fund in question – see Figure 3.1. While informative about the final value of the investment, this type of graph does not throw much light on the progress since inception. The reason is that the whole graph is conditioned on the terminal value, so that a large percentage loss at the beginning (−17.46% in November 1987, when the amount invested is small) will appear smaller than a small percentage loss towards the end (−6.53% in April 2000, when the amount invested is large).

We can partially solve this problem by using a logarithmic scale rather than a linear scale on the *y*-axis. However, a better tool to visualize and summarize a large data set is the *relative frequency histogram*. It consists in grouping similar returns together and calculating their frequency. The advantage of grouping is that it hides some of the random noise that is not likely to be meaningful, while at the same time preserving the structure of the data.

To build it, we must proceed as follows:

- Define a set of mutually exclusive and exhaustive intervals, such that each observed return must fall into one and only one interval.
- Count the number of observed returns falling within each interval, and divide the result by the total number of all returns. This gives the relative frequency or percentage of observed returns in each interval.

Table 3.1 Monthly returns (%) for a given hedge fund since its inception

	Jan	Feb	Mar	Apr	May	Jun	Jul	Aug	Sep	Oct	Nov	Dec
1986								0.47	−5.84	1.04	−0.20	−0.17
1987	5.33	10.63	−2.81	−2.13	−1.37	5.81	2.37	3.27	−2.01	−9.56	−17.46	1.43
1988	1.20	4.34	2.35	3.17	−2.30	5.39	−0.88	−1.65	2.25	2.34	−2.65	3.51
1989	4.72	0.88	0.88	1.93	2.85	0.99	1.44	2.41	−0.34	−3.55	−0.01	0.39
1990	−3.53	−1.85	4.23	−3.35	4.85	0.93	−0.22	−7.97	1.36	2.33	1.34	1.45
1991	5.13	1.70	0.76	0.49	0.93	−0.69	2.10	5.02	2.65	2.35	−1.26	1.24
1992	3.12	1.24	−0.40	1.15	−0.03	−2.49	0.07	0.41	11.87	2.73	1.89	1.95
1993	1.07	2.43	0.34	4.13	1.97	4.61	4.53	1.11	−1.15	5.18	−0.26	8.49
1994	0.45	−6.87	−2.95	−5.45	0.08	−1.19	−1.44	0.51	2.09	−2.31	−2.24	−1.30
1995	−2.05	−0.88	3.43	0.44	0.34	1.25	1.24	3.40	1.74	−1.91	3.62	2.86
1996	4.24	0.86	−0.14	3.32	2.79	−1.70	−6.69	2.90	2.54	1.10	5.22	0.24
1997	4.38	1.63	−2.51	−0.20	4.53	1.95	5.58	0.76	3.76	−0.46	1.08	1.80
1998	0.02	3.80	5.23	−0.04	0.51	2.96	1.57	−7.67	−0.76	−2.73	1.29	2.90
1999	2.07	0.27	2.03	3.95	1.10	0.57	2.17	0.42	−1.02	1.17	7.02	7.24
2000	5.13	2.24	7.38	−6.53	−4.65	−0.86	3.69	2.60	2.00	−0.36	−1.84	3.57
2001	0.23	0.66	−1.43	0.97	0.63	0.55	−1.40	0.16	−0.60	−1.37	0.35	0.99
2002	−0.76	−0.64	−0.11	0.23	0.29	−1.05	−1.32	0.68	−0.38	−0.64	−0.85	1.76
2003	0.18	0.16	−0.72	0.03	1.84	−0.13						

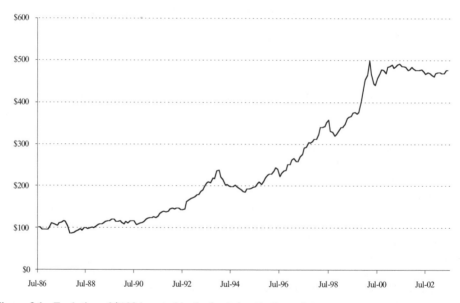

Figure 3.1 Evolution of $100 invested in the fund since its inception

- Finally, plot a bar chart, where each bar corresponds to a particular interval of the returns measured (plot horizontally) and the height of a bar represents the relative frequency of occurrence for a particular interval (plot vertically).

As an illustration, Figure 3.2 shows the histogram of monthly returns for our fund. We can observe that the data produce a nice mound or bell shape, with right and left tails that taper off roughly symmetrically, except for one spike deep in the left tail. The minimum value is around −18%, the maximum value is around +12%, and the central peak lies at around 1%.

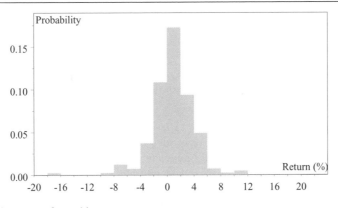

Figure 3.2   Histogram of monthly returns

Clearly, the histogram is a useful device to provide an overall picture of the information present in the series of monthly returns and to explore the shape of the corresponding distribution. It gives us a picture of what the returns look like without having to deal in detail with the collection of raw returns of Table 3.1.

3.1.1   Central tendency statistics

Histograms are usually the first step implemented to understand the nature of a series of returns. However, when analyzing and comparing funds, it is more convenient to use statistics to summarize the return series rather than a graph. This is precisely the role of measures of central tendency (also called measures of location) such as the mean (or average), the median and the mode. All of them provide information about the observations in the middle of a data set.

The *arithmetic average return* is computed simply by summing the return in each sub-period $(R_{0,1}, R_{1,2}, \ldots, R_{T-1,T})$ and dividing the total by the number of sub-periods (T). Each sub-period should have the same length (e.g. one day, one month). Mathematically:

$$\bar{R}^{(A)} = \frac{1}{T}(R_{0,1} + R_{1,2} + \cdots + R_{T-1,T}) \tag{3.1}$$

or equivalently:

$$\bar{R}^{(A)} = \frac{1}{T}\sum_{t=1}^{T} R_{t-1,t} \tag{3.2}$$

As an illustration, for the fund of Table 3.1, one would obtain an arithmetic mean return equal to:

$$\bar{R}^{(A)} = \frac{1}{203}(0.47\% - 5.84\% + \cdots -0.13\%) = 0.82\%$$

An alternative measure of the mean return is the *geometric mean return*, which represents the return that, once compounded, would produce the same holding period return for a given investment. Its formula is more complicated than the arithmetic average, because it accounts for the effect of compounding. It multiplies all the sub-period returns, expressed as $(1 + R_{t,t+1})$, where $R_{t,t+1}$ is the percentage return between time t and time $t + 1$, and takes the root corresponding to the number of sub-periods (T). Mathematically:

$$\bar{R}^{(G)} = [(1 + R_{0,1})(1 + R_{1,2}) \cdots (1 + R_{T-1,T})]^{1/T} - 1 \tag{3.3}$$

or equivalently:

$$\bar{R}^{(G)} = \left[\prod_{t=0}^{T-1} (1 + R_{t,t+1}) \right]^{1/T} - 1 \tag{3.4}$$

Using the same data, the geometric mean return of our fund would be equal to:

$$\bar{R}^{(G)} = (1.0047 \times 0.9416 \times \cdots \times 0.9987)^{1/203} - 1 = 0.77\%$$

Both the arithmetic mean and the geometric mean returns calculated above are monthly figures – they are calculated from monthly data. Annualizing them yields an annual arithmetic mean return of 10.33% and an annual geometric mean return of 9.64%.

As this example shows, the arithmetic mean and the geometric mean yield different results. Which one should be preferred? Fund managers usually prefer using the arithmetic mean. It is easier to calculate than the geometric mean and results in higher values, which makes their fund look better.[1] However, in reality, the choice between the arithmetic mean and the geometric mean should depend on the context. The arithmetic mean return should be considered appropriate only if the objective is to measure a one-period mean return. On the other hand, if the goal is to obtain the mean return over several successive periods, then the geometric mean is a better measure because it takes compounding into account.

In most situations, the arithmetic mean return may be sufficient as a quick approximation to the geometric mean return for rough comparisons of performance. But in the case of applications requiring more precision, the approximation will break down and the geometric mean should be used. As an illustration, consider a hypothetical hedge fund that gained +50% every month for the first 11 months of its existence, and that collapsed the next month (−100%). What can we say about this fund? The overall return was −100%, that is, the investors lost their entire initial investment. The geometric mean return is −100%. Yet the arithmetic average monthly return is still 37.5%, i.e. [(11 × 50%) − 100%]/12.

Hence, the key point to remember is that it is improper to interpret the arithmetic mean return as a measure of the effective mean return over an evaluation period, because it does not account for compounding effects.[2]

Box 3.1

Note that, due to their additive nature, continuously compounded returns are easier to average than simple returns. The geometric mean in the domain of simple returns becomes an arithmetic mean in the domain of continuously compounded returns. Hence, to average a series of continuously compounded returns, it is sufficient to add them up and divide the result by the number of values:

$$\bar{r}^{(A)} = \frac{1}{T} \sum_{t=1}^{T} r_{t-1,t} \tag{3.5}$$

The result is a continuously compounded return. Taking the exponential will bring us back to the domain of simple returns, and provides the geometric mean return:

$$\bar{R}^{(G)} = \exp(\bar{r}^{(A)}) - 1 \tag{3.6}$$

---

[1] The only situation where the two averages would be equal is if all monthly returns are identical.
[2] The proper interpretation of the arithmetic mean rate of return is as follows: it is the average value of withdrawals, expressed as a fraction of the initial net asset value, that can be made at the end of each sub-period while keeping the initial net asset value intact.

The presence of outliers, that is, very high or very low returns, can significantly affect the value of the average. In this case, the *median return* is a better measure of central tendency. The median, as already stated, is simply the middle value in a data set.[3] As an illustration, if we again take our data set, the median monthly return would be 0.88% per month, with 101 values below it and 101 values above it.

A median value that is different from the arithmetic mean signals an asymmetric return distribution. In our case, we have 0.82% for the arithmetic mean return and 0.88% for the median monthly return. This implies that the return distribution is skewed to the left. That is, below average returns occur more frequently than above average returns. We will see shortly other indicators of asymmetry.

Finally, the last average statistic we will mention in this chapter is called the *mode*. It represents the most frequently occurring observation. It is not widely used in practice for returns, which can take any value, but rather used for variables that can only take a limited set of values, or that have been grouped in prespecified categories.

3.1.2 Gains versus losses

Several fund managers like to compare their *average gain* with their *average loss.* The average gain is the simple return average (arithmetic mean) of the periods with a gain. It is calculated by summing all observed positive returns and then dividing the total by the number of gain periods. Similarly, the average loss is a simple average (arithmetic mean) of the periods with a loss. It is calculated by summing all observed negative returns and then dividing the total by the number of loss periods. In our example, the average monthly gain would be equal to +2.40%, while the average loss would be −2.24%.

The *gain-to-loss ratio* is a simple ratio of the average gain divided by the average loss (in absolute value) over a given period. Fund managers often use it to compare winning period returns with losing period returns. Although it is a rather intuitive measure, its interpretation is subject to caution because (i) it hides the relative number of winning and losing periods, and (ii) it does not account for compounding. In our previous example, the gain-to-loss ratio would be 2.40/2.24 = 1.07, which means that on average, the gains are slightly higher than the losses. However, when one looks at the time series, it is obvious that the manager of the fund had mostly winning (positive) months. Whether this is luck or good management remains to be seen, but for sure it does not transpire from the gain-to-loss ratio.

3.2 MEASURING RISK

We are all familiar with the quip that if you put someone's feet in a bowl of ice and his head under the grill, his feet will be frozen and his head burned, but on average, his body temperature will remain "normal". This image is often used to convey the dangers of using averages to represent a large volume of information. The same principle applies to hedge funds.

Analyzing funds solely on the basis of the average returns they generated is certainly a straightforward way to make comparisons – see for instance the league tables showing fund managers ranked according to their returns over the last months or years. But returns alone do not tell the whole story. Central tendency statistics such as the mean return may provide a good indicator of the average behavior of a sample of returns, but two funds with the same

---

[3] In the event that there is an even number of data points, the median is calculated by taking the average (mean) of the two middle points. Hence, in any case, unlike the average, the median is not affected by the presence of outliers: if we made the smallest value even smaller or the largest value even larger, it would not change the value of the median.

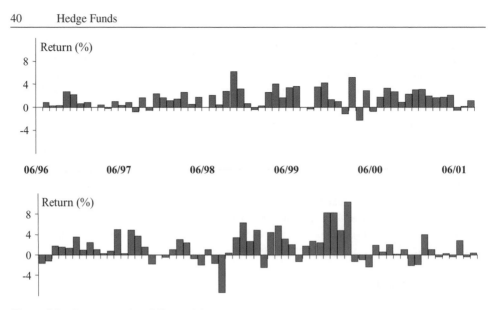

Figure 3.3   Same mean, but different risks!

mean return may also have very different behavior, depending on how representative the mean return is with respect to each individual return. Hence, we need some additional measure(s) to indicate the degree to which individual returns are clustered around, or deviate from, the mean return.

By way of illustration, consider Figure 3.3, which represents the monthly returns of two hedge funds over the period July 1996 to August 2001. The first fund is a market neutral fund active in utility stocks. The second is a long/short fund that focuses on the technology, healthcare and retail sectors.

These two funds have the same average annualized return over the period (about 19%). However, their behavior differs greatly. In the case of the first fund, the average is quite representative of the individual monthly returns, while the second fund's returns fluctuate widely around their average. Most investors would probably agree that risk is essential and deem the second fund more risky than the first over the period in question. But what do they mean exactly by "more risky"?

3.2.1   What is risk?

It is difficult to reach a consensus on how to define risk. Indeed, different investors have different concerns, depending on the nature of their portfolio, the nature of the institution that employs them and their own risk aversion. They therefore perceive risk differently. A pension fund may see risk as the failure to meet its liabilities. An asset manager may perceive risk as a deviation from his benchmark. A statistician may define risk as a potential deviation from the average. And a private investor may consider risky any situation where he may lose money.

As a consequence, ways of measuring risk have proliferated, to the point that they have become a matter of confusion for investors, essentially for two reasons. First, different risk measures will produce different rankings for the same set of funds. Second, there is little or no conceptual cohesion between the different approaches to measuring risk, which seem to have been developed completely independently of each other.[4] The reason for this muddle is that different risk measures basically answer different questions. Indeed, there is no fundamental reason for the answer to the question "What is the fund that has the lowest probability of loss?" being the same as the answer to "What is the fund that has the smallest average deviation from its benchmark?" Nevertheless, all these definitions share common characteristics. They combine uncertainty with the possibility of a loss, disappointment or unsatisfactory outcome.

We attempt below to clarify the issue by discussing in turn the major risk measures that are applied in the hedge fund universe, starting with the simplest. We consider their goals and essential properties, compare their advantages and deficiencies, and illustrate their application. Once again, we attempt to favor intuition over mathematical developments, with the exception of providing a calculation formula for each risk measure.

3.2.2   Range, quartiles and percentiles

The simplest measure of risk is the dispersion of observed returns. The latter is measured by the *range*, which is the distance between the highest and the lowest observed returns. For example, the range of returns for the fund originally introduced in Table 3.1 is 29.33% (the minimum return is -17.46% and the maximum return is $+11.87\%$).

This range is easy to measure using a histogram – see Figure 3.2. However, the range is extremely sensitive to the presence of outliers in the data. Furthermore, it only provides information about the maximum and minimum returns, but does not say anything about all the other returns in between. This is why economists often prefer using percentiles to measure the variability of a distribution.

Suppose a series of returns is arranged in ascending order. The *p*th *percentile* is a number such that $p\%$ of the returns of the set fall below and $(100 - p)\%$ of the returns fall above it.[5] The median, by definition, is the 50th percentile. The 25th percentile, the median and the 75th percentile are called *quartiles*. They are often used to describe a data set because they divide the data set into four groups, with each group containing a quarter (25%) of the observations. Alternatively, we could also divide the returns into five equal-size sections and measure *quintiles*, or in 10 equal-size sections and measure *deciles*. Another quantity often reported is the inter-quartile range, which is equal to the 75th percentile minus the 25th percentile. It is useful because it is less influenced by extreme values, as it limits the range to the middle 50% of the values.

A graphical way to represent the median, quartile distribution and extremes of data is the box plot, also known as the box-and-whiskers plot. This is especially helpful in determining visually whether or not there are significant differences between several sets of returns. As an illustration, Figure 3.4 shows the box plot for the fund originally described in Table 3.1. The first quartile is -0.64%, the median is 0.88% and the third quartile is 2.39%.

---

[4] See for instance Booth *et al.* (1999).

[5] When determining the *p*th percentile, problems similar to those for the median usually occur, because most probably the set of observed returns will not contain a value that divides the distribution exactly into proportions of p and $1 - p$, respectively. There are then two possibilities. Either that variable value can be taken as the quartile that leads to proportions closest to the required ones (this is the only possible strategy on an ordinal level of scale), thus an error in the proportions has to be accepted but the quartile is an observed return. Or an interpolation rule can be applied to those two variable values leading to the two proportions closest to the required ones, thus only a virtual value for the quartile is calculated but it has the advantage of dividing the distribution exactly as required. The less data a set contains, the bigger these problems become.

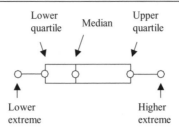

Figure 3.4   A box-and-whiskers plot

3.2.3   Variance and volatility (standard deviation)

Intuitively, over a single period, the risk of an investment should be associated with the possible dispersion of returns around their arithmetic mean, denoted $\bar{R}$. The larger the dispersion, the greater the potential risk. While the concept is attractive, its implementation is not. Indeed, the formula for calculating the "average" dispersion around the mean return is not simple.

At first glance, if we have a series of T returns and we want to measure the dispersion of returns around the mean return, an appealing measure would be the average deviation, calculated algebraically as the expected deviation of the fund's returns from their mean:

$$\text{AD} = \text{E}(R - \bar{R})$$
$$= \frac{1}{T} \sum_{t=1}^{T} (R_{t-1,t} - \bar{R})$$

(3.7)

The problem with this definition is that, whatever the observed returns, this formula will always return a zero value. The reason is simply that the average is by definition at the middle of all observations, so that negative deviations exactly offset positive deviations. This will not get us very far.

To avoid this problem, we may use the *mean absolute deviation*, which is calculated as the expected absolute deviation from the mean:

$$\text{MAD} = \text{E}\,|\,R - \bar{R}\,|$$
$$= \frac{1}{T} \sum_{t=1}^{T} |\,R_{t-1,t} - \bar{R}\,|$$

(3.8)

The term "absolute", represented by vertical dashes in the formula, means that even the negative differences occurring for data smaller than the average are counted as positive (e.g. a $+3\%$ difference stays $+3\%$, but a -3% difference becomes $+3\%$). The average deviation is not very difficult to calculate, and it is intuitively appealing. Some statisticians also use the median instead of the mean. However, the mathematics of absolute values do not have very attractive properties in subsequent statistical analysis, particularly when optimizing portfolios. Hence, we had better look for an alternative approach to the problem.

A well-known statistical measure, the *variance*, solves the problem of the deviations averaging to zero. Denoted by the Greek letter σ^2, the variance is calculated as the average squared deviation from the mean return:

$$\sigma^2 = \text{E}(R - \bar{R})^2$$
$$= \frac{1}{T-1} \sum_{t=1}^{T} (R_{t-1,t} - \bar{R})^2$$

(3.9)

Squaring the deviations has several advantages. First, squaring makes each term positive so that values above the mean return do not cancel out values below the mean return. Second, squaring adds more weighting to the larger differences, and in many cases this extra weighting is appropriate since points further from the mean return may be more significant in terms of risk.[6] Furthermore, the mathematics of variance are relatively manageable in subsequent statistical calculations (e.g. portfolio optimization). It is therefore not surprising that the first papers in finance adopted variance as a risk measure.

However, the return differences are squared, so that the units of variance are not the same as the units of return. Hence, it is necessary to take the square root of the variance to come back to the same units as the returns. The corresponding quantity is called the *standard deviation* and is denoted by the Greek letter σ:

$$\sigma = \sqrt{\frac{1}{T-1} \sum_{t=1}^{T} (R_{t-1,t} - \bar{R})^2} \qquad (3.10)$$

In finance, the standard deviation is referred to as the *volatility*.

If we apply equation (3.10) to the return series of Table 3.1, we obtain a volatility figure equal to 3.23%. This corresponds to the volatility of monthly returns. Like returns, volatility figures are generally annualized. To annualize, one needs to multiply the volatility estimated using equation (3.10) by the square root of the observation frequency ($\sqrt{12}$ for monthly observations, $\sqrt{360}$ for daily, etc.). In our case, the annual volatility of the fund would be 11.19% ($3.23 \times \sqrt{12}$).

3.2.4 Some technical remarks on measuring historical volatility/variance

At this point, it is worth making a few technical remarks on the calculation of the volatility. These remarks are not fundamental for the remainder of the chapter, but they provide some answers to questions that are usually left unanswered.

Why $(T-1)$ rather than T?
First, it may be wondered why we divide by $(T-1)$ rather than T when computing the variance in equation (3.9). The reason is purely technical, and lies in the difference that exists between a sample and a population.

We are working with a sample of T historical returns of a given fund. From this sample, we are trying to infer the variance of the population, that is, the variance of all possible returns (past and future) of the fund in question. The population is not observable, so its variance is not measurable. Hence, we need to estimate it using a statistic that we can produce with our sample.

We could measure the variance of the sample using the more natural formula:

$$\tilde{\sigma}^2 = \frac{1}{T} \sum_{t=1}^{T} (R_{t-1,t} - \bar{R})^2 \qquad (3.11)$$

where we divide by T rather than $(T-1)$. The value $\tilde{\sigma}^2$ effectively represents the variance of the series of returns that we have. The problem is that we can show that $\tilde{\sigma}^2$ is a biased estimator of the variance of the population. That is, if you consider all possible samples of size T and average all of the resulting variances, this average will not be the population variance.

---

[6] As a side effect, the variance and standard deviation are very sensitive to extreme returns.

The reason is that when we calculate the sample variance, we have already calculated the sample mean return. Hence, in reality, we do not have T different returns free to vary, but only $(T - 1)$ if the mean return is to stay constant. In a sense, the Tth return is already specified by the $(T - 1)$ other returns and the mean return. Hence, since there are only $(T - 1)$ choices ("degrees of freedom"), we need to divide by $(T - 1)$ rather than T when estimating the population variance.

Which average, geometric or arithmetic, should we use?

The second remark concerns the type of average return to use in the calculation of the variance. Should we use the arithmetic or the geometric average? So far, we have used the arithmetic average because we were only considering single-period applications. However, from a theoretical point of view, the real answer is rather surprising: neither of them. Because of the compounding property of simple returns, it does not make any sense to add up simple return differences. We should compound these differences, not add them up. And the use of an arithmetic average or geometric average does not change the question in any way.

The correct calculation of volatility is actually much easier using continuously compounded returns, due to their additive property. First, calculate the standard deviation of continuously compounded returns (σ_{cc}):

$$\sigma_{cc} = \sqrt{\frac{1}{T-1} \sum_{t=1}^{T} \left(r_{t-1,t} - \bar{r}^{(A)} \right)^2} \qquad (3.12)$$

where $\bar{r}^{(A)}$ is the arithmetic average of continuously compounded returns. Note that we do not need to compound returns, because they are continuously compounded.

Then, go back to the simple return universe by taking the exponential of the log-return standard deviation:

$$\sigma = \exp(\sigma_{cc}) - 1 \qquad (3.13)$$

This will provide a return volatility estimate that accounts for all compounding effects. As an illustration, the volatility we would obtain for the fund of Table 3.1 is 3.32%, versus 3.23% using the simple returns and equation (3.9). In practice, the difference between the correctly calculated volatility and the one given by equation (3.9) is usually negligible, so that most people prefer to ignore it and stick to the simpler formula. This is acceptable as long as all volatilities are wrongly calculated in the same way. Hence, all volatilities will be biased the same way, so apples will be compared with apples in a sense, even though they may be bruised.

How about the annualization procedure?

You guessed it. The method commonly used – multiplying the monthly standard deviation by the square root of 12 – is also only an approximation, which becomes inaccurate when the compounding effect is marked. The problem with this procedure is that the annualized return used in the calculation is itself a non-compounded return, determined from a series of returns that are in reality compounding.

As an illustration of the problem, consider a fictive investment strategy that has an average return of 100% per month with a monthly volatility of 100%. If the return distribution is normal, one can show that there is a 15% probability of negative monthly returns. When proceeds are reinvested every month, the expected value for the annual return is $(1 + 100\%)^{12} - 1 = 4095\%$. Applying the $\sqrt{T}$ rule to find the annual volatility gives $\sqrt{12} \times 100\% \approx 346\%$. The distribution for the annual return is narrow, and the probability of having negative returns has become negligible. Clearly, there is something wrong with the $\sqrt{12}$ rule. Whatever the accumulated capital is at the end of the 11th month, for the 12th month, we should expect again about a 15% probability of losing all of it since all the capital is reinvested for the 12th month.

How many data points?

Finally, another important question in assessing volatility is the choice of an observation period and the frequency of the observed data. Depending on the choices made, a variety of estimates for the volatility figure can be obtained. The difficulty when using historical volatility is the implicit trade-off between the number of observations chosen (T) and the window of data used. If volatility is stationary over time, then the choice of T is irrelevant, and T should be chosen as large as possible to maximize accuracy in the estimation process, since more information will enhance estimation. If volatility is not stationary, a compromise has to be found between using long measurement intervals that will give stable figures, but are very slow to reflect structural changes, and using short measurement intervals that reflect changing circumstances rapidly, but are very noisy. In a sense, the choice is between accurately estimating a biased quantity and inaccurately estimating the real value. The issue is particularly important with hedge funds, whose returns are only observable on a monthly basis. As a rule of thumb, a volatility figure calculated with less than 24 data points makes no sense and should be considered as irrelevant.

3.2.5   Back to histograms, return distributions and z-scores

Interpreting an average return or a volatility figure using a histogram is relatively easy, particularly if the histogram is similar to a bell-shaped curve. In this case, it is tempting to approximate the histogram to a normal return distribution – see Figure 3.5.

The normal distribution, also known as the Gaussian distribution, is the most widely used general-purpose distribution, because it has several very attractive statistical properties:

- All normal distributions have the same general shape, the "bell-shaped curve". Each normal distribution is characterized by only two parameters: the mean and the standard deviation. Once these parameters are known, the distribution is completely specified.
- In a normal distribution, the mean (average), median and mode are equal, so that the distribution is symmetrical around the mean. That is, if we draw a vertical line through the

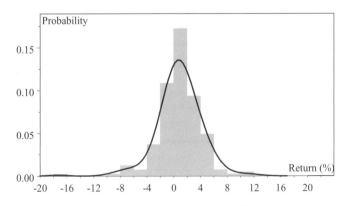

Figure 3.5   Histogram of returns and the corresponding normal distribution

mean, one side of the distribution is a mirror image of the other. Furthermore, half of the observations are above the average return and half below the average return.

- A theorem called the central limit theorem tells us that sums of random variables are approximately normally distributed if the number of observations is large. Thus, even when the distribution is not exactly normal, it may still be convenient to assume that a normal distribution is a good approximation. In this case, all the statistical procedures developed for the normal distribution can still be used.

When an empirical distribution is approximated to a normal distribution, in a sense, the density curve of the normal distribution acts as a smoothed-out histogram, or an "idealized" picture of the original distribution. In particular, the area under the normal density curve gives the proportion of observations that fall within a particular range of values. The proportions obtained from the density curve will not equal the observed proportions exactly, but if the normal is a good approximation, the proportions should be close enough to the originals.

This is particularly useful, because the area under any normal density curve is perfectly determined: 68.26% of the total number of observations fall within one standard deviation of the mean, 95.44% within two standard deviations of the mean, and 99.73% within three standard deviations of the mean. These percentages (as well as those for other multiples of the volatility) are easily found in a standard normal distribution table. With their help, it is relatively easy to estimate the probability of any range of returns.

Say for instance that our target return is 5%, and the distribution of returns has a mean of 8% and a volatility of 12%. A quick calculation shows us that 5% is 0.25 standard deviations below the mean of 8%, as $(5\% - 8\%)/12\% = -0.25$. This value is called a z-score, or standard score. It is often used to compare values from different data sets (e.g. different mean and volatility) or to compare values within the same data set. Basically, it is the number of standard deviations by which a given value is above or below the mean.

Looking in a statistical table for the standard normal distribution, we can observe that 40.15% of the area under a normal distribution is to the left of the mean minus 0.25 standard deviations. Hence, assuming normally distributed returns, there is a 40.15% chance of experiencing a return that is less than 5% (Figure 3.6).

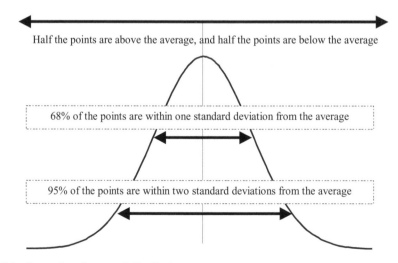

Half the points are above the average, and half the points are below the average

68% of the points are within one standard deviation from the average

95% of the points are within two standard deviations from the average

Figure 3.6   Properties of a normal distribution

Assuming normally distributed returns is extremely appealing to researchers and practitioners alike because normal distributions have well-known mathematical properties that make them easy to process and understand. However, in practice, it is worth considering how good such an approximation is. Empirical observation of financial markets has often revealed that large movements occur more frequently than would be expected if returns were normally distributed. For instance, the 1987 equity crash recorded negative returns that were over 20 standard deviations from the mean (relative to the conventional measures of volatility just prior to the crash). In addition, most return distributions are also skewed, meaning that there is a greater likelihood of the portfolio yielding either higher or lower returns than would be expected under normal distribution conditions.

A histogram is again an effective graphical tool for visualizing such deviations from normality in a data set. In addition, two statistics, known as skewness and kurtosis, may be used to quantify these effects.

Skewness is the third central moment of a distribution.[7] It measures the symmetry of a return distribution around its mean. Zero skewness indicates a symmetrical distribution. A positively skewed distribution is the outcome of rather small losses but larger gains, so it has a long tail on the right-hand side of the distribution, which is usually desirable. Conversely, a negatively skewed distribution is the outcome of many small gains but larger losses, so it has a long tail on the left-hand side of the distribution, which is usually not desirable.

Mathematically, the skewness is calculated as:

$$\text{Skewness} = \frac{T}{(T-1)(T-2)} \sum_{t=1}^{T} \left(\frac{R_{t-1,t} - \bar{R}}{\sigma} \right)^3 \tag{3.14}$$

where T is the number of observations. The measure is free of units but preserves the sign of the deviation of the observation from the mean. As a reference, the standard normal distribution is perfectly symmetrical and has a skewness coefficient equal to zero.

Kurtosis is the fourth central moment of a distribution. It measures the degree of peakedness and heaviness of the tails of a distribution. On the one hand, distributions where a large proportion of the observed values lie towards the extremes are said to be "platykurtic" or display positive kurtosis. Graphically, they display a distinct peak near the mean, decline rather rapidly, and have heavy tails. If, on the other hand, the observed values are clustered near the mean, the distribution is said to be "leptokurtic" or display negative kurtosis. Graphically, they display a flat top near the mean rather than a sharp peak – a uniform distribution would be the extreme case. In contrast, a normal distribution is said to be "mesokurtic" and has a kurtosis value equal to 0.

Formally, the kurtosis is defined as:

$$\text{Kurtosis} = \frac{T(T+1)}{(T-1)(T-2)(T-3)} \sum_{t=1}^{T} \left(\frac{R_{t-1,t} - \bar{R}}{\sigma} \right)^4 - \frac{3(T-1)^2}{(T-2)(T-3)} \tag{3.15}$$

where T is the number of observations.[8] The measure is free of units but is always positive regardless of the sign of the deviation of the observation from the mean.

The normal distribution has skewness and kurtosis values equal to zero. Thus, it is fully described by its first two central moments, the mean and standard deviation. Distributions

---

[7] The mean is the first central moment and the variance, which equals the standard deviation squared, is the second central moment.
[8] Note that some analysts do not subtract the second term from the kurtosis. As a result, when T is large, the threshold value for the normal distribution becomes 3 rather than 0.

that exhibit skewness and kurtosis need more than the mean and standard deviation to be characterized.

Box 3.2

Once again, one may wonder why we are dividing by $(T - 1)$, $(T - 2)$, etc. in equations (3.14) and (3.15). The reason is similar to the $(T - 1)$ argument for the variance. We are working with a sample of returns, and we are trying to estimate the skewness and kurtosis of the population. One can show that the more intuitive estimators

$$\tilde{S} = \frac{1}{T} \sum_{t=1}^{T} \left(\frac{R_{t-1,t} - \bar{R}}{\sigma} \right)^3 \tag{3.16}$$

and

$$\tilde{K} = \frac{1}{T} \sum_{t=1}^{T} \left(\frac{R_{t-1,t} - \bar{R}}{\sigma} \right)^4 - 3 \tag{3.17}$$

work perfectly in the sample, but are biased estimators of the skewness and kurtosis of the population.

Armed with the estimated skewness and kurtosis of a distribution, it is possible to run a battery of statistical tests to verify if the assumption of normality is plausible. Among these, the Bera–Jarque test (Jarque and Bera, 1987) is one of the most popular. As an illustration, Table 3.2 shows the calculation of skewness, kurtosis and the Bera–Jarque test for the fund we introduced in Table 3.1, as well as for the MSCI World index. We clearly see that in general, the normality assumption is rejected for the fund. It is only when we remove some outliers (e.g. August 1998, October 1987) that the normality assumption cannot be rejected. By comparison, the hypothesis of normal distribution seems generally more plausible with the MSCI World.

Box 3.3

The Bera–Jarque test evaluates the hypothesis that a series of returns has a normal distribution with unspecified mean and variance, against the alternative hypothesis that the series of returns does not have a normal distribution. Intuitively, for a normal distribution, the sample skewness should be near 0 and the sample kurtosis should be near 3. The Bera–Jarque combines skewness and kurtosis into a single statistic and determines whether the latter is unusually different from its expected value.

The Bera–Jarque statistic is defined as:

$$\text{JB} = \frac{T}{6} \left[\text{Skewness}^2 + \frac{\text{Kurtosis}^2}{4} \right] \tag{3.18}$$

The Bera–Jarque statistic follows a chi-square distribution with two degrees of freedom. If the value of JB calculated from a sample is greater than a critical value, the null hypothesis of asymptotic normality is rejected. The relevant critical value depends on the level of significance desired. For instance, for a level of significance of 5%, the critical value is 5.99; for a level of significance of 1%, the critical value is 9.21. Note that the Bera–Jarque test is an asymptotic test, and should not be used with very small samples.

Table 3.2 Skewness, kurtosis and Bera–Jarque normality test. The trimmed sample corresponds to the whole sample minus the 2% most extreme values (positive or negative)

	Whole sample		Trimmed sample	
Since fund inception	Fund	MSCI World	Fund	MSCI World
Average (%)	0.82	0.75	0.86	0.80
Volatility (%)	3.23	4.48	2.71	4.09
Skewness	−0.91	−0.51	−0.35	−0.29
Kurtosis	5.88	1.10	1.20	−0.01
Min return (%)	−17.46	−16.96	−7.97	−10.98
Max return (%)	11.87	11.77	8.49	10.55
Number of observations	203	203	199	199
Bera–Jarque	320.51	18.93	16.00	2.70
Normality	Rejected	Rejected	Rejected	Not rejected
	Whole sample		Trimmed sample	
Since January 1994	Fund	MSCI World	Fund	MSCI World
Average (%)	0.65	0.57	0.67	0.62
Volatility (%)	2.71	4.30	2.53	4.05
Skewness	−0.34	−0.54	−0.28	−0.40
Kurtosis	1.37	0.34	1.24	−0.14
Min return (%)	−7.67	−13.32	−6.87	−10.98
Max return (%)	7.38	9.06	7.24	8.93
Number of observations	114	114	112	112
Bera–Jarque	11.09	6.05	8.69	3.14
Normality	Rejected	Not rejected	Not rejected	Not rejected

Normal distributions are therefore nothing more than an ideal type rarely encountered in practice. Without outliers, in normal market conditions, fund and index returns may seem to be normally distributed. However, as soon as a few market crashes and rallies occur, the normality assumption vanishes. This implies that there is still a great deal of research needed to fully understand the processes at work. We simply do not yet know what are the appropriate models to characterize most financial series – we have approximations that may work in certain situations, but are clearly not the true model.[9]

3.3 DOWNSIDE RISK MEASURES

3.3.1 From volatility to downside risk

Intuitively, volatility seems an appealing measure of risk. It is easily calculated, based on well-known statistical concepts, and is easily interpretable: it measures how consistently a series of returns was delivered in the past. Naturally, the implicit theory is that the more consistently

---

[9] This explains why most econometric techniques rely on asymptotic convergence to normality as the sample of returns gets larger, and not on finite sample normality. For a large sample, the asymptotic normal distribution of the estimated parameters is established by the central limit theorem, but nothing similar exists for small samples. Note also that the standard assumption in theoretical finance is that the continuously compounded returns $r_{t,t+1}$ are independent and identically normally distributed. This implies that the simple returns, $R_{t,t+1}$, as well as the prices or net asset values, are independent and identically log-normally distributed.

returns occurred in the past, the more likely it is that the investor will receive similar returns in the future. However, volatility also has some drawbacks as a measure of risk.

First, volatility measures only the dispersion of returns around their historical average. Since positive and negative deviations from the average are penalized equally in the calculation process, the concept only makes sense for symmetrical distributions. Most investors will feel comfortable with this symmetry assumption, because they recall the normal distribution from their introduction to statistics. However, in practice, most return distributions are neither normal nor even symmetrically distributed. This creates problems, because even though two investments may have the same mean and volatility, they may differ significantly in terms of their higher moments such as skewness and kurtosis. This is particularly the case for (i) dynamic trading strategies, such as portfolio insurance and stop losses; (ii) strategies involving buying or selling options; and (iii) strategies that actively manage their leverage. All these strategies are likely to be used by hedge funds and they create asymmetries and "fat tails" in return distributions that render the volatility less meaningful and require asymmetric risk considerations.

Second, it is questionable how relevant the dispersion of returns around an average is from an investor's standpoint. Indeed, this runs contrary to the way most investors feel about returns. Few investors fret about their portfolios doubling. Most only perceive risk as a failure to achieve a specific goal, such as the risk-free rate or a benchmark rate. The level of this rate may vary from one investor to another, but the failure carries certain consequences. For instance, a pension fund that fails to achieve a minimum return may have to raise contributions. It would only consider "risk" as the downside of the return distribution, the upside being "success", "talent" or just "luck". Volatility clearly does not capture this distinction.

Finally, the third argument against volatility is that investors are often more adverse to negative deviations than they are pleased with positive ones of the same magnitude.[10] This calls for a heavier weight on negative returns, whereas in calculating volatility, deviations above and below the mean return are given weights equal to their probability of occurring. Therefore, even when the distribution is symmetrical, volatility will not be in line with investors' perceptions.

As a result of these limitations, misleading conclusions may easily be drawn when analyzing an investment using standard deviation alone. Just as an illustration, consider the case of a position combining a long stock protected by an at-the-money put option. Even though we assume a normally distributed stock return distribution, the protected stock distribution is not normal any more, but is positively skewed. Its downside risk is limited, while its upside potential is still virtually unlimited. The problem when using the volatility of such a position is simply that it no longer measures the risk! Since the downside is limited, an increase in the volatility can simply arise from outliers on the right side of the distribution, that is, from an increased probability of higher returns. Uncertainty is therefore greater, but risk clearly remains the same.

These major drawbacks of volatility as a measure of risk explain why investors and researchers have developed several alternative risk measures.

Unlike standard deviation, downside risk measures attempt to define risk more in accordance with the investor's perception. That is, they consider that returns above a prespecified target represent an opportunity rather than a financial risk, while variability of returns below this target is precisely what we should call risk – see Figure 3.7.

---

[10] This is called "prospect theory", and was originally conceptualized by Kahneman and Tversky (1979).

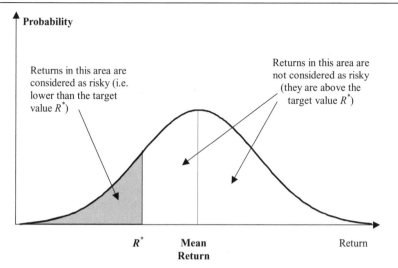

Figure 3.7   Measuring downside risk on the return distribution

Hence, investors should be interested in minimizing downside risk rather than volatility for at least two reasons: (i) only downside risk or safety first is relevant to an investor and (ii) security distributions may not be normally distributed, so that variance does not perform well as a risk measure. Therefore a downside risk measure would help investors make proper decisions when faced with non-normal security return distributions.[11]

3.3.2   Semi-variance and semi-deviation

The calculation of a downside risk measure parallels that of variance and standard deviation. Starting from a sample of T returns $(R_{0,1}, R_{1,2}, \ldots, R_{T-1,T})$, the difference between each return $R_{t-1,t}$ and the prespecified target rate of return R^* is computed. These differences are then squared and averaged. This gives a form of downside variance. Taking the square root yields the downside risk.

Mathematically:

$$\text{Downside risk}_P = \frac{1}{T}\sqrt{\sum_{t=1}^{T} d_{t-1,t}^2} \qquad (3.19)$$

where

$$d_{t-1,t} = \begin{cases} R^* - R_{t-1,t} & \text{if } R_{t-1,t} < R^* \\ 0 & \text{otherwise} \end{cases} \qquad (3.20)$$

Unlike standard deviation, downside risk accommodates different subjective views of risk by changing the target rate R^*. However, it is obvious that the choice of a specific target rate will have a large influence on the downside risk measure, and therefore on its accuracy and

---

[11] When distributions are normally distributed and, more generally, when distributions are symmetrical, both the downside risk measure and the variance provide the same measure of risk. In a sense, the downside risk will be equal to the upside potential.

stability.[12] In practice, investors often set R^* equal to the average (historical) return, zero, or a given moving target such as the risk-free rate or any benchmark rate.

- When R^* is set equal to the average return, the corresponding downside risk measure is called the below-mean semi-deviation, or *semi-deviation*; its square is called the below-mean semi-variance or *semi-variance*. Markowitz (1959) already considered it as a valuable alternative to volatility for those who are concerned about below average performance, but he did not apply it in his groundbreaking analysis. The reasons were essentially that (i) computing power in the 1950s was insufficient to deal with the corresponding calculations and (ii) with normally distributed returns, semi-deviation is proportional to volatility and provides no greater insight into the relative risk of different assets or portfolios. Subsequently, the improvement in computing power and the gradual realization that returns were not normal led to the development of semi-deviation-based portfolio theories. However, semi-deviation has the major drawback that it is only observable *ex post*, i.e. once things have happened, because it requires the average return.
- When the target rate R^* is set at zero, the corresponding measure captures the variability of negative returns (i.e. losses). This measure is often used in the case of risk-averse private clients who are particularly worried about the risk of losing money.
- Finally, when the target rate R^* is set equal to a moving target such as the risk-free rate or a market index, the corresponding measure captures the variability of returns below a benchmark. It is called the below-target semi-deviation and its square is called the below-target semi-variance. This measure of risk is of particular interest to institutional investors, who typically have minimum return requirements and are benchmarked against reference indices.

After proposing the semi-variance measure, Markowitz (1959) stayed with the variance measure because it was computationally simpler. In addition, all the modern portfolio theories developed in the 1960s assumed normally distributed returns, that is, a particular case in which the below-mean semi-variance should be one-half of the variance.[13] Nevertheless, research on semi-variance did continue, both by practitioners and by academics. Other more intuitive downside risk statistics were developed to provide investors with more information than simply a downside deviation number. They also offer insight into the causes of the risk. These include:

- The *downside frequency*, which tells investors how often returns fall below the minimum target return. It helps investors to assess accurately the likelihood of a bad outcome.
- The *gain standard deviation*, which is similar to the standard deviation except that it calculates an average (mean) return only for the periods with a *gain* and then measures the variation of only the *gain* periods around this gain mean. In a sense, the gain standard deviation measures the volatility of upside performance.
- The *loss standard deviation*, which measures the volatility of downside performance. It calculates an average (mean) return only for the periods with a loss and then measures the variation of only the losing periods around this loss mean.

---

[12] Stability implies that, whatever the target rate chosen, the value of the downside risk will change by only an infinitesimal amount as we vary the target rate. Graphically, this means that the graph of the downside risk as a function of the target rate is approximately horizontal around the chosen point (or "locally stable", as some would say).

[13] In fact, taking the variance and dividing it by the below-mean semi-variance yields an alternative measure of skewness. If the ratio is not equal to 2, then there is evidence that the distribution is skewed or asymmetric.

Although downside risk measures can provide additional insight into the risk profile of potential investments, downside risk is only slowly gaining acceptance in the financial community. There are essentially two reasons for this. First, as we mentioned earlier, in the context of normal distributions, downside risk measures are simply proportional to volatility and do not add much information. Most investors feel comfortable assuming normal distributions, even though this is not very realistic in practice. Second, many practitioners have just adopted standard deviation as a risk measure and they are reluctant to embrace another measurement tool that could yield conflicting results. This is accentuated by the fact that there are a number of ways to calculate downside risk, each of which can potentially yield different results. It is therefore essential that individuals interpreting downside risk statistics understand the calculation methodology, because downside risk statistics calculated using different assumptions are not comparable.

3.3.3   The shortfall risk measures

The starting point of *shortfall risk measures* is a target return denoted R^* and predefined by the investor. Risk is then to be considered to be the possibility of not attaining this target return. Special cases of shortfall risk measures are the shortfall probability, the shortfall expectation and the shortfall variance.

The shortfall probability is the probability of a fund's returns dipping below the target R^*. Mathematically:

$$\text{Risk} = \Pr(R_{t,t+1} < R^*) \tag{3.21}$$

The target rate R^* may be static (e.g. equal to zero) or stochastic (e.g. equal to an inflation rate, the risk-free rate or a market index return). The concept is therefore relative rather than absolute. Investment strategies that minimize the shortfall probability are referred to as "probability maximizing strategies", in that they maximize the probability of reaching the investment goal.

Note that the shortfall probability only evaluates the probability of a shortfall with respect to the target but does not evaluate the potential extent of this shortfall. Hence, to assess how severe an undesirable event might be, shortfall probabilities are often accompanied by an indication of the maximum loss or the average shortfall (that is, the expected value of the underperformance, conditional on being below the benchmark rate), as well as by the shortfall variance (that is, the variance of the underperformance, conditional on being below the benchmark rate).

3.3.4   Value at risk

Value at risk (VaR) is a relatively recent risk measure in finance, but its equivalent has been used for several years in statistics. Simply stated, the value at risk of a position is the maximum amount of capital that the position can expect to lose within a specified holding period (e.g. 10 days or one month) and with a specified confidence level (e.g. 95% or 99%). In terms of probability theory, VaR at the $p\%$ confidence level is the $(1 - p)\%$ quantile of the profit and loss distribution. Note that VaR is often expressed as a percentage loss rather than as an absolute dollar loss to facilitate comparisons.

An example will make this clearer – see Figure 3.8. Say we want to compute the one-month 99% value at risk of the Morgan Stanley Capital Index USA, from December 1969 to October 2000, using monthly non-annualized data. All that needs to be done is to observe the series of one-month returns for the stock, build up the corresponding return distribution, and exclude

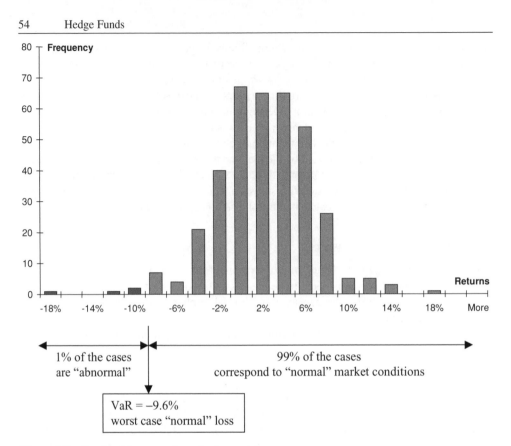

Figure 3.8   Graphical interpretation of value at risk

1% of the cases as being "abnormal" market conditions. The worst-case remaining return (−9.6%) is the value at risk of the index, expressed in percentage terms. It corresponds to the 1% percentile of the return distribution, i.e. 1% of the observed values are lower than the VaR and 99% are higher than the VaR.

When the distribution of returns is a normal distribution,[14] VaR is simply equal to the average return minus a multiple of the volatility (e.g. for a confidence level of 99%, VaR is equal to the average return minus 2.33 times the standard deviation). In this case, the concept of VaR does not generate any new information; it is just a different, less technical form of risk reporting, in which the term volatility is replaced by the perhaps easier to understand term value at risk. However, it is well known that in practice, the assumption of a normal distribution is questionable for most assets, and particularly for hedge funds. It is therefore not surprising that VaR has become the standard tool in risk management for banks and other financial institutions.

However, without the assumption of a normal distribution, VaR is a very problematic risk measure. In particular, VaR may violate second-order stochastic dominance and therefore does not always describe risk aversion in the traditional sense – see Guthoff *et al.* (1998). But more importantly, VaR is not sub-additive – see Artzner *et al.* (1997, 1999). That is, the sum of

---

[14] More generally, this holds for all elliptic probability distributions.

Table 3.3 The VaR is not necessarily sub-additive.
In this example, the VaR of the combined
investments is larger than the sum of individual VaRs

Scenario	Loss X_1	Loss X_2	Loss $X_1 + X_2$
1	0	0	0
2	0	0	0
3	0	0	0
4	0	0	0
5	0	0	0
6	0	0	0
7	0	0	0
8	0	0	0
9	0	−1	−1
10	−1	0	−1
VaR$_{85\%}$	0	0	−1

the risks of two separate funds (X and Y) may be lower than the risk of the pooled portfolio
(X + Y). Mathematically:

$$VaR(X + Y) \geq VaR(X) + VaR(Y) \tag{3.22}$$

Consider as an illustration two funds X_1 and X_2 and 10 possible scenarios. Table 3.3 shows the
losses of funds X_1 and X_2 in each scenario. Clearly, the value at risk at an 85% confidence level
violates the sub-additivity property. This creates an incentive to divide the two-fund portfolio
into single-fund sub-portfolios to lower the apparent level of risk. This lack of sub-additivity
makes VaR a problematic criterion for portfolio optimization, the internal allocation of capital,
and for the design of VaR-type risk-adjusted compensation schemes.

Last, but not least, VaR does not provide any information about the expected size of the loss
beyond the considered "normal market conditions". This is why VaR is often complemented
by the *expected shortfall* (or conditional VaR), which measures the expected loss of a portfolio
conditional on the portfolio loss exceeding the VaR. An interesting discussion of expected
shortfall is Rockafellar and Uryasev (2002). Note that one can easily show that the expected
shortfall is sub-additive.

3.3.5 Drawdown statistics

Another key measure of track record quality and/or strategy risk is the notion of drawdown,
which is defined as the decline in net asset value from the highest historical point. Often
expressed as a percentage loss, it can be interpreted as the "regret" an investor would have for
not selling at the highest price (see Figure 3.9).

There are in fact several ways of calculating drawdown statistics. An individual *drawdown*
is basically any losing period during an investment record. The *maximum drawdown* or "*peak
to valley*" is therefore the maximum loss (in percentage terms) that an investor could have
experienced within a specific time period. The *uninterrupted drawdown* calculates the length
and severity of an uninterrupted drop. The *recovery time* or *drawdown duration* is the time
taken to recover from a drawdown and come back to the original level. By looking at the size

Table 3.4 List of drawdowns experienced by the CSFB/Tremont since its inception in January 1994

Peak date	Trough date	Decline (%)	Recovery date	Decline duration (months)	Recovery duration (months)
Jan-94	Apr-94	−9.13	Jul-95	3	15
Sep-95	Oct-95	−0.11	Nov-95	1	1
Jan-96	Feb-96	−3.59	Apr-96	1	2
Jun-96	Jul-96	−4.13	Sep-96	1	2
Feb-97	Mar-97	−1.41	Apr-97	1	1
Jul-97	Aug-97	−1.26	Sep-97	1	1
Sep-97	Oct-97	−1.64	Dec-97	1	2
Dec-97	Jan-98	−1.21	Feb-98	1	1
Jul-98	Oct-98	−13.81	Nov-99	3	13
Dec-99	Jan-00	−0.1	Feb-00	1	1
Feb-00	May-00	−7.74	May-01	3	12
Jun-01	Jul-01	−0.02	Aug-01	1	1
Aug-01	Sep-01	−0.83	Nov-01	1	2
Jan-02	Feb-02	−0.56	Mar-02	1	1
May-02	Jul-02	−2.18	Dec-02	2	5

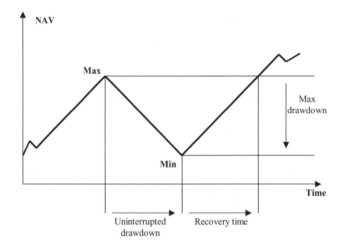

Figure 3.9 The drawdown concept

and duration of past drawdowns (expressed as a percentage of portfolio value), an investor can realistically assess the pain he would feel with that fund manager, were the situation to recur.

Drawdowns have one major advantage over volatility: they refer to a physical reality, and as such they are less abstract. In the United States, the Commodity Futures Trading Commission requires managed futures advisors to disclose their maximum drawdown. However, a large number of hedge fund managers voluntarily disclose this statistic to evidence the quality of their track record. As an illustration, Table 3.4 shows the list of drawdowns experienced on the CSFB/Tremont hedge fund index since its inception in 1994.

Despite their intuitive nature, maximum drawdown statistics should be used with caution, for at least two reasons:

- Other things being equal, maximum drawdowns will be greater as the frequency of the measurement interval becomes smaller. Investments that are marked to market daily, such as managed futures or traditional assets, may thus appear at a disadvantage to less frequently valued investments (e.g. hedge funds). Hence, it is never appropriate to compare maximum drawdowns between time series with different reporting intervals without making an appropriate correction.
- Other things being equal, maximum drawdowns will be greater for a longer time series, so that managers with longer track records will tend to have deeper maximum drawdown figures. Hence, it is never appropriate to compare maximum drawdowns between time series with different time lengths.

In addition, one should remember that the maximum drawdown is a single number derived from a single string of data without any sort of averaging process. Because of the uniqueness of that observation, the result is highly error-prone and thus not necessarily very useful in building statistical inferences for the future. From a statistical perspective, a better risk measure would be the average of a series of largest drawdowns. Last, but not least, one should remember that the maximum drawdown cannot identify the current risk in a portfolio until after losses occur.

3.4   BENCHMARK-RELATED STATISTICS

Although they are sold as absolute performers, hedge funds often produce ratios that compare their performance with that of a selected market index or benchmark. Some of these ratios do not rely on any statistical or financial theory, but are just intuitive by nature. Others find their roots in the origins of financial theory. In the following, we will only list the essential ones.

3.4.1   Intuitive benchmark-related statistics

Among the popular ratios on the investor side are the following:

- The *capture indicator*, which is the average of the captured performance (that is, the average ratio between the fund's returns and the benchmark's returns). It is somewhat hard to interpret, because conclusions depend upon the sign of the benchmark's returns.
- The *up capture indicator*, which is calculated as the fund's average return divided by the benchmark average return, considering only periods when the benchmark was up. The greater the value the better.
- The *down capture indicator*, which is the fund's average return divided by the benchmark average return, considering only periods when the benchmark was down. The smaller the ratio the better.
- The *up number ratio*, which measures the number of periods in which the fund was up when the benchmark was up, divided by the number of periods in which the benchmark was up. The larger the ratio the better.
- The *down number ratio*, which measures the number of periods in which the fund was down when the benchmark was down, divided by the number of periods in which the benchmark was down. The smaller the ratio the better.
- The *up percentage ratio*, which measures the number of periods in which the fund outperformed the benchmark when the benchmark was up, divided by the number of periods when the benchmark was up. The larger the ratio the better.

Table 3.5   Intuitive benchmark-related statistics for the fund of Table 3.1

Capture indicator	1.09
Up capture	0.46
Down capture	0.13
Up number ratio	0.77
Down number ratio	0.50
Up percentage ratio	0.29
Down percentage ratio	0.79
Percent gain ratio	1.11
Negative months over total	34%

- The *down percentage ratio*, which is a measure of the number of periods in which the fund outperformed the benchmark when the benchmark was down, divided by the number of periods when the benchmark was down. The larger the ratio the better.
- The *percent gain ratio*, which is a measure of the number of periods in which the fund was up divided by the number of periods in which the benchmark was up. The larger the ratio the better.
- The *ratio of negative months over total months*, which is also a good indicator of the downside risk of a fund, although it neglects the absolute size of returns in positive and negative months.

As an illustration, Table 3.5 shows the values obtained for the fund considered in Table 3.1. The benchmark is the MSCI World.

3.4.2   Beta and market risk

Another interesting relative risk measure is called beta and is denoted by the Greek symbol β. Simply stated, beta measures how risky a fund may be as compared to the overall stock market, typically approximated to the Standard & Poor's 500 or the MSCI World. A fund that moves in harmony with the market is said to have a beta of 1.0. Other things being equal, if the market goes up 10%, the fund is expected to go up 10%. If the market goes down 10%, the fund is expected to go down 10%. When a fund has a beta that is less than one, it is supposed to move less in price than the market in general. Conversely, a fund with a beta higher than one is supposed to move more in price than the market in general. Hence, beta measures the risk of a fund by telling us how much its market price changes compared to changes in the overall stock market. A fund with a beta of more than one tends to be riskier than the market, while a fund with a beta of less than one is less risky.

As an illustration, the beta of the fund we considered in Table 3.1 was 0.30 against the MSCI World, which is rather low. This is not really surprising, because most hedge funds claim to deliver absolute performance, that is, returns that are independent of market conditions. Hence, they should display low levels of beta in general (Figure 3.10).

It is essential at this stage to understand that beta focuses only on the impact of the overall stock market, and ignores all other influences, which are considered as specific risk. In a sense, beta is an incomplete explanation of risk and returns. A low beta fund does not necessarily mean low risk. It simply means low exposure to the market, or more simply, low market risk. A fund that has a low beta and a high volatility is an indication that most of the risk carried by the fund is not coming from market movements, but is completely specific.

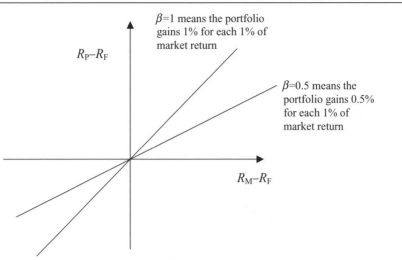

$\beta=1$ means the portfolio gains 1% for each 1% of market return

R_P-R_F

$\beta=0.5$ means the portfolio gains 0.5% for each 1% of market return

R_M-R_F

Figure 3.10   Interpreting beta as the slope of a regression line when plotting the excess returns of a portfolio ($R_P - R_F$) against the excess returns of the market ($R_M - R_F$)

3.4.3   Tracking error

Tracking error is one of the most commonly used measures in traditional fund management, where performance is usually evaluated against a prespecified benchmark portfolio. Tracking error quantifies precisely the degree to which the performance of a fund differs from that of its benchmark. The lower the tracking error, the more the fund resembles its benchmark's risk and return characteristics. Although the concept is simple, readers should be aware that there are several definitions of the tracking error in financial literature.

Tracking error is sometimes defined as differences between the fund returns and the benchmark portfolio returns – see Hwang and Satchell (2001). For this definition, a positive tracking error is synonymous of outperforming the benchmark:

$$\text{TE}_{\text{SD}} = \sqrt{\frac{1}{T} \sum_{t=1}^{T} \left(R_{t-1,t} - R_{t-1,t}^{\text{benchmark}} \right)} \tag{3.23}$$

Tracking error can be defined as the standard deviation of the returns difference between the fund and the benchmark portfolio. In this case, a high tracking error reflects a large deviation (either positive or negative) from the benchmark:

$$\text{TE}_{\text{SD}} = \sqrt{\frac{1}{T-1} \sum_{t=1}^{T} \left(R_{t-1,t} - R_{t-1,t}^{\text{benchmark}} \right)^2} \tag{3.24}$$

Rudolf *et al.* (1999) argue that the quadratic form of TE_{SD} is difficult to interpret, and that portfolio managers typically think in terms of linear and not quadratic deviation from a benchmark. Hence, they suggest a linear version of the tracking error expressed in terms of mean absolute deviations (MAD) of the differences between portfolio returns and the benchmark portfolio returns. In this case, a high tracking error also reflects a large deviation (either positive or negative) from the benchmark:

$$\text{TE}_{\text{MAD}} = \frac{1}{T-1} \sum_{t=1}^{T} \left| R_{t-1,t} - R_{t-1,t}^{\text{benchmark}} \right| \tag{3.25}$$

All of these definitions can be used for *ex ante* tracking error (using forecast active and benchmark returns) as well as *ex post* tracking error (using realized active and benchmark returns). In all cases, the benchmark is key as it is the *de facto* position of neutrality for the fund manager. If a manager were to simply follow the benchmark, the expectation would be that his performance should equal the performance of the benchmark, and his tracking error should be nil.

Note that so far, the notion of tracking error has not yet entered the hedge fund world. But things are likely to change in the near future, as some institutional investors will certainly attempt to track some of the recently created investable hedge fund indices.

4
Risk-Adjusted Performance Measures

If you can't measure it then you can't manage it.

Most comparisons of hedge funds concentrate exclusively on total return figures. They openly ignore risk measures and risk-adjusted performance and claim to care only about absolute returns. Even worse, they provide no means of establishing the extent to which good past performance has been due to chance as opposed to skill. Nevertheless, these comparisons are widely used by marketers to show that their funds are superior to the competition. A 50% return over one year sounds better than 10%, right?

Needless to say, when the funds or indices in question exhibit different risk characteristics, naive comparisons of this nature become extremely misleading. Investors who rely solely on returns to pick a hedge fund may not be prepared for the wild ride that lies ahead. Investing is by nature a two-dimensional process based not only on returns, but also on the risks taken to achieve those returns. The two factors are opposite sides of the same coin, and both should be taken into consideration in order to make sound investment decisions.[1]

Comparing funds that have the same risk characteristics or the same return characteristics is straightforward: at equal risk, more return is always better; at equal return, less risk is always preferable. Difficulties start when we have two or more funds with different expected returns and risks. In particular, given that a higher expected return is desirable but a higher risk is not, how should one compare a high-return, high-risk fund with another fund that has a lower return and a lower risk? The question, then, is this: on a relative scale, how much additional return is sufficient compensation for additional risk? This is precisely where risk-adjusted performance measures are helpful.[2]

Condensing return and risk into *one* useful risk-adjusted number is one of the key tasks of performance measurement. When correctly done, performance measurement reduces the rugged terrain of investment to a level playing field; it thus becomes possible to compare the performance of a given fund with other funds having *similar* risk characteristics, as well as with other funds having *different* risk characteristics. It also opens the door to the correct measurement of excess performance over a benchmark – the famous so-called "alpha". These aspects are of prime interest to both investors and money managers, as members of the former group typically select members of the latter group on the basis of their past performance statistics, and will reward them with incentive fees calculated on the basis of their future performance.

In practice, we have a number of performance measures at our disposal that will help us to choose between risky investments.[3] The list is so long that it almost seems as if each hedge fund

---

[1] Unfortunately, depending on the market conditions, investors tend to concentrate their attention more on either return or risk, but rarely on both at the same time. When markets rose as they did through much of the 1990s, many investors worried only about missing out on the market's huge gains felt comfortable just to be participating. After all, double-digit returns every year were good enough for anyone, right? However, with the end of the equity cult, as fear overtook greed, investors were somehow forced to rediscover risk.

[2] Note that in the following, we tend to anthropomorphize hedge funds. We should keep in mind that when we evaluate their performance, we are in fact judging the performance of their manager, who takes the investment decisions for the portfolio.

[3] See, for instance, Amenc and le Sourd (2003) for a survey.

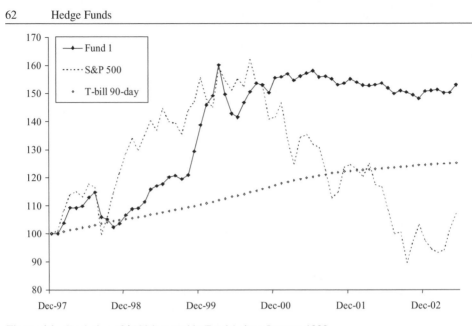

Figure 4.1   Evolution of $100 invested in Fund 1 since January 1998

manager can choose his own measure. How should we select just one to use in our evaluations? Or do we really need them all? Or, perhaps more importantly, can we identify which approach is best? Below we review various measures of risk-adjusted performance, describe their logic, strengths and weaknesses, and answer some key, but typically ignored, questions. As we shall see, each performance measure answers a specific question; there is no all-round champion. There is, however, a performance measure for each specific goal.

We illustrate our review by looking at a sample of five hedge funds over the January 1998– May 2003 period, making no claim that the sample or the period is representative of anything in particular. The selection simply consists of funds that have very different qualitative and quantitative characteristics in different market conditions. As the names of the funds are not relevant to the exercise, they have been omitted. Instead, each is identified by a number.

Fund 1 is a fund of hedge funds that aims at producing long-term risk-adjusted capital appreciation. It focuses on several strategies, e.g. long/short, global macro, arbitrage and managed futures. Its portfolio is diversified, with around 25 to 30 managers. The total fund size is $1 billion (Figure 4.1).

Fund 2 invests and trades primarily in US equities, both long and short. Stock selections are opportunistic, bottom-up, and are based on fundamental analysis. The portfolio is widely diversified, with 200 to 250 stocks and a maximum of 4% allocation per position, inclusive of both long and short positions. The portfolio is actively traded. The fund size is larger than $3 billion (Figure 4.2).

Fund 3 invests primarily in US equities and bonds, both long and short. In selecting investments for the fund, the investment manager emphasizes both individual stock selection and general economic analysis. The portfolio is widely diversified, with a maximum of 2.5% allocation per position, and historically a long bias. The fund size is larger than $2 billion (Figure 4.3).

Fund 4 is a relative value, fixed income, arbitrage fund. The fund trades actively, with 15 to 25 different strategies (yield curve arbitrage, options, OTC derivatives, short swaps

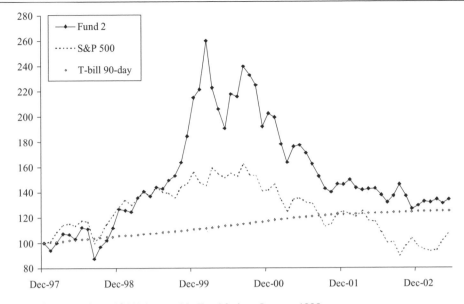

Figure 4.2   Evolution of $100 invested in Fund 2 since January 1998

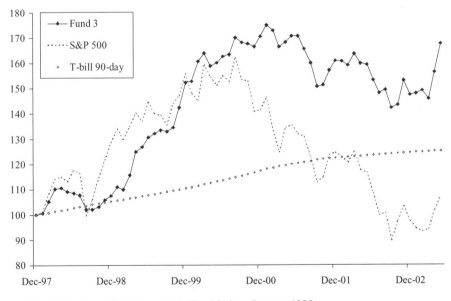

Figure 4.3   Evolution of $100 invested in Fund 3 since January 1998

and long corporate credit, etc.). Its portfolio typically contains 50 to 100 positions, mostly from G10 countries (in fact, 90% in the US fixed income market). The fund size is $1.8 billion and the maximum leverage 20 times (Figure 4.4).

Fund 5 seeks maximum capital appreciation, mainly in the USA, with the flexibility of investing internationally. Its primary asset class is equity, although it may use derivatives from time to time. The fund utilizes a bottom-up approach in security selection and does not place

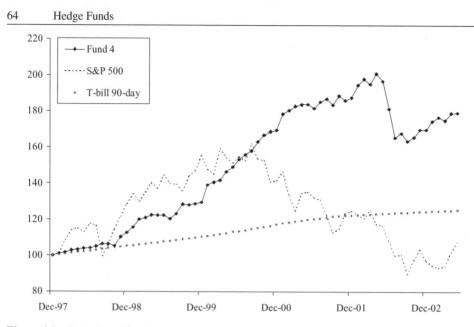

Figure 4.4   Evolution of $100 invested in Fund 4 since January 1998

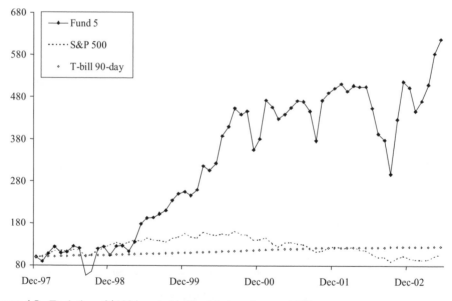

Figure 4.5   Evolution of $100 invested in Fund 5 since January 1998

major bets on the direction of the market. It invests in a concentrated number of stocks, both long and short. The fund size is $120 million, the maximum leverage is two times, and the least we can say is that the manager is rather aggressive (Figure 4.5).

The risk and return figures differ widely between funds. For instance, it is relatively difficult to compare directly the return of Fund 5 (39.96% p.a.) with the return of Fund 1 (8.16% p.a.),

Table 4.1 Average return and volatility calculation for our five different hedge funds (all data are annualized)

	Fund 1	Fund 2	Fund 3	Fund 4	Fund 5
Mean return (%)	8.16	5.56	9.98	11.36	39.96
Volatility (%)	9.55	29.48	11.45	8.95	79.53
Best month (%)	7.38	17.44	8.10	7.49	80.90
Worst month (%)	−7.67	−21.17	−5.80	−8.81	−53.57
% of positive months	65%	49%	60%	78%	65%

Table 4.2 Sharpe ratio calculation for five different hedge funds (all data are annualized; the T-bill rate has an average return of 4.23% p.a. over the period)

	Fund 1	Fund 2	Fund 3	Fund 4	Fund 5
Mean return (%)	8.16	5.56	9.98	11.36	39.96
Volatility (%)	9.55	29.48	11.45	8.95	79.53
Sharpe ratio	0.41	0.05	0.50	0.80	0.45

because of their different volatility level (79.53% versus 9.55%). Thanks to the performance measures we review below, we will be able to do an apples-to-apples comparison (Table 4.1).

4.1 THE SHARPE RATIO

Devised by William Sharpe (1966), a Nobel Prize-winning economics professor, the Sharpe ratio undoubtedly remains the most commonly used measure of risk-adjusted performance.

4.1.1 Definition and interpretation

The definition of the Sharpe ratio is remarkably simple. The Sharpe ratio measures the amount of "excess return per unit of volatility" provided by a fund. It is calculated by dividing the excess return[4] of the fund by its volatility. Algebraically, we have:

$$\text{Sharpe ratio}_P = \frac{R_P - R_F}{\sigma_P} \qquad (4.1)$$

where R_P is the average return on portfolio P, R_F is the risk-free asset, and σ_P is the standard deviation of returns on portfolio P. All numbers are usually expressed on an annual basis, so the Sharpe ratio itself is expressed on an annual basis.[5]

As an illustration, Table 4.2 shows the Sharpe ratios calculated for our five hedge funds. The interpretation of the Sharpe ratio is straightforward: the higher the ratio the better. A high

---

[4] Excess return here means return above the risk-free rate. The risk-free asset is often specified as Treasury bills, even though in his 1966 study, Sharpe used the yield on 10-year Treasury bonds as a risk-free proxy. Note that the use of a zero risk-free rate in calculating the Sharpe ratio is neither especially realistic nor the standard way in which this measure is commonly used. Nevertheless, it is sometimes encountered, because the benefits of the simplicity and comparability that it provides outweigh these two considerations.

[5] If this is not the case, some caution is necessary, as the Sharpe ratio is in fact time-dependent. As a first-order approximation, return increases proportionally with time, while volatility increases proportionally with the square root of time. Hence, the overall Sharpe ratio increases proportionally with the square root of time. An annual Sharpe ratio will therefore be $\sqrt{12}$ bigger than a monthly Sharpe ratio.

Sharpe ratio means that the fund in question delivered a high return for its level of volatility, which is always good. In contrast, a Sharpe ratio of 1.0 indicates a return on investment that is proportional to the risk taken in achieving that return, and a Sharpe ratio lower than one indicates a return on investment that is less than the risk taken. In our case, over the period in question, we can see that Fund 5 was in fact better than Fund 1 because it offered a reward of 0.45% p.a. per unit of volatility, while Fund 1 only offered 0.41% p.a. However, the best fund in the group appears to be Fund 4, with a reward of 0.80% p.a. per unit of volatility – which corresponds to a Sharpe ratio of 0.80.

How can one interpret this 0.80 figure? Consider for instance the case of an investor who holds the risk-free asset (4.23% return, no volatility). If this investor agrees to purchase Fund 4 shares (11.36% return, 8.95% volatility), the incremental return is 7.13% (11.36% minus 4.23%) and the incremental risk is 8.95% (8.95% minus 0%). Hence, the ratio of incremental return to incremental risk is 7.13%/8.95% ≈ 0.80. In other terms, the investor is willing to accept an increase in volatility of 1% as long as this increase is rewarded by 0.80% return. This is precisely what a Sharpe ratio equal to 0.80 says.

Now, if our investor decides to allocate 50% of his portfolio to Fund 4 and the rest to the risk-free asset, he would get a portfolio with a return of 7.80% and a volatility of 4.48%. Compared to the risk-free asset, the incremental return is 3.57%, the incremental risk is 4.48%, and the Sharpe ratio is still 0.80. And if our investor decides to allocate 150% of his portfolio to Fund 4 and finance the extra 50% position by borrowing at the risk-free rate, he would get a portfolio with a return of 14.93% and a volatility of 13.43%. Compared to the risk-free asset, the incremental return is 10.70%, the incremental risk is 13.43%, and the Sharpe ratio is again 0.80. This clearly shows that the Sharpe ratio of a fund is not influenced by its leverage. All leveraged and unleveraged versions of Fund 4, and more generally, all leveraged and unleveraged versions of any portfolio, will have the same Sharpe ratio.

Graphically, in a mean return/volatility space, the Sharpe ratio is the slope of the line joining the risk-free asset to the fund being examined – see Figure 4.6. The equation of this line can be expressed as:

$$\text{Return} = \text{Risk-free rate} + (\text{Sharpe ratio} \times \text{volatility})$$

That is, in the case of Fund 4:

$$\text{Return} = 4.23\% + (0.80 \times \text{volatility})$$

The financial literature often refers to this line as the *capital allocation line*.[6] Each point on this line corresponds to a particular allocation between the risk-free asset and Fund 4. Stated differently, any portfolio on this line can be created by leveraging or de-leveraging Fund 4. It is clear from Figure 4.6 that any other fund combined with the T-bills will never reach the capital allocation line of Fund 4.

4.1.2   The Sharpe ratio as a long/short position

More recently, Sharpe (1994) revised the definition of the Sharpe ratio and suggested a new interpretation in terms of differential return with respect to a benchmark. Let R_P and R_B be the

---

[6] When the fund considered is a proxy for the stock market, the capital allocation line is referred to as the *capital market line*. It represents the set of portfolios that are made up of only T-bills and of the market index.

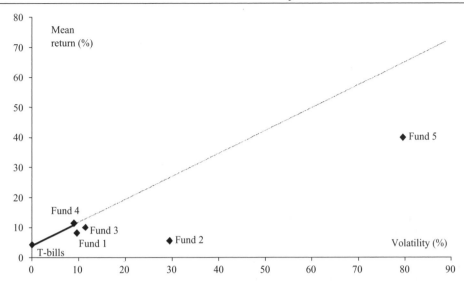

Figure 4.6 Risk/return trade-off achievable by leveraging (solid line) or de-leveraging (dotted line) Fund 4. It shows that all combinations of Fund 4 and the risk-free asset generate higher returns at the same level of risk than any combination of another fund and the risk-free asset

average returns on a fund P and on a benchmark portfolio B respectively. The differential return between the fund and its benchmark is defined as $(R_P - R_B)$. From a financial perspective, these differential returns correspond to a zero investment strategy that consists in going long on the fund in question and short on the benchmark. Alternatively, one could also swap the return on the benchmark for the return on the fund and *vice versa*.

The revised Sharpe ratio – also called the information ratio – compares the average differential return with its volatility. The latter is nothing more than the tracking error of the fund P with respect to the benchmark B. Algebraically:

$$\text{Information ratio}_P = \frac{R_P - R_B}{\text{TE}_P} \tag{4.2}$$

When the benchmark equals the risk-free rate, the information ratio equals the traditional Sharpe ratio.

The beauty of this new definition is that it allows for a more general interpretation. Let us consider the benchmark as a hypothetical initial investment and let us try to select an asset that improves on the benchmark in risk–expected return terms. In this framework, a higher information ratio represents a better departure from the benchmark because it implies an expected return larger than the return for relatively little extra risk – see Figure 4.7. Hence, we should always pick the asset that has the highest information ratio.

4.1.3   The statistics of Sharpe ratios

Most of the time, Sharpe ratios are measured and reported without any information about their statistical significance. Once again, this is regrettable. The building blocks of the Sharpe ratio – expected/average excess returns and volatility/tracking error – are unknown quantities that must be estimated statistically from a sample of returns. They are therefore subject to

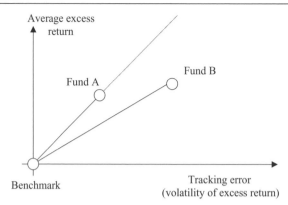

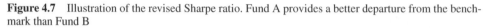

Figure 4.7   Illustration of the revised Sharpe ratio. Fund A provides a better departure from the benchmark than Fund B

estimation error, which implies that the Sharpe ratio itself is also subject to estimation error.[7] Thus, we should always verify the statistical significance of Sharpe ratio estimates before stating any conclusion about the performance of a fund.

The financial literature describes several approaches to dealing with the uncertainty surrounding Sharpe ratios.

- The first approach is the Jobson and Korkie (1981) test for the equality of the Sharpe ratios of any two portfolios. It is the first formal test of the significance of performance, but it requires normality of asset returns, which is often not the case for individual hedge funds.
- The second approach is the Gibbons, Ross and Shanken (1989) test to verify *ex ante* portfolio efficiency. Although there is a substantial theoretical difference between the two concepts of portfolio performance and portfolio efficiency, there is a close relationship between them. In particular, the test shows whether the adjunction of new assets in a universe effectively results in a significant improvement of performance, by comparing the maximum Sharpe ratios obtained for the original universe with those for the augmented universe. This test has often been applied in the literature, for instance to examine the *ex ante* efficiency of portfolios, to test the benefits of adding international investments to a domestic portfolio, or to compare equally weighted with optimized portfolios – see for instance Rubens *et al.* (1998) or Cheng and Liang (2000).
- Finally, the third approach is that described recently by Lo (2002). Although still at its early stages, this line of research is the most promising. It derives the statistical distribution of the Sharpe ratio using standard econometric methods. The derivation is made under several different sets of assumptions for the statistical behavior of the return series on which the Sharpe ratio is based – e.g. mean reversion, momentum and other forms of serial correlation. Lo finds that all these effects can have a non-trivial impact on the Sharpe ratio estimator itself. For instance, positive serial correlation can yield annualized Sharpe ratios that are overstated by more than 65%, therefore resulting in inconsistent rankings.

Whatever the approach, it is crucial that performance is investigated over a sufficiently long period of time. Without a minimum sample size, determining portfolio performance becomes

---

[7] Sharpe himself (1994) pointed out that the Sharpe ratio can be interpreted as a *t*-statistic to test the hypothesis that the return on the portfolio is equal to the risk-free return.

a hazardous task, and it is difficult to really assess whether performance was due to luck or skill – or lack of it.

Box 4.1

The Jobson and Korkie (1981) test statistic can be formulated as follows. Let μ_1 and μ_2 be the mean *excess* returns of the portfolios under investigation, σ_1 and σ_2 the return volatility of the two portfolios, and $\sigma_{1,2}$ the covariance of the two portfolio returns. The excess returns are assumed to be serially independent and normally and independently distributed.

Jobson and Korkie use the following Z-statistic:

$$Z = \frac{\sigma_1 \mu_2 - \sigma_2 \mu_1}{\sqrt{\theta}} \tag{4.3}$$

where θ is the asymptotic variance of the expression in the numerator, calculated as follows:[8]

$$\theta = \frac{1}{T}\left[2\sigma_1^2\sigma_2^2 - 2\sigma_1\sigma_2\sigma_{1,2} + \frac{1}{2}(\mu_1\sigma_2)^2 + \frac{1}{2}(\mu_2\sigma_1)^2 - \frac{\mu_1\mu_2}{\sigma_1\sigma_2}\sigma_{1,2}^2\right] \tag{4.4}$$

Jobson and Korkie show that the Z-statistic is approximately normally distributed, with a zero mean and a unit standard deviation for large samples under the null assumption that the two Sharpe ratios are equal.

A significant Z-statistic would reject the null hypothesis of equal risk-adjusted performance and would suggest that one of the investment portfolio strategies outperforms the other. However, Jobson and Korkie note that the statistical power of the test is low, especially for small sample sizes. As illustrated by Jorion (1985), at a 5% significance level, the test fails to reject a false null hypothesis up to 85% of the time. Thus, a statistically significant Z between two portfolios can be seen as strong evidence of a difference in risk-adjusted performance.

Box 4.2

The Gibbons, Ross and Shanken (1989) test compares the estimated maximum Sharpe ratio for the original universe (denoted Sharpe$_1$) with the estimated maximum Sharpe ratio for the augmented universe (denoted Sharpe$_2$). The authors show that the statistic

$$W = \left[\frac{\sqrt{1 + \text{Sharpe}_2^2}}{\sqrt{1 + \text{Sharpe}_1^2}}\right]^2 - 1 \tag{4.5}$$

follows a Wishart distribution, which is a generalization of the χ^2-distribution. Under the null hypothesis that the Sharpe ratio of the extended universe is not different from the Sharpe ratio of the original universe, the statistic W should not be statistically different from zero. Since increasing the number of assets in a universe can only improve the maximum Sharpe ratio, we are only concerned with positive values of W. Any large positive deviation from zero implies that the two Sharpe ratios are actually different.

---

[8] Note that the original Jobson and Korkie (1981) paper contains typographic errors in this expression, which led to an underestimation of the asymptotic variance, i.e. the null hypothesis is rejected too often.

Working with a Wishart distribution is not so convenient. Fortunately, a simple transformation suggested by Morrison (1976) shows that the statistic

$$F = \frac{T(T - N - 1)}{N(T - 2)} W \tag{4.6}$$

has a central F-distribution with $(N, T - N - 1)$ degrees of freedom, where T is the number of returns observed and N is the number of assets in the original universe. As with any F-statistic, N must be low in relation to T for the test to have good discriminatory power.

4.2   THE TREYNOR RATIO AND JENSEN ALPHA

Two other widely used performance measures are the Treynor ratio and the Jensen alpha (frequently simply called "alpha"). Both find their roots in financial theory, more specifically in the Capital Asset Pricing Model (CAPM) developed by Sharpe (1964).

4.2.1   The CAPM

Centerpiece of modern financial economics, the CAPM was originally developed to (i) explain the rationale for diversification; (ii) provide a theoretical structure for the pricing of assets with uncertain returns in a competitive market; and (iii) explain the differences in risk premiums across assets. A rigorous exposition of the CAPM principles and results is far beyond the scope of this book and may easily be found in the literature.[9] In the following paragraphs, therefore, we limit ourselves to recalling briefly the intuition behind the CAPM, listing its major conclusions, and then proceeding directly to their implications in terms of performance measurement.

The fundamental premise of the CAPM is that the volatility of an asset can be split into two parts: a systematic risk and a specific risk. The systematic risk part is the risk of being affected by general market movements. It represents the part of an asset's volatility that is perfectly positively or negatively correlated with the market. The specific risk, on the other hand, is specific to each asset. It represents the remaining part of an asset's volatility that is not correlated with the market.

When investors form portfolios, the systematic risk parts of individual assets are simply added up to give the systematic risk of the whole portfolio. This risk is non-diversifiable and will be present in all portfolios. The specific risk parts do not add up, however, but rather tend to compensate each other, particularly when the assets considered are negatively correlated. This is the impact of diversification. Hence, in a well-diversified portfolio, each asset's specific risk should be eliminated by diversification, so that the total portfolio's specific risk should be insignificant.

The second premise of the CAPM is that risk-averse and rational investors do not want to subject themselves to a risk that can be diversified away. Rather, they attempt to optimally construct their portfolios from uncorrelated assets in order to eliminate specific risk. As a consequence, investors should not care about the total volatility of individual assets, but only about the systematic risk component – the only risk that remains in the final portfolio.

The logical consequence of the foregoing is that there should be no reward for non-systematic risk. Although measurable at the individual asset level, specific risk will disappear at the

---

[9] See for instance Newman et al. (1992), Bodie et al. (1999), Sharpe et al. (1998), Elton and Gruber (1995), or Danthine and Donaldson (2001).

portfolio level. So why would the market ever reward something that does not exist any more in a well-diversified portfolio? At equilibrium, investors should only be rewarded for the systematic risk they take, not for the non-systematic risk they have eliminated. This is precisely what the CAPM says.

The CAPM asserts that the expected return on a given asset should be equal to the risk-free interest rate plus a risk premium. The latter depends linearly on the market risk exposure (i.e. the beta of the asset) and the market risk premium (i.e. what the market portfolio pays above the risk-free rate for taking market risk). Therefore, the expected return on a risky asset should be given by:

$$E^{CAPM}(R_P) = R_F + \beta_P[E(R_M) - R_F] \tag{4.7}$$

where R_P and R_M are respectively the percentage returns on the portfolio P and on the market portfolio M, R_F denotes the risk-free rate, β_P is the beta of portfolio P with respect to the market portfolio M, and $E(\cdot)$ denotes the unconditional expectation operator.

Equation (4.7) is the most important conclusion derived from the CAPM. It states that expected returns are linearly related to market risk (beta), but not, as often believed, to total risk (volatility). Other things being equal, a high beta asset should produce a higher expected return than the market and a low beta asset should produce a lower return. Similarly, increasing the market risk premium should increase the return of all assets with positive beta. In that respect, one could say that the CAPM philosophy is the exact opposite of traditional stock picking, as it attempts to understand the market as a whole rather than look at what makes each investment opportunity unique.

Note that equation (4.7) can easily be rewritten in terms of risk premiums by simply subtracting the risk-free rate from both sides of the security market line (SML) equation. This yields

$$E^{CAPM}(R_P) - R_F = \beta_P [E(R_M) - R_F] \tag{4.8}$$

Graphically, in a return-beta space, the CAPM implies that all fairly priced securities and portfolios should plot along a line. This line is the SML. Its intercept with the vertical axis should be the risk-free rate, and its slope should be equal to the market risk premium. The more risk-averse investors are, the steeper the slope and the higher the expected return for a given level of systematic risk (Figure 4.8).

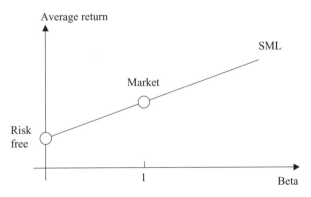

Figure 4.8   The security market line (SML)

By construction, the risk-free asset and the market portfolio should fall exactly on the SML, with betas of zero and one respectively. Consequently, any asset on the SML can be "replicated" by an appropriate mix of the risk-free asset and the market. This property – called the two-fund separation theorem – is particularly useful in creating a passive benchmark, when assessing the performance of an actively managed portfolio.

4.2.2 The market model

The CAPM and its graphical equivalent, the SML, give predictions about the expected relationship between risk and return. Theoretically, they should only be interpreted strictly as *ex ante* predictive models. However, when doing performance analysis, the framework is different. Performance must be assessed *ex post*, based on a sample of observed past data. What we need then is an explanatory model, and the *ex ante* CAPM must be transformed into an *ex post* testable relationship. The latter usually takes the form of a time series regression of excess returns of individual assets on the excess returns of some aggregate market index. It is called the *market model*, and can be written as:

$$R_i = \alpha_i + R_F + \beta_i[R_M - R_F] + \varepsilon_i \tag{4.9}$$

where R_i and R_M are the realized returns on security i and the market index, respectively, α_i is the expected firm-specific return and ε_i is the unexpected firm-specific return. If the CAPM holds, and if markets are efficient, α_i should not be statistically different from zero, and ε_i should have a mean of zero. The coefficients α_i and β_i correspond to the slope and the intercept of the regression line.

Alternatively, equation (4.9) can also be rewritten in terms of risk premiums:

$$R_{i,t} - R_F = \alpha_i + \beta_i[R_{M,t} - R_F] + \varepsilon_{i,t} \tag{4.10}$$

As we will see shortly, this equation constitutes the source of two major performance measures of financial portfolios, namely, Jensen's alpha (1968) and the Treynor ratio (1966).

Most practitioners tend to confuse the CAPM with time series regression. Although the two models look similar, they are fundamentally different. The market model is just an ad hoc, convenient, single-factor model fitted to observed data (Figure 4.9), while the CAPM is an

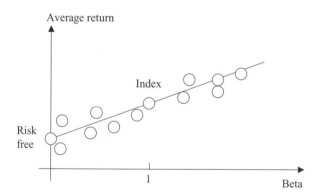

Figure 4.9   The market model

economic equilibrium model. Furthermore, the market model uses a simple market index as a proxy for the entire (non-observable) market portfolio of the CAPM. We come back to these differences in Chapters 7 and 8, when considering factor models.

An interesting interpretation of the market model is given by rearranging the terms in equation (4.9) to obtain:

$$R_i = \alpha_i + (1 - \beta_i)R_F + (\beta_i)R_M + \varepsilon_i \qquad (4.11)$$

The terms $(1 - \beta_i)$ and β_i can be interpreted as weights in a portfolio. Thus, equation (4.11) means that the return on a portfolio is made up of four components: (i) an asset-specific expected return α_i; (ii) an allocation to the risk-free asset; (iii) an allocation to the market portfolio; and (iv) an error term, which on average should be zero. We come back to this interpretation in Chapter 8.

Several commercial firms provide estimates of beta but their data should be treated with caution. These firms often ignore the risk-free rate as well as dividends, and simply estimate betas by regressing the returns on stocks against the return on the market:

$$R_i = \alpha_i^* + \beta_i^* R_M + \varepsilon_i^* \qquad (4.12)$$

This shortcut generally has no practical impact on the estimate of beta, but the corresponding alpha is useless for performance evaluation, as it differs significantly from the original alpha.

4.2.3 The Jensen alpha

According to the CAPM, it is impossible for an asset to remain located above or below the SML. If an asset produces a return that is higher than it should be for its beta, then investors will rush in to buy it and drive up its price, lowering the return and returning it to the SML. If the asset is located below the SML, then investors will hurry to sell it, driving down the price and hence increasing the return. Consequently, if all assets are fairly priced, deviations from the SML should not occur, or at least should not last very long.

Nevertheless, active fund managers are typically in search of assets that deviate from the SML. They attempt to identify them before the market reacts, so that they can profit from the mispricing. If they are successful, they will achieve a return that is above what could be expected, given the market risk taken. Hence, their portfolios will also be located above the SML. Conversely, unsuccessful managers will achieve a return that is lower than what could be expected, given the market risk taken. Hence, their portfolios will be located below the SML. This suggests a straightforward way of measuring performance, namely, the Jensen alpha, named after Harvard professor Michael Jensen (1968).

The Jensen alpha is defined as the difference between the realized return and the return predicted by the CAPM:

$$\alpha_P = R_P - E^{CAPM}(R_P) \qquad (4.13)$$

That is:

$$\alpha_P = [R_P - R_F] - \beta_P[R_M - R_F] \qquad (4.14)$$

Hence, the Jensen alpha is measured as the difference between the effectively realized risk premium and the expected risk premium. According to the CAPM, only market risk should

Table 4.3   Jensen alpha calculation for five different hedge funds

	Fund 1	Fund 2	Fund 3	Fund 4	Fund 5
Jensen alpha	0.36	0.44	0.54	0.59	4.09

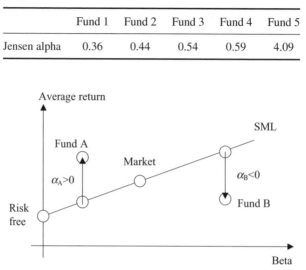

Figure 4.10   Undervalued and overvalued securities with the SML

be rewarded, so the alpha should be nil. If this is not the case, the alpha can be interpreted as an indicator of superior performance when it is positive or of poor performance when it is negative (Figure 4.10).

Graphically, a security with an alpha of zero will plot on the SML. A security with a positive alpha (e.g. Fund A in Figure 4.10) will plot above the SML. It generates more return than it should, given its systematic risk (measured by beta). A security with a negative alpha (e.g. Fund B in Figure 4.10) will plot below the SML. It generates less return than it should, given its systematic risk (measured by beta).

The Jensen measure can also be interpreted as the profitability of a net arbitrage position that goes long on the evaluated fund and goes short on both the risk-free asset and the market in proportions that neutralize market risk. For example, consider a fund with a beta of 0.6. Then Jensen's alpha measures the average profit of investing $1 in the fund, obtaining the funds from borrowing $0.40 (shorting the risk-free asset) and shorting $0.60 worth of the market portfolio. If the alpha is positive, that means an investor who initially holds a portfolio made up of $0.60 worth of the market portfolio and $0.40 of the risk-free asset can improve his portfolio by diverting a small fraction of his wealth to the fund in question. If the alpha is negative, the investor should avoid the fund.[10]

When confronted with several funds, the alpha decision rule is of course to choose the investment that maximizes the value added, that is, the investment with the highest alpha. We will therefore prefer investment A over B if $\alpha_A > \alpha_B$. As an illustration, Table 4.3 shows the Jensen alpha calculations for our five hedge funds. Note that the alpha is calculated from monthly returns, so that it is itself a monthly figure. Clearly, according to the Jensen alpha, Fund 5 dominates the sample.

---

[10] If possible, he should even sell the fund short and invest the proceeds in the original portfolio. However, in practice, most funds cannot be sold short.

Box 4.3

It is possible to derive a precise interpretation of Jensen's alpha in terms of optimal portfolio choice by relating it to the Sharpe ratio. Suppose an investor initially holds a combination of an index portfolio tracking the market and the risk-free asset, in proportions w_M and $(1 - w_M)$. This investor considers whether he should add fund P to his portfolio. In other words, he considers whether he should take a small fraction w_P of his wealth and invest it in portfolio P, while reducing the fractions held in the risk-free asset and the index to $(1 - w_P)(1 - w_M)$ and $(1 - w_P)w_M$ respectively.

It can then be shown that the derivative (in the financial calculus sense) of the Sharpe ratio of the resulting portfolio with respect to ε, evaluated at $w_P = 0$ (no investment yet), is:

$$\left. \frac{\partial \text{Sharpe}}{\partial w_P} \right|_{w_P=0} = \frac{\alpha}{w_M \sigma_M^2} \tag{4.15}$$

4.2.4 The Treynor ratio

In the market model, the value added (or withdrawn) by a manager is measured by the alpha, while the market risk exposure is measured by the beta. Jack L. Treynor, one of the fathers of modern portfolio theory and former editor of the *Financial Analysts Journal*, suggested comparing the two quantities:

$$\text{Treynor ratio}_P = \frac{\alpha_P}{\beta_P} \tag{4.16}$$

Replacing α_P by its definition and simplifying gives

$$\text{Treynor ratio}_P = \frac{R_P - R_F}{\beta_P} \tag{4.17}$$

All returns are usually expressed on an annual basis, so the Treynor ratio itself is expressed on an annual basis. The risk-free asset is often specified as Treasury bills, and beta is often measured against a diversified market index (e.g. S&P 500). Note that the derivations implicitly assume $\beta_P \neq 0$.

In a sense, the Treynor ratio is a reward-to-risk ratio similar to the Sharpe ratio. The key difference is that it looks at systematic risk only, not total risk. Higher values of the Treynor ratio are always desirable as they indicate greater return per unit of (market) risk. As an illustration, Table 4.4 displays the Treynor ratios obtained for our five hedge funds. We observe once again that Fund 4 seems to dominate the sample, with a Treynor ratio equal to 113.02, thanks to its relatively low beta (0.06).

4.2.5 Statistical significance

Once again, a crucial element in the Jensen alpha and Treynor ratio is the question of statistical significance. In particular, the quality of the regression used to obtain the beta coefficient should be scrutinized. First, are the coefficients statistically different from zero? Second, how high is the explanatory power of the regression? We come back to these issues when considering single and multi-factor models in Chapters 7 and 8. However, as an illustration, consider Table 4.5,

Table 4.4 Treynor ratio calculation for five different hedge funds
(the T-bill rate has an average return of 4.23% p.a. over the period)

	Fund 1	Fund 2	Fund 3	Fund 4	Fund 5
Mean return (%)	8.16	5.56	9.98	11.36	39.96
Beta (S&P 500)	0.19	0.64	0.43	0.06	2.08
Treynor ratio	20.22	2.07	13.36	113.02	17.15

Table 4.5 Statistical significance of the market model coefficients

	Fund 1	Fund 2	Fund 3	Fund 4	Fund 5
R^2 of regression	0.16	0.22	0.54	0.02	0.43

which displays a statistic called the R-square. Roughly stated, the R-square (R^2) measures the quality of the regression model used to calculate the Jensen alpha and the Treynor ratio.

We saw previously that Fund 4 seems to dominate the sample with a Treynor ratio equal to 113.02, thanks to its relatively low beta (0.06). However, we now see that the R^2 of the regression that provided this beta is only 0.02. This implies that the S&P 500 behavior only explains 2% of the variance of Fund 4. Do we feel confident in basing our conclusions on a model that has such a low explanatory power? Not likely! Hence, we should be cautious and always assess the quality of our models before accepting their conclusions.

4.2.6 Comparing Sharpe, Treynor and Jensen

Investors frequently wonder why there are differences between the fund rankings provided by the Sharpe ratio, the Treynor ratio and the Jensen alpha. The three measures are indeed different. On the one hand, both the Treynor ratio and the Jensen alpha issue from the CAPM and measure risk the same way. However, the Treynor ratio provides more information than Jensen's alpha. In particular, two securities with different risk levels that provide the same excess returns over the same period will have the same alpha but will differ with respect to the Treynor ratio. The difference comes from the fact that the Treynor ratio provides the performance of the portfolio per unit of systematic risk. On the other hand, the Sharpe ratio focuses on a different type of risk – total risk, as opposed to systematic risk. It penalizes funds that have a high volatility and therefore funds that have non-systematic risk. Hence, in general, the ranking of Sharpe ratios will usually be different from that of Treynor ratios or Jensen alphas. Intuitively, it is only when applied to well-diversified traditional portfolios that the three measures will result in similar rankings because most of the risk will be systematic. In the case of hedge funds, the non-systematic component is usually large, so very different rankings may be obtained.

It is relatively easy to derive the exact conditions that must hold for the Sharpe ratio and the Treynor ratio to provide the same ranking. Consider two funds, A and B, such that fund A has a higher Treynor ratio than fund B. That is:

$$\frac{R_A - R_F}{\beta_A} > \frac{R_B - R_F}{\beta_B} \tag{4.18}$$

Replacing the betas with their definitions and rearranging terms, we find that

$$\frac{1}{\rho_{A,M}} \frac{R_A - R_F}{\sigma_A} > \frac{1}{\rho_{B,M}} \frac{R_B - R_F}{\sigma_B} \tag{4.19}$$

where $\rho_{i,M}$ denotes the correlation between fund i and the market. Therefore, the Treynor ratio will provide the same ranking as the Sharpe ratio only for assets that have identical correlations to the market.

Similarly, we can derive the conditions that must hold for the Sharpe ratio and the Jensen alpha to provide the same ranking. Consider two funds, A and B, such that fund A has a higher alpha than fund B. That is:

$$\alpha_A > \alpha_B \tag{4.20}$$

Replacing the alphas with their definitions and rearranging terms yields

$$\sigma_A \left[\frac{R_A - R_F}{\sigma_A} - \rho_{A,M} \frac{R_M - R_F}{\sigma_M} \right] > \sigma_B \left[\frac{R_B - R_F}{\sigma_B} - \rho_{B,M} \frac{R_M - R_F}{\sigma_M} \right] \tag{4.21}$$

Hence, the Treynor ratio will provide the same ranking as the Sharpe ratio only for assets that have identical correlations to the market *and* the same volatility. Most of the time, this condition will not be encountered so the rankings will be different.

Another frequent question from investors is: "Which measure should be used to evaluate portfolio performance?" The simple answer is: "It depends." To evaluate an entire portfolio, the Sharpe ratio is appropriate. It is simple to calculate, does not require a beta estimate and penalizes the portfolio for being non-diversified. To evaluate securities or funds for possible inclusion in a broader or master portfolio, either the Treynor ratio or Jensen's alpha is appropriate. However, they require a beta estimate and assume that the master portfolio is well diversified.

4.2.7 Generalizing the Jensen alpha and the Treynor ratio

As we will see, the market model is one of the simplest asset pricing models possible. It expresses everything in terms of a single factor, the market portfolio. However, one can easily extend the market model, for instance by including additional factors or by postulating some non-linear relationships. In this case, alpha will be defined as the difference between the realized return and the new model-predicted return.

A particular and unfortunate case of what precedes is the tendency of some investment practitioners to use the term "alpha" to describe the extent to which a portfolio's returns have exceeded expectations, or simply to measure returns in excess of those over a benchmark index (e.g. S&P 500). In a CAPM framework, this implicitly assumes that the beta of the considered portfolio is in fact equal to one, which is often not verified.

In the context of multi-factor models the Treynor ratio has also been generalized by Hübner (2003). Conceptually, the generalized Treynor ratio is defined as the abnormal return of a portfolio per unit of weighted average systematic risk. In a linear multi-index, these requirements are fulfilled by normalizing the risk premia using a benchmark portfolio and by rotating the factors to obtain an orthonormed hyperplane for risk dimensions. This performance measure is invariant to the specification of the asset pricing model, the number of factors or the scale of the measure.

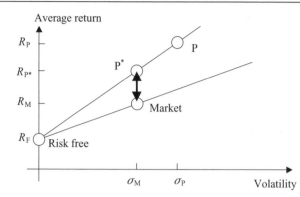

Figure 4.11   The M^2 performance measure when the fund has a higher volatility than the market ($\sigma_P > \sigma_M$). The adjusted portfolio P* is a mix of T-bills and P

4.3 M^2, M^3 AND GRAHAM–HARVEY

More recently, several researchers have provided new perspectives on measuring portfolio performance. Although not yet as popular as the Sharpe ratio or Jensen's alpha, these measures are gaining ground in the hedge fund industry.

4.3.1   The M^2 performance measure

Despite near universal acceptance among academics and institutional investors, the Sharpe ratio is too complicated for the average investor. The reason is that it expresses performance as an excess return per unit of volatility, while most investors are used to dealing with absolute returns. This motivated Leah Modigliani from Morgan Stanley and her grandfather, the Nobel Prize winner Franco Modigliani, to develop and suggest a replacement for the Sharpe ratio.[11] The new performance measure, called M^2 after the names of its founders, expresses performance directly as a return figure, which should ease its comprehension.

The key idea of the M^2 performance measure is to adjust all funds by leveraging or de-leveraging them using the risk-free asset, so that they all have the same volatility – typically the market volatility. Say for instance that we want to compare the performance of a fund (named P) with the performance of the market (named M). In general, we observe that $\sigma_P \neq \sigma_M$, so that we cannot compare the two assets by just looking at their returns. According to M^2, we need to form a portfolio P* composed of the original fund P and T-bills (with return R_F and no volatility) that has the same standard deviation as M. Then, one can simply compare the adjusted funds and the market solely on the basis of the return.

There are two possible situations. If the fund has a higher volatility than the market ($\sigma_P > \sigma_M$), then portfolio P* will contain a mix of T-bills and the original fund P. This is the de-leveraging situation illustrated in Figure 4.11. In this case, we have:

$$\frac{\sigma_M}{\sigma_P} = \frac{R_{P*} - R_F}{R_P - R_F} \tag{4.22}$$

---

[11] See Modigliani (1997) and Modigliani and Modigliani (1997).

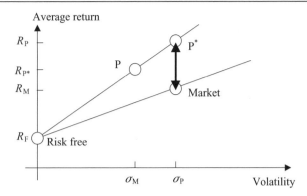

Figure 4.12   The M^2 performance measure when the fund has a lower volatility than the market ($\sigma_P <$ σ_M). The adjusted portfolio P* is made up of portfolio P and a loan at the risk-free rate

Solving for R_{P*} yields

$$M^2 = R_{P*} = \frac{\sigma_M}{\sigma_P}(R_P - R_F) + R_F \tag{4.23}$$

If the fund has a lower volatility than the market ($\sigma_P < \sigma_M$), then portfolio P* will contain a short position in T-bills and a long position in the original fund P. This is the leveraging situation illustrated in Figure 4.12. In this case:

$$\frac{\sigma_M - \sigma_P}{\sigma_M} = \frac{R_{P*} - (R_P - R_F)}{R_{P*}} \tag{4.24}$$

*Disregard there
this is no
adjustment needed
for fund volatility
lower than market vol.*

Solving for R_{P*} yields

$$M^2 = R_{P*} = \frac{\sigma_M}{\sigma_P}(R_P - R_F) - R_F \tag{4.25}$$

In both cases, the resulting portfolio P* is compared with the market solely on the basis of return. In essence, for a fund P with a given risk and return, the M^2 measure is equivalent to the return the fund would have achieved if it had the same risk as the market. Thus, the fund with the highest M^2 will have the highest return for any level of risk – very much like the fund with the highest Sharpe ratio.

As an illustration, Table 4.6 shows the calculation of M^2 for our sample of five funds. The benchmark volatility level was set at 20.75%, which corresponds to the S&P 500 volatility over the period in question. The T-bill rate has an average return of 4.23% p.a. over the period. The ranking we obtain with M^2 is the same as the ranking of the Sharpe ratio. This confirms that the M^2 performance measure is essentially a new variant of the Sharpe ratio. It is just easier to interpret, because it is expressed directly in terms of return.

It is worth noting that any reference point other than the volatility of the market could equally well be chosen. With M^2, the market simply provides a standard risk level to which all portfolios are scaled so that they can be compared "apples to apples". The economic significance of the market, if any, is left aside.

Arun Muralidhar from J.P. Morgan Investment Management argues that M^2 is not a sufficient rule for making decisions on how to rank funds or structure portfolios. It is true that M^2 accounts for differences in standard deviations between a portfolio and a benchmark, but not for the

Table 4.6 Calculating M^2 for our sample of hedge funds

	Fund 1	Fund 2	Fund 3	Fund 4	Fund 5
Mean return (%)	8.16	5.56	9.98	11.36	39.96
Volatility (%)	9.55	29.48	11.45	8.95	79.53
Sharpe ratio	0.41	0.05	0.50	0.80	0.45
Portfolio P*					
% of fund	217.3%	70.4%	181.2%	231.8%	26.1%
% of T-bills	−117.3%	29.6%	−81.2%	−131.8%	73.9%
σ_{P*}	20.75	20.75	20.75	20.75	20.75
$M^2 = R_{P*}$	12.77	5.17	14.65	20.76	13.55

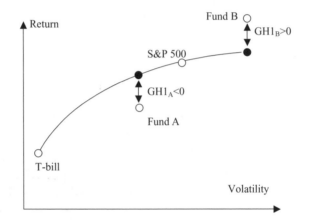

Figure 4.13 Interpreting GH1 by leveraging or de-leveraging the S&P 500

differences in correlation. He therefore suggests a new performance measure called M^3 that corrects for the difference in correlations. Although interesting from a theoretical perspective, M^3 has never really been applied in practice.

4.3.2 GH1 and GH2

In parallel with Modigliani and Modigliani, John Graham and Campbell Harvey have developed two simple approaches to adjust the risk of compared portfolios so as to end up with the same volatility. Both of them are also based on a leveraging/de-leveraging approach.

The first approach suggested by Graham and Harvey consists in leveraging or de-leveraging the market to match the volatility of the fund examined. The performance measure GH1 is then defined as the difference between the mean fund return and the mean return on the volatility-matched portfolio. Figure 4.13 details the geometry of the measure applied to two funds. Combining the S&P 500 with Treasury bills to match the volatility of Fund A yields a portfolio with a higher return than Fund A. Hence, GH1 for Fund A is negative, which indicates underperformance. In contrast, leveraging the S&P 500 to match the volatility of Fund B yields a portfolio with a lower return than Fund B. Hence, GH1 for Fund B is positive, which indicates outperformance.

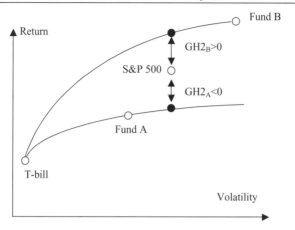

Figure 4.14   Interpreting GH2 by leveraging or de-leveraging the analyzed funds

The second approach suggested by Graham and Harvey consists in leveraging or de-leveraging the fund examined to match the volatility of the market. The performance measure GH2 is then defined as the difference between the mean return on the volatility-matched portfolio and the mean market return. Figure 4.14 details the geometry of the measure applied to the same two funds. Leveraging Fund A with Treasury bills to match the volatility of the market yields a portfolio with a lower return than the market. Hence, GH2 for Fund A is negative, which indicates underperformance. In contrast, combining Fund A with Treasury bills to match the volatility of the market yields a portfolio with a higher return than the market. Hence, GH2 for Fund B is positive, indicating outperformance.

The sets of portfolios obtained by mixing T-bills and other assets form curves rather than straight lines. This is because Graham and Harvey reject the usual assumption that the T-bill return has zero variance and zero covariance with the portfolio being evaluated. In reality, the usual assumption does hold if the maturity of the T-bills coincides exactly with the evaluation period. That is, the cash is effectively a zero-coupon instrument maturing exactly at the end of the evaluation period. In practice, though, this is often not the case, and there is likely to be a non-zero correlation between the interest rate changes and asset returns, which gives the curve. Depending on the level of correlation, this could lead to misleading inferences about the performance, particularly for low volatility funds where substantial leverage is needed to achieve the market volatility. However, the impact is generally negligible for well-diversified portfolios.

The two Graham and Harvey measures look very similar but in fact they provide different perspectives:

- GH1 is similar to the Jensen alpha measure, except that with Jensen, the benchmark portfolio (beta times the market index) has the same market exposure (beta) as the analyzed portfolio, but not necessarily the same total volatility.[12]
- GH2 is similar to the M^2 measure, but does not rely on the assumption of zero risk for the cash proxy.

---

[12] To obtain a striking example of the advantage of the Graham and Harvey measures, consider the case of a fund that randomly selects between a 200% long in the market and a 200% short in the market position, with an average zero exposure over a measurement period. If the alpha of this fund is positive (say 1%), then the strategy will be identified as superior. However, the volatility-matched portfolio is likely to be a leveraged version of the market portfolio with twice the variance of the market. Hence, the random strategy would appear as a clear underperformer according to the GH1 measure.

4.4 PERFORMANCE MEASURES BASED ON DOWNSIDE RISK

Dissatisfaction with the variance as a risk measure, coupled with other behavioral evidence, has led some researchers to propose alternative risk-adjusted performance measures. Several of these are based on the downside risk approach – see for instance Sortino and van der Meer (1991), Fishburn (1977), Sortino and Price (1994), Marmer and Ng (1993), or Merriken (1994).

4.4.1 The Sortino ratio

Frank Sortino, Director of the Pension Research Institute and a professor emeritus at San Francisco State University, reconsidered the issue of performance measurement from the perspective of downside risk. His contention was that the most important risk was not volatility, but rather the risk of not achieving the return in relation to an investment goal. Hence, he suggested replacing the Sharpe ratio by the Sortino ratio, which measures the incremental return over a minimum acceptable return (MAR) divided by the downside deviation (as opposed to the standard deviation) below the MAR.

Algebraically, we have:

$$\text{Sortino ratio}_P = \frac{R_P - \text{MAR}}{\text{DD}_P} \tag{4.26}$$

where R_P and MAR are respectively the average percentage returns on portfolio P and a minimum acceptable return, and DD_P is the downside deviation of returns of portfolio P below the MAR. All numbers are usually expressed on an annual basis, so the Sortino ratio is annualized.

As an illustration, Table 4.7 shows the Sortino ratios of our five funds calculated with respect to different minimum acceptable returns. If the goal of the investor is to avoid losing money, the MAR is set at zero and Fund 4 ranks as the best fund. If the goal of the investor is to achieve at least the risk-free rate, the MAR is set equal to the T-bill rate and Fund 5 comes out on top.

Table 4.7 Sortino ratio calculations for our five different hedge funds (all data are annualized)

	Fund 1	Fund 2	Fund 3	Fund 4	Fund 5
Mean return (%)	8.16	5.56	9.98	11.36	39.96
Volatility (%)	9.55	29.48	11.45	8.95	79.53
Sharpe ratio	0.41	0.05	0.50	**0.80**	0.45
MAR = 0%					
Downside deviation	5.23	16.70	5.86	5.50	30.90
Sortino (MAR = 0)	0.75	0.08	0.98	**1.30**	1.16
MAR = Risk-free rate					
Downside deviation	15.09	25.55	15.69	14.13	37.54
Sortino (MAR = R_F)	0.26	0.05	0.37	0.50	**0.95**
MAR = Mean return					
Downside deviation	6.23	17.52	7.29	6.60	35.18
Sortino (MAR = mean)	**1.14**	0.41	0.98	1.08	0.20

Finally, if we use the mean return of each fund as the reference MAR, Fund 1 becomes the best performing fund.

Clearly, the Sortino ratio can accommodate different degrees of target returns. However, there are different downside deviations for different minimum acceptable rates and hence different Sortino ratios and different rankings of the funds under consideration. It is therefore essential to specify the minimum acceptable rate used to calculate any Sortino ratio, as well as to use the same rate for different funds in order to be able to perform comparisons.

4.4.2   The upside potential ratio

Instead of searching for the manager who had the highest average return over some period of time, some, if not most, investors would prefer to find those managers who had the highest average returns above their MAR. Hence, Sortino *et al.* (1999a,b) suggested replacing the excess return used in the denominator of the Sortino ratio by the upside potential. The latter is defined as the expected return in excess of the MAR and can be thought of as the potential for success. The ratio of the upside potential to the downside risk is termed the "upside potential ratio".

An important advantage of using the upside potential ratio rather than the Sortino ratio is the consistency in the use of the reference rate for evaluating both profits and losses. An upside potential ratio of 1.6, for instance, means that the fund has 60% more upside potential than downside risk, where the term "risk" refers to the same concept.

As an illustration, Table 4.8 shows the upside potential ratios of our five funds calculated with respect to different minimum acceptable returns. If the goal of the investor is to avoid losing money, the MAR is set at zero and Fund 3 ranks as the best fund. If the goal of the investor is to achieve at least the risk-free rate, the MAR is set equal to the T-bill rate and Fund 5 comes out on top. Finally, if we use the mean return of each fund as the reference MAR, Fund 1 becomes the best performing fund.

Table 4.8   Upside potential ratio calculations for our five different hedge funds (all data are annualized)

	Fund 1	Fund 2	Fund 3	Fund 4	Fund 5
Mean return (%)	8.16	5.56	9.98	11.36	39.96
Volatility (%)	9.55	29.48	11.45	8.95	79.53
Sharpe ratio	0.41	0.05	0.50	**0.80**	0.45
MAR = 0%					
Upside potential	1.97	6.52	2.77	1.80	12.13
Downside deviation	5.23	16.70	5.86	5.50	30.90
Upside potential ratio	0.38	0.39	**0.47**	0.33	0.39
MAR = Risk-free rate					
Upside potential	6.40	9.15	6.17	5.51	17.54
Downside deviation	15.09	25.55	15.69	14.13	37.54
Upside potential ratio	0.42	0.36	0.39	0.39	**0.47**
MAR = Mean return					
Upside potential	2.89	6.73	3.19	2.41	15.40
Downside deviation	6.23	17.52	7.29	6.60	35.18
Upside potential ratio	**0.46**	0.38	0.44	0.37	0.44

Table 4.9 RoVaR ratio calculations for our five different hedge funds (all data are annualized)

	Fund 1	Fund 2	Fund 3	Fund 4	Fund 5
Mean return (%)	8.16	5.56	9.98	11.36	39.96
$\text{VaR}_{1M,99\%}(\%)$	−6.94	−16.97	−5.42	−8.17	−33.06
RoVaR ratio	1.18	0.33	**1.84**	1.39	1.21
$\text{VaR}_{1M,95\%}(\%)$	−2.55	−10.16	−3.80	−2.01	−16.27
RoVaR ratio	3.20	0.55	2.63	**5.65**	2.46

4.4.3 The Sterling and Burke ratios

The Sterling and Burke ratios are widely advertised by commodity trading advisors, because those ratios illustrate what they believe they do best: namely, let their profits ride and stringently cap their losses.

The *Sterling ratio* goes one step further than the Sortino ratio by looking at the drawdowns to measure risk. It is defined as

$$\text{Sterling}_P = \frac{\bar{r}_P - r_F}{\overline{\text{dwn}}} \qquad (4.27)$$

where $\overline{\text{dwn}}$ is the average of the most significant drawdowns during the observation period. What a "significant" drawdown is remains to be defined. Some analysts use the maximum drawdown rather than the average drawdown.

Burke (1994) proposed using the square root of the sum of the squares of each drawdown, in order to penalize deep extended drawdowns as opposed to numerous mild ones. The Burke ratio is defined as:

$$\text{BU}_P = \frac{R_P - R_F}{\sqrt{\sum_{i=1}^{N} (\text{dwn}_i^2)}} \qquad (4.28)$$

4.4.4 Return on VaR (RoVaR)

Another measure that is popular particularly among practitioners is the return on value at risk, or RoVaR. This is defined simply as the return on the portfolio (R_P) divided by the absolute[13] value at risk (VaR_P):

$$\text{RoVaR}_P = \frac{R_P}{|\text{VaR}_P|} \qquad (4.29)$$

As in the case of the Sortino ratio, the RoVaR ratio can be customized to cater for different holding periods as well as different levels of confidence for the VaR. As an illustration, Table 4.9 shows the RoVaR of our five funds using a one-month historical value at risk calculated at 99% and at 95% confidence. Once again, the ranking differs, because the risk definitions are different.

---

[13] The VaR is usually expressed in absolute terms, so the RoVaR ratio is positive if the expected return is positive.

Box 4.4

In the case of normally distributed returns, it is relatively easy to express the RoVaR of a portfolio as a function of the Sharpe ratio, as the VaR typically depends on the mean return (R_P) and on the volatility of the portfolio (σ_P). More precisely:

$$VaR_P = -(R_P + k\sigma_P)$$

where $-k$ is the standard normal variable reflecting the confidence level on which the VaR is predicated (for example, $k = -1.645$ if we have a 95% confidence level). It follows that:

$$RoVaR_P = -\frac{R_P}{(R_P + k\sigma_P)}$$

Using equation (4.1) to replace R_P, we obtain

$$RoVaR_P = -\frac{[R_F + \text{Sharpe}_P\,\sigma_P]}{k\sigma_P + R_F + \text{Sharpe}_P\,\sigma_P}$$

This shows that there is a link between the RoVaR and the Sharpe ratio. It also evidences that we should not expect the same ranking of funds from both measures. As an illustration, if the risk-free rate R_F is zero, we have:

$$RoVaR_P = -\frac{[\text{Sharpe}_P]}{k + \text{Sharpe}_P}$$

As k can take any value, there is no reason for the RoVaR and the Sharpe ratio to provide equal rankings.

4.5   CONCLUSIONS

Over the last few decades, a number of sophisticated measures have been developed to monitor the risk-adjusted performance of hedge funds. These measures have much in common as regards their underlying framework and financial intuition, but they rely on different calculation techniques and parameters. Hence, when applied to a series of hedge funds, they often produce different rankings.

From the performance evaluator's point of view, this array of performance measures offers a rich choice but at the same time makes the selection of a method difficult – if at all possible. Not surprisingly, for some years, unscrupulous product marketers have taken advantage of this difficulty. They simply considered hedge fund performance measurement as a game, following one guiding principle: "Give me a fund and I will find the performance measure and the time period that makes it look attractive."

Today, hedge fund investing is no longer a game but a serious business. Each investor embarking on a hedge fund investment has his own strategic rationale and critical objectives, which will define his perception of risk. Hence, rather than waiting for all the pieces of the puzzle to fall into place, he should carefully assess his current situation in order to be proactive in his choice of a performance measure. Only by knowing what he is looking for can he identify the performance measure that best suits his requirements. Then, and only then, will the historical analysis of portfolio performance provide much more than just good marketing information.

5
Databases, Indices and Benchmarks

A long-term investment is a short-term investment that performed badly.

Due to the private nature of hedge funds, it is relatively difficult to obtain adequate information about the operations of individual funds or reliable summary statistics about the industry as a whole. Hence, for a long time, gaining insight into the performance characteristics of the hedge funds was no simple matter. Quantitative and qualitative information on hedge funds has only recently become more readily available, thanks to the creation of hedge fund databases and indices.

5.1 HEDGE FUND DATABASES

Since hedge funds cannot advertise, being included in a database and therefore on the radar screens of consultants is very important in terms of visibility. Thus, many hedge funds release monthly return information to specialized databases, such as Hedge Fund Research, TASS and Altvest. These databases collect information, and then sell it back to anyone interested in buying it – accredited investors, banks, funds of funds, consultants, and even lucky academics. Some of these data consumers may at some point become hedge fund investors, and this is the major motivation for managers to give out information on a consistent basis.

Most of the large data vendors provide additional services, ranging from fund selection and screening to asset allocation and product structuring. In addition, they use their databases to calculate a number of hedge fund indices that are widely used in the industry, particularly for strategic asset allocation and benchmarking and also for validating the superiority of hedge funds over traditional asset classes.

Unfortunately, as we shall see, the existing hedge fund databases and their derived hedge fund indices are not necessarily representative of the entire (non-observable) hedge fund universe. Each database and/or index is built up from different funds according to different methods of construction, and is likely to be affected to a greater or lesser degree by several biases and inaccuracies. As a consequence, the performance of indices supposed to measure the same strategy will evolve at differing paces, which may seriously confuse investors. Some claim that properly accounting for these biases and inaccuracies may, in fact, change the perception of hedge funds. Without adopting this extreme viewpoint, it is important to be aware of the existence of biases and know their estimated extent, as well as some of the solutions that have recently been suggested in the financial literature (Tables 5.1 and 5.2).

5.2 THE VARIOUS BIASES IN HEDGE FUND DATABASES

The biases in hedge fund data come from two main sources. First, there are the biases in the way each database is constructed. Some of these biases are natural, in that they are inherent to the data collecting process. They can be eliminated, usually at the cost of complicated calculations,

Table 5.1   Major hedge fund and commodity trading advisors databases

Database	Short description	Number of funds/CTAs
Altvest/InvestorForce	Originally developed by Altvest, this database was acquired by InvestorForce. It is now a commercial hedge fund website that provides information on alternative investments as well as integrated analytical and reporting tools	Over 2600
Barclays Hedge Fund and CTA Database	Barclays offers the newest, fastest growing, most accurate and up-to-date hedge fund/CTA database available	Over 2200
CISDM/Zurich/MAR	Originally created by Managed Account Reports, this database was sold to Zurich Capital Markets in March 2001 and gifted to the University of Massachusetts Center for International Securities and Derivatives Markets in August 2002	Over 2500
Daniel B. Stark & Co.	Daniel B. Stark & Co.'s CTA & Futures Fund Manager Database contains 12 years of information on commodity trading advisers and futures funds	Over 420 CTAs Over 200 futures funds
Eurekahedge	Eurekahedge Advisors is an advisory firm registered with the Securities and Futures Commission of Hong Kong	Over 330 in Asia Over 500 in Europe 734 funds of funds
Eurohedge InvestHedge AsiaHedge	Managed by HedgeFund Intelligence – an independent publishing group – with the Bank of Bermuda, these online databases provide performance data and contact information on European funds, and funds of hedge funds	Over 650 in Europe 700 funds of funds
Financial Risk Management (FRM)	This proprietary database belongs to FRM, an independent investment management group dedicated to the construction and management of customized hedge fund portfolios. The database has been used in some academic research	About 8000
Hedge Fund Research (HFR)	HFR is an SEC-registered investment adviser specializing in structuring and managing fund of funds and multiple manager portfolios. It is a leading supplier of data on hedge funds	Over 2500

but some will subsist as long as it remains impossible to observe the entire universe of hedge funds. Second, there is the problem of stale or, worse, "managed" hedge fund prices being reported by the managers directly. In extreme cases, these biases generate errors that make the data absolutely useless.

5.2.1   Self-selection bias

The self-selection bias is really innate to the private nature of the hedge fund industry. While mutual fund performance data must be disclosed to the public, hedge funds, as private investment pools, are not required to disclose performance or asset information to anyone other than their

Table 5.2 Major hedge fund and commodity trading advisors databases

Database	Short description	Number of funds/CTAs
Hennessee	Hennessee is an SEC-registered investment adviser that provides only alternative investment advisory services	About 3000
Morgan Stanley Capital Indices (MSCI)	Introduced in 2002, the MSCI Hedge Fund Indices offer transparency in index construction and maintenance for qualified investors, a comprehensive hedge fund classification framework, and an extensive, growing and reliable database	More than 1300
TASS/Tremont	Founded in London in 1990, TASS Investment Research is the information and research subsidiary of Tremont, and one of the leading providers of data, information and market intelligence to the hedge fund industry. The TASS database is one of the oldest and largest hedge fund databases in the industry	Over 3000
Tuna/Hedgefund.net	Hedgefund.net is a free hedge fund website that provides information on alternative investments to more than 35 000 accredited investors worldwide	About 4000
US Offshore Funds Directory	An annual printed source of information on hedge funds	About 1000
Van Hedge Fund Advisors	A research and hedge fund advisory firm	Over 5000

current investors. Plus, the hedge fund managers themselves decide what information is to be provided in their prospectuses. Of course, some hedge fund managers may opt to report performance information to data providers, but this is only done on a voluntary basis. Hence, the sample of hedge funds observed will not constitute a true random sample of the general population.

This situation is likely to create a bias, because the characteristics and performance of reporting funds may differ from those of non-reporting funds. As an example, smaller funds with good track records have a strong incentive to report to databases, because this will increase their visibility and may attract new investors. Conversely, managers with sub-par performance will not report to databases because they do not want to compare badly with better performing peers. Thus, at first glance, the conclusion would be that the reporting funds should have a better performance than the non-reporting funds. Consequently, databases where poorly performing hedge funds are likely to be missing should have a bias towards the best performing funds.

However, there are also a large number of very good, well-established hedge fund managers who do not report to databases because they do not need to or do not want to. Some have been successful in achieving the business desired, they already manage the assets they want, and they may have long lists of investors waiting to enter the fund. So, why take on the burden of reporting on a regular basis to a third party? Others are afraid that if they communicate their performance to a data vendor, they will be included in that data vendor's index and automatically raise the performance of that index, so their individual performance will appear less differentiated. The conclusion then would be that databases might have a bias towards only the average and below-average hedge funds.

In reality, the self-reporting bias may be positive or negative depending on the circumstances. As long as the non-reporting funds remain unobservable, it is not possible to quantify exactly the impact[1] of the bias. However, since investment talent combined with the ability to identify and take advantage of market opportunities is usually in short supply, it seems reasonable to assume that non-reporting managers with a poor performance outnumber those with a good performance.

5.2.2 Database/sample selection bias

Selecting a database or a sample of hedge funds to work with is also likely to be a major source of performance bias. Every existing database is incomplete. The reason is that most databases, samples and studies only cover funds that meet some specific criteria, such as a minimum asset base, an audited track record, or a few years of existence. Although rational and easily justifiable from an investment perspective, these criteria create a sample selection bias towards particular segments of funds. As an illustration:

- The worst hedge fund managers will never appear in databases simply because they do not survive long enough – most databases require at least two years of existence. The result is likely to be an upward bias in databases in comparison with the entire universe.
- Several data vendors (e.g. HFR) exclude particular investment styles such as managed futures funds from their database. The reason is that they consider them as being different from true hedge funds. However, this sentiment is not universally shared, and other databases (e.g. TASS, MAR) include them alongside hedge funds. The same problem applies to funds of hedge funds, which are sometimes excluded to avoid double counting the assets (once in the fund, and once in the fund of funds), and sometimes included.

In addition to these explicit selection biases, there are also implicit biases. For instance, managers may agree to report to one or two databases, but rarely to all the existing databases. Hence, the sample sets being different, there may be wide differentials in the statistics calculated by various databases. Differences in the data collection methods among databases may be the source of another bias. Some databases allow managers to directly input and revise their prices, while others collect data directly from the administrators. Needless to say, the latter source is far more reliable,[2] but more difficult to obtain.

5.2.3 Survivorship bias

Survivorship bias is probably one of the most discussed biases in the performance analysis literature. Simply stated, survivorship bias results from the tendency of some funds to be excluded from performance studies and databases due to the fact that they no longer exist. Most database vendors started collecting data in the middle of the 1990s, or even later in some cases. Historical returns from these databases are therefore conditioned by survival and may

---

[1] Note that a similar bias has already been studied in economics. In fact, James Heckman, a Nobel Prize winner in 2000, developed a procedure for correcting this type of bias in linear regression models. The key insight in Heckman's work is that, if we can estimate the probability that a fund will be willing to report on a voluntary basis, we can use this probability estimate to correct the linear regression models.

[2] Liang (2000) made the noteworthy observations that (i) out of the 1162 funds in the HFR database and the 1627 funds in the TASS database, there were only 465 common funds and that (ii) only 47% of the performances recorded for the common funds were strictly identical. For the other 53% of the funds, there were several significant differences in the net asset value, incentive fee, management fee and investment styles.

be overstated, while historical risk may be understated. This assumes, of course, (i) that funds that disappeared did so for performance reasons and (ii) that data on funds that disappear for performance or financial reasons are dropped from the database.

A good illustration of how survivor bias can skew inferences is the "marathon analogy". Say only 100 runners out of a field of 1000 contestants in a marathon actually finish. Bearing in mind that there were 1000 starters, if a person finished 100th out of these 100, what is his or her rank: last, or in the top 10%? The same question obviously applies to hedge funds. Indeed, it is important to realize that the hedge funds that contributed to the successful performance of the industry over the last 10 years are for the most part not the same funds that are still available today.[3]

Survivorship bias is not peculiar to funds and managed portfolios. It also exists in other asset classes, such as equity. As an illustration, Foster and Kaplan (2001) evidenced that only 74 stocks out of the 500 that made up the S&P 500 in 1950 survived until the year 2000, and only 18 companies of the Forbes 100 list published in 1917 were still present on the Forbes 100 list of 1987. But the phenomenon is magnified with mutual and hedge funds, because the annual attrition rate is much larger than for stocks. As an illustration, in 1986, the then existing 586 equity funds tracked by Lipper Analytical Services returned 13.4%. By 1996, the 1986 performance had magically improved to 14.7%, because 24% of the funds had disappeared or been merged into other funds. Of course, the poor returns investors had received from the defunct funds did not disappear; they just went unreported as if they had never existed. Brooks and Kat (2001) stated that around 30% of newly established funds do not survive the first three years, primarily due to poor performance.

Using four survival models, Gregoriou (2002) conducted survival analysis of hedge funds from the Zurich Capital Markets database from 1990 to 2001. He found that the median life of a hedge fund is 5.5 years and that most long-lived funds tend to be large in size, with high returns, low leverage and low minimum purchase requirements. Funds appear to fail more after the first year, and the conditional fail rate continues to be relatively high for several years before it eventually decreases. Not surprisingly, funds of hedge funds had the longest median survival time at 7.5 years.

Several data vendors now retain historical data about funds that have been liquidated or have stopped reporting for other reasons, so survivorship bias should gradually disappear. However, it still exists for historical data prior to the creation of the database and is influenced heavily by the decision to keep tracking disappeared funds. Other data vendors (e.g. HedgeFund.net) explicitly state that they do not care about survivorship bias and keep removing from their database the past performance of funds that have ceased operations.

Note that the motives for disappearing from a database are numerous and cover a variety of situations:

- The fund is liquidated, typically after a series of large and sudden losses.
- The fund is closed, typically after a long period of below-par performance that drives net asset values well below previous high water marks for the payment of performance-based fees.
- The fund is merged with another hedge fund. This is typically the case of small non-performing funds that are absorbed into other funds.

---

[3] Brown *et al.* (2001) observed that 50% of hedge fund managers disappear within 30 months, and only 4% have been in business for 10 years.

Table 5.3 Estimates of the survivorship bias on average return

Study	Survivorship bias (% p.a.)	Sample
Malkiel (1995)	0.5% or 1.5%	Mutual funds
Bares *et al.* (2001)	1.3%	FRM (incl. FoF), 1996–1999
Ackerman *et al.* (1999)	0.16%	HFR and MAR databases, including funds of funds, 1989–1999
Brown *et al.* (1999)	3%	Hand-collected data from the US Offshore Funds Directory, 1989–1995
Brown *et al.* (1998)	2.6%	Offshore hedge funds
Fung and Hsieh (2000b, 2001b)	3%	TASS database, 1994–1998
Fung and Hsieh (1997b)	3.4%	CTA funds from TASS database
Liang (2000, 2001)	2.2% to 2.4%	TASS database
Edwards and Caglayan (2001)	1.85%	MAR (incl. FOF), 1991–1998
Barry (2003)	1.4%	TASS database, 1994–2001

- The fund stops reporting, but may still be active. In practice, people often refer to funds that exit from a database but still exist as "defunct funds", whereas a "dead fund" is one that has exited from the database and stopped operations.

In theory, correcting for survivorship bias is fairly easy. We just need to obtain data for the entire set of funds that existed over the period under review and then calculate the annual performance of the average fund in the complete sample. The latter is then compared with the annual average performance of surviving funds (the ones that are still operating at the end of the sampling period). The return difference gives us the survivorship bias. This is the methodology that was adopted by Malkiel (1995) for mutual funds. With hedge funds, however, the entire sample of funds is not observable, as there are no disclosure or registration requirements. Hence, survivorship bias cannot be measured directly and needs to be estimated from samples of surviving funds and samples of dead funds.

The literature on hedge funds provides a series of estimates of the survivorship bias. They vary from 0.16% in Ackermann *et al.* (1999) to 3.0% in Fung and Hsieh (2000b) – see Table 5.3. As demonstrated by Liang (2000), these differences are easy to explain if one considers the compositional differences in the databases (e.g. the proportion of dead funds retained), the inclusion of funds of funds (less susceptible to overall failure), and the starting date of the studies (leading databases only retain returns on dead funds that died after 1994).

The consensus in the industry appears to be that since 1994, the TASS and MAR databases better reflect the (unobservable) hedge fund universe than the HFR database. In addition, the attrition rate increased significantly in 1998, as well as during the bear market of 2000–2003. In these circumstances, one should imagine a potential survivorship bias of around 3–4% per annum. However, as illustrated by Brown and Goetzmann (1995) and Brown *et al.* (2001), survivorship is also likely to impact higher moments of the distribution of returns as well as the degree of serial correlation.

5.2.4 Backfill or instant history bias

Another important source of bias is the backfill bias, also called the instant history bias. It occurs whenever funds joining a given database are allowed to backfill their historical returns,

Table 5.4 Estimates of the backfill bias on average return

Study	Backfill bias (% p.a.)	Sample
Fung and Hsieh (2000b, 2001b)	1.4%	TASS database, 1994–1998
Edwards and Caglayan (2001)	1.2%	MAR (incl. FOF), 1991–1998
Barry (2003)	1.4%	TASS database, 1994–2001

therefore entering the database with "instant history", even though they were not part of the database in previous years.

This is equivalent to granting a free option to hedge fund managers, namely, the option to decide when to be included in the database with all or part of the fund's track record. Since it is in each fund's interest to display the most positive performance possible, most managers will go through an incubation period during which they will not report any performance figures. Then, if the mean performance displayed by a fund during its incubation period is better than that of funds that have belonged to the corresponding database for a long time, the manager will request its inclusion in the database with all its track record. Naturally, this is likely to bias the past performance upward. As an illustration, Barry (2003) studied the TASS database and observed that 80% of hedge funds backfill at least six months of data, 65% of all funds backfill at least 12 months and 50% backfill more than two years. More worrying is the observation by Liang (2000) that out of the 465 funds listed in common by the HFR and TASS databases, only 154 (or 33.1%) have the same starting date in both databases.

Different databases are not exposed to instant history bias in the same way. Both HFR and CSFB say they do not allow data to be backfilled, but some firms do let funds put the past few years of returns into the database, and this practice distorts the data.

The backfill bias may be estimated for a particular database by averaging the returns since inception and comparing them to the average returns since the fund's inclusion date. Academic research seems to suggest an estimate of 1.2–1.4% per annum using this methodology. However, correcting historical performance by removing the track record between the inception date and the database inclusion date is not necessarily recommended, as it may create a new style bias of the truncated data set vis-à-vis the original. For instance, over the period 1999–2000, it would remove a large proportion of returns to new funds, most of which were long-bias equity hedge funds that outperformed other funds during that period (Table 5.4, Figure 5.1).

5.2.5 Infrequent pricing and illiquidity bias

Another serious problem with hedge fund data is the natural tendency for managers to "manage" optimally their monthly net asset value in order to smooth their returns. The problem is particularly acute for two categories of hedge funds:

- Hedge funds holding illiquid securities or securities that are difficult to price, such as very small cap stocks, emerging market bonds, over-the-counter securities and distressed assets. The marking to market of these assets is often difficult, due to the small trading volume and/or unavailability of effectively traded prices daily. Consequently, some fuzziness and subjectivity comes into play in the determination of fair net asset values. As an illustration, if a security does not trade on the first and last days of the month, the manager will often assign a price, which could be the price at which the security last traded (hence stale) or, worse, a price which the manager thinks is reasonable.

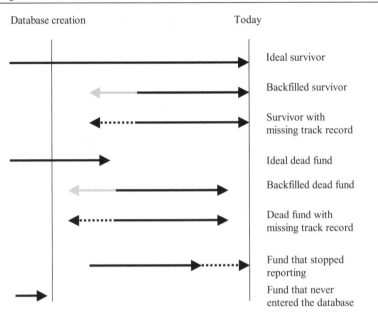

Figure 5.1 The different types of funds in a database

- US onshore limited partnerships, as the vast majority of these funds value their own portfolio. Only 30% use third-party administrators, and in most of the cases, they only use the so-called NAV-light service, which is simply an administrator rubber-stamping the prices supplied by the fund itself.

Box 5.1

The Capital Market Risk Advisors (CMRA) survey on NAV/fair value practices, whose results are discussed in Rahl (2001), provides a good illustration of the potential magnitude of the valuation differences that different pricing approaches create. Overall, only 13% of respondents recognized that they were making adjustments of some kind to the "market" prices they received from their valuation sources. These adjustments were small in most cases, but could reach 30% of the net asset value in the largest cases. This is not so surprising when one learns that on 31 December 2000, the differences between the prices provided by five dealers of collateralized mortgage obligations (CMOs[4]) to a hedge fund ranged from 6% to 44%. With this type of price difference, the different methodologies for incorporating dealer quotes (using the average of the dealer quotes, the median, the worst, the best, etc.) can give rise to wide differences in valuation. The least honest managers will obviously use this opportunity to underestimate or overestimate the periodic changes in value of their portfolios in order to smooth their monthly returns, or even worse, to fraud.

More worrying are the results of the Investor Risk Committee of the International Association of Financial Engineers and CMRA survey of institutional investors, hedge

---

[4] Collateralized mortgage obligations are investment grade bonds that are backed by a pool of mortgage loans with a fixed maturity. The rules for the distribution of the principal payments and interest from the underlying collateral are specified in the CMO prospectus.

funds and funds of funds on hedge fund transparency and valuation practices. About 50% of investors and 20% of funds of funds do not know whether their funds are making any adjustments to NAV, and only 94% of funds of funds versus 50% of investors receive details on most or all of their hedge funds' valuation policies.

If a manager, consciously or not, tends to smooth his returns (and systematically understates the volatility of his portfolio and its correlations with traditional indexes), then there will be an associated systematic overstatement of risk-adjusted returns.[5] Consequently, when fed into an optimizer, these returns will look very attractive, and there will be an over-allocation to investment styles and managers that make use of less liquid securities. This phenomenon is referred to as the illiquidity bias.

Finally, a multi-period sampling bias may occur if the historical period analyzed is too short. Ackermann *et al.* (1999) argue in favor of an estimation period of at least 24 monthly observations, whereas Fung and Hsieh (2000b) require at least 36 historical returns for each fund in their analysis.

5.3   FROM DATABASES TO INDICES

Although hedge fund databases are marred by all the above-mentioned biases, they remain extremely useful tools. In the late 1980s and early 1990s, when hedge funds were identified with the likes of George Soros' Quantum Fund and Julian Robertson's Tiger Fund, there was no source of information other than the complacent self-reports of fund managers, which were generally not easily accessible for investors. The industry was hampered by a lack of information transparency, making an informed investment decision difficult. In those days, the appeal of hedge funds was their exclusivity: only those with the right contacts and sufficiently large amounts of money could buy a ticket on the hedge fund train.

It is only in the last decade that hedge funds have matured from being cowboy investments for the rich to being a serious alternative to the traditional asset classes. The massive inflow of capital has brought an end to the relatively confidential nature of alternative investment strategies, which can no longer reasonably be regarded as a marginal activity within the asset management industry. Thanks to the creation of hedge fund databases, investors have progressively gained access to uniform, accurate and timely measures of valuation, return and risk at the fund level. But what about the industry level? There seems to be an index for just about anything these days, so why not an index for hedge funds? Boosted by the rising interest of institutional investors and the explosion in the number of managers and trading styles, a plethora of indices have sprung up to measure performance at the industry level.

5.3.1   Index construction

The least we can say is that hedge fund indices were initially regarded with skepticism. Indeed, there seems to be an inherent contradiction between the target of absolute performance generally shown by the alternative investment world and the fundamental idea of an index. But the contradiction is only perceived. In reality, the logic and potential benefits of a hedge fund index are essentially the same as for any other asset class:

---

[5] Asness *et al.* (2001) have focused on this problem and observe that once the data is adjusted, the effective risk (market exposure) of the corresponding hedge fund rises significantly.

- An index provides a broadly representative picture of the composition, valuation, performance and risks of the hedge fund industry over time, as well as its correlations with other asset classes. It is particularly useful in improving the soundness of the strategic allocation process, for instance in determining how much to allocate to hedge funds in a global diversified portfolio. It also helps people to better understand the performance profiles of different strategies, thus countering the negative publicity surrounding hedge funds.
- Not all hedge fund managers are equally skilled, and the evidence suggests that the dispersion in returns between good and bad managers is widening with time. An index provides a benchmark against which the performance of managers can be measured in a fair way.
- An index provides the basis for constructing a passive investment product, i.e. index funds, for investors seeking controlled exposure to the asset class through a single, efficient, convenient investment without carrying specific risks. Given the unique challenges of hedge fund investing, the potential benefits of an index-based, passive investment product are especially compelling. Moreover, its existence would open the possibility of creating hedge fund derivatives to participate in a particular investment style.
- An index provides the standardized data needed to measure the risk–return profile of any fund compared with the index. In particular, it allows investors to take active bets in a conscious way by voluntarily diverging from the index.

However, the difficulties involved in the development of quality indexes, which are already evident in the traditional universe, are exacerbated in the case of hedge funds. First, indices built from databases of individual hedge funds inherit all the database biases. Consequently, the performance of the index (based on the observed hedge funds in the database) will not necessarily match that of the unobservable hedge funds in the whole universe of funds. Second, the correct classification of observed funds based on their investment style is difficult. All existing classifications are ambiguous and arbitrary. Not only are the borders between the strategies and funds blurred, they are constantly changing.

Consequently, although the need for and value of a hedge fund index is clear, none of the indices constructed so far have gained universal acceptance in the marketplace. This is not surprising, given the diversity and complexity of the hedge fund industry. Consider just a few of the criteria that an index must meet, and the unique challenges that arise in trying to construct an index. To gain acceptance, a hedge fund index should be clearly positioned with respect to a series of key principles:

- *Transparency* – The list of funds included in an index and the weight assigned to each fund should be fully disclosed and readily obtainable. Guidelines for altering the index, its components or their weights should be specified in advance and be reasonable according to common sense. The prices or returns used to compute the indices should also be available (possibly for a fee) so that index returns can be independently verified and explained.
- *Index coverage and representativity* – Ideally, an index should represent the whole hedge fund universe accurately. However, this raises the question of being comprehensive versus being appropriate. A comprehensive index will include as many funds as possible, ideally the whole universe. An appropriate index will exclude funds that a typical institutional investor would not hold, for instance because the track record is too short, the size too small or the reputation of the manager unsavory. It may also favor the purity of the investment style at the expense of covering a larger number of funds.
- *Weighting* – An important question with hedge fund indices is the weighting scheme. Should the index weight funds by market capitalization (i.e. assets under management) or assign

an equal weight to all funds? In the traditional investment world, capitalization weighted indices have won the battle. They correspond more to the intuitive vision of investing, that is, (i) investors tend to allocate more to larger companies and (ii) in the absence of rebalancing, good performance results in an increase of the relative weight of a company in the index. This corresponds to a momentum-type strategy, where more money is naturally allocated to winners. In contrast, equally weighted indices are rebalanced every month by removing money from well-performing funds and putting it into poorly performing ones ("selling winners and buying losers"). This corresponds to a contrarian strategy and is an artifact of equally weighted indices.

However, in the hedge fund world, there is only one index provider that systematically uses capitalization weighted indices. This apparent success of equally weighted indices is founded on a series of reasons:

○ Hedge fund indices are still in their infancy. It is worth recalling that the Dow Jones index at the beginning was a simple, equally weighted average of a few companies' share prices. This was justified by the lack of computing power at that time. More than a century later, the Dow Jones is still widely used, but it is completely unrepresentative of the US economy in general; investors prefer the Standard & Poor's 500. A similar evolution is likely to take place in the hedge fund universe.
○ Standardizing for asset size is problematic in index construction. The assets under management of hedge funds are difficult to determine, since many managers combine managed accounts and onshore/offshore vehicles. Moreover, hedge funds may have different levels of leverage and those levels may vary over time, with the result that the real asset size may also vary significantly.
○ Some claim that capitalization weighted indices create a distorted picture, as "hot money" flows into a successful fund or strategy, which creates a temporary over-weighting. Although this is true, the same remark somehow applies to equally weighted indices, as the majority of new funds are usually created in the most successful strategies. Furthermore, equally weighted indices often double or triple the weight of individual funds by considering separately the different versions of the same fund (e.g. limited partnership, different series of shares for the offshore fund, managed accounts), which is not much better.

As you have probably guessed, our preference goes clearly to asset weighted indices, which effectively measure the performance of the average dollar invested in the industry – just as the Standard & Poor's 500 measures the performance of the average dollar invested in the US stock market. Equally weighted indices are less useful, unless one wants to measure the performance of the average manager in the industry (Figure 5.2).

• *Investability* – The question of investability is a thornier one. Some claim that, to be useful to investors and advisers, a hedge fund index should represent the world of funds that are actually open to new investment, not the history of funds that are already closed, and that can provide adequate capacity to absorb new investment for the foreseeable future. While making perfect sense from an investment perspective, this goes against the idea of measuring the universe performance by encompassing the largest possible number of funds. It seems that there is no clear answer to the question. An index could adopt either attitude. It simply needs to be clearly situated in terms of its investability policy.
• *Timely reporting* – It is necessary to obtain the index performance in a reasonable amount of time after the end of the month in question.
• *Stability of performance over time* – Once published, the performance of an index should not be revised retroactively.

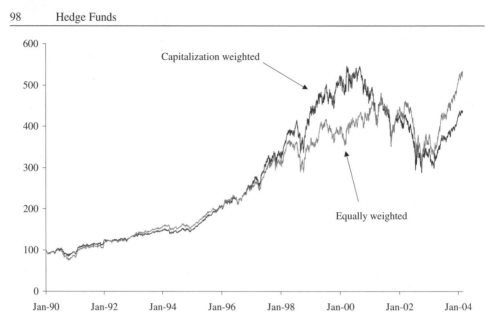

Figure 5.2 Comparison between S&P 500 normal and S&P 500 equally weighted

Despite the formidable task of getting information from hedge fund managers, a growing number of firms are now involved in the creation and publication of hedge fund indices, including leading traditional index providers such as Standard & Poor's and Morgan Stanley Capital Indices. Hence, the lack-of-index issue that once deterred many institutions from embracing hedge funds is now slowly being swept away. The proliferation of new hedge fund indices has even resulted in a new difficulty: that of choosing one.

5.3.2 The various indices available and their differences

For investors, selecting the right index is a real challenge, since the wrong choice may create disappointment resulting from unexpected risks and the lack of compliance with actual needs. The difficulty is that the strengths and weaknesses of competing indices are rarely evidenced, which makes the whole process that much more confusing. Rivalry has always been present in the clubby world of index design and maintenance, but it has always been subtle, even fraternal, in nature. Each index provider claims to have the best set of hedge fund indices, but none will criticize explicitly other indices. Thus there is not one index that can be considered definitive. Even worse, investors are increasingly concerned by the use of specific indices to enhance the marketing presentation of hedge fund products. Consequently they are losing trust in hedge fund indices and remain suspicious about which one to use. In order to step back from this vicious circle, we provide below a comparison of the major index providers as well as the structure and essential construction rules of their indices.

5.3.2.1 ABN Amro

ABN Amro, in conjunction with Eureka Hedge Fund Advisors, publishes the Eurekahedge indices, which form a set of equally weighted indices tracking the performance of Asian hedge funds. There are currently three indices available: the ABN EH index, the ABN EH Japan

Altvest indices
Altvest Hedge Fund Index

Currency trading	Fund of funds	Relative value
Emerging markets	Health care	→ Long/short equity
Event-driven	Macro	→ Capital structure arbitrage
→ Merger arbitrage	Short selling	
→ Distressed securities	Technology	

Figure 5.3   The classification used by Altvest

index and the ABN EH Asia ex-Japan index. The constituent funds all have minimum assets under management of $40 million. Rebalancing occurs "periodically", as material changes in assets under management become known.

5.3.2.2   Altvest

Altvest is a subsidiary of InvestorForce Inc., an information-providing company that targets institutional investors, consultants and money managers. Since the year 2000, Altvest has produced a family of 14 hedge fund indices from a database of about 2000 hedge funds, with data going back to 1993.

Altvest's indices consist of a master index, which is built from all funds in the database, and 13 sub-indices comprising funds that are included in the master index (see Figure 5.3). To map funds with categories, Altvest assigns each fund to the category in which the largest percentage of its assets is invested. If a fund changes category, its past performance remains with its previous sub-index and future performance is included in the new index. Note that a fund can be simultaneously included in several sub-indices. For example, a fund of funds specialized in technology stocks appears in both the "fund of funds" and the "technology" sub-indices. Additionally, the "event-driven" sub-index includes all funds from both the "merger arbitrage" and "distressed securities" sub-indices, and the "relative value" sub-index includes all funds from the "long/short equity" and "capital structure arbitrage" sub-indices.

Although only recently created, Altvest became popular when Calpers, the largest public pension plan in the United States, announced that it would be using Altvest's capabilities to manage its one billion dollar position in alternative investments. Since then, Altvest has also created an innovative technology platform that allows investors and consultants to search for information on alternative investments online. The information is updated online on a daily basis and provided through the web, which means it is available as soon as managers report their performance. Historical data is frozen after a month, so that it can never be modified by the addition or removal of new funds.

5.3.2.3   CISDM/Zurich/MAR

Founded in 1979, Managed Account Reports (MAR) is a subsidiary of Metal Bulletin plc, a London Stock Exchange listed publishing and information providing company. It has tracked managed futures investments since 1979 and hedge funds since 1994.

CISDM hedge fund benchmarks

CISDM event-driven median
→ Distressed securities sub-median
→ Risk arbitrage sub-median
CISDM Global emerging median
CISDM Global international median
CISDM Global established median
→ Global established growth sub-median
→ Global established small-cap sub-median
→ Global established value sub-median

CISDM global macro median
CISDM market neutral median
→ Market neutral arbitrage sub-median
→ Market neutral long/short sub-median
→ Market neutral mortgage-backed sub-median
CISDM sector median
CISDM short-sellers median
CISDM fund of funds median
→ Fund of funds diversified sub-median
→ Fund of funds niche sub-median

CISDM trading adviser benchmarks

CISDM Trading Adviser Qualified Universe Index
CISDM Trading Adviser Qualified Universe Index (Equal-weighted)

Currency advisers sub-index
Diversified advisers sub-index
European advisers sub-index
Financial advisers sub-index

Stock index advisers sub-index
Discretionary advisers sub-index
Systematic advisers sub-index
Trend-follower advisers sub-index

CISDM futures fund benchmarks

CISDM Fund/Pool Qualified Universe Index

Guaranteed fund sub-index
Private pool sub-index
Public fund sub-index

Offshore fund sub-index
Multi-adviser fund sub-index
Single adviser fund sub-index

Figure 5.4 The classification used by CISDM

MAR used to publish a series of monthly hedge fund and managed futures indices that had the particularity of considering the median performance rather than the average (see Figure 5.4). With the acquisition of the company's alternative investment fund databases and related intellectual property by Zurich Capital Markets in March 2001, MAR's range of managed futures and hedge fund benchmarks was re-branded under the Zurich name. Zurich then announced its intention of boosting support for the MAR databases by "improving reported performance data, modernizing the technological platforms behind the databases and expanding the hedge fund categories, strategies and styles".

However, in August 2002, Zurich Capital Markets decided to donate its database to the Center for International Securities and Derivatives Markets (CISDM) at the University of Massachusetts, Amherst. This confirmed the CISDM's role as the premier university research center for the study of alternative investments. The new database is called the CISDM Database and continues to be operated by MAR. It is listed monthly in MarHedge, a publication of Metal Bulletin plc.

5.3.2.4 CSFB/Tremont

CSFB/Tremont Index LLC is a joint venture between Credit Suisse First Boston and Tremont Advisors Inc. The former is one of the world's leading global investment banking firms and the latter is a diversified financial services company specializing in hedge fund consulting, information and research, and investment products.[6] The two companies joined forces to produce a series of hedge fund indices in 1998, with data going back to 1994.

The selection of funds for the CSFB/Tremont indices is done every quarter. The process starts by considering all 3000 United States and offshore hedge funds contained in the TASS database, with the exception of funds of funds and managed accounts. In order to qualify for inclusion in an index, a hedge fund must (i) have at least $10 million under management; (ii) provide audited financial statements;[7] and (iii) meet the CSFB/Tremont reporting requirements in terms of disclosure and transparency. In August 2003, only 448 funds met these three requirements. The qualifying funds are then divided into various categories based on their investment style, with the final constraint that the index in all cases should represent at least 85% of the assets under management in the corresponding universe. Funds are re-selected on a quarterly basis as necessary and the indices are calculated and rebalanced monthly.

The weight of each fund in an index is given by the relative size of its assets under management. This makes the CSFB/Tremont indices the first asset weighted indices for hedge funds and implies a more accurate depiction of the industry. The composition of the indices is public and available on the web.

In addition to the standard indices, in August 2003, CSFB/Tremont launched a series of investable indices, based on a sample of 60 funds. These 60 funds are selected from the funds included in the broader index. They are generally the six largest funds by assets under management in each of the 10 sectors comprising the CSFB/Tremont hedge fund index. To be a member of the investable index, funds must fulfill the following criteria:

- Be a member of the CSFB/Tremont hedge fund index.
- Be domiciled outside the United States (for access by non-US investors).
- Have no lockup restriction.
- Be open to new investments and redemptions, with reasonable terms regarding the size of the investment as well as the time limits.[8]
- Be free of any investigation or review by a regulatory body or other authority for such reasons as wrongdoing or breach of any law, regulation or rule.

In August 2003, the aggregate assets under management by the 60 investable index constituents were equal to approximately $55 billion, making it the industry's largest investable hedge fund index (Figure 5.5).

5.3.2.5   EACM

Evaluation Associates Capital Markets (EACM) is an investment advisory firm based in Norwalk, CT. It specializes in hedge funds and multi-manager investment programs for institutional and high net worth clients. In January 1996, EACM launched a new benchmark for alternative investment strategies called the EACM100® Index, as well as indices for five broad strategies and 13 underlying sub-strategies, with data going back to 1990.

---

[6] Oppenheimer Funds, a US-based provider of traditional investment products managing assets of $127 billion, recently acquired Tremont Advisors Inc. for $140 million.

[7] Which implies that the fund has been in business for at least a year!

[8] The minimum amount, if any, for initial investment in a fund has to be less than or equal to the greater of (i) the product of $50 000 000 and its prospective weight in the index and (ii) $100 000. The minimum amount, if any, for subsequent investments in the same fund must be less than or equal to the lesser of (i) the product of $10 000 000 and its prospective weight in the index and (ii) $200 000. Redemptions must be feasible no less frequently than monthly or, in the case of funds in the event-driven and convertible arbitrage sectors, no less frequently than quarterly.

CSFB/Tremont indices
Hedge Fund Index

Convertible arbitrage	Event-driven	Long/short equity
Dedicated short bias	→ Event-driven: distressed	Managed futures
Emerging markets	→ Event-driven: multi-strategy	Multi-strategy
Equity market neutral	→ Event-driven: risk arbitrage	
Fixed income arbitrage	Global macro	

CSFB/Tremont investable indices
Hedge Fund Index

Convertible arbitrage	Event-driven	Long/short equity
Dedicated short bias	Fixed income arbitrage	Managed futures
Emerging markets	Global macro	Multi-strategy
Equity market neutral		

Figure 5.5   The classification used by CSFB/Tremont

EACM indices
EACM 100® Index

Relative value	Equity hedge funds	Global asset allocators
→ Long/short equity	→ Domestic long biased	→ Discretionary
→ Convertible hedge	→ Domestic opportunistic	→ Systematic
→ Bond hedge	→ Global/international	Short sellers
→ Multi-strategy		
Event-driven		
→ Deal arbitrage		
→ Bankruptcy/distressed		
→ Multi-strategy		

Figure 5.6   The classification used by EACM

EACM's indices are computed from an equally weighted composite of non-audited performance information provided by a set of about 100 hedge funds. These funds are selected by EACM as being representative of their style, and the index may be rebalanced at the beginning of each calendar year. However, EACM does not disclose individual fund names or their weightings, which they consider proprietary (Figure 5.6).

5.3.2.6   HFR

Hedge Fund Research (HFR) is a veteran of the hedge fund industry. The Chicago-based firm publishes a series of 37 equally weighted monthly performance HFRI indices based on both onshore and offshore funds from the HFR database. These indices are net of fees and free of

---

HFRI
HFRI Fund Weighted Composite Index

Convertible arbitrage	Macro
Distressed securities	Market timing
Emerging markets (total)	Merger arbitrage
→ Emerging markets: Asia	Regulation D
→ Emerging markets: Eastern Europe/CIS	Relative value arbitrage
→ Emerging markets: global	Sector (total)
→ Emerging markets: Latin America	→ Sector: energy
Equity hedge	→ Sector: financial
Equity market neutral	→ Sector: health care/biotech
→ Equity market neutral: statistical arbitrage	→ Sector: miscellaneous
Equity non-hedge	→ Sector: real estate
Event-driven	→ Sector: technology
Fixed income (total)	Short selling
→ Fixed income: arbitrage	Fund of funds
→ Fixed income: convertible bonds	→ Fund of funds: conservative
→ Fixed income: diversified	→ Fund of funds: diversified
→ Fixed income: high yield	→ Fund of funds: market-defensive
→ Fixed income: mortgage-backed	→ Fund of funds: strategic

Figure 5.7   The classification used by HFR

survivorship bias after 1994.[9] Funds are assigned to categories based on the descriptions in their offering memoranda. There is no minimum required asset size, nor minimum length of track record for fund inclusion in the index. The weighting scheme is revised on a monthly basis to include new funds and to eliminate defunct ones. The indices are updated three times a month (flash estimate, mid- and end month). The trailing four months are left as estimates and are subject to change. All performance prior to that is locked and is no longer subject to change (Figure 5.7).

Since March 2003, HFR has also published a series of HFRX indices (one composite index and eight primary investable indices). The styles covered are convertible arbitrage, distressed securities, event-driven, equity hedge, equity market neutral, macro, relative value and merger arbitrage. Rebalanced on a quarterly basis, the HFRX indices are designed to offer full transparency, investability, daily repricing and consistent fund selection.[10] All HFRX indices are composed of hedge funds that are open for investment and that passed extensive qualitative screening and due diligence (Figure 5.8).

5.3.2.7   HedgeFund.net/Channel Capital Group

Channel Capital Group Inc., based in New York City, owns and operates HedgeFund.net, one of the web's most popular sites for hedge fund information and performance data. HedgeFund.net produces a set of 32 hedge fund indices (called the Tuna indices) from a database of around 4000 onshore and offshore funds, with data going back to 1976. It also produces four aggregated indices using the same data (see Figure 5.9).

---

[9] Most HFR indices were created in 1994 and were backfilled until 1990.

[10] The fund selection is based on cluster analysis, a statistical technique that we will review in Chapter 9.

HFRX
HFRX Global Hedge Fund Index

	Event-driven
Convertible arbitrage	Macro merger arbitrage
Distressed securities	Relative value arbitrage
Equity hedge	
Equity market neutral	

Figure 5.8 The classification used by HFR (investable indices)

HedgeFund.net (Tuna indices)
Hedge Fund Aggregate Index
Aggressive Aggregate Index
Equity Hedge Aggregate Index
Relative Value Aggregate Index

Aggressive growth	Fund of funds	Regulation D
Convertible arbitrage	Healthcare sector	Risk arbitrage
Country-specific	Long only	Short bias
CTA	Long/short hedged	Short-term trading
Distressed	Macro market neutral	Small/micro cap
Emerging markets	Market timer	Special situations
Energy sector	Opportunistic	Statistical arbitrage
Event-driven	Options arbitrage	Technology sector
Finance sector	Options strategies	Value
Fixed income	Other	Venture capital/private equity
Fixed income arbitrage	Other market neutral	

Figure 5.9 The classification used by HedgeFund.net

The Tuna indices are calculated as an equally weighted average of the performance of all funds within the corresponding category. Fund managers themselves select the category to which they want to be assigned. The funds that compose the indices are disclosed on the website of HedgeFund.net.

5.3.2.8 Hennessee

The Hennessee Group LLC is a New York-based research and consulting firm. It produces a set of 23 equally weighted indices and four composite indices, based on a sample of about 500 hedge funds selected from a database of about 3000 funds. Most of these indices were created in 1987 but became publicly available only in 1992.

To be included in the index, a fund should (i) have at least \$100 million of assets, or at least \$10 million of assets and a track record of more than 12 months, and (ii) satisfy the Hennessee Group LLC reporting requirements. Funds are assigned to categories based on "manager's core competency", and the performance of dead funds stays in the indices to reduce survivorship bias.

An interesting feature of the Hennessee indices is that they include several funds that are closed to new subscriptions, and that therefore do not report to other agencies. This is possible only because clients of the Hennessee Group are effectively investing in these funds (Figure 5.10).

Hennessee Hedge Fund Indices
Hennessee Hedge Fund Index
Hennessee Correlated Index
Hennessee Non-Correlated Index
Hennessee Global/Macro Index

Convertible arbitrage	Healthcare/biotech	Pacific rim
Distressed	High yield	Regulation D
Emerging markets	International	Short biased
Europe	Latin America macro	Technology
Event-driven	Market neutral	Telecom and media
Financial equities	Merger arbitrage	Value
Fixed income	Multiple arbitrage	
Growth	Opportunistic	

Figure 5.10   The classification used by Hennessee

InvestHedge indices
InvestHedge Composite

Global multi-strategy $

Arbitrage $	US equity $	Asia Pacific funds of funds $
Global equity $	European equity Euro	Global-macro-currency-debt $
	Emerging markets hedge $	

Eurohedge indices

European long/short $	Fixed income & high yield	Combined arbitrage
European long/short £	Global equity	→ Event-driven
European long/short Euro	Managed futures	→ Mixed arbitrage
Macro		→ Stat. & quant. arbitrage
		→ Convertible & equity arbitrage

AsiaHedge indices
AsiaHedge Composite

Asia including Japan US$	Japan long/short US$	Australia long/short AU$
Asia excluding Japan US$	Japan long/short Yen	Emerging markets

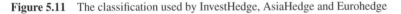

Figure 5.11   The classification used by InvestHedge, AsiaHedge and Eurohedge

5.3.2.9   InvestHedge, AsiaHedge and Eurohedge

HedgeFund Intelligence is an independent publishing group that focuses on providing information about the hedge fund industry, collecting performance data and organizing hedge fund conferences. Its major characteristic is its independence, as it neither manages money nor advises investors, and the company is 100% owned by its directors and staff. HedgeFund Intelligence produces a series of European and global hedge fund indices with data going back to the year 2000, as well as a series of Asian hedge fund indices going back to 2001 (Figure 5.11).

LJH Global Investments		
LJH Global Hedge Index		
Asian hedge	Event-driven	Risk arbitrage
Convertible arbitrage	Fixed income arbitrage	Risk arbitrage
Distressed securities	European hedge	Short only
Domestic hedge	Global macro	Technology
Emerging markets	Hedge index	
Emerging markets fixed income	Market neutral equity	

Figure 5.12   The classification used by LJH Global Investments

5.3.2.10   LJH Global Investments

LJH Global Investments is a consulting and advisory firm based in Naples, FL. It has developed a set of 16 indices of various hedge fund styles (see Figure 5.12).

Each index is calculated as the performance of an equally weighted sample of 25 to 50 hedge funds. These funds are selected and mapped to a specific strategy by LJH Global Investments. They must provide audited statements and pass some due diligence tests. The composition of each index is revised on a regular basis but is not disclosed.

5.3.2.11   Morgan Stanley Capital Indices

Morgan Stanley Capital Indices (MSCI) is a leading provider of global equity and fixed income indices used by institutional investors worldwide. Cashing in on its pre-eminent place in traditional asset class indices, MSCI teamed up with Financial Risk Management (FRM) to cover the hedge fund field in July 2002 with a new database of about 1500 hedge funds (Figure 5.13).

In parallel with its database, MSCI has created the industry's most comprehensive and detailed classification framework for hedge funds – the MSCI Hedge Fund Classification Standard. This standard uses multiple characteristics of funds to classify them, grouped together in several dimensions:

- The first dimension covers the investment process employed to generate returns, such as directional trading, relative value, security selection, credit specialist and multi-process. Each process group includes several sub-categories – see Figure 5.13.
- The second dimension covers the asset class used to generate returns. This includes equities (split into equity and convertibles), fixed income (split into credit-sensitive, credit-insensitive and mortgage-backed securities), commodities, currencies (split into developed and emerging markets), real estate and options.
- The third dimension is the geographic location of the funds' investments. The categories announced are Europe, North America, Japan, Pacific ex-Japan and emerging markets, as well as broader global developed and global categories.

In addition, secondary classification characteristics are the Global Industry Classification Standard (GICS) and capitalization size for equity-oriented strategies, and fixed income focus for credit-oriented strategies. This gives a very large number of potential combinations, but it allows for a very precise definition of the strategy followed by a hedge fund, such as: "relative

Primary Characteristics					Secondary Characteristics	
Investment Process		Asset Class	Geography			
Process Group	Process		Area	Region		
Directional Trading	Discretionary Trading	Commodities	Developed Markets	Europe	GICS Sector	Consumer Discretionary
	Tactical Allocation	Convertibles		Japan		Consumer Staples
	Systematic Trading			North America		Energy
	Multi-Process			Pacific ex Japan		Financials
				Diversified		Health Care
Relative Value	Arbitrage	Equity				Industrials
	Merger Arbitrage	Fixed Income	Emerging Markets	EMEA		Information Technology
	Statistical Arbitrage	Diversified		Asia Pacific		Materials
	Multi-Process			Latin America		Telecom Services
				Diversified		Utilities
Security Selection	Long Bias					No Industry Focus
	No Bias		Global Markets	Europe		
	Short Bias			Asia ex Japan	Fixed Income Focus	Asset-Backed
	Variable Bias			Asia		Government Sponsored
Specialist Credit	Long-Short Credit			Diversified		High Yield
	Distressed Securities					Investment Grade
	Private Placements					Mortgage-Backed
	Multi-Process					Sovereign
						No Fixed Income Focus
Multi-Process	Event-Driven				Capitalization Size	Mid and Large Cap
Group	Multi-Process					Small Cap
						Small and Mid Cap
						No Size Focus

Figure 5.13   The MSCI hedge fund Classification Standard SM
Source: MSCI.

value–convergence arbitrage–fixed income–global–developed" or "directional trading–long bias–equity–Europe–financial sector–mid cap".

Equally weighted indices are calculated for any strategy where the number of funds is relevant. It is worth noting that MSCI is the first hedge fund index provider to make data on constituent hedge funds available and linked directly to the index, enabling clients subscribing to the indices and fund database to analyze index performance and risk characteristics fund by fund.

MSCI also provides three composite indices based on fund size. The Broad Hedge Fund Composite Index covers funds in excess of $15 million, the Core Fund Index considers only funds in excess of $100 million within a given strategy, and the Small Fund Index includes funds between $15 million and $100 million.

In total, this results in more than 160 MSCI hedge fund indices at the time of writing these lines. Given the prominence of the sponsor, these indices should become widely accepted.

More recently, MSCI also launched its Hedge Invest Index, which consists of a diverse sample of hedge funds that represent a broad range of hedge fund strategies and have weekly liquidity. Published every Friday, the index contains only open funds that have committed to liquidity and capacity terms with Lyxor Asset Management.[11] MSCI is responsible for

---

[11] Lyxor Asset Management (Lyxor) is a subsidiary of the Société Générale Group dedicated to structured funds activities, including management of alternative investment funds. As of June 2003, Lyxor managed a total of $26.7 billion, of which $9.8 billion were in alternative investments, and employed 93 professionals, 60 of whom were dedicated to alternative investment products.

designing and maintaining the index, classifying funds into strategies and publishing the index and constituent data. Lyxor is responsible for establishing each individual fund on their managed account platform, conducting initial due diligence, monitoring the investment mandate of each hedge fund manager and providing fund valuations independent of each fund's external adviser.

The MSCI Hedge Invest Index is clearly structured for use as the basis of index-linked financial products. As of July 2003, the index contained 64 funds in 11 investment processes. The number of funds in the index is expected to increase over time.

5.3.2.12   Standard & Poor's

Standard & Poor's (S&P), the other global leader in index development, is a newcomer to the field of hedge fund indices but has the ambition of becoming a major player. Since October 2002, it has published a main hedge fund index, as well as four sub-indices covering in total nine investment strategies (macro, equity long/short, managed futures, special situations, merger arbitrage, distressed, fixed income arbitrage, convertible arbitrage and equity market neutral).

The aim of the S&P index is to become the leading, transparent, investable index for hedge funds. Equally weighted, the index only contains 40 funds, which has prompted some skepticism from rivals who often consider it as a sort of fund of funds. The main index actually includes fewer than 1% of the known universe. But S&P insists that, according to its statistical research, 30 to 40 funds reliably reporting their performance data can accurately represent a much larger universe.

The S&P hedge fund index has been built from the beginning as an investable index. The funds included have to go through a very stringent quantitative and qualitative filtering process. The quantitative screening assesses each fund's representativity, while the qualitative screening addresses the quality and tenure of the funds, the risk and operating controls, and the capacity to accept new investments. A fund can be removed at any time from the index if it becomes closed to new investment, if it no longer represents its respective strategy, or if it fails to pass the due diligence reviews of Albourne Partners, a hedge fund consultant to S&P. The high level of transparency requested from the fund managers includes daily pricing, which enables S&P to calculate and publish the index on a daily basis. Derivatives Portfolio Management (DPM) is in charge of verifying the valuations.

For purposes of analysis, S&P constructed a *pro forma* version of the index that is based on the index constituents as of September 2002, using monthly performance data from January 1998 through September 2002 from the fund companies themselves. The *pro forma* version is rebalanced to its original equal weights annually in August.

Recently, Standard & Poor's granted PlusFunds, a developer of passive hedge fund investment products, an exclusive license to develop investment products tracking the S&P hedge fund indices. Each manager of a hedge fund included in the index has agreed to manage a separate account identical to his or her private hedge fund (Figure 5.14).

5.3.2.13   Van Hedge Fund Advisors International

Van Hedge Fund Advisors International is a research and advisory services firm based in Nashville, TN. It maintains a database of about 5000 funds (2650 US and 2350 offshore), primarily used to identify hedge funds for investors, and on request, to design custom hedge fund portfolios.

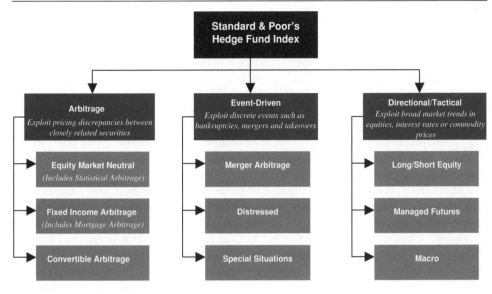

Figure 5.14   The S&P hedge fund classification approach
Source: Standard & Poor's.

Figure 5.15   The classification used by Van Hedge Fund Advisors

Van Hedge Fund indices were initially compiled in 1994 and published for the first time in 1995, with data going back to 1988. Van Hedge tracks the performance of 14 strategies, plus a global index, based on a sub-sample of about 750 offshore and onshore hedge funds (see Figure 5.15). Funds are assigned to categories based on their offering memorandums and interviews with their managers.

5.3.2.14   Zurich Capital Markets

Zurich Capital Markets (ZCM) was originally a wholly owned New York-based subsidiary of the Zurich Financial Services Group.[12] Over the years, ZCM has established itself as an attractive niche provider of services to hedge fund investors and managers, and has made several attempts at creating series of investable hedge fund indices.

---

[12] Founded in 1872 and with its headquarters in Zurich, Switzerland, Zurich Financial Services is an insurance-based financial services provider with an international network. It has offices in approximately 60 countries and employs about 68 000 people.

In October 1999, ZCM and Hedge Fund Research created a joint venture named ZCM/HFR Index Management for the purpose of offering hedge fund indices as well as funds of funds tracking these indices. The new company designed the methodology and started publishing indices tracking five strategies (merger arbitrage, convertible arbitrage, distressed securities, equity hedge and event-driven). However, the concept never attracted more than $300 million from investors, mostly from Zurich Capital Markets. The major problem was that the methodology was rather opaque. To quote: ". . . each index is constructed as a diversified allocation to a collection of separately-managed accounts, weighted and rebalanced via a proprietary methodology developed by the joint-venture". The joint venture terminated in December 2000. ZCM bought back the investment platform of ZCM/HFR for an undisclosed sum and stopped calculating these indices.

In March 2001, following the acquisition of an alternative investment fund database and intellectual property from Managed Account Reports LLC, Zurich Capital Markets in partnership with Schneeweis Partners LLC again started offering five hedge fund indices. The five strategies selected were the same as those of the former ZCM/HFR hedge fund indices, that is, merger arbitrage, convertible arbitrage, distressed securities, equity hedge and event-driven. Each index is built from an equally weighted portfolio of 10 to 15 hedge funds. These funds are carefully selected for the "purity" of their investment style, which manifests itself primarily in manager correlation with other pure style managers as well as specific style-related benchmarks. In addition, each selected fund must have had at least $25 million under management for at least two years, and must be likely to be considered for investment by institutional or sophisticated investors. The composition of the portfolio is public, and rebalancing is carried out on a quarterly basis, under the supervision of an independent committee.

In parallel, ZCM launched the Zurich Institutional Benchmark Series, a fund of hedge funds, with the goal of replicating the performance of the indices with modest tracking error and at relatively low cost. It collected $315 million in the first month, and had a target size of $2–3 billion by the end of 2002. One of its particularities is that it invests with the managers represented in each index through managed accounts, in order to have a complete view of the assets (with Zurich acting as custodian).

In June 2003, however, Zurich Financial Services announced its intention to focus on its core insurance activities and decided to divest itself of the ZCM business line. In July, BNP Paribas and Zurich Financial Services signed an agreement for the transfer of certain structured products from ZCM to BNP Paribas, including structured products linked to alternative investment funds managed by ZCM. This transaction should enable BNP Paribas, already a European leader in structured fund-of-funds products, to become one of the top players in this business in the United States. At the time of writing, the future of the Zurich indices is not known yet, but it does not look so bright.

5.3.3   Different indices–different returns

The different hedge fund indices available on the market are built from different data sets, conform to diverse selection criteria and style classifications, and use different methods of construction. As a result, the observed performance varies considerably depending on the index used, and investors cannot rely on competing hedge fund indices to obtain a true and fair view of hedge fund performance (Table 5.5).

Table 5.5 Comparison between the major hedge fund index providers

	Altvest	CSFB	EACM	Hennessee	HFR	HF.Net	MAR	S&P	Van Hedge	Zurich
Managed futures		X				X	X	X		
Global macro	X	X		X	X	X	X	X	X	
Long/short equity	X	X	X		X	X		X		X
Dedicated short	X	X	X	X	X	X	X		X	
Emerging markets	X	X		X	X	X	X		X	
Market neutral		X		X	X	X	X	X	X	
Fixed income arb.		X		X	X	X		X	X	
Convertible arb.		X	X	X	X	X		X		X
Merger arb.	X	X	X	X	X	X	X	X		X
Distressed	X	X	X	X	X	X	X	X	X	X
Funds of funds	X				X	X	X		X	X
Event-driven	X	X	X	X	X	X	X			X
Relative value	X		X		X	X				
Special situations						X		X	X	
Regulation D				X	X	X				
Aggressive growth						X			X	
Value		X				X			X	
Energy					X	X				
Financial			X	X	X	X			X	X
Technology	X			X	X	X			X	
High yield				X	X					
Healthcare	X			X	X	X			X	
International					X		X			
Market timing						X	X		X	
Opportunity			X	X		X			X	
Statistical arb.					X	X				

Several papers have explicitly mentioned the measurement and interpretation problems that surround some hedge fund indices.[13] However, the first study that systematically documented the heterogeneity existing between *all* hedge fund indices is that of Amenc and Martellini (2001b, 2003a). Some of their results are spectacular. For instance, for the long/short equity strategies, Zurich Capital Markets reports a +20.48% return in February 2000 (non-annualized), while EACM reports a −1.56% return (non-annualized) for the same month and the same strategy. This represents a difference of 22.04% for indices that are supposed to be representative of the same strategy. Similar situations occur with other indices and other strategies, and using quarterly figures does not necessarily smooth out the differences. As an illustration, the maximum difference is 30.08% for long/short or 16.52% for relative value, as opposed to, respectively, 22.04% or 10.47% at the monthly level.

The average correlations between the indices that focus on the same strategy are usually acceptable. However, the lowest correlations are extremely low, and even sometimes negative (case of Zurich and EACM long/short equity indices once again). These low correlations

---

[13] See for instance Brittain and Lyster Watson & Co. (2001), Brooks and Kat (2001), Fung and Hsieh (2002a) or Schneeweis *et al.* (2001).

Table 5.6 Performance comparison between the major hedge fund index providers

Strategy	Date	Worst index performance	Best index performance	Spread (%)
Convertible arbitrage	Oct-98	CSFB: −4.67	Hennessee: 0.08	4.75
Dedicated short	Feb-00	Van Hedge: −24.3	EACM: −3.09	21.20
Distressed	Aug-98	HF Net: −12.08	Van Hedge: −4.70	7.38
Emerging markets	Aug-98	MAR: −26.65	Altvest: −7.2	19.45
Event-driven	Aug-98	CSFB: −11.77	Altvest: −6.71	5.06
Fixed income arbitrage	Oct-98	HF Net: −10.78	Van Hedge: 0.2	10.98
Funds of funds	Dec-99	MAR: 2.41	Altvest: 10.42	8.01
Global macro	May-00	Van Hedge: −5.80	HF Net: 12	17.80
Long/short equity	Feb-00	EACM: −1.56	Zurich: 20.48	22.04
Market neutral	Dec-99	Hennessee: 0.2	Van Hedge: 5.2	5.00
Merger arbitrage	Sep-98	Altvest: −0.11	HFR: 1.74	1.85
Relative value	Sep-98	EACM: −6.07	Van Hedge: 4.40	10.47

Source: Amenc and Martellini (2001b).

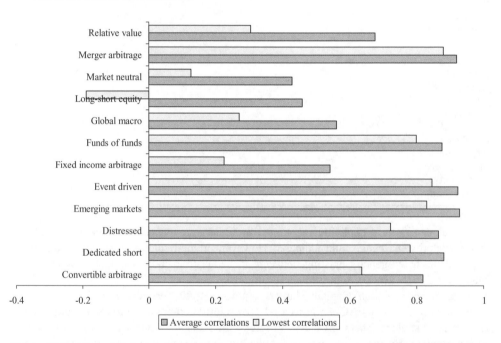

Figure 5.16 Measuring the average and lowest correlation between the indices for each hedge fund strategy
Source: Amenc and Martellini (2001b).

seem to occur more frequently in the case of "pure alpha" strategies, such as equity market neutral, long/short, global macro and fixed income arbitrage. In contrast, some strategies seem more homogenous and consistent in their behavior (e.g. merger arbitrage) (Table 5.6, Figure 5.16).

While not surprising, these results are bothersome because they clearly indicate that hedge fund indices fail to agree on what they measure. This is likely to result in significantly different

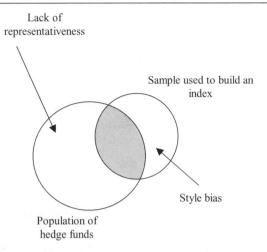

Figure 5.17   The biases in hedge fund indices

portfolios, depending on what indices are used to model the asset class during the asset allocation process. Furthermore, the major inconsistencies between indices seem to occur precisely when reliable information is most needed, that is, during periods of market crisis (August/September 1998, February 2000, etc.).

In addition to the problems described above, Amenc and Martellini mention two other biases that affect hedge fund indices:

- The lack of representativeness, as (i) the existing databases only cover a relatively small fraction of the hedge fund population and (ii) some indices only cover a tiny portion of a database. For instance, Zurich Capital Markets and S&P use only 60 hedge funds to build their indices, that is, less than 1% of the total universe.
- The presence of a style bias. Most indices use the managers' self-proclaimed styles to classify funds, but in reality, nothing guarantees that a manager will follow a single investment style and avoid drifting away from it. As opportunities disappear in the original strategies, it is common practice for some hedge fund managers to start looking at other markets – see Lhabitant (2001). As a result, all competing indices for a given style are likely to encompass funds that should not be included.

These two biases can be represented as in Figure 5.17. As an illustration, Figure 5.18 shows what we obtain using the TASS, HFR and CISDM hedge fund databases.

Such disturbing evidence poses serious problems. The heterogeneous picture provided by the set of existing hedge fund indices confuses investors and sheds suspicion on results based on a single hedge fund index. Today, it is probably still the major obstacle to the institutionalization of the alternative investment industry. It affects not only portfolio analysis involving hedge funds but also empirical tests of asset pricing theory.

5.3.4   Towards pure hedge fund indices

Rather than building a new index and claiming that the newcomer is better than all the existing ones, Amenc and Martellini (2003a) and the EDHEC Risk and Asset Management Research

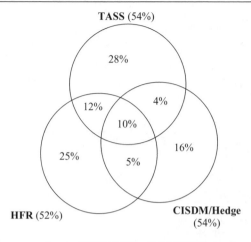

Figure 5.18   The universe according to TASS, HFR and CISDM/Hedge (we thank Drago Indjic from Fauchier Partners for providing these results)

Center recently suggested an original solution to the problem of hedge fund indices' heterogeneity and lack of representativeness. They use *all* the relevant information contained in *all* the competing indexes available and compile them to produce a set of optimal alternative indexes. Optimal here means stable, more representative, easy to replicate, non-commercial and with fewer biases.

In a sense, each EDHEC index can be seen as a sort of "index of the existing indices". However, the methodology used to calculate the EDHEC index goes far beyond a simple average of the existing indices. It relies on a statistical technique called principal component analysis (PCA), which transforms a number of correlated variables (in our cases, the indices) into a smaller number of uncorrelated variables called *principal components*. The first principal component accounts for as much of the variability in the data as possible, and each succeeding component accounts for as much of the remaining variability as possible.

Without going into too much detail, the intuition behind the EDHEC methodology is as follows. In theory, there exists one true pure index that represents adequately what the hedge fund industry is doing. In practice, this index is not observable, because no one has yet gained access to the complete set of data that its calculation requires. Instead, there are several observable indices that are calculated by various index providers on a sub-set of the complete data set. Each of these indices can be represented as the true pure index, plus some noise capturing the existence of biases and lack of full representativeness. The idea of PCA is to combine optimally all indices in order to eliminate the noise as far as possible. That is, PCA will build a portfolio of the existing indices that best captures the common behavior of the group of observed indices. Implicitly, the common behavior identified by PCA should correspond to the true pure index.

In summarizing the group of observed indices into one single portfolio of indices, some information is lost, particularly where the heterogeneity of information provided by competing index providers is the most extreme. However, PCA ensures that the loss is minimal, in the sense that no other linear combination of competing indices implies a lower information loss. On average, Amenc and Martellini (2003a) observe that pure style indices are able to capture about 80% of the behavior of the time series of competing indices.

Table 5.7   The performance of EDHEC indices

	October 2003 (%)	YTD 2003 (%)	Annual average return since inception (%)	Annual volatility since inception (%)	Sharpe ratio
Convertible arbitrage	1.46	9.20	10.69	3.79	1.76
CTA Global	1.04	7.35	9.05	10.10	0.50
Distressed securities	2.67	22.99	14.32	4.50	2.29
Emerging markets	2.59	24.98	14.46	8.76	1.19
Equity market neutral	1.15	5.22	6.22	1.27	1.76
Event-driven	1.91	17.07	8.47	4.94	0.91
Fixed income arbitrage	0.35	6.54	7.51	2.14	1.64
Funds of funds	1.52	9.16	4.81	3.00	0.27
Global macro	1.11	13.57	8.19	3.87	1.08
Long/short equity	3.65	17.85	2.77	7.40	−0.17
Merger arbitrage	1.11	6.82	3.07	3.17	−0.29
Relative value	1.59	9.62	7.22	3.87	0.83
Short selling	−6.56	−21.41	4.98	17.89	0.05

How good is the resulting index? Amenc and Martellini prove two theorems that provide the answer to this question. First, a portfolio of competing indices encompasses more individual funds and is always less biased than the average of the set of indices it is extracted from. Second, a portfolio of indices is always more representative than any competing index. The empirical tests confirm the theory and suggest that PCA-based indices do achieve the improvement of representativeness they were designed for (Table 5.7).[14]

EDHEC recently launched its new model (www.edhec-risk.com) and is now introducing the concepts to industry players and institutional investors. The least one can say is that the first reactions were extremely positive. In particular, passive strategies and products aimed at capturing the average return of a specific hedge fund universe could greatly benefit from the new set of indices.

To demonstrate the usefulness of their new pure indices, the EDHEC researchers constructed portfolios made up of single funds that replicate the EDHEC alternative indexes. On average, there were 25 funds in each portfolio, drawn randomly (without replacement) from several databases. The weights given to the funds were chosen in order to minimize the tracking error with respect to the EDHEC index. For the sake of comparison, the same procedure was applied with respect to the HFR and the CSFB/Tremont indices.

The tracking errors obtained are represented in Table 5.8. They confirm the superiority of the EDHEC indices in terms of ability to be replicated by a hedge fund portfolio. In particular, the low difference observed between the in-sample and out-of-sample tracking errors confirms that the tracking error is stable over time and remains at acceptable levels. These results, as well as others published on the EDHEC website, confirm that the new indices are ideal candidates to help investors to allocate a significant part of their portfolio to the alternative class. According to many researchers and investors, they even qualify as potential benchmarks – benchmarks that help to assess past performance on a risk-adjusted basis and help to identify the current risk characteristics of hedge fund strategies.

---

[14] Amenc and Martellini suggest and test other methodologies to help build a pure style index or index of the indices for a given style, such as Kalman filtering and minimum bias with or without positivity constraints. More detail can be found in their original paper.

Table 5.8   Trackability of the EDHEC alternative indices

	EDHEC in sample (%)	EDHEC out of sample (%)	CSFB in sample (%)	HFR in sample (%)
Convertible arbitrage	0.73	1.05	2.23	0.74
Emerging markets	2.34	3.39	4.61	3.19
Event-driven	0.95	1.36	2.40	1.03
Fixed income arbitrage	1.11	1.25	0.83	2.70
Global macro	0.12	2.23	0.17	0.13
Long/short equity	1.90	3.25	4.02	2.07
Market neutral	0.73	0.86	1.03	2.28

Source: EDHEC Risk.

5.4   FROM INDICES TO BENCHMARKS

One of the most controversial topics on the hedge fund front these days is that of benchmarking returns. At first glance, the terms "hedge funds" and "benchmarks" would seem to be conflicting. Hedge fund managers are hired for their skills. They should be allowed to roam wherever their value-creating instincts take them, unfettered by benchmarks that discourage unconventional investment ideas. Their portfolios should aim to produce positive absolute returns rather than to outperform a given benchmark. For many years, the perceived success of hedge funds nourished this anti-benchmark view, and as a consequence fostered the mystique, which the alternative investment industry had an enormous vested interest in maintaining. Not surprisingly, the most active opponents of benchmarks were often those who benefited the most from looser scrutiny.

However, with the continued growth of the alternative investment industry, the rising interest of institutional investors and the explosion in the number of managers and trading styles, the demand for benchmarks to measure performance has been rising. The term "benchmarks" should be understood here in the Association for Investment Management and Research (AIMR) sense, that is, as "an independent rate of return (or hurdle rate) forming an objective test of the effective implementation of an investment strategy". People want to be able to measure the performance of managers with whom they place their money but, without benchmarks, how can an investor really monitor a hedge fund's performance and formulate expectations on an ongoing basis? How can he assess whether a manager possesses sustainable skill in generating superior results, or if his performance just derives from the asset class or the particular market he is invested in?

Performance benchmarks are important for three key reasons: they help measure the investment performance of institutional fund managers, they provide clients and trustees with a reference point for monitoring that performance, and they can also have the effect of modifying the behavior of portfolio managers. As investors have become more and more interested in this field, and as so many new hedge funds have come on to the market, it has become more important to maintain a clearer perspective by looking for an assessment of the average performance of the industry. Investing in a hedge fund is largely a matter of purchasing alpha, which is a manager's skill in identifying market inefficiency and exploiting it. Credible benchmarks, or at least references, are therefore necessary to assess alpha in a correct way. Benchmarks are also a good general tool to aid in the planning, implementation and review of investment policies. They provide a common language of communication between the investor and the investment manager, and provide an objective means with which to assess return and risk as well as to interpret and monitor a fund's behavior.

5.4.1   Absolute benchmarks and peer groups

Originally, hedge fund managers avoided the benchmark question by establishing absolute return targets. These were loosely defined as a flat, stated rate of return which was theoretically achievable in any market environment (e.g. 15%). Hedge fund peer group universes were also used, but only as a supplemental form of comparative performance measurement.

In the year 2000, markets became increasingly challenging for hedge fund managers as well, and they started seriously underperforming relative to historical industry norms. In this new environment, benchmarking to an absolute return in its purest sense was almost impossible. Hence, several hedge fund managers started repositioning their targets in terms of an interest rate, plus a spread (e.g. Libor+6%). However, this did not account for the huge fall in interest rates that the financial world was going to experience. Today, the new semi-absolute returns do not equate to the old calculations. Indeed, yesterday's 15% is far from today's Libor+5%, which effectively amounts to 6%.

Many managers also turned to a traditional index such as the S&P 500[15] to benchmark the performance of their fund.[16] Although popular because of the recent performance of traditional assets, this type of index is a poor candidate for benchmarking hedge funds. There are three reasons for this:

- *Trading strategy* – Hedge funds normally adopt a dynamic trading strategy that can involve very short-term positions, sometimes buying and selling in the market on an intra-day basis. Hedge funds also change their market exposures significantly depending on market conditions. Traditional indices, in contrast, correspond to a policy of buying and holding stocks for an extended period.
- *Leverage* – Hedge funds typically leverage their bets by margining their positions and by using short sales, whereas the use of leverage is not accounted for in traditional indices.
- *Non-benchmark assets* – Hedge funds typically invest in shares of companies that are not included in the S&P 500, but that make up the rest of the US or world stock and bond markets.

Consequently, the relationship between hedge fund returns and the returns on a traditional benchmark is complex and not linear, causing a loose observable correlation between hedge funds and traditional indices. To make matters worse, investors often set multiple benchmarks, which may conflict with each other (e.g. outperform cash in the short term and equity in the long term, while being correlated to neither of them). This leads to dissatisfaction on the part of both the client and the manager. In our opinion, a fund and its benchmark should exhibit similarities, and not be completely uncorrelated. Therefore, we tend to reject this type of comparison as being unfair.

On the investor side, many people started relying on relative peer group comparisons as their primary method of benchmarking. At first glance, peer groups offer several advantages:

---

[15] The S&P 500 is a widely recognized benchmark that comprises the 500 largest, publicly traded corporations in the United States.

[16] A point to remember is that, even with a hedge fund manager of superior caliber, it should be arithmetically impossible for the average invested dollar to consistently beat a correctly defined benchmark. By definition, without fees, about half of the managers should beat the benchmark and the other half should not. If all managers beat the benchmark, it is probably because the benchmark is not adequate.

they look at the effective performance of other practitioners, they reflect the differences or similarities between managers in their trading decisions, and they take fully into account the transaction and trading costs. However, peer groups suffer from a strong arbitrary selection bias, given the lack of an established oversight process for determining universe participants in the peer group, and whether the universe accurately represents the entire asset class. They also suffer heavily from survivor bias, as disappearing managers are regularly deleted from the peer group. Last but not least, they are usually not considered as a viable passive investment strategy, so a portfolio manager will have no neutral position to take if he has no particular view on the market.

For these reasons, we believe that peer groups are useful as a means of comparing the results of similar managers within a given portfolio or the performance of funds within a narrow universe, but are inadequate to assess the performance of a manager in general. What is needed is a set of effective benchmarks.

5.4.2   The need for true benchmarks

Webster's New Collegiate Dictionary defines a benchmark as "a point of reference from which measurements may be made" or "something that serves as a standard by which others may be measured". In the context of hedge fund performance, a benchmark should serve as a point of reference or standard to measure and evaluate the economic performance of a manager or a strategy. It should allow for better decision-making in hiring, retaining and firing managers, as well as for a better understanding of a strategy in general. It is a crucial tool in determining asset allocation policy, implementing portfolio decisions and evaluating performance. The danger, of course, is that investors start focusing too much on short-term performance. Hence the importance of selecting an appropriate market benchmark.

Ideally, each hedge fund should be assigned a benchmark that takes into account all the details of its strategy, e.g. the markets and assets traded, the leverage and the directional bias (net long versus net short), in order to get a real picture of which economic environments will favor or punish a given manager's actions. Jeffery Bailey's (1992a) essential elements of a manager benchmark represent a useful checklist. They are as follows:

- *Unambiguous* – The names and weights of securities constituting the benchmark should be clearly delineated.
- *Investable* – The option to forgo active management and simply hold the benchmark as an asset should be available.
- *Measurable* – The benchmark's return should be readily calculated on a reasonably frequent basis, typically at least monthly for hedge fund strategies.
- *Appropriate* – The benchmark should be consistent with the manager's investment style.
- *Reflective of current investment options* – The manager should have current investment knowledge of, and opinion about, the securities that make up the benchmark.
- *Specified in advance* – The benchmark should be constructed prior to the start of an evaluation period.

These properties look like common sense, but it is often the case in practice that benchmarks of individual hedge funds do not possess some of these properties, particularly the fourth and fifth ones.

In addition to dedicated fund benchmarks, it is also necessary to have benchmarks at the industry level. Credible benchmarks are useful as broad-based measures of what the industry is doing, and could help people better understand funds' performance profiles and counter negative publicity about hedge funds. In line with Bailey, we suggest five properties that an ideal benchmark at the market level should have. These are:

- *Simplicity* – The industry benchmark should be easy to understand and easy to calculate. If the process is complicated or non-transparent, acceptance of the benchmark may be negatively impacted.
- *Replicability* – There should be a straightforward investment strategy that performs in line with the benchmark.
- *Comparability* – The industry benchmark should be calculated in a way that allows comparisons with individual managers (e.g. use of closing vs. opening prices, fees, taxes, timing of reporting).
- *Representativity* – The benchmark should effectively represent the performance of the underlying market. In particular, a good benchmark should include all the "big names" to be credible.

Once again, most of these properties are common sense. But the latter unfortunately often goes by the board when it comes to investing, particularly in alternative assets. Fortunately, the next part of the book – and particularly Chapter 8 – will help us to understand the true nature of hedge fund returns and will therefore throw some light on the vexed question of how benchmarks should be defined at the fund or at the strategy level.

Part II
Understanding the Nature of Hedge Fund
Returns and Risks

6

Covariance and Correlation

Use a hammer the wrong way, and you will smash your thumb.

Correlation and regression are obviously two related topics, interwoven to the point that most people have difficulty differentiating them. Both correlation and regression estimate and describe mathematically the relationship that may exist between one variable (called the *dependent variable*) and a set of variables (called *independent variables*). This task makes them among the most used and misused tools in quantitative analysis.

Indeed, many investors often use correlation to analyze the relationship between two assets, without being aware of the hidden underlying assumptions. Many people also find regression difficult to understand – but nevertheless use it or have to use it for predictive purposes. This situation is not really surprising. Firstly, correlation and regression are often taught as part of a basic statistics course, and very few of us remember anything from this class. Secondly, with the advent and proliferation of user-friendly software for statistical analysis, many of these techniques are now available to the practitioner at the touch of a key, which results in a laissez-faire attitude. "If the graphs look professional, the statistics are probably too. So why bother with what is inside the box?"

Needless to say, this is a risky attitude. The basics of correlation and regression can and should be understood before going further in this book. But do not worry – what follows is written for those who have little or no knowledge of statistics. The goal is to provide a general overview of correlation and regression, rather than an elegant statistical treatment of their properties. It will also serve as a refresher for people who vaguely remember what entered their minds maybe more than 20 years ago. The need for understanding springs from the fact that these topics are important in the next steps of the risk and return analysis that will be done.

There are many ways to be fooled by numerical summaries, as we shall see. Therefore, the easiest way to gain insight into the concepts of correlation and regression is to use graphs. In this chapter, we will focus essentially on correlation. Chapter 7 takes up the subject of regression.

6.1 SCATTER PLOTS

One of the best tools for understanding the association of two variables such as x and y is a *scatter plot*, or scatter diagram. It is especially helpful when the number of data points is large – studying a list of too many values is virtually hopeless. A scatter plot is a plot of the values of the dependent variable against the corresponding values of the independent variable. The independent variable is usually represented on the abscissa (x-axis, or horizontal axis), while the dependent variable is represented on the ordinate (y-axis, or vertical axis), so that each point on the scatter plot corresponds to an observed couple (x_i, y_i).

Scatter plots are primarily used as data visualization tools. They show where the majority of data values are concentrated, and may help to identify patterns or clusters in the data. They

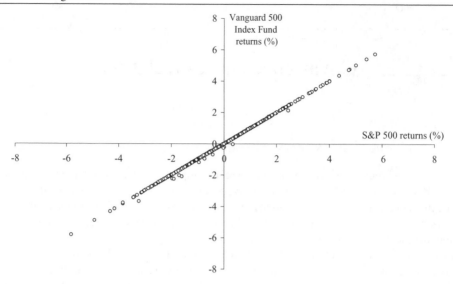

Figure 6.1   Scatter plot of the daily returns on the Vanguard 500 Index Fund against the daily returns of the S&P 500 index, January 2000 to June 2003

facilitate the detection of outliers and can also reveal relationships or associations between two variables. Such relationships manifest themselves by any non-random structure in the plot. Correlation, one of our two topics, measures how closely a scatter plot follows a straight line.

As an illustration, Figure 6.1 shows the scatter plot of the daily returns on the Vanguard 500 Index Fund (y-axis) against the daily returns of the S&P 500 index (x-axis). The Vanguard 500 Index Fund's objective is to track the performance of the S&P 500 index. It is therefore not really surprising to observe that there is an almost perfect linear relationship between the two series of returns, the scatter around the line being zero. The slope of the line is positive and very close to one. Small returns of the S&P correspond closely to the same small returns of the Vanguard fund; large returns of the S&P correspond to almost the same large returns of the Vanguard fund. Hence, there is a perfect co-relation (that is, a perfect correlation) between the S&P 500 and the Vanguard 500 Index Fund.

In contrast, Figures 6.2 and 6.3 show the scatter plots of the daily returns on the Vanguard 500 Index Fund (y-axis) against the daily returns of the Dow Jones Industrial Average index (x-axis) and the Nasdaq Composite index (x-axis), respectively. Both graphs evidence a positive linear relationship between x and y, with relatively little scatter around the line. The slope of the line is positive (small values of x correspond to small values of y; large values of x correspond to large values of y). Hence, there is still a positive co-relation (that is, a positive correlation) between x and y. However, this correlation is less perfect than in Figure 6.1. This is due to the differences that exist between the Dow Jones Industrial, the Nasdaq Composite and the S&P 500 indices.

Finally, Figure 6.4 shows the scatter plot of the daily returns on the Vanguard 500 Index Fund (y-axis) against the daily returns of the Nikkei 225 index (x-axis). The graph demonstrates the absence of a clear linear relationship between x and y. One can easily observe that for a given value of x, the corresponding values of y fall all over the graph. This lack of predictability

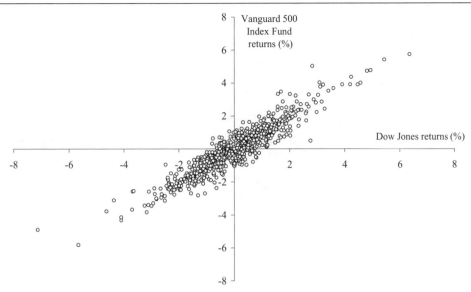

Figure 6.2 Scatter plot of the daily returns on the Vanguard 500 Index Fund against the daily returns of the Dow Jones Industrial Average index, January 2000 to June 2003

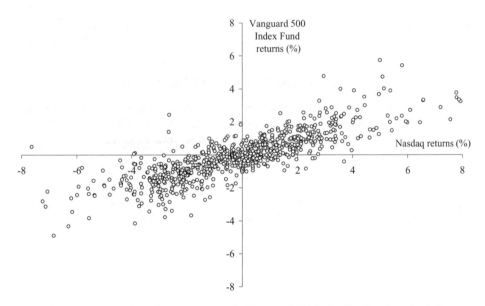

Figure 6.3 Scatter plot of the daily returns on the Vanguard 500 Index Fund against the daily returns of the Nasdaq Composite index, January 2000 to June 2003

in determining y from a given value of x, and the associated amorphous, non-structured appearance of the scatter plot, leads to the summary conclusion that there is no co-relation, or no clear relationship, between x and y.

Scatter plots usually display clearly the strength of the relationship between two quantitative variables. But our eyes are generally not good judges of how strong a relationship is. Thus we

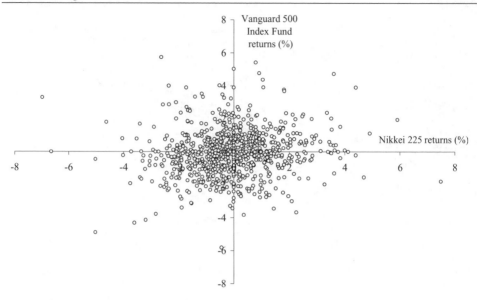

Figure 6.4 Scatter plot of the daily returns on the Vanguard 500 Index Fund against the daily returns of the Nikkei 225 index, January 2000 to June 2003

need to define a quantitative measure of the association. This is precisely where covariance steps in.

6.2   COVARIANCE AND CORRELATION

Covariance and correlation are fundamental statistical concepts that lie hidden behind most of the theories and tools used in finance. Simply stated, they measure the extent to which two random variables X and Y are related to each other, or tend to vary together.

6.2.1   Definitions

To understand the notion of covariance we need to go back to the variance, since covariance and variance are closely linked. Remember that the variance is calculated as the average squared deviation from the mean return. For a variable X, we have:

$$\sigma_X^2 = E(X - \bar{X})^2$$
$$= \frac{1}{N-1} \sum_{i=1}^{N} (X_i - \bar{X})^2$$

(6.1)

Now, we want to measure co-variation, that is, how much two variables X and Y change together or contrarily. In statistics, the quantity that measures the degree of joint variation between two variables is called the covariance. It can be seen as an extension of the variance concept to the case of two variables, in the sense that it measures jointly the deviation of one variable from its mean *and* the deviation of the second variable from its mean. Covariance between X and Y is denoted $\sigma_{X,Y}$ and is calculated as the average of the product of the deviations of X and Y

Table 6.1   Variance–covariance matrix for the Vanguard 500 Index Fund and various indices

	Vanguard	S&P	DJ	Nasdaq	Nikkei
Vanguard	2.03	2.02	1.85	3.01	0.24
S&P	2.02	2.02	1.84	3.01	0.24
DJ	1.85	1.84	1.90	2.36	0.24
Nasdaq	3.01	3.01	2.36	6.28	0.40
Nikkei	0.24	0.24	0.24	0.40	2.41

from their respective means:[1]

$$\sigma_{X,Y} = E((X - \bar{X})(Y - \bar{Y}))$$

$$= \frac{1}{N-1} \sum_{i=1}^{N} (X_i - \bar{X})(Y_i - \bar{Y})$$

(6.2)

When the two variables deviate from their means in the same way most of the time, these products will be positive. For example, if both residuals are negative (both X and Y are below their respective means), the product is still positive. Thus a large covariance indicates a strong positive relationship between X and Y. And a large negative covariance (products mostly negative) indicates two variables doing the opposite thing, or a strong negative relationship. Finally, a covariance near zero indicates no linear relationship at all between X and Y.

Covariance information between a series of N variables is usually presented in the form of a variance–covariance matrix. The latter is a square table, where the entry at the ith line and jth column represents the covariance between the ith and the jth variable:

$$\begin{pmatrix} \sigma_{1,1} & \sigma_{1,2} & \sigma_{1,3} & \cdots & \sigma_{1,N} \\ \sigma_{2,1} & \sigma_{2,2} & \sigma_{2,3} & \cdots & \sigma_{2,N} \\ \sigma_{3,1} & \sigma_{3,2} & \sigma_{3,3} & \cdots & \sigma_{3,N} \\ \vdots & \vdots & \vdots & & \vdots \\ \sigma_{N,1} & \sigma_{N,2} & \sigma_{N,3} & \cdots & \sigma_{N,N} \end{pmatrix}$$

By definition, covariance is symmetric, as $\sigma_{X,Y} = \sigma_{Y,X}$. Also, the covariance of any variable with itself ($\sigma_{X,X}$) is that variable's variance (σ_X^2). Hence, the variance–covariance matrix is symmetric, and the terms on the diagonal are simply the variance of the variables considered. This explains why some people only report the "lower off-diagonal" of the variance–covariance matrix.

Table 6.1 displays the variance–covariance matrix between the Vanguard 500 Index Fund and the various indices that we examined earlier on. We can see that in practice, the size of the covariance does not tell us much. The reason is that it depends mostly on the size of X and Y. Hence, without knowing the scales or units of measurement of X and Y, there is no way of distinguishing what is "large" and what is "near zero". To obtain a more direct indication of how two components co-vary, we need to scale covariance.

---

[1] Note that if we replace Y by X in the covariance formula, we get the variance of X. Thus, the variance is the covariance of a variable with itself.

One can show that in absolute terms, the covariance between two variables is always smaller than the product of the two variables' standard deviation. Consequently, there are lower and upper limits to the covariance, given by

$$-\sigma_X \sigma_Y \leq \sigma_{X,Y} \leq +\sigma_X \sigma_Y \qquad (6.3)$$

If we divide this relation by $\sigma_X \sigma_Y$, we get

$$-1 \leq \frac{\sigma_{X,Y}}{\sigma_X \sigma_Y} \leq +1 \qquad (6.4)$$

and thus we obtain the Pearson product–moment correlation coefficient, named after its originator Karl Pearson. It is calculated as the ratio of the co-variation (i.e. covariance) between X and Y that is actually observed to the co-variation (i.e. covariance) that would exist if the variables X and Y were perfectly correlated:

$$
\begin{aligned}
r_{X,Y} &= \frac{\text{Observed covariance}}{\text{Maximum possible covariance}} \\
&= \frac{\text{Covar}(X, Y)}{\sqrt{\text{Var}(X) \times \text{Var}(Y)}}
\end{aligned}
\qquad (6.5)
$$

The Pearson product–moment correlation coefficient has the great advantage of being instantly interpretable. It is a measure of linear association that ranges over a scale of 1 to -1. Often symbolized by the lowercase Roman letter $r_{X,Y}$, it indicates both the direction of the relationship between the two variables X and Y and its magnitude.

- Perfect positive correlation is seen at $r_{X,Y} = +1$. It occurs when all the points (X_i, Y_i) fall exactly on an upward sloping line, signifying a perfect linear relationship between X and Y. Note that the slope of the line does not matter here, as long as it is positive.
- Perfect negative correlation is seen at $r_{X,Y} = -1$. It occurs when all the points (X_i, Y_i) fall exactly on a downward sloping line, signifying a perfect negative linear relationship between X and Y. Again, the slope of the line does not matter here, as long as it is negative.
- Complete absence of a correlation is represented as $r_{X,Y} = 0$, which is observed when there is no linear relationship between X and Y. In a sense, any information about X is useless in predicting Y, and *vice versa*.

These three particular values of correlation, $+1$, -1 and 0, are hardly observable in real life. But the rule of thumb is easy to understand. As the absolute value of the correlation coefficient increases in magnitude, the points on the scatter plot become more tightly concentrated about a straight line. This line will have a positive slope for positive correlations and a negative slope for negative correlations. Hence, two variables are positively associated when above-average values of one tend to accompany above-average values of the other and below-average values also tend to occur together. Two variables are negatively associated when above-average values of one tend to accompany below-average values of the other, and *vice versa*. The term "average" refers here to the respective average of the two variables considered.

Table 6.2 Pearson's r correlation matrix for the Vanguard
500 Index Fund and various indices

	Vanguard	S&P	DJ	Nasdaq	Nikkei
Vanguard	1.00	1.00	0.94	0.85	0.11
S&P	1.00	1.00	0.94	0.85	0.11
DJ	0.94	0.94	1.00	0.68	0.11
Nasdaq	0.85	0.85	0.68	1.00	0.10
Nikkei	0.11	0.11	0.11	0.10	1.00

Table 6.3 Absolute value of the correlation
coefficient and the strength of the corresponding
association

Absolute value of correlation	Strength of association between variables
0.80–1.00	Very strong association
0.60–0.79	Strong association
0.40–0.59	Moderate association
0.20–0.39	Weak association
0.00–0.19	Little if any association

As with covariance, we can summarize all the correlations of a series of N variables in a symmetric correlation matrix. The terms on the diagonal $(r_{i,i})$ are always equal to 1:

$$\begin{pmatrix} r_{1,1} & r_{1,2} & r_{1,3} & \cdots & r_{1,N} \\ r_{2,1} & r_{2,2} & r_{2,3} & \cdots & r_{2,N} \\ r_{3,1} & r_{3,2} & r_{3,3} & \cdots & r_{3,N} \\ \vdots & \vdots & \vdots & & \vdots \\ r_{N,1} & r_{N,2} & r_{N,3} & \cdots & r_{N,N} \end{pmatrix}$$

Table 6.2 displays the correlation matrix between the Vanguard 500 Index Fund and the various indices that we examined earlier on. We can see clearly the perfect correlation between the S&P 500 and the Vanguard 500 Index Fund, as well as the low correlation of the Nikkei with all the other indices/funds.

Figure 6.5 shows a series of scatter plots for different degrees of correlation. Two things should be noted. First, at least from a visual perspective, a correlation even as high as $r = 0.6$ does not look much different from a correlation of $r = 0$. However, this does not mean that a small correlation is worthless, as we shall see later. Second, although the correlation cannot exceed $r = 1$ in magnitude, there is still a lot of variability left when the correlation is as high as $r = 0.90$.

The sign of the correlation coefficient determines whether the correlation is positive or negative. The magnitude of the correlation coefficient determines the strength of the correlation. Table 6.3 may be used to describe the strength of association suggested by the absolute value of a correlation coefficient. However, as we shall see later, a very high correlation value may

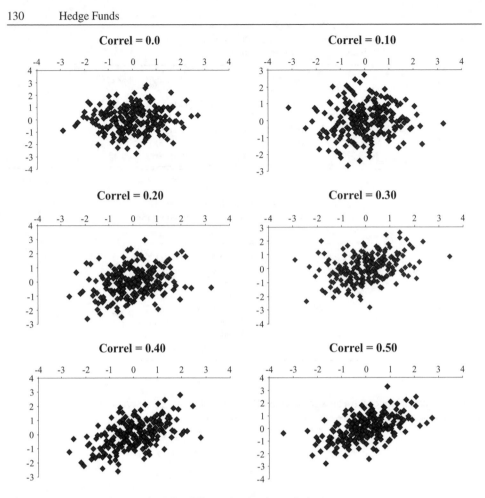

Figure 6.5   Scatter plots obtained for different levels of correlation

be the result of chance, and thus not significant. On the other hand, a very low correlation value may be significant, meaning that there is only a small but effective association between variables.

Note that while correlation coefficients are usually reported as a value between -1 and $+1$, squaring them makes them easier to understand. The square of the correlation coefficient is called the coefficient of determination. It is equal to the percentage of the variance in the dependent variable that is related to the variation in the independent variable. A correlation of $+0.5$ or -0.5 means that 25% of the variance in the dependent variable is related to the variation in the independent variable (as $\pm 0.5^2 = 0.25$). Similarly, a correlation of $+0.7$ or -0.7 means that 49% of the variance in the dependent variable is related to the variation in the independent variable. We will come back to this property when considering regression.

Covariance – and its standardized version, correlation – play a crucial role in the construction of portfolios of hedge funds. The reason is that the variance of a portfolio depends essentially on the covariance between the funds in the portfolio. Thus, by combining funds with less than

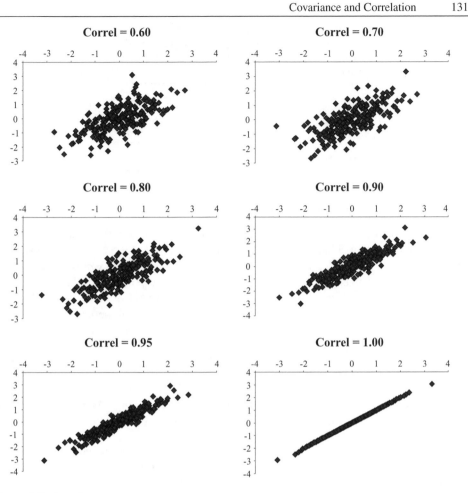

Figure 6.5   *(cont.)*

perfect positive correlation, it is possible to reduce portfolio risk without sacrificing any of the portfolio's return.

6.2.2   Another interpretation of correlation

An alternative intuitive approach to interpreting correlation consists in comparing the X and Y observations with their respective means $\bar{X}$ and $\bar{Y}$. We can simply count the number of observations that are above their mean, as well as the number of observations that are below their mean, and report the result in a table – see for instance Table 6.4.

With a strong positive correlation between X and Y (correlation close to 1), one would expect most of the data points to be in the "above–above" and "below–below" quadrants. With a strong negative correlation between X and Y (correlation close to -1), one would expect most of the data points to be in the "below–above" and "above–below" quadrants. And if the two variables were not really related (correlation close to zero), one would expect to see an equal number of points in each quadrant.

Table 6.4 Another way of interpreting the
correlation coefficient between the Vanguard 500
Index Fund and the daily returns of the Dow Jones
index

	Dow Jones	
Vanguard Index Fund	Below mean	Above mean
Above mean	44	419
Below mean	398	50

6.2.3 The Spearman rank correlation

Pearson correlation calculations are based on the assumption that both X and Y values are sampled from populations that follow a Gaussian distribution, at least approximately. With large samples, this assumption is not too important. But a small sample size is likely to result in premature conclusions. In particular, a single extreme data point (an outlier) can have a powerful effect on the correlation coefficient when the sample size is small, as we shall see later in this chapter. To mitigate this problem, the Pearson r correlation coefficient is sometimes replaced by the Spearman rank correlation, which is less sensitive to outliers. The Spearman rank correlation is calculated using ranks[2] rather than on the original data itself.

As an illustration, say we have a sample of N data points (X_i, Y_i). The procedure can be summarized as follows:

1. Assign a rank $X_{(i)}$ to each X_i observation. That is, $X_{(i)} = 1$ for the smallest X observation and $X_{(i)} = N$ for the largest one. When two or more observations are equal, the average rank is used.
2. Assign a rank $Y_{(i)}$ to each Y_i observation. That is, $Y_{(i)} = 1$ for the smallest Y observation and $Y_{(i)} = N$ for the largest one. When two or more observations are equal, the average rank is used.
3. Subtract the two sets of ranks to get a series of differences $d_{(i)} = X_{(i)} - Y_{(i)}$.
4. Square the values of $d_{(i)}$.
5. Use the formula

$$r^* = 1 - 6 \sum_{i=1}^{N} \frac{d_{(i)}^2}{N(N^2 - 1)} \qquad (6.6)$$

where N is the number of ranks.

Spearman's rank correlation coefficient, like all other correlation coefficients, takes a value between -1 and $+1$, and can be interpreted in the same way as Pearson's r correlation co-efficient. A positive correlation is one in which the ranks of both variables increase together. A negative correlation is one in which the ranks of one variable increase as the ranks of the other variable decrease. A correlation of $+1$ or -1 will arise if the relationship between the two variables is exactly linear. A correlation close to zero means there is no linear relationship between the ranks.

---

[2] That is, each variable is ranked separately by putting the values of the variable in order and numbering them: the lowest value is given rank 1, the next lowest is given rank 2, and so on.

Table 6.5 Spearman rank correlation matrix for the
Vanguard 500 Index Fund and various indices

	Vanguard	S&P	DJ	Nasdaq	Nikkei
Vanguard	1.00	1.00	0.93	0.85	0.13
S&P	1.00	1.00	0.93	0.85	0.14
DJ	0.93	0.93	1.00	0.68	0.12
Nasdaq	0.85	0.85	0.68	1.00	0.13
Nikkei	0.13	0.14	0.12	0.13	1.00

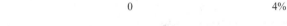

Figure 6.6 The risk of a portfolio can be represented as a vector

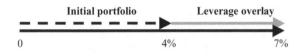

Figure 6.7 Leveraging the initial portfolio increases the length of the risk vector

As an illustration, Table 6.5 displays the Spearman rank correlation matrix between the Vanguard 500 Index Fund and the various indices that we examined earlier on. The matrix is very similar to the Pearson r matrix, because the sample size is relatively large (911 observations).

6.3 THE GEOMETRY OF CORRELATION AND DIVERSIFICATION

A visual way to understand the power of correlation and its consequences in finance – in particular the need for diversification – is through geometry. Say we visualize the risk of an asset as a vector, whose length is measured in terms of units of risk. So, if a 1-cm vector equals one unit of risk, a 4-cm vector equals four units of risk, i.e. a volatility of 4%. Let us call that vector the initial portfolio. We want to consider the impact of adding new assets – regrouped in an overlay portfolio – into the initial portfolio (Figure 6.6).

If we leverage the initial portfolio, we simply extend the length of its vector accordingly. For instance, if we leverage the initial portfolio of Figure 6.6 by 75% (i.e. a 1.75 to 1 leverage, or 1.75 dollars invested for each dollar of capital), we would add three units of risk to the total and reach a total risk of seven units, i.e. a volatility of 7%. Note that the angle between the initial portfolio and the new leverage overlay is $0°$, and the correlation between the new leveraged portfolio and the initial portfolio is exactly one (Figure 6.7).

Similarly, a perfect hedge of 75% of the initial portfolio would move the vector back three units of risk towards the origin. In this case, the angle between an initial portfolio and the hedge overlay is $180°$, and the correlation coefficient is -1. The final risk would be one unit (i.e. a volatility of 1%) (Figure 6.8).

At this point, we may suspect that there exists a functional relationship between the angle formed by the two vectors and their correlation coefficient. This is true. But let us see what

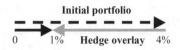

Figure 6.8 Hedging the initial portfolio decreases the length of the risk vector

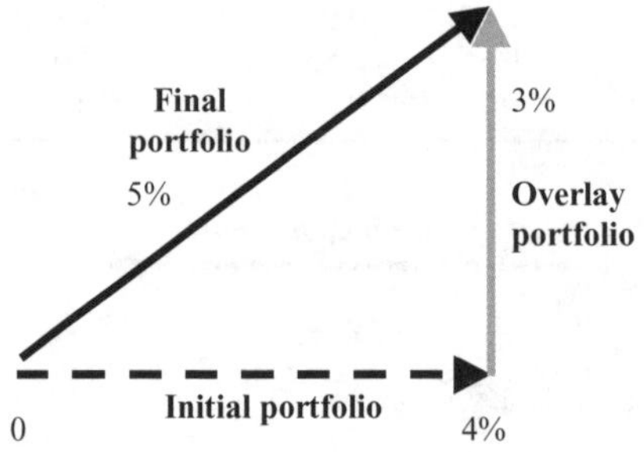

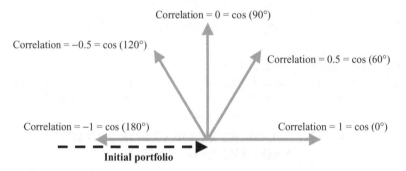

Figure 6.9 The geometry of risk when the overlay portfolio is orthogonal (i.e. uncorrelated) to the initial portfolio

Figure 6.10 The geometry of diversification. Each correlation coefficient corresponds to the cosine of the angle with the initial portfolio

happens if we have zero correlation between the overlay and the initial portfolio. In this case, the overlay portfolio can be visualized as a straight line with a 90° angle with the benchmark portfolio, and the total portfolio risk would be the hypotenuse. Using the Pythagorean theorem ($A^2 + B^2 = C^2$, where C is the hypotenuse), we can calculate that the total risk equals 5% (Figure 6.9).

The beauty of this geometric analysis is that it works for any correlation value. In fact, the angle between the two vectors can be seen as a function of the cosine of the correlation coefficient. You should note, however, that the acuteness of the angle is not linearly proportional to the correlation. Nevertheless, understanding the geometry of risk gives investors a powerful way to visualize diversification (Figure 6.10).

So far, we have plotted our portfolios as points on a two-dimensional graph. But we can also consider, at least in theory if not in imagination, plotting our data as two points in an N-dimensional space (consider $N = 3$ if you have trouble with this idea). If we do this, and we draw a line from the origin to each point, we will have two lines, one for the benchmark and one for the overlay. Then a concept similar to the correlation coefficient is the cosine of the angle formed by the two vectors, which varies from -1 for $180°$ through 0 for $90°$ to 1 for $0°$. We have:

$$r_{X,Y} = \cos(\theta)$$

If $r_{X,Y} > 0$, the angle is acute. If $r_{X,Y} = 1$, the angle is 0 and the lines point in the same direction. If $r_{X,Y} < 0$, the angle is obtuse. If $r_{X,Y} = -1$, the angle is $180°$ and the lines point in opposite directions. And if $r_{X,Y} = 0$, the angle is a right angle, and we have orthogonal lines.

6.4   WHY CORRELATION MAY LEAD TO WRONG CONCLUSIONS

Correlation is an extremely convenient tool to measure the strength of the relationship between two variables and express it as a single number that is independent of the units used to make the measurement. It is straightforward to calculate – most spreadsheets and statistical packages offer a correlation function – and easy to understand. It is not surprising therefore that correlation is often the first exploratory tool used by analysts to compare funds, discover and describe similarities, or validate the existence of hypothesized relationships. There is little doubt that the correlation coefficient in its many forms has become the workhorse of quantitative research and analysis of hedge funds. Unfortunately, when incorrectly used, the concept of correlation can easily become a minefield for the unwary and lead to incorrect conclusions. In the following, we will review some of the pitfalls involved in the use and interpretation of correlation.

6.4.1   Correlation does not mean causation

It is surprising to observe how often causal implications sneak insidiously into interpretations of correlation. Correlation and causation are two separate notions that represent different paradigms with different logical interpretations and implications. A correlation is established when research reveals that one characteristic or tendency is found to occur along with another characteristic or tendency. What does it mean to say that two events are positively correlated? Roughly, events of type A and events of type B are correlated if and only if the following conditions are satisfied: (i) whenever an event of type A occurs, an event of type B occurs and *vice versa*; and (ii) whenever there is no event of type A, there is no event of type B and *vice versa*. That is, events of type A and events of type B tend to occur together or not at all. For instance, one could observe that a hedge fund tends to have high returns when the volatility of equity markets is high, or inversely, that the volatility of equity markets tends to be high when the hedge fund returns are high.

It is important to realize that in such a conclusion, the issue of causation is not relevant; the emphasis is on the co-occurrence. All we have really established is that the two characteristics (volatility and high returns) tend to be found together. No reliable inference can be made as to whether the presence of one characteristic causes the other characteristic to occur, or *vice versa*. Such a connection, called causation, cannot be established solely from a high level of correlation. Several traps lie on the road from co-occurrence to causation.

First, a high correlation may be purely fortuitous; it hence constitutes no proof of causation. Did you notice for instance that Elizabeth Taylor's marriages in 1951, 1953, 1958, 1960, 1965, 1976 and 1977 all coincided with stock market gains? Did you know that the GDP-adjusted S&P 500 index coincides well with the number of 45–50-year-olds in the country? Over the period 1946–1997, the correlation of the two variables is 0.927. What does this tell us? Clearly, data mining software will easily find a data series that is highly correlated with any figure, even if there is no causality.

Second, a high correlation may be the result of a common cause. A celebrated example of this principle is the ice cream–snakebite connection. Studies have shown that the number of snakebites typically increases in the summer months. Studies have also shown that the consumption of ice cream increases in the summer months. A study comparing snakebites and ice cream consumption might very well reveal that the two are highly correlated; the more ice cream consumed, the higher the number of snakebites. Having said that, it obviously cannot be inferred that ice cream lovers run a greater risk of being bitten by a snake, or that a snakebite will automatically bring you a free ice cream. Nevertheless, the two variables are correlated. The reason is that both are influenced by a third variable, the rise of temperature. Snakes go out in summer, and so do ice cream lovers. Hence, correlation is visible, but there is no causality.

Therefore, it should be clear that *correlation does not necessarily imply causality*. In fact, causality cannot be inferred by data analysis alone. Rather, one must infer that a causal relationship exists on the basis of an underlying causal theory that explains the relationship between the two variables. In a second step, one may verify empirically that the relationship exists.[3]

Another point worth noting is that sequences are no more a source of causality than correlations. The *post hoc ergo propter hoc* (after this therefore because of this) fallacy is based upon the mistaken notion that, simply because one thing happens after another, the first event was a cause of the second. In reality, many events follow sequential patterns without being causally related. Coincidences happen. To establish the probability of a causal connection between two events, controls must be established to rule out other factors such as chance or some unknown causal factor. And anecdotes are not sufficient because they rely on intuition and subjective interpretation.

6.4.2 Correlation only measures linear relationships

Another essential aspect of correlation is that it measures only the strength of a *linear* relationship. Correlation cannot capture non-linear relationships, no matter how strong they are, or it may capture them in an incorrect way. We must be wary that a weak correlation coefficient may mask a strong non-linear relationship.[4] Consider the following case, for example. Say X is a normally distributed random variable with mean zero and variance equal to one. Let $Y = X^2$. There is a perfect non-linear relationship between Y and X, as shown in Figure 6.11.

Now, let us calculate the covariance coefficient between X and Y:

$$\begin{aligned}
\text{Covar}(X, Y) &= \text{E}[(X - \bar{X})(Y - \bar{Y})] \\
&= \text{E}(XY) - \text{E}(X\bar{Y}) - \text{E}(\bar{X}Y) + \text{E}(\bar{X}\bar{Y}) \\
&= \text{E}(X^3) - \bar{Y}\text{E}(X) - \bar{X}\text{E}(Y) + \bar{X}\bar{Y} \\
&= 0
\end{aligned} \tag{6.7}$$

The covariance of X and Y is *exactly equal* to zero. So is the correlation coefficient. Even though the association is perfect – one can predict Y exactly from X – the correlation coefficient r

---

[3] Conversely, a weak correlation does not guarantee that a causal relationship does not exist. Rather, lack of correlation could occur if (i) there are insufficient or inaccurate data; (ii) the data do not allow multiple causal relationships to be sorted out; or (iii) the tested model is badly specified. Consequently, we may have weak correlations, but strong causal connections.

[4] Note that a strong non-linear correlation need not imply causation!

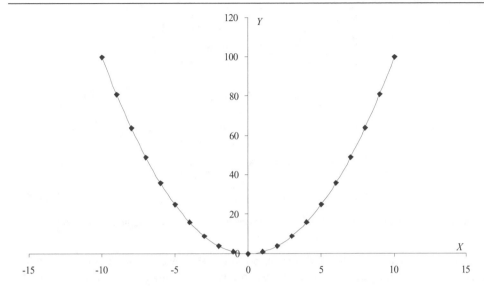

Figure 6.11   Perfect non-linear relationship between variables Y and X

is exactly zero. This is because the association is purely non-linear. Without looking at the scatter plot, many analysts would simply conclude that the two variables are independent of each other, which is wrong. What happens is that the two variables are linearly unrelated to each other, which is quite different.

The inability of correlation to capture non-linear relationships is particularly important for hedge funds. As we shall see later, a wide range of hedge fund strategies – especially the "non-directional" ones – exhibit non-linear risk–return payoffs, and this may significantly bias downward their correlation with other asset classes.

6.4.3   Correlations may be spurious

Another major problem with the use of correlation is the spurious correlation fallacy, whose occurrence is pervasive, but generally unnoticed.

Karl Pearson was the first to use the term "spurious correlation" in 1896 to "distinguish the correlations of scientific importance from those that were not". Today, the term is used to describe a correlation between two variables that are not causally connected. In fact, most of the time, it is not the correlation itself that is spurious, but the inference from the existence of a significant correlation coefficient of the existence of a significant causal relationship.[5] Our previous ice cream and snakebites example is an illustration of such a spurious correlation.

The problem with spurious correlation is that analysts tend, for psychological reasons, to overestimate the importance of positive evidence and underestimate the importance of negative evidence for their favored hypothesis. Hence, when confronted with a spurious correlation that confirms their expectations, analysts tend to simply accept the correlation as valid and, even worse, they start making false causal claims. Ideally, what we would need in such a case is some kind of statistic that produces a number indicating the probability of the correlation being

---

[5] In short, were it not for convention, we would use the term "misleading associations" rather than "spurious correlation".

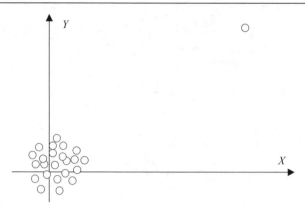

Figure 6.12   An extremely perturbing outlier may result in a correlation coefficient close to one

spurious. Unfortunately, such a statistic does not yet exist. However, this does not rule out the possibility of revealing all kinds of spurious correlation. Common sense at least should be brought into play to confirm and/or disprove the results of empirical observation.

6.4.4   Correlation is not resistant to outliers

In finance, and particularly with hedge funds, returns that are considered as outliers are frequently encountered. By outliers, we mean returns that depart distinctly from the pattern set by the majority of the returns. Outliers are actually an ill-defined concept, without clear boundaries; nevertheless, they are in general unusually large or unusually small values compared to the others. The months of October 1987, September 1998 and March 2000 provide good examples of such outliers.

An outlier may be the result of an error in measurement, in which case it will distort the interpretation of the data, having undue influence on many summary statistics. In this case, the outlier can safely be removed from the initial data set.[6] But an outlier may also be the consequence of a genuine structural property of the data. In that case, the outlier is important because it indicates an extreme behavior of the process under study. Such outliers should not be routinely removed without further justification.

One of the problems with genuine outliers is that, if they are located sufficiently far away, their presence can bias the summary statistics away from values representative of the majority of the sample. The problem is especially important with younger hedge funds, which often (i) have small samples of return data and (ii) use a combination of leverage and aggressive positions. Then, even a single outlier can distort the classical covariance and correlation estimates, making them virtually useless. That is, correlation for the vast majority of the data can be very erroneously reported.

Figures 6.12 and 6.13 show two extreme examples of scatter plots with a large outlier. In Figure 6.12, the outlier makes the correlation coefficient nearly one; without it, the correlation coefficient would be nearly zero. In Figure 6.13, the outlier makes the correlation coefficient nearly zero; without it, the correlation coefficient would be nearly one.

A first solution to control the influence of outliers is to calculate additional correlation coefficients, such as:

---

[6] The literature on the rules for rejection of outliers is extensive – see for instance Barnett and Lewis (1994).

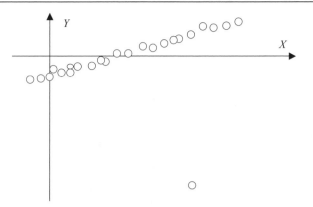

Figure 6.13   An extremely perturbing outlier may result in a correlation coefficient close to zero

- The correlation during negative/positive market returns.
- The correlation during the N worst/best market returns.
- The volatile correlation, i.e. the correlation between a fund and a benchmark when the latter had extreme positive or negative returns. A volatile correlation higher than the classical correlation means that the fund is more exposed to market downturns or to volatile markets, which usually results in significant skewness and kurtosis.

As an illustration, the classical correlation between the MSCI World index and the CSFB/Tremont hedge fund index is 0.47. It falls to 0.36 when the MSCI World index displays negative performance, and even 0.03 when the MSCI World index displays positive performance. In volatile markets, the correlation rises to 0.46, and it even reaches 0.63 during the 10 worst months of the MSCI World.

In this context, an interesting graph to monitor is the marginal contribution of each return in the sample to the volatile correlation. As an illustration, Figure 6.14 shows the influence of each return of the CSFB/Tremont hedge fund index on the value of its volatile correlation with the MSCI World. In this example, it is obvious that September 1998 makes an extremely high contribution to the final value of the correlation.

The next step in dealing with the presence of outliers is generally to use robust statistical methods. These methods are explicitly designed to avoid being influenced by outliers. They are applicable to a wide range of problems, including estimation of covariance and correlation matrices. However, the improved immunity to noise and outliers offered by robust techniques is usually obtained at the expense of a considerable increase in computation. An introduction to this thrilling field of econometric theory is to be found in Huber (1981).

6.4.5 Correlation is limited to two variables

Last but not least, it must be borne in mind that correlation measures the linear relationship between two variables, and two variables only. In the real world, however, very few pairs of variables are isolated. Most are part of larger wholes or combinations of interrelated and co-varying parts, and these wholes in turn are still parts of other wholes (as a cell is part of a leaf, which is part of a tree, that is part of a forest). Things usually co-vary in large clusters or patterns of interdependence and causal influences – which regression and factor analysis will have the job of unraveling. To isolate two variables, compute the correlation between them

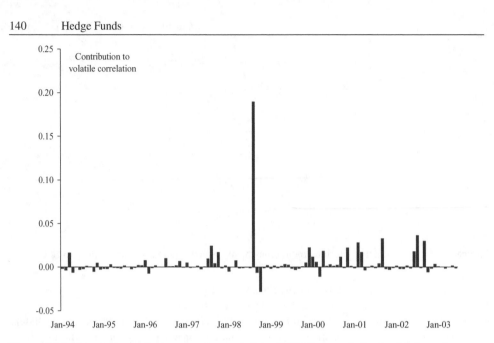

Figure 6.14   Marginal contribution of each return of the CSFB/Tremont hedge fund index to its correlation with the MSCI World

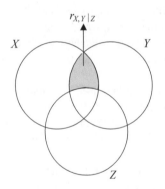

Figure 6.15   Graphical illustration of how the partial correlation between X and Y controlling for Z removes the Z influence and only considers the pure interaction between X and Y

and interpret that correlation as measuring the relationship between the two variables alone can therefore be misleading.

Note that it is possible to control for the effect of a third variable (say Z) when examining the correlation of X and Y. This is termed *partial correlation*, and is calculated as:

$$r_{X,Y|Z} = \frac{r_{X,Y} - (r_{X,Z} - r_{Y,Z})}{\sqrt{\left(1 - r_{X,Z}^2\right)\left(1 - r_{Y,Z}^2\right)}} \tag{6.8}$$

In a sense, $r_{X,Y|Z}$ is the correlation between variables X and Y with the influence of variable Z removed from both variables. This is illustrated in Figure 6.15. However, partial correlation only solves the problem for three variables, but not for more. Hence, we will have to use multiple factor analysis and more advanced techniques when the number of variables exceeds three.

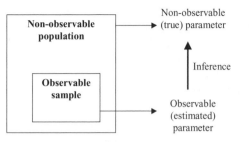

Figure 6.16   Sample versus population

6.5   THE QUESTION OF STATISTICAL SIGNIFICANCE

In dealing with investments, many people often forget what statistical significance really means and consequently may easily misinterpret given results. How often, for instance, do we see conclusions drawn from a single correlation coefficient estimated in a single sample, without any verification of the statistical significance of that coefficient? How can one be sure (i) that the correlation coefficient is statistically different from zero and (ii) that the result we obtained is not due to chance?

6.5.1   Sample versus population

The problem of statistical significance is that we are working with a random sample – or a sample that we believe approximates a random representative sample – taken from a population.[7] In a sense, a sample is a relatively small window through which we hope to see the outlines of some larger, more inclusive reality (Figure 6.16). In some cases, the glimpse provided by the sample may truly represent the larger reality, while in other cases it may misrepresent it, leading to erroneous conclusions.

What can we say about an entire population when all we have is a sample that we hope is representative? All we can do is use statistics (averages, variances, correlation coefficients, etc.) derived from the sample to estimate the value of the same statistics for the population. But the sample is only an approximation of the population, so the sample statistics are also only an approximation of the population statistics. If we draw a different sample, we may get a different value. This phenomenon is called sampling error. The only way we could really get the population value is to measure everyone in the population, which is usually not feasible.

Suppose, for example, that we have a sample estimate for a statistic – statisticians talk about a "point estimate" – but we are not really sure whether that statistic would be valid for the entire population. Fortunately, it is possible to use the sample estimate to calculate a range within which the population value is likely to fall. For most applications, "likely" means 95% or 99% of the time, and the corresponding range is called the 95% or 99% *confidence interval*. The values at each end of the interval are called the *confidence limits*.

---

[7] The term "population" as used here means all the possible observations. For instance, if the variable investigated is the series of monthly returns on the S&P 500, the population contains all the returns since the inception of the index until its disappearance – basically, until S&P stops calculating it. This population contains several returns that are unknown today, as they will only occur in the future. The largest observable sample is the set of monthly returns since the inception of the index until today. A smaller sample would cover a shorter period of time.

Confidence intervals are more informative than point estimates, since they provide a range of plausible values for the unknown parameter. The width of the confidence interval gives us some idea of the degree of uncertainty about the (unknown) true value. In plain English, we would say that the confidence interval is the likely range of the true value.[8]

Few phrases have a more convincing ring than "the results are statistically significant". Many people get excited when they see the word "significant," without really understanding what it means. When a statistic is regarded as significant, this simply means that it is confidently considered to be reliable (i.e., it didn't happen by fluke). It does not mean that the finding is important or that it has any decision-making value. A confidence level of 95% and above is usually considered to have *statistical significance*. In other words, most analysts are willing to admit that a relationship is statistically significant if the possibility of that relationship being purely due to chance is less than 5%. Hence, the link between confidence interval and statistical significance is extremely strong, as both are founded on estimating the likelihood of an event.

6.5.2 Building the confidence interval for a correlation

The procedure for computing a confidence interval for a correlation coefficient is somewhat tricky. The reason is that the Pearson's r is not normally distributed – it is trapped between -1 and $+1$ – so that we cannot use the standard inferential tests. Fortunately, a transformation has already been worked out for converting correlation coefficients into a new set of values that are close enough to normal for our purposes. Therefore, Pearson's r must first be converted to a new variable, called Fisher's Z. The confidence interval is computed using Fisher's Z, and then converted back to Pearson's r.

The procedure can be summarized as follows:

1. Compute the sample's correlation coefficient r.
2. Convert the value of r to Z by using the following transformation:

$$Z = \frac{1}{2} \ln \left(\frac{1+r}{1-r} \right) \tag{6.9}$$

where $\ln(\cdot)$ is the natural or base-e logarithm. Fisher's Z is approximately normally distributed, no matter what the population r might be. Its standard deviation is $\sigma_Z = 1/\sqrt{(N-3)}$, where N is the number of pairs of return observations.
3. Compute the confidence interval of Z as you would for any normal distribution. For instance, for a 95% confidence interval, we know that the confidence interval is $[Z - 1.96\sigma_Z, Z + 1.96\sigma_Z]$.
4. Transform the end points of the Z confidence interval back to r by using the inverse transformation:

$$r = \frac{e^{2Z} - 1}{e^{2Z} + 1} \tag{6.10}$$

By way of example, suppose we have a sample of 64 monthly returns for two hedge funds. In this sample, we observe a correlation of $r = 0.68$ between the respective performances of the funds. The corresponding Fisher Z is 0.83. For $N = 60$ points (i.e. 5 years of monthly data),

---

[8] It should be noted that the confidence interval does not measure the variability of the true value in the population, and has nothing to do with the standard deviation of the true value, as is too often said. The true value in the population is a fixed number, with no uncertainty. We do not know it, but it is not a random variable. The confidence interval defines the range where the true value is most likely to be, based on what we observe in a sample.

Table 6.6 Impact of the sample size on the confidence interval for the correlation coefficient

Measured correlation (*r*)	Number of observations		Correlation confidence interval
0.68	4	(4 months)	−0.81 to 0.99
0.68	12	(1 year)	0.17 to 0.90
0.68	60	(5 years)	0.51 to 0.80
0.68	120	(10 years)	0.57 to 0.77
0.68	240	(20 years)	0.61 to 0.74
0.68	2 400	(200 years)	0.66 to 0.70
0.68	4 800	(400 years)	0.66 to 0.69
0.68	24 048	Since J.C.	0.67 to 0.69

Note: J. C. = Jesus Christ.

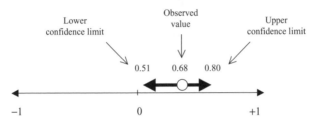

Figure 6.17 Interpreting the confidence interval for the correlation coefficient

the Fisher Z has a volatility of $1/\sqrt{(60-3)} = 0.132$. Multiplying by 1.96 gives 0.260, which is half the width of the confidence interval for Fisher's transformed Z. Coming back to the original units yields the 95% confidence limits, which are 0.51 and 0.80. This means that if our sample was representative, there is a 95% chance that the correlation between the performance of the two hedge funds is between 0.51 and 0.80. Figure 6.17 shows these results graphically. The confidence interval is the length of the arrow between the upper and lower limits.[9] You would report this result formally as follows: "The correlation between the performance of the two hedge funds was 0.68; the 95% confidence interval was 0.51 to 0.80." Less formally, we could say: "The correlation sample was 0.68, and the likely range for the population's correlation is 0.51 to 0.80."

If you are unhappy with the large width of the confidence interval, you will need to obtain more data to narrow it. Intuitively, a larger sample will help because it is potentially more representative of the entire population. Table 6.6 shows how the width of the confidence interval for the correlation coefficient depends on the number of returns. Note that you cannot say anything useful about the population correlation with only four months of data, as the possible range goes from −0.81 to +0.99. With 12 months you already get the idea that the correlation could be moderately positive. With 60 months the correlation is definitely positive and probably large, although it could also be moderate. The sample of 240 months (i.e. 20 years of data!) nails it as a large effect, and observing a hedge fund since J.C. gives almost too much precision.

---

[9] It should be noted that the confidence limits in this example are not spaced equally on either side of the observed value. That happens with non-normally distributed statistics like the correlation coefficient. When a statistic is normally distributed, the observed value falls in the middle of the confidence interval.

If the confidence interval does not include the zero value, the correlation is said to be *statistically significant*. In the above exhibit, the results for the sample sizes of 12 and above are all statistically significant, whereas the sample with 4 months is not. That is, for smaller sample sizes, given our estimates coming from the sample, we cannot exclude the fact that the true value of the correlation is equal to zero, as zero is in the confidence interval. As the sample size gets larger, it becomes clear that the true correlation is likely to be different from zero.

6.5.3   Correlation differences

In some cases, it is desirable to compare two correlation coefficients and check for their effective difference. For instance, we may want to test whether the correlation of a hedge fund with a market index has increased over recent years. The simplest procedure consists in measuring two correlation coefficients over two distinct periods, and calculating their difference. The sign of the difference indicates whether there has been a correlation increase or decrease. But similarly to the single correlation case, the question of statistical significance arises once more: is the correlation difference really different from zero?

The procedure for computing a confidence interval on the difference between two independent correlations is similar to the procedure for computing a confidence interval on one correlation. The first step is to convert both correlation values from Pearson's r to Fisher's Z. Then a confidence interval is constructed based on the general formula for a confidence interval where the statistic is $Z_1 - Z_2$. Finally, the upper and lower limits of the confidence interval are converted back from Fisher's Z to Pearson's r.

The procedure can be summarized as follows:

1. Compute the sample correlation coefficients r_1 and r_2.
2. Convert the value of r_i to Z_i by using the following transformation:

$$Z_i = \frac{1}{2} \ln\left(\frac{1 + r_i}{1 - r_i}\right) \tag{6.11}$$

where $\ln(\cdot)$ is the natural or base-e logarithm. The statistic $Z = Z_1 - Z_2$ is approximately normally distributed no matter what the population might be. Its standard deviation is

$$\sigma_{Z_1 - Z_2} = \sqrt{\frac{1}{N_1 - 3} + \frac{1}{N_2 - 3}} \tag{6.12}$$

where N_1 is the number of pairs of returns used to estimate r_1 and N_2 is the number of pairs of returns used to estimate r_2.
3. Compute the confidence interval of $Z_1 - Z_2$ as you would for any normal distribution. For instance, for a 95% confidence interval, we know that the confidence interval is $[(Z_1 - Z_2) - 1.96\sigma_{Z_1 - Z_2}, (Z_1 - Z_2) + 1.96\sigma_{Z_1 - Z_2}]$.
4. Transform the end points of the Z confidence interval back to r by using the inverse transformation:

$$r = \frac{e^{2Z} - 1}{e^{2Z} + 1} \tag{6.13}$$

Note that the above routine can only be used if the two correlation coefficients are measured from independent samples (i.e. different groups of returns). If the same returns are used for

Table 6.7   Change in correlation between Dinvest Total Return and the
CSFB/Tremont Global Macro index

	Jan 94 to Dec 98	Jan 99 to Jun 03
Correlation (r_i)	0.70	0.26
Number of returns	60	55
Z_i	0.88	0.27
$Z_1 - Z_2$	0.61	
$\sigma_{Z_1 - Z_2}$	0.19	
Conf. interval of $Z_1 - Z_2$	[0.24; 0.97]	
Conf. interval of $r_1 - r_2$	[0.24; 0.75]	

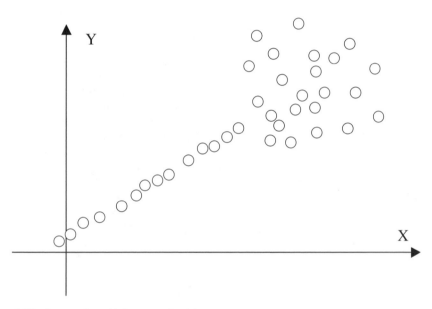

Figure 6.18   Scatter plot with heteroscedasticity

both correlation coefficients (e.g. the samples overlap), then the assumption of independence would be violated and we would have to use a more complicated test.

As an illustration, we applied the above test to the correlation between the returns of the fund Dinvest Total Return and the CSFB Tremont Global Macro index over two different periods: January 1994 to December 1998, and January 1999 to June 2003. These periods were selected on purpose because the fund changed its strategy at the end of the year 1998 and shifted its major focus from global macro to long/short equity. As we can see from Table 6.7, the correlation with the Global Macro index is 0.70 in the first period and 0.26 in the second period. The 95% confidence interval for the difference between the two correlation coefficients does not include zero, so we are confident in saying that the correlation is really different between the two periods.

6.5.4 Correlation when heteroscedasticity is present

When a time series of returns displays a volatility that changes over time, it is said to be heteroscedastic. On a scatter plot, heteroscedasticity results in large variations of the scatter in Y, depending on where the slice through the scatter plot is taken. As an illustration, Figure 6.18 shows a scatter plot with heteroscedasticity. The volatility of Y clearly increases for low values of X – the scatter on the left-hand side of the plot is much greater than that in the strip on the right.

Beyond a visual inspection of the scatter plot, quite a few tests for heteroscedasticity are available. These include (i) the Goldfeld–Quandt test, (ii) White's test, (iii) the Breusch–Pagan test and (iv) Engle's ARCH test.[10]

In practice, investors are not concerned about hedge fund correlation during market upswings. Rather, they require a low correlation during market downswings. During financial crises, it is very likely that returns will exhibit heteroscedasticity, as the volatility generally increases. Several researchers have also presented evidence that correlation coefficients tend to increase substantially during these periods. Although appealing, this conclusion needs to be tempered, as the estimate of the standard correlation coefficient r may be biased in the presence of heteroscedasticity.

The problem is that the direction of the bias depends on the time series properties of the returns. For instance, Loretan and English (2000), Ronn *et al.* (2000) and Forbes and Rigobon (2002), among others, show that under some conditions, the bias on the estimated correlation will be upward.[11] Yoon (2003), on the other hand, shows that heteroscedasticity may cause the correlation coefficients to be biased downward when returns follow a particular time series process. There is still room for doubt, therefore, so we shall simply say that the time series behavior of returns should be more thoroughly studied before investigating the impact of a crisis on correlation.

---

[10] The situation is somewhat complicated by the fact that there are different types of heteroscedasticity and thus not all the tests may lead to the same conclusion. For a review of these tests, see Greene (2000).

[11] Forbes and Rigobon (2002) also show that, once adjustments for the bias caused by heteroscedasticity are made, there is little change in correlation coefficients after recent financial crises.

7

Regression Analysis

In a strong wind, turkeys can fly...

As basic to statistics as the Pythagorean theorem is to geometry, regression analysis is one of the most widely used, and misused, techniques in economics and finance – as well as in several other fields. For long, regression has been confined to the world of equities and bonds. With the increased availability of hedge fund data, regression analysis techniques are now commonly applied to alternative investments.

The term "regression" is in itself a misnomer. In general usage, the word has negative overtones, as underscored by the definition contained in the *Thesaurus of Psychological Index Terms* of the American Psychological Association. Regression is "a return to earlier, especially to infantile, patterns of thought or behavior, or stage of functioning, e.g. feelings of helplessness and dependency in a patient with a serious physical illness". Fortunately, in finance, regression analysis means something else. Simply stated, it encompasses the set of statistical techniques for investigating and modeling the functional dependence of a dependent variable Y on one or several independent variables called predictors and denoted $X_1, X_2, \ldots, X_k$.

Scatter plots, correlation, covariance and regression analysis are intimately related, but have very different roles. On the one hand, as evidenced in the previous chapter, a scatter plot provides a visual picture of the relationship between a *response variable* and an *explanatory variable*. Most of the time, this picture is too detailed and essentially qualitative, but it is useful in that it provides some insight into the structure of a data set. If, using the scatter plot, we find evidence of a relationship between some variables, then we can use correlation or covariance to measure the strength and direction of this association. Correlation and covariance quantify how consistently the two variables vary together, but do not help us to describe exactly the specific relationship that exists between the two variables. This is precisely the role of regression analysis, which can be seen as an extension of the correlation, covariance and scatter plot concepts. It fits a curve through our data on the scatter plot, and describes it by means of an equation that has some explanatory power and, in most cases, some predictive power. We mentioned earlier that dimension reduction was a leitmotif of statistics. In the same spirit, the dominant theme of regression analysis is dimension reduction *with minimal loss of information*.

Although the computations that underlie regression appear more complicated than those of descriptive statistics, we believe it is possible to understand regression analysis without fully comprehending all its underlying proofs and theories. In fact, it is not only possible, but essential. We therefore provide below an overview of the most basic techniques of regression analysis – how they work, what they assume, and how they may go awry when some key assumptions do not hold.

The general equation that underlies any regression is:

$$\text{Observed data} = \text{Predictable component} + \text{Unpredictable component}$$

"Observed data" are the observed values of the dependent variable, e.g. in our case the returns on a hedge fund. The "predictable component" consists of the predictions generated by the regression equation, and the "unpredictable component" consists of the residuals or unpredictable parts of the data.[1] The general idea in regression analysis is of course to move as much information as possible into the predictable component, leaving the unpredictable component with no important information or particular pattern.

In order to introduce the fundamental ideas in the simplest of all settings, we focus first on simple linear regression. The term "simple" means that we consider a two-variable framework, that is, we use only one independent variable (X) to explain changes in the dependent variable (Y). The term "linear" means that we consider only the case of linear relationships between our two variables. Later on, we will consider more advanced techniques such as multiple, stepwise and non-linear regressions.

7.1   SIMPLE LINEAR REGRESSION

In order to understand regression analysis, it is necessary to be aware of the differences that exist between the "true model" that governs the world and our estimate of this model.

7.1.1   Reality versus estimation

Consider for instance the Leveraged Brothers Fund, a fictive but reputed hedge fund whose investment policy is to invest all its capital every month in the S&P 500 on a leveraged basis of 2:1. That is, every month, the fund manager borrows an amount equal to the fund's capital, and invests that capital plus the borrowed amount in the S&P 500 index. To keep things simple, assume that (i) the loan costs 0.3% interest per month; (ii) the fund manager can trade at no cost; and (iii) the fund does not charge any fee.

The performance of the Leveraged Brothers Fund can be expressed as a simple linear function of the S&P 500 return:

$$R_{\text{Fund}} = a + (b \times R_{\text{S\&P500}}) \qquad (7.1)$$

with $a = -0.3$ and $b = 2$. This is the "true" model that describes our fund.

Now, say that the Leveraged Brothers Fund is completely opaque, with managers unwilling to provide significant information regarding its portfolio or its strategy. We are analysts trying to analyze the strategy followed by Leveraged Brothers Fund by comparing its returns ($Y = R_{\text{Fund}}$) to the MSCI World returns ($X = R_{\text{MSCI World}}$). The model we assume is:

$$R_{\text{Fund}} = \hat{a} + (\hat{b} \times R_{\text{MSCI World}}) \qquad (7.2)$$

The estimation of the two parameters $\hat{a}$ and $\hat{b}$ yields $\hat{a} = 0.35$ and $\hat{b} = 2.04$ – we will see later how these values are obtained. This is our estimated model. Obviously, our model is wrong, but the only way to correct it is by having some private information about what the fund is really doing.

Figure 7.1 compares the true (unknown) model and our estimated model. Clearly, our model is not far from reality. But it is not reality. Hence, a summary of the primary problems addressed by regression is as follows:

---

[1] Note that statisticians usually use the word prediction in a technical sense. Prediction in this sense does not refer to "predicting the future" (statisticians call that forecasting) but rather to guessing the response from the values of the regressors in an observation taken under the same circumstances as the sample from which the regression equation was estimated.

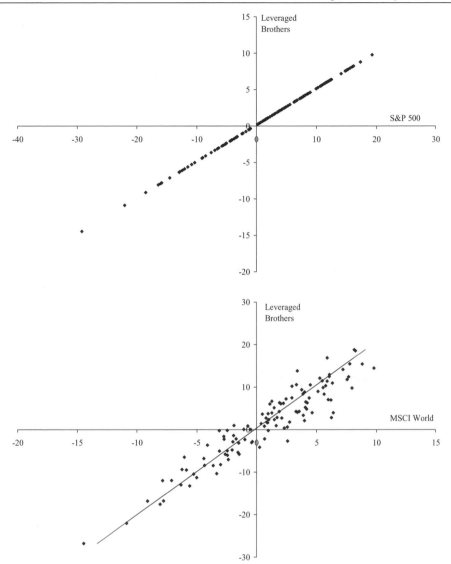

Figure 7.1   Comparing the "true" model (top) with our estimated model (bottom)

(i) How can we build a model that summarizes well a set of observable information (the past returns of the fund) without approximating too much? In particular, how can we identify the index that corresponds to the X variable in the "true" model (e.g. select the S&P 500 rather than the MSCI World)?

(ii) How can we efficiently use the set of information that we possess to estimate the parameters of our model ($\hat{a}$ and $\hat{b}$) and calibrate it to reality?

(iii) How can we assess the quality of our model compared with what we can observe from the "true" unknown model, and in particular how can we be sure that what we have estimated (i.e. $\hat{a}$ and $\hat{b}$) is not only due to chance or the lack thereof?

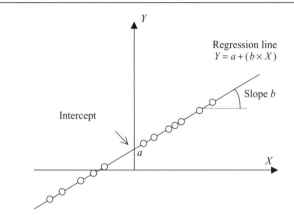

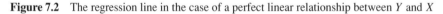

Figure 7.2   The regression line in the case of a perfect linear relationship between Y and X

Note that in our previous example, if we had used the S&P 500 returns rather than the MSCI World returns as an explanatory variable, our estimated model would equal the true model. But this is only an illusion. In reality, the true model will be much more complicated than the one followed by the Leveraged Brothers Fund, so that it is unlikely that we would identify it by chance or accident.

7.1.2   The regression line in a perfect world

Now that we have explained the difference that exists between the "true model" that governs the world and our estimate of this model, let us focus on the process of identifying the estimated model. For the sake of simplicity, let us assume that there exists a "true" linear relationship between two variables Y and X, which is given by

$$Y = a + (b \times X) \tag{7.3}$$

The parameters a and b provide a quantitative description of the relationship between X and Y. On a scatter plot, with X on the horizontal axis and Y on the vertical axis, we can draw a line through the data that connects all points. This line is called the regression line – see Figure 7.2.

The intercept a is the intersection point of the regression line with the vertical axis. It represents the value of Y when X is equal to zero. The slope b represents the change in Y per unit X. A positive slope means that for every unit increase in X the response variable Y has an increase of b units. Conversely, a negative value of b indicates that for every unit increase in X, the variable Y decreases by b units. Hence, in a perfect world, each observation Y_i is perfectly determined if one knows the value of X_i and the two parameters a and b.

In practice, however, the exact values of parameters a and b are usually unknown. The goal of regression analysis is to estimate these two parameters using a sample of N pairs of observations (Y_i, X_i), with $i = 1, \ldots, N$. We will denote the estimates of a and b by $\hat{a}$ and $\hat{b}$. Ideally, $\hat{a}$ and $\hat{b}$ should be as close as possible to the true values a and b.

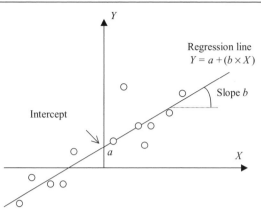

Figure 7.3   The regression line in the case of an approximate linear relationship between Y and X. The slope b represents the average change in Y when X increases by one unit. The intercept a corresponds to the average value of Y when X equals 0

7.1.3   Estimating the regression line

If the model we assumed corresponds to the "true" model, estimating $\hat{a}$ and $\hat{b}$ is no problem at all. We just need two sample points and a ruler to join them and we have our regression line. Indeed, further sample points on the scatter plot would lie exactly along the same straight line and convey no additional information. Thus, the slope of the estimated regression line ($\hat{b}$) will be exactly equal to b, and its intercept ($\hat{a}$) will be exactly equal to a. However, in reality, things will not be so simple.

A first problem is that the observed values of X and Y may be affected by various errors that cause the observed values to deviate from what they should be. These typically include data errors (mistakes in the recording and reporting of prices), non-synchronicity (arising from the need to use multiple simultaneous prices), liquidity premiums (arising from the potential impact of differential liquidity on assets), and/or discreteness (arising from the quoting, trading and reporting of prices in discrete increments, etc.). Consequently, if we take a ruler and draw a straight line through the scatter plot, the data will never fit that line perfectly. Some points will be above the line and some will be below – see Figure 7.3.

A second, more fundamental, problem is that most relationships in the real world are rather more of a non-linear nature.[2] In such a case, linear regression analysis should be seen as a first-order *approximation* of the *reality*. That is, our model is unlikely ever to reproduce the underlying truth exactly but we can expect that, in the right circumstances, our estimates will be "close" to the truth.[3] In this situation as well, if we take a ruler and draw a straight line through the scatter plot, some points will be above the line and some will be below – see Figure 7.3.

If we believe that the true relationship between X and Y is not exactly linear, we need to adjust our original model by adding an error term. The specification of the relationship between

---

[2] Although it may be possible to transform certain types of non-linear relationships into linear ones, this requires knowledge of the true functional relationship between Y and X, which we often do not possess. We will come back to that topic when considering non-linear regression.

[3] There are several examples of such linear approximations in finance beyond linear regression. For instance, the delta of an option or the duration of a bond can be seen as first-order approximations of reality.

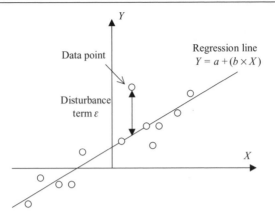

Figure 7.4 The regression line in the case of an approximate linear relationship between Y and X. For each data point, the disturbance term ε is represented as the vertical distance to the regression line

X and Y then becomes

$$Y = a + (b \times X) + \varepsilon \tag{7.4}$$

where ε is a random variable that accounts for the discrepancies that emerge between the actual, observed values of Y and the values that are predicted by the "true" model. Obviously, the error term ε should have an expected value of zero; if this is not the case, the model is biased (Figure 7.4).[4]

Equation (7.4) describes how the world evolves according to us. Now, remember the question of what is observable and what is not. For the time being, the parameters a and b are still unobservable and unknown, so the error component ε is also unobservable. Based on a sample of observed points (X_i, Y_i), the task of regression analysis is precisely to produce the best estimate of the two parameters a and b, that is, identify the regression line, from which we can estimate the error terms.

If we find that all the data points do not exactly form a line on the scatter plot, but rather a cloud, we are faced with the task of figuring out which line best represents the scatter plot. The exact theoretical answer to that question is beyond the scope of this book. Here we will just provide the intuition the reader needs to proceed.

Any line drawn through the scatter plot with slope $\hat{b}$ and intercept $\hat{a}$ predicts

$$\hat{Y} = \hat{a} + (\hat{b} \times X) + \hat{e} \tag{7.5}$$

while the reality is

$$Y = a + (b \times X) + \varepsilon \tag{7.6}$$

with a, b and ε unknown. The difference between the predicted $\hat{Y}$ and the observed Y is again an error term. For an observed pair (X_i, Y_i), this error term can easily be calculated:

$$\hat{e}_i = Y_i - \hat{Y}_i = Y_i - \hat{a} - (\hat{b} \times X_i) \tag{7.7}$$

See Figure 7.5.

---

[4] An expected error different from zero implies that the model systematically underestimates or overestimates reality. As the bias is systematic, it is easy to correct by adjusting the value of a downward or upward. In practice, basic regression analysis techniques assume that the error term is normally distributed, with zero mean and constant variance.

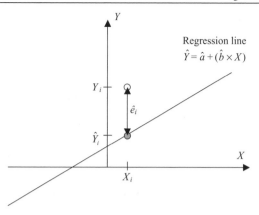

Figure 7.5   The approximate linear relationship between Y and X

Obviously, the regression line should attempt to minimize a function of all the error terms. In other words, we should choose the slope $\hat{b}$ and intercept $\hat{a}$ of our regression line in such a way as to minimize a function of all the error terms in the sample. The simplest mathematical function to consider is the sum of errors. Unfortunately, minimizing the sum of errors is not an attractive criterion. It can be shown that any line that goes through the center of the scatter plot (the point with coordinates $\bar{X}$ and $\bar{Y}$, corresponding to the mean of X on the horizontal axis and the mean of Y on the vertical axis) always minimizes the sum of errors. Furthermore, large negative errors and large positive errors would cancel out, so the sum could be at a minimum even though the line selected fitted the data very poorly. A different function of all the errors to be minimized must therefore be used.

Many different functions come into consideration. Each has its advantages and disadvantages, its strengths and weaknesses. Some may not be appropriate in any circumstances; others may be appropriate only in specific situations.[5] However, the most commonly used approach to regression – called ordinary least squares (OLS) and proposed by the German scientist Karl Gauss – attempts to minimize the sum of the squared errors. That is:

$$\text{Choose } \hat{a} \text{ and } \hat{b} \text{ to minimize } \sum_{i=1}^{N} \hat{e}_i^2$$

or equivalently, the variance of the individual errors:[6]

$$\text{Choose } \hat{a} \text{ and } \hat{b} \text{ to minimize } \sigma_{\hat{e}}^2$$

One virtue of the OLS approach is that it is very easy to employ computationally. In particular:

- It gives simple closed-form solutions for the parameters $\hat{a}$ and $\hat{b}$. Algebraically, we have:

$$\hat{b} = \frac{\text{Covar}(X, Y)}{\text{Var}(X)} = \frac{\sum_i (X_i - \bar{X})(Y_i - \bar{Y})}{\sum_i (X_i - \bar{X})^2} \tag{7.8}$$

and

$$\hat{a} = \bar{Y} - \hat{b} \times \bar{X} \tag{7.9}$$

---

[5] For a technical discussion of alternative functions of the residuals, see for instance Rousseeuw and Leroy (1987).

[6] As the errors have zero mean, minimizing the sum of squared errors or minimizing the variance of errors yields the same result.

- It severely penalizes large individual errors[7] and ensures that all errors remain small on average.
- It has some attractive statistical properties under plausible assumptions about the error terms. When using OLS, one can show (i) that the regression line always passes through the points of means $(\bar{X}, \bar{Y})$; (ii) that the errors have zero covariance with the sample of X values and also with the predicted $\hat{Y}$ values; and (iii) that the estimates $\hat{a}$ and $\hat{b}$ are the best linear unbiased estimators of the true values a and b.

These desirable properties make the OLS approach the most widely used in practice when performing regression analysis.[8]

7.1.4   Illustration of regression analysis: Andor Technology

As an illustration, let us analyze the behavior of a long/short equity fund using regression analysis. The fund considered is Andor Technology Offshore Fund, the flagship fund of Andor Capital Management. With $2.5 billion of assets, Andor Technology is the largest technology hedge fund in the world. Managed by Daniel C. Benton, it attempts to take advantage of changes in the technology industry by identifying long-term secular trends.

Andor Technology is known in the industry for the quality of its fundamental research, as well as for the aggressiveness of its bets. In particular, it shorts stocks to make money, not just to protect its long positions. For instance, a few months after the Nasdaq crash of March 2000, the fund clearly shifted from a net long to a net short market exposure. The latter was maintained until late in 2003, which is extremely uncommon among technology funds. This allowed Andor to maintain its positive performance through the years 2000, 2001 and 2002. However, during the first half of 2003, the net short exposure, although slightly reduced, generated significant losses as the market recovered – see Figure 7.6. By using regression analysis, we can attempt to recognize the shift from net long to net short that occurred at Andor Technology.

First, we consider a sample period going from January 1994 to July 2003, and regress the monthly returns on Andor Technology (Y) over that period with the returns of the Nasdaq (X). A visual inspection of the scatter plot reveals that although it is possible to draw a regression line, the line does not fit the scatter plot very well – see Figure 7.7. Nevertheless, for the sake of illustration, we continue the regression analysis based on this sample.

Using for instance the Excel regression toolkit (provided with the Data Analysis package), we obtain the results of Table 7.1. This output is typical of that from a regression package. The intercept and the slope of the regression line come under "Coefficients" in the bottom part of the table. They are equal to 2.43 and 0.17, respectively. Hence, according to the regression, Andor Technology captured on average about 17% of any movement of the Nasdaq, plus a fixed return of 2.43% per month.

7.1.5   Measuring the quality of a regression: multiple R, R^2, ANOVA and p-values

The estimated coefficients of a regression describe the nature of the relationship between the two variables X and Y. However, knowing the slope and the intercept of a regression line does not tell us anything about how well the line fits the data. How widely do the actual values of Y

---

[7] A side-effect of minimizing the squared residuals is that the intercept and slope of the regression line may be dramatically affected by the presence of outliers.

[8] Other techniques, in particular the generalized methods of moments (GMM), are less restrictive in their approach, but they are mathematically cumbersome and they do not provide the best linear unbiased estimators of a and b. Nevertheless, they are useful in some particular situations, e.g. models where there is autocorrelation/heteroscedasticity in the error terms – see Greene (2000).

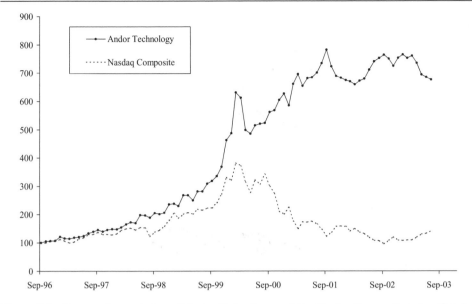

Figure 7.6 Comparative evolution of Andor Technology and the Nasdaq Composite index, October 1996 to July 2003

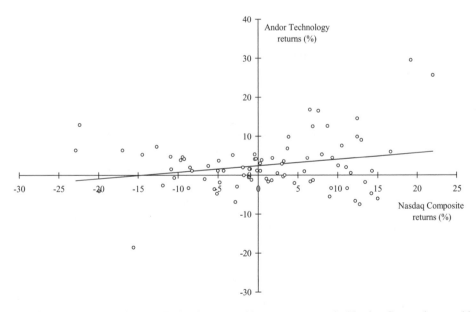

Figure 7.7 Scatter plot of Andor Technology monthly returns versus the Nasdaq Composite monthly returns, October 1996 to July 2003

differ from the values predicted by our model? The "best" regression line may have little or even no explanatory power at all, or simply be the result of chance. Visual inspection of the scatter plot is useful, but it does not allow us to identify precisely the quality of the regression. Therefore, we need to consider additional quantitative indicators to tell how well the regression summarizes our scatter plot.

Table 7.1   Regression of Andor Technology monthly returns versus the Nasdaq Composite monthly returns, October 1996 to July 2003

Regression statistics	
Multiple R	0.23
R-square	0.05
Adjusted R-square	0.04
Standard error	6.76
Observations	82

(handwritten annotations: $\dfrac{209.21}{3870.18}$; $\sqrt{45.76} = 6.76$)

ANOVA

	df	SS	MS	F	Significance F
Regression	1.00	209.21	209.21	4.57	0.04
Residual	80.00	3660.97	45.76		
Total	81.00	3870.18			

(handwritten: $45.76 = \dfrac{3660.97}{80}$; $4.57 = \dfrac{209.21}{45.76}$)

	Coefficients	Standard error	t-stat	p-value	Lower 95%	Upper 95%
Intercept	2.43	0.75	3.24	0.00	0.94	3.93
Nasdaq	0.17	0.08	2.14	0.04	0.01	0.32

Several technical measures are produced as part of a regression output and usually serve as indicators of confidence in the results of the regression. For instance, the *multiple R* is the correlation between the observed Y and the model predicted $\hat{Y}$. It ranges between 0 and 1 – by construction, it will never be negative. The higher the multiple R, the better.

Another popular indicator of the quality of the regression is the R-square (R^2), also called the *coefficient of determination*. It indicates the percentage of the total variation observed in the dependent variable (Y) that can be explained using the linear model prediction ($\hat{Y}$) compared to just using the mean ($\bar{Y}$). Stated differently, we decompose the variability in the response, Y, into the portion that we can explain with our linear prediction and error. Specifically, we have:

$$\sum_{i=1}^{N}(Y_i - \bar{Y})^2 = \sum_{i=1}^{N}(\hat{Y}_i - \bar{Y})^2 + \sum_{i=1}^{N}(Y_i - \hat{Y}_i)^2 \qquad (7.10)$$

or equivalently:

$$\text{SS(Total)} = \text{SS(Model)} + \text{SS(Error)} \qquad (7.11)$$

where SS stands for "sum of squares". Then, R^2, which is the square of the usual correlation coefficient, is calculated as the ratio of the variance captured by the fitted model to the variation variance in Y:

$$R^2 = \frac{\text{Explained variance}}{\text{Total variance}} = \frac{\sum_{i=1}^{N}(\hat{Y}_i - \bar{Y})^2}{\sum_{i=1}^{N}(Y_i - \bar{Y})^2} \qquad (7.12)$$

where Y are the observed values for the dependent variable, $\bar{Y}$ is the average of the observed values and $\hat{Y}$ are predicted values for the dependent variable (the predicted values are calculated using the regression equation).

For a given set of data, the larger the value of R^2, the more accurate is the regression.[9] Since $0 \leq R^2 \leq 1$, an R^2 close to 1 means that we have a very good fit – i.e. X explains most of the variance in Y. Note that this does not necessarily mean a causal explanation, merely a statistical one. Conversely, an R^2 close to 0 implies that X does not explain Y any better than the sample mean $\bar{Y}$. It may indicate that there is no relationship, or that the relationship is not linear.

Finally, a useful indicator is the *standard error* of the estimate, which indicates how closely the actual observations coincide with the predicted values on the regression line. If we accept the hypothesis that error terms are normally distributed, then about 68.3% of the observations should fall within ± 1 standard error units of the regression line, 95.4% should fall within ± 2 standard error units, and 99.7% should fall within ± 3 standard error units.

In the case of Andor Technology, the multiple R is equal to 0.23, a rather low figure. The R^2 is equal to 0.05, or 5%, meaning that the Nasdaq composite only explains 5% of the variations of Andor Technology. This is obviously a very weak relationship. And the standard error is rather large (6.76). At this stage, we are entitled to wonder if the amount of variance explained by our model is significantly greater than that which could be attributable to chance.

The analysis of variance (ANOVA) table is used to test the significance of the overall regression results.[10] The two hypotheses confronted are:

Null hypothesis H_0 There is no linear relationship between X and Y

versus

Alternative hypothesis H_a There is a linear relationship between X and Y

The relevant information for us is to be found in the last two columns of the ANOVA table. The test statistic is called the F-ratio – it was developed by R.A. Fisher in 1924, and later named in his honor by G.W. Snedecor. It is defined as the ratio of the explained to the unexplained variance:

$$F = \frac{\sum_{i=1}^{N} (\hat{Y}_i - \bar{Y})^2}{\sum_{i=1}^{N} (Y_i - \hat{Y}_i)^2} \times (N - 2) \tag{7.13}$$

We can reject the null hypothesis if the computed/observed F is greater than or equal to a critical value, which can be obtained by looking at a table of the F-distribution.[11] Alternatively, we can simply look at the last column of the ANOVA table, where we find a p-value. If the p-value is small enough (say less than 5%), this means that it is unlikely that the slope was non-zero purely by chance. In our case, the p-value is 4%, so we reject the null hypothesis. Hence, our model has a low explanatory power (low R^2), but the little that is explained is significant.

---

[9] One drawback of the R^2 measure is that there does not seem to be a consensus among researchers as to what constitutes a "good" R^2. Some researchers will draw conclusions from regression results despite the fact that only 10% or 20% of the total variation observed is explained by their model, others will be thrilled to report an R^2 greater than 30%, and yet others will hardly comment on the fact that R^2 was 70%. Thus, the R^2 measure is very much subject to personal evaluation.

[10] An ANOVA table always has the same structure, and we refer the interested reader to Greene (2000) for further details on the subject.

[11] The F-ratio follows an F-distribution with $k - 1$ and $N - k$ degrees of freedom, where N is the number of observations and k the number of parameters estimated.

This clearly shows that, when summarizing a linear regression, it is important to quote both the coefficient of determination and the p-value. With the small sample sizes often encountered in hedge fund studies, the coefficients of a regression can have substantial values yet can still fail to be significant (i.e. do not have a small p-value), or *vice versa*.

Box 7.1

To understand the F-ratio construction, consider equation (7.11). The degrees of freedom of each sum of squares are as follows:

- Degrees of freedom total = DF(Total) = number of observations – 1 = $N - 1$.
- Degrees of freedom model = DF(Model) = number of explanatory variables in the model = K.
- Degrees of freedom error = DF(Error) = DF(Total) – DF(Model) = $N - 1 - K$.

The mean squares are simply the sums of squares divided by the degrees of freedom (e.g. MS(Total) = Var(Y)).

The overall F-ratio is defined as F = MS(Model)/MS(Error), which under the null hypothesis stated above will follow an F-distribution with numerator degrees of freedom = DF(Model) and denominator degrees of freedom = DF(Error). In the particular case of $K = 1$ (single regression), we obtain the F-ratio defined in equation (7.13).

7.1.6   Testing the regression coefficients

Assuming that the regression model provides a good fit, another important question is whether all individual terms are needed. In particular: (i) is the intercept coefficient significantly different from zero; and (ii) is the slope coefficient significantly different from zero?

We must bear in mind that each coefficient in the regression is estimated, and is therefore affected by some uncertainty. This uncertainty is measured by the standard error of each coefficient, which is given in the bottom part of Table 7.1. For instance, for the intercept coefficient ($\hat{a} = 2.43$), we have a standard error of $\sigma_{\hat{a}} = 0.75$.

Armed with this information, we can use three different approaches to test whether the intercept is significantly different from zero:

- We can divide the estimated coefficient by its standard error. This gives a t-ratio, or t-statistic, which is reported by most regression software (bottom of Table 7.1). It tells us how many standard error units the coefficient is away from zero. As a rule of thumb, a t-statistic with an absolute value larger than 1.96 means that the corresponding coefficient is statistically different from zero (it is more than two standard deviations away from its mean[12]).
- We can simply look at the p-value (bottom of Table 7.1). If it is small enough (say less than 5%), then we accept the idea that the corresponding coefficient is statistically different from zero.
- We can build a 95% confidence interval by adding ± 1.96 times the standard error to the estimated coefficient. If zero is not included in this interval, this means that we can exclude the fact that the corresponding coefficient may be equal to zero. In our Excel output, the 95% confidence interval is pre-calculated (bottom of Table 7.1, right-most columns).

---

[12] The exact threshold critical value can be obtained by looking at the tables for the t-distribution in a statistics textbook.

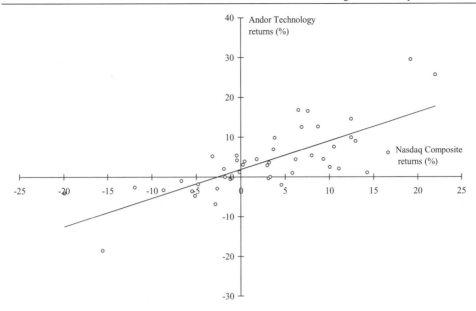

Figure 7.8   Scatter plot of Andor Technology monthly returns versus the Nasdaq Composite monthly returns, October 1996 to July 2000

All these approaches are founded on the hypothesis of normally distributed errors with constant variance. In our case, the three approaches produce the result that both the slope and the intercept are significantly different from zero. However, in the light of the scatter plot or the R^2, we should not be very confident about using a model that has only 5% explanatory power. Furthermore, we know that Andor Technology dramatically changed its asset allocation from net long to net short a few months after the Nasdaq crash, but we have not used that information so far. So, we probably need to work a little bit more on our model.

7.1.7   Reconsidering Andor Technology

The simplest way of incorporating that information is to split the period in two, and run a separate regression on each sub-period. The first period goes from October 1996 to July 2000, and the second from August 2000 to August 2003. Using again the Excel regression toolkit (in the Data Analysis package), we obtain the results displayed in Figure 7.8 and Table 7.2 for the first period and the results shown in Figure 7.9 and Table 7.3 for the second period. The results are strikingly different for the two periods.

In the first period, Andor Technology displayed a correlation of 0.76 with the Nasdaq Composite. It captured about 72% of the movements of the Nasdaq, plus a fixed component of 1.86% per month. Both coefficients are significant. The R^2 of the regression is 57%, also statistically significant (the p-value is 0). In the second period, Andor Technology displayed a correlation of −0.88 with the Nasdaq Composite. It captured about 36% of the movements of the Nasdaq, but in the opposite direction, plus a fixed component of 0.22% per month. Only the first coefficient is significant. The R^2 of the regression is 77%, also statistically significant (the p-value is 0).

Table 7.2   Regression of Andor Technology monthly returns versus the Nasdaq Composite monthly returns, October 1996 to July 2000

Regression statistics

Multiple R	0.76
R-square	0.57
Adjusted R-square	0.56
Standard error	5.47
Observations	45

ANOVA

	df	SS	MS	F	Significance F
Regression	1.00	1711.21	1711.21	57.11	0.00
Residual	43.00	1288.45	29.96		
Total	44.00	2999.66			

	Coefficients	Standard error	t-stat	p-value	Lower 95%	Upper 95%
Intercept	1.86	0.86	2.15	0.04	0.11	3.60
X variable 1	0.72	0.10	7.56	0.00	0.53	0.91

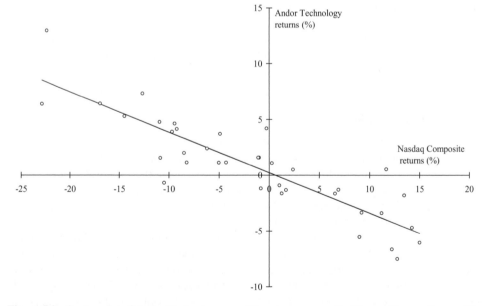

Figure 7.9   Scatter plot of Andor Technology monthly returns versus the Nasdaq Composite monthly returns, August 2000 to July 2003

Table 7.3 Regression of Andor Technology monthly returns versus the Nasdaq Composite monthly returns, August 2000 to July 2003

Regression statistics

Multiple R	0.88
R-square	0.77
Adjusted R-square	0.77
Standard error	2.08
Observations	37

ANOVA

	df	SS	MS	F	Significance F
Regression	1.00	512.23	512.23	118.61	0.00
Residual	35.00	151.15	4.32		
Total	36.00	663.38			

	Coefficients	Standard error	t-stat	p-value	Lower 95%	Upper 95%
Intercept	0.22	0.35	0.65	0.52	−0.48	0.93
X variable 1	−0.36	0.03	−10.89	0.00	−0.43	−0.29

This example clearly illustrates the power of regression analysis when it is combined with some qualitative information about what a fund is doing. While it would have taken a considerable amount of time to figure out what happened at Andor Technology just by running regressions on different periods, the qualitative information about the change in net exposure allowed us to immediately split our sample and verify the information.

This example also highlights a feature of regression analysis. If the explanatory power is low, the error term ε and the intercept coefficient $\hat{a}$ capture all the unexplained variations. Hence, a large intercept with a low explanatory power is often a strong signal that the regression model is badly specified. Unfortunately, when the intercept is positive, many investors confuse it with a strong signal that the fund has added value over the index it is compared with. We come back to this point in the next chapter, when measuring the value added by a fund manager.

7.1.8 Simple linear regression as a predictive model

Explaining what happened in the past is extremely interesting, at least from an academic point of view. But to make money on financial markets, it is necessary to forecast. If there is a strong linear association between two variables, it is very tempting to use a linear regression model to predict the value of the dependent variable. Before getting there, however, we must heed the following important warnings:

- A prediction based on a regression model is conditional upon knowing (or predicting) the future value of the independent variable, i.e. future returns of the Nasdaq in our Andor Technology example.
- A regression line is usually calibrated on past data. If the relationship between X and Y changes, the regression will not be reliable for prediction. Remember the Andor Technology case, which shifted from a net long to a net short exposure within a month.

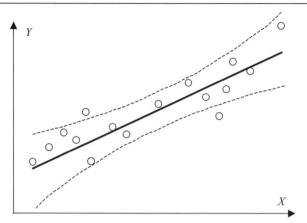

Figure 7.10   The standard error measures the scatter in the actual data around the estimated regression line

- A regression line is usually calibrated on a limited set of data. We should be cautious, as prediction outside the range of the data – called extrapolation – is risky and often not appropriate.
- A strong association between X and Y says nothing about the existence of a cause-and-effect relationship between them. It may be that the observed association is purely due to chance, or that Y influences X rather than the opposite.

Now, assume that we have determined that X effectively causes Y and that this relationship will persist in the future. If our regression model is

$$\hat{Y} = \hat{a} + (\hat{b} \times X) + \hat{e} \tag{7.14}$$

then the predicted value of Y for a value of $X = X^{new}$ is

$$E(Y^{new}) = \hat{a} + (\hat{b} \times X^{new}) \tag{7.15}$$

How precise is this prediction? It should be recalled that (i) $\hat{a}$ and $\hat{b}$ are only estimates of the true and unknown coefficients a and b, and they inherently have some uncertainty; (ii) the error term $\hat{e}$ has an expected value of zero, but is not always zero. Consequently, $\hat{Y}^{new}$ is also a random variable, hence it also has a sampling distribution. Therefore, when using a regression to forecast, rather than just to provide a point estimate, it is better to provide a prediction interval that indicates the range of most likely values for the dependent variable.

As an illustration, Figure 7.10 shows the 95% confidence interval or 95% prediction interval of the regression line. Note that the dashed lines that demarcate the confidence interval are curved. This does not mean that the confidence interval includes the possibility of curves as well as straight lines. Rather, the curved lines are the boundaries of all possible straight lines. Figure 7.11 shows four possible linear regression lines (solid) that lie within the confidence interval (dashed).

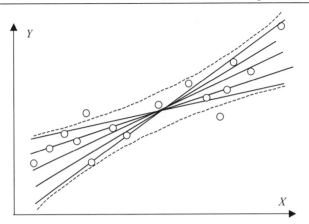

Figure 7.11   An example of several "possible" linear regression lines

7.2   MULTIPLE LINEAR REGRESSION

Simple linear regression is a very useful tool to ascertain the causal effect of one variable upon another. Unfortunately, almost no dependent variable in the real world is affected by only one independent variable. Most of the time, we need to quantify the impact of several influences upon a single dependent variable. One possible solution is to perform a regression analysis with one independent variable, and then test whether a second independent variable is related to the residuals from this regression, continue with a third variable, etc. However, a problem with this approach is that we are putting some variables in privileged positions, because they enter the analysis first. In contrast, multiple regression analysis is precisely a technique that extends simple regression to allow several independent variables to enter the analysis simultaneously.

7.2.1   Multiple regression

Let $X_1, X_2, \ldots, X_k$ denote k different independent variables whose relationship with a response variable Y is to be investigated. A multiple linear regression model may be written as

$$Y = a + (b_1 \times X_1) + (b_2 \times X_2) + \cdots + (b_k \times X_k) + \varepsilon \qquad (7.16)$$

where:

Y is the dependent or explained variable
$X_1, X_2, \ldots, X_k$ are independent or explanatory variables (called regressors)
ε is an error term that is uncorrelated to all regressors

The task of estimating the parameters $a, b_1, \ldots, b_k$ is conceptually identical to the earlier task of estimating only a and b for a single linear regression. The difference is that we can no longer think of regression as choosing a line that goes through a scatter plot. The regression equation now represents a (hyper)plane in a $(k + 1)$-dimensional space.[13]
  If this idea is a bit overwhelming, consider the following. When $k = 2$, the regression equation is a line in a two-dimensional plane, as illustrated already in Figure 7.4. When $k = 2$,

---

[13] There are k dimensions, one for each independent variable, plus one dimension for the dependent variable Y.

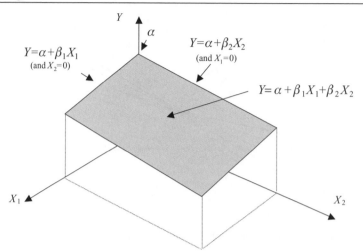

Figure 7.12 A three-dimensional representation of the regression approach

the regression tries to fit a plane through a cloud of points in three dimensions, as illustrated in Figure 7.12. The least-squares objective is to minimize the sum of squared vertical distances between the points and the plane.[14] The intercept of that plane with the Y-axis (where $X_1 = X_2 = 0$) corresponds to the constant term a, its slope in the (X_1, Y) dimension corresponds to the coefficient b_1, and its slope in the (X_2, Y) dimension corresponds to the coefficient b_2.

When $k = 3$, the regression tries to fit a three-dimensional space through a cloud of points that spans four dimensions. This seems like science fiction for most of us. Though most sober people are unable to visualize more than three dimensions, mathematics can. Clearly, a four-or-more variable model is very difficult to represent graphically, but the concept remains the same. Multiple regression analysis is in fact capable of dealing with an arbitrarily large number of explanatory variables.

Similarly to simple regression, the interpretation of the coefficient estimates in a multiple regression is relatively simple. If all other variables are held constant and X_i increases by one unit, then coefficient b_i captures the average change that will result in Y. To put it slightly differently, b_i is an estimate of the effect of variable X_i on Y, holding everything else constant. The coefficient a is the average value of Y when $X_1 = X_2 = \cdots = X_k = 0$. The estimation can still be done according to the principles of ordinary least squares. The equations for the OLS estimates of the regression equations are only a little more complicated algebraically. We will not go into such detail here.

7.2.2 Illustration: analyzing the Grossman Currency Fund

As an illustration, let us analyze the return of the Grossman Currency Fund, the fund founded by Sanford J. Grossman, the former Steinberg Trustee Professor of Finance at the Wharton School and former president of the American Finance Association. The feature of this currency trading fund is its systematic approach: its trading strategy is 100% computerized, model-driven and

---

[14] Note that this regression model also allows us to analyze the partial relationships between Y and individual X_i variables. That is, we can consider the relationship between Y and a given X_i, controlling for all other explanatory variables. In Figure 7.12, these partial relationships are represented by their corresponding regression lines in the (X_1, Y) and (X_2, Y) planes.

Table 7.4   Regression of Grossman Currency Fund monthly returns versus the CHF/US$, EUR/US$ and JPY/US$ relative variations, August 2001 to July 2003

Regression statistics

Multiple R	0.75
R-square	0.57
Adjusted R-square	0.50
Standard error	2.17
Observations	24

ANOVA

	df	SS	MS	F	Significance F
Regression	3.00	124.22	41.41	8.82	0.00
Residual	20.00	93.92	4.70		
Total	23.00	218.14			

	Coefficients	Standard error	t-stat	p-value	Lower 95%	Upper 95%
Intercept	0.01	0.50	0.03	0.98	−1.02	1.05
X_1 (EUR/US$)	−1.24	0.43	−2.84	0.01	−2.14	−0.33
X_2 (JPY/US$)	1.13	0.24	4.65	0.00	0.62	1.63
X_3 (CHF/US$)	0.22	0.40	0.56	0.58	−0.61	1.06

the model's decisions are never overridden. A trading desk executes the trade recommended by the system and has only intra-day discretion as to the specific timing orders are placed, as opposed to the direction and amount of trades.

We regress the Grossman Currency Fund returns against the relative variations in CHF/US$, EUR/US$ and JPY/US$ exchange rates, from August 2001 to July 2003. The results are summarized in Table 7.4. Note that all the exchange rates considered are expressed as the amount of foreign currency obtained for one US dollar. Hence, a positive variation in the exchange rate means the US dollar strengthened against the foreign currency (i.e. you need more currency units to buy one US dollar).

The regression has an R^2 equal to 0.57, which is relatively high for a model with only three explanatory variables applied to a macro fund. However, a drawback of the R^2 measure is that, as additional variables are added to a regression, the R^2 tends to increase even if there is no causal relation between the added variables and the dependent. The reason is that R^2 is not adjusted for the number of independent variables in the regression model. Hence, the more variables you have, the better the R^2. To correct for this bias, it is advisable to use the R-adjusted for multiple regression. Simply stated, R-adjusted is R^2 plus a penalty for the number of explanatory variables in the model. It is calculated as:

$$R\text{-adj} = 1 - (1 - R^2) \times \frac{N-1}{N-K-1} \tag{7.17}$$

where N is the number of observations and K is the number of explanatory variables. Unlike the coefficient of determination, R-adjusted may decrease if variables are entered that do not add significantly to the model fit.

Table 7.5   Regression of Grossman Currency Fund monthly returns versus the EUR/US$ and JPY/US$ relative variations, August 2001 to July 2003

Regression statistics

Multiple R	0.75
R-square	0.56
Adjusted R-square	0.52
Standard error	2.13
Observations	24

ANOVA

	df	SS	MS	F	Significance F
Regression	2.00	122.77	61.38	13.52	0.00
Residual	21.00	95.37	4.54		
Total	23.00	218.14			

	Coefficients	Standard error	t-stat	p-value	Lower 95%	Upper 95%
Intercept	0.02	0.49	0.03	0.98	−1.00	1.03
X_1 (EUR/US$)	−1.03	0.23	−4.40	0.00	−1.52	−0.55
X_2 (JPY/US$)	1.15	0.23	4.88	0.00	0.66	1.63

The R-adjusted for our example is equal to 0.50, which is still high. It means that 50% of the variance of the Grossman Currency Fund is explained in a linear way by the variation of three exchange rates.

The F-stat, which measures the ratio of explained variance to unexplained variance, is also adjusted for the degrees of freedom:

$$F = \frac{\sum_{i=1}^{N} (\hat{Y}_i - \bar{Y})^2}{\sum_{i=1}^{N} (Y_i - \hat{Y}_i)^2} \times \frac{N - K - 1}{K} \tag{7.18}$$

The F-stat of our example equals 8.82, and its p-value is 0.00, so that the hypothesis that there is no (linear) relationship can be rejected, and the multiple correlation (0.75) can be called statistically significant.

When looking at the individual coefficients, the regression yields a negative coefficient ($b_1 = -1.24$) for the EUR/US$ variations, which suggests a long exposure to the euro – the fund captured on average 124% of the EUR/US$ variations, but in the opposite direction.[15] Similarly, we can observe a short exposure to the yen ($b_2 = 1.13$, which means that the fund captured on average 113% of the JPY/US$ variations) and a short exposure to the Swiss franc ($b_3 = 0.22$, which means that the fund captured on average 22% of the CHF/US$ variations). However, we also see that while the t-stats for b_1 and b_2 are above 1.96 in absolute value, the t-stat for b_3 is 0.56. This signals that the Swiss franc exposure is non-significant. Consequently, we can drop the corresponding variable (CHF/US$ exchange rate variations) from the model

---

[15] Remember that all the exchange rates considered are expressed as the amount of euros for one US dollar, so that a negative coefficient means you lose money when the US dollar appreciates against the euro, or equivalently, that you are long euros.

and run the regression again using only the EUR/US$ and JPY/US$ exchange rate variations as explanatory variables.[16] The new results are summarized in Table 7.5.

The new model confirms our previous findings, with a significant long exposure to the euro ($b_1 = -1.03$) and a significant short exposure to the yen ($b_2 = 1.15$). The variations in these two currencies explain about 52% of the variations of the fund, which is not bad for a model with only two independent variables.

An interesting observation is that the intercept coefficient (0.02) is not statistically different from zero (t-stat $= 0.03 < 1.96$). Hence, from a logical perspective, we should remove the corresponding term from the model and re-estimate the model without any intercept. However, as we will see in the next chapter, although not significant, the intercept is often left in the model because it has a specific financial interpretation – it measures the value added, if any, by the manager.

7.3   THE DANGERS OF MODEL SPECIFICATION

Properly used, regression analysis is an extremely powerful tool to analyze the relation between two variables. However, several pitfalls lie in the path of the unwary. Regression models should be properly specified and meet the basic regression assumptions in order to be usable. But in reality, all our models are misspecified to some extent – our theories are always a simplification of reality and all of our measures are imperfect. Hence, our task should be to seek models that are reasonably well specified in order to keep our errors relatively modest. This is precisely where some input from qualitative analysis can prove useful.

In brief, model specification involves two categories of choice: (i) the set of variables that we include in a model; and (ii) the functional form of the relationships we specify. We describe below the major sources of model misspecification in the first category, namely, the exclusion of a relevant variable, the inclusion of an irrelevant variable and the multi-collinearity, heteroscedasticity and autocorrelation of the independent variables. Later, at the end of this chapter, we will address the issue of alternative functional forms (e.g. non-linear relationships).

7.3.1   The omitted variable bias

> As I was going up the stair,
> I met a man who wasn't there.
> He wasn't there again today.
> I wish, I wish he'd go away!

This childhood poem reminds us that the absence of something can be just as tangible as the presence of something. Unfortunately, the remark also applies to regression analysis. When a variable that ought to be included in a regression is left out, the estimated effect of the variables we include in the model is likely to be in error. This creates an "omitted variable bias", which may affect the validity of the whole regression.

To understand the consequences of this bias, two cases should be considered:

- If the omitted variable is uncorrelated with the other explanatory variables considered, its (omitted) contribution is captured only by the intercept and the error term. In that case, the

---

[16] Note that only one variable can be dropped at a time. If a variable is dropped from a model, the model must be refitted before dropping a further variable.

omission may have two consequences. First, it biases the intercept upward or downward, because the intercept captures any deviation of the error term from a zero mean. Second, it may also violate the assumptions necessary for the regression, and in particular the normality assumption for the error terms (as error terms now include a part of the omitted variable). In that case, any inference based on the regression will be suspect.

- If the omitted variable is correlated with some of the explanatory variables considered, then the coefficients of these explanatory variables will be biased upward or downward because they reflect not only an estimate of the effect of the variable with which they are associated, but also partly the effects of the omitted variable.[17] If the correlation is not perfect, then it is likely that the intercept and the error term will also be affected, as in the previous case, and we will end up with worthless results.

Hence, omitting relevant variables is in any case likely to result in severe problems. At best, it will complicate hypothesis testing. At worst, it will invalidate the whole outcome of the regression.

Box 7.2   The mathematics of omission

The consequences of omitted variable bias are more insidious than a first glance might reveal. As an illustration, consider the following example. Say the true model is

$$Y = a + (b_1 \times X_1) + (b_2 \times X_2) + \varepsilon \tag{7.19}$$

while the model we estimate is

$$Y = a^* + (b_1^* \times X_1) + \varepsilon^* \tag{7.20}$$

For the sake of illustration, say the omitted variable (X_2) can be considered as a function of X_1 in a conditional or auxiliary regression:

$$X_2 = c + (d \times X_1) + e \tag{7.21}$$

Then, the true model becomes

$$Y = a + (b_1 \times X_1) + (b_2 \times \underbrace{(c + (d \times X_1) + e)}_{X_2}) + \varepsilon \tag{7.22}$$

Rearranging terms yields

$$Y = \underbrace{[a + (b_2 \times c)]}_{a^*} + \underbrace{[b_1 + (b_2 \times d)]}_{b_1^*} \times X_1 + \underbrace{[(b_2 \times e) + \varepsilon]}_{e^*} \tag{7.23}$$

So, we clearly see that $E(a^*) \neq a$ and $E(b^*) \neq b$. Remember that the coefficient d is equal to the covariance between X_1 and X_2, divided by the variance of X_1, and that the coefficient b_2 is equal to the covariance between X_2 and Y, divided by the variance of X_2. Thus, the coefficient b_1 will be biased by two factors: (i) the extent of the correlation between X_1 and X_2 and (ii) the extent of the correlation between Y and X_2.

---

[17] For a formal derivation of the bias in the multivariate case, see Greene (2000).

The first *symptom of an omitted variable* is a low R^2 statistic. This signals that our model does not capture some aspects of the process that generates the dependent variable. However, this is a necessary but not a sufficient condition for the presence of an omitted variable bias – the unexplained variation could also be random noise.

Another way of detecting omitted variables is the regression specification error test (RESET) suggested by Ramsey (1969). The intuition behind this test is that the residuals from a regression with omitted variables will include a systematic component, reflecting the net influence of the omitted variables. Thus, the residuals from the suspect regression should be carefully examined to see if they are related to an omitted variable.[18]

Finally, there is the common situation where we know that a relevant variable ought to be included, but none is available. For instance, how can we measure the risk aversion of the market? Although we all see what we mean by this concept, there is no variable that explicitly measures it. The solution is then to replace the otherwise omitted variable by a proxy variable. Proxies are imperfect substitutes for the variables they replace. In our risk-aversion example, we could use as a proxy the inflows to equity mutual funds, or the spread between BBB and AAA bonds, or any other variable that tracks risk aversion closely. This introduces the possibility of *measurement error*, but the consequences of the latter are preferable to those of specification bias.

7.3.2   Extraneous variables

In a sense, the problem of extraneous variables is the opposite of the omitted variable bias. It occurs when the regression includes an independent variable that has no impact on the dependent variable.

Here again, two cases should be distinguished:

- If the extraneous variable is uncorrelated with the other independent variables, it will not interfere with the impact of the relevant variables on the dependent variable. So, there will be no bias. The undesired variable will be easily recognized by its low and non-significant t-stat. We then simply exclude the undesired variable and reassess the regression with the relevant, remaining variables only.
- If the extraneous variable is correlated with some of the other independent variables, its effect will be subtler. It will not interfere with the impact of the relevant variables on the dependent variable, but it will eat up one degree of freedom and make it harder for the equation to accurately "assign" the variance of Y to the X's and sort out the effects of independent variables. This will reduce the precision of the estimates.

In short, the problem of extraneous variables is less acute than that of omitted variables. With extraneous variables, OLS estimation still yields unbiased coefficient estimates and hypothesis testing continues to be valid; but the standard errors are larger (i.e. the coefficients are less precise) than if we had dropped the irrelevant variables.

To avoid the presence of extraneous variables, we need to apply common sense when defining the independent variables and carefully inspect their correlation with the dependent variable. If, despite these checks, we obtain a model with a high R^2 but very large uncertainty around the regression parameters, it is likely that some extraneous variable has slipped in.

---

[18] Unfortunately, the Ramsey test is a general misspecification test and does not distinguish between omitted variables and incorrect functional form.

7.3.3 Multi-collinearity

Commonly, different independent variables in a multiple regression model are related. However, when this relationship is too strong, some problems arise when testing and fitting the model. This is referred to as multi-collinearity. When two independent variables are highly correlated, they both convey essentially the same information. In this case, neither may contribute significantly to the model once the other has been included. But together they contribute a lot. So, the adjusted-R value is high (the overall model fits the data well), the p-value of the F-test is low (the good fit is unlikely to be a coincidence), but neither X variable makes a significant contribution. And if both variables were removed from the model, the fit would be much worse.

If the goal is simply to predict Y from a set of X variables, then multi-collinearity is not a great problem. The predictions will still be accurate, and the adjusted-R will quantify how well the model predicts the Y values. But if the goal is to understand how the various X variables impact Y, then multi-collinearity is a big problem. In particular, multi-collinearity increases the standard error of the estimates, which reduces the t-statistics and thus reduces the degree of confidence that can be placed in the estimates. The confidence intervals may even include zero, which means that you cannot even be confident that an increase in the X value is associated with an increase, or a decrease, in Y.

The only way out is to identify the variables that create the multi-collinearity and remove one of them. A basic approach is to calculate the correlation coefficient for each pair of predictor variables. Large correlation figures (both positive and negative) usually point to the source of the trouble.

7.3.4 Heteroscedasticity

One of the classical assumptions of regression analysis is that residuals are dispersed randomly and homogenously throughout the range of the estimated dependent variable – this feature is called homoscedasticity. Put another way, the variance of residual error should be constant for all values of the independent(s). If this assumption is violated, the errors are said to be heteroscedastic; it can be shown that the parameter estimates are still consistent but they are no longer efficient. Thus, inferences based on the standard errors are likely to be misleading.

There are several methods of testing the presence of heteroscedasticity. The most commonly used is the time-honored inspection of the residuals. This involves looking for patterns in a plot of the residuals from the regression. A homoscedastic model will display a uniform cloud of dots, whereas heteroscedasticity will result in patterns such as a funnel shape, indicating greater error as the dependent variable increases. More formal tests are the Breusch–Pagan (1979) test, the Goldfeld–Quandt test and White's (1980) general test.[19]

There are essentially two methods of dealing with heteroscedasticity: either (i) entirely re-specify the model; or (ii) use the *weighted least-squares* regression option. This is a regression technique in which smaller residuals are weighted more when calculating the regression coefficients' confidence intervals. In addition, most regression packages implement White's (1980) correction for heteroscedasticity. The correction computes the proper estimate of the variance when OLS is applied in the presence of heteroscedasticity, and uses it for inference.

---

[19] See Greene (2000) for more details on these tests.

7.3.5 Serial correlation

Last but not least, serial correlation is another well-known potential problem in regression analysis. One of the assumptions of OLS regression is that the disturbance term relating to any observation is not influenced by the disturbance term relating to any other observation. Put simply, the error terms of the OLS equation estimate must be distributed independently of each other and hence the covariance between any pair of error or residual terms must be zero. Should this covariance not be zero, then the residuals are said to be autocorrelated and a linear relationship between present and past error terms can be observed.

As an illustration, in a simple regression of Y on X, we would have

$$Y_t = a + (b \times X_t) + \varepsilon_t \tag{7.24}$$

but also

$$\varepsilon_t = \rho \varepsilon_{t-1} + \upsilon_t \tag{7.25}$$

As we can see, the error term ε is not independently distributed. Consequently, the regression estimates will still be unbiased, but inefficient – the variance of the errors will be seriously underestimated and the confidence intervals too large. Ergo, reliable inferences cannot be made from the regression results.

There are many causes of serial correlation in regressions involving time series data. In particular, there is usually some momentum effect built into most time series. This is particularly true for hedge funds that invest in non-liquid assets (e.g. distressed securities).

The test for serial correlation included in most software packages is the Durbin–Watson test, which detects only first-order serial correlation. It is calculated as

$$DW = \frac{\sum\limits_{t=2}^{N} (\varepsilon_t - \varepsilon_{t-1})^2}{\sum\limits_{t=2}^{N} \varepsilon_t^2} \tag{7.26}$$

where ε is the estimated residual from the OLS regression and N is the sample regression size. The value of DW ranges from 0 to 4. Values close to 0 indicate extreme positive serial correlation; values close to 4 indicate extreme negative serial correlation; values close to 2 indicate no serial correlation. As a rule of thumb, DW should be between 1.5 and 2.5 to indicate independence of observations.[20] Positive serial correlation means that standard errors of the coefficients are too small. Negative serial correlation means that standard errors are too large.

In addition to the Durbin–Watson test, there exist several other tests, depending on the type of serial correlation hypothesized. Most statistical and/or econometric software packages also enable the user to automatically correct for serial correlation, for instance by using generalized least squares (GLS) estimation rather than the usual ordinary least squares (OLS).[21]

---

[20] The exact critical values depend on the sample size. Please refer to Greene (2000).

[21] In the first iteration of GLS, the estimated OLS residuals are used to estimate the error covariance matrix. In the second iteration, GLS estimation minimizes the sum of squares of the residuals weighted by the inverse of the sample covariance matrix.

7.4 ALTERNATIVE REGRESSION APPROACHES

In addition to the traditional linear approach, a large number of alternative approaches to regression also exist.

7.4.1 Non-linear regression

In some instances, there may be reason to believe that changes in explanatory variables will have differential effects on the dependent variable as the values of the explanatory variables change. For instance, graphs of original data against a predictor, or residuals against a predictor, may show curvature or more generally a non-linear pattern. Failure to account for non-linearity can lead to either overstatement or understatement of the effect of a change in the value of an explanatory variable on the dependent variable. In that case, the use of a non-linear regression model should be considered.

The goal of non-linear regression is to adjust the values of the variables in the model to find the curve – and not the line – that best predicts Y from X. More simply, the goal is to find the curve that comes closest to the points. That is, the model minimizes the sum of the squares of the vertical distances of the points from the regression curve.

To use non-linear regression, a mathematical model based on some theory must first be defined. The first step is to choose a model. For instance, a *polynomial regression* fits data to this equation:

$$Y = a + (b_1 \times X) + (b_2 \times X^2) + \cdots + (b_k \times X^k) + \varepsilon \tag{7.27}$$

Any number of terms can be included. If we stop after the second term, it is called a first-order polynomial equation, which is identical to the equation for a straight line. If we stop after the third term, it is called a second-order, or quadratic, equation. If we stop after the fourth term, it is called a third-order, or cubic, equation.

Polynomial regression can be used to create a standard curve for interpolation, or to create a smooth curve for graphing. But polynomial regression is rarely useful in modeling a relationship, because it is highly unstable to extrapolate. The uncertainty increases as we approach the maximum and minimum values of our measurements; this is why the confidence bands become too wide in these regions. Hence, as a rule, power and other transform terms should be added only if there is a theoretical reason to do so. A further caveat is that fitting polynomial models almost invariably produces multi-collinearity problems. This can be countered by using centering when introducing power terms (subtracting the mean from each score, i.e. replacing X by $X - \bar{X}$). Correlation and unstandardized coefficients will not change as a result of centering.

7.4.2 Transformations

In the past, when non-linear regression was not readily available, researchers when necessary used to transform their data to make a linear graph, and then analyze the transformed data with linear regression. Our opinion of this approach is very simple: it is outdated and should not be used any more.

There are at least two reasons to avoid systematically transforming variables. First, linear regression assumes that the scatter of points around the line follows a normal distribution and that the standard deviation is the same at every value of X. These assumptions are not necessarily true with the transformed data. Thus, the results of the linear regression may be incorrect. Second, a transformation may alter the relationship between X and Y, in particular the bounded nature of some variables. This is likely to result in incorrect modeling. Thus, since non-linear regression is easy, there is no reason to force data into a linear form.

However, transformations can be very useful when appropriately used. Although it is usually inappropriate to analyze transformed data, it is often helpful to *display* data after a linear transform. The human eye and brain evolved to detect edges (lines), not to detect rectangular hyperbolas or exponential decay curves. Hence, transforming and plotting the transformed data is usually useful in discovering the nature of the original non-linear relationship.

7.4.3   Stepwise regression and automatic selection procedures

When using regression analysis, we usually want to reduce the number of explanatory variables so that the resulting regression equation is easy to understand, interpret and work with. Thus we only want to include the most significant variables. Overall, we want as few variables as possible in the final regression equation, while at the same time retaining the ability to effectively predict Y.

When there are a large number of potential explanatory variables for a multiple regression, there is no substitute for the use of good judgment in choosing which ones to include in the model. Testing all possible subsets of the set of potential independent variables is usually not feasible.[22] But there is a useful procedure, known as stepwise regression, which can aid by determining the statistically optimal combination of independent variables based solely on the t-statistics of their estimated coefficients.

There are essentially three modes of operation of stepwise regression:

- The *backward elimination* approach starts with all the independent variables in the model. At each step, at most one variable is eliminated from the model. For a variable to be eliminated: (i) it must have the smallest t-statistic of all variables still in the model and (ii) the t-statistic must be smaller than a specified threshold value. When all the variables remaining are significant, we are left with the regression equation.
- The *forward selection approach* starts with no independent variable – at first, the model only contains the intercept. At each step, only one variable can be added to the model. For a variable to be added: (i) it must have the largest t-statistic (in absolute value) when it alone has been added to the model and (ii) this t-statistic must be greater than a specified threshold value. The procedure stops when, of the variables not yet added, none have a t-statistic greater than the threshold value, or when there are no more variables to add.
- *Stepwise regression* combines forward selection and backward elimination in the following way. It starts with no independent variable – at first, the model only contains the intercept. At each step the forward selection method is used in an attempt to add a variable to the model. If no variables are added the process stops. After a variable has been added to a model already containing at least one variable, then one step of the backward elimination method is employed on the model containing all of the entered variables. If a variable is removed, it is returned to the collection of unentered variables and the process continues until no more variables are selected for inclusion or deletion.

---

[22] If there are K potential independent variables (besides the constant), then there are $2^K - 1$ distinct sub-sets of them to be tested (counting the full set but excluding the empty set which corresponds to the mean model).

Properly used, stepwise regression puts more power and information at the user's fingertips than does the ordinary multiple regression option. It is especially useful for sifting through large numbers of potential independent variables and/or fine-tuning a model by poking variables in or out. However, improperly used, it may converge on a poor model while giving a false sense of security. It is a bit like doing carpentry with a chain saw: you can get a lot of work done quickly, but you may end up doing more harm than good if you don't read the instructions, keep cool and maintain a firm grip on the controls.

In addition, it is wise to remember that a model selected by automatic methods can only find the "best" combination from among the set of variables included: if some important variables or lags or transformations thereof are omitted, no amount of searching or ranking will compensate. Furthermore, stepwise regression has severe problems in the presence of collinearity – it will not necessarily produce the best model if there are redundant predictors.

Hierarchical multiple regression is similar to stepwise regression but the researcher, not the computer, determines the order of entry of the variables. F-tests are used to compute the significance of each added variable (or set of variables) to the explanation reflected in R^2.

7.4.4   Non-parametric regression

Non-parametric regression, also known as non-parametric smoothing or local regression, is a variant of regression analysis that builds on classical methods, such as linear and non-linear least squares regression. However, in contrast to these techniques, non-parametric regression makes minimal assumptions about the dependence of the average Y on the X's.

With non-parametric regression, we simply assume that the dependent variable Y is explained by a function $f(\cdot)$ of the independent variable(s):

$$Y = f(X_1, \ldots, X_k) + \varepsilon \tag{7.28}$$

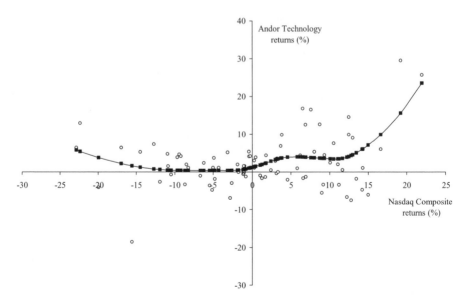

Figure 7.13   LOWESS regression of Andor Technology monthly returns versus the Nasdaq Composite monthly returns, October 1996 to July 2003

but the function $f(\cdot)$ is left unspecified.[23] The goal is precisely to estimate the shape of the regression function $f(\cdot)$ directly by a data-driven technique rather than to estimate parameters.

There are numerous techniques for non-parametric regression, particularly when there is only one independent variable. One of the most popular is called LOWESS (locally weighted smoothing scatter plots, sometimes called LOESS). It combines much of the simplicity of linear least squares regression with the flexibility of non-linear regression. The idea of LOWESS is to fit a low-degree polynomial at each point in a data set. The fit is particular, in the sense that (i) it only considers a sub-set of the data (the closest data points to the current point) and (ii) it uses weighted least squares, i.e. it gives more weight to points near the current point and less weight to points further away.

In general, the local polynomials' fit to each sub-set of the data is almost always of first or second degree, that is, either locally linear (in the straight line sense) or locally quadratic. Using a zero-degree polynomial turns LOWESS into a weighted moving average. Higher degree polynomials tend to overfit the data in each sub-set and are numerically unstable, making accurate computations difficult.

As an illustration, Figure 7.13 displays the result of a LOWESS regression with a polynomial of degree two applied to Andor Technology, over the October 1996 to July 2003 period. The output of LOWESS, as for most non-parametric regressions, is a function that fits the data well, but is not easily represented by a mathematical formula. This makes it difficult to transfer the results of an analysis to other people. In order to transfer the regression function to another person, we would need the data set and software for LOWESS calculations.

---

[23] Although most methods of non-parametric regression implicitly assume that $f(\cdot)$ is a smooth, continuous function – see Cleveland (1979) and Cleveland and Devlin (1988).

8
Asset Pricing Models

Finance is the only place where one can win a Nobel prize by linearizing.

On the surface, the relationship between risk and return seems straightforward: both should move in the same direction. A rational investor should accept a higher risk only if it is rewarded by a higher expected return, and decreasing risk should result in lower expected returns.

In practice, risk is usually approximated to volatility, which is a measure of uncertainty. Yet, risk and uncertainty are not exactly the same concept. In the case of risk, we know all the possible outcomes and the probability of their occurring, but we do not know which outcome will occur for sure. In the case of uncertainty, on the other hand, we are unaware either of the possible outcomes or of the probability of their occurring, or both. In a sense, risk and uncertainty are polar extremes, but many situations in the real world have elements of both: we usually believe that we have some knowledge of both probabilities and outcomes. In this context, quantifying precisely the risk–return relationship is hard – if we knew exactly how and when risk is rewarded, it would not be called risk any more.

Investing without knowing what the risks are and how much reward we can expect for taking them is a daunting task. Fortunately, financial theory includes a large body of research called asset pricing, which focuses uniquely on formalizing the relationship between risk and expected returns. For instance, asset pricing explains why the long-term expected return on a short-term government bond should be smaller than the long-term expected return on a stock, or more generally, why two different assets have different expected returns. In addition, asset pricing can help us understand why expected returns may change with time and how the returns on various assets vary together.

Asset pricing has the particularity of being a self-sufficient field of research. Theorists develop models with testable predictions, and empiricists document pricing puzzles. That is, they identify stylized facts that fail to fit established pricing theories and these facts then stimulate the development of new theories. Thanks to this fertile cycle, over the last 50 years, asset pricing has given birth to some of the greatest success stories of neo-classical economic analysis. Among these, we may cite the Capital Asset Pricing Model (CAPM), the Arbitrage Pricing Theory (APT) and the Black–Scholes (1973) option pricing formula. All these models have provided answers and insights that are now indispensable not only to researchers but also to all practitioners in financial markets. Part of their success is obviously attributable to their ability to identify arbitrage opportunities and generate trading ideas. If a market does not obey a model's predictions, academics usually decide that the model needs improvement and go back to work. But practitioners are happy to live with the idea that markets are sometimes wrong and do not price correctly some assets, because it means potential trading opportunities for the shrewd investor.

The taxonomy of asset pricing models comprises two major categories, namely, absolute pricing models and relative pricing models. Absolute pricing models are most common in academic settings. They include fundamental equilibrium models and consumption-based models, as well as most macroeconomic models. Absolute pricing models price each asset individually, by reference to its exposure to fundamental sources of risk. They use asset pricing theory positively to give an economic explanation for why prices are what they are and why agents have such risk exposures, or in order to predict how prices might change if the policy or economic structure changes. Relative pricing models, in contrast, should be considered as a means of exploring the evidence rather than of arriving at a profound behavioral explanation of financial markets. In a sense, they aim at providing a simple representation of how the world works. They price each asset by reference to the prices of some other assets, which are exogenous – the pricing model does not ask where they come from. The Black–Scholes formula is a classic illustration of such a model. It calculates an option price as a function of its underlying asset price, regardless of whether the latter is fairly valued by the market or not.

Not surprisingly, pure theoreticians of finance dislike relative pricing models. They claim that only absolute pricing is worthy of study. Summers (1985), for example, compares financial economists with "ketchup economists", obsessed only with the relative prices and interrelationships between different sized bottles of ketchup. He concludes, "They ignore what seems to many to be the more important question of what determines the overall level of asset prices". Needless to say, most practitioners strongly disagree with that opinion. On a day-to-day basis, they need positive and pragmatic models that capture the way the world works, not normative models that state how the world should be. It is naturally this path that we will explore in this chapter.

Most of the asset pricing models we consider below are relatively simple. All fall into the relative pricing category. They price hedge funds relative to the market or other risk factors, and do not really focus on what determines the underlying factors, the market or factor risk premium, or the risk exposures taken by hedge fund managers. Hence, they are relatively easy to understand and apply in practice, provided enough data is available. Most of them are based on a two-step approach.

First, they assume that hedge fund returns are specific functions of carefully selected macro- and microeconomic factors. The selection of relevant factors and the determination of the relationship that links them to fund returns is the key to this approach. Just because a certain fundamental characteristic aligns with past performance does not mean that this characteristic represents a systematic risk factor that the market compensates with some return. This is precisely where the difference between correlation and asset pricing models lies.

Second, using multiple regression analysis, they assess the sensitivity of hedge fund returns to these factors and attempt to validate or invalidate empirically their initial assumption. It is important to realize at this stage that testing any asset pricing model is in fact a joint test of market efficiency *and* of the validity of the pricing model. Since we do not know if the asset pricing model in question is valid, the acquisition of returns in excess of what the model says may indicate that the hypothesized model is wrong and not that the market is inefficient.

8.1   WHY DO WE NEED A FACTOR MODEL?

Before going any further, let us explain briefly why factor models are useful, not only for asset pricing, but also for portfolio management, risk measurement and, more generally, for any discipline that needs information about the co-movements of different assets (i.e. uses the covariance and/or the correlation matrix).

8.1.1 The dimension reduction

Technically, an asset pricing factor model does no more than condense the dynamics of a large series of fund returns into a smaller series of explanatory factors, whose influence is common to all funds. In a sense, the small set of factors and factor exposures[1] provides a parsimonious representation of the large set of funds. That is, it explains most of the variance and covariance of the funds considered.

To understand the importance of this dimension reduction, consider the following example. Suppose we have to monitor a universe of $N = 1000$ hedge funds. We may decide to analyze each individual hedge fund and its particularities rather than trying to build a "one-size-fits-all" factor model. And when building portfolios, we may simply analyze the correlation or covariance between the returns of all funds, so that we can figure out which funds will complement well other funds in terms of diversification. However, monitoring a universe of a thousand funds implies estimating (among other things) a covariance matrix of one million terms ($N \times N$). Even bearing in mind that the covariance matrix is symmetrical, so that we only need to estimate $N \times (N - 1)/2$ terms, this still represents 499 500 terms. This is a manifestation of the so-called curse of dimensionality. The time series necessary to estimate so many parameters from historical data with an acceptable degree of measurement error is enormous, as is the computation time. And we have not yet talked about out-of-sample forecasting, which is necessary to build portfolios with a good diversification of risks in the future! Clearly, we have to find another approach.

The element that requires the largest number of estimates is the covariance matrix. It is therefore the crux of the matter. To simplify the analysis of individual funds as well as the process of portfolio construction, we need to simplify the estimation of the covariance matrix. One possible solution is to make some simplifying assumptions about its structure, that is, assumptions about the interrelationships among funds. This is exactly what factor analysis does. Factor analysis determines from a statistical perspective the interrelationships among a large number of variables (e.g., fund returns) and expresses these interrelationships in terms of their common underlying dimensions (the factors). The output of factor analysis is a factor model, where the return of each fund is represented as the sum of two mutually orthogonal components: a component that is common to all funds, and a component that is idiosyncratic to each fund. The common component is driven by a small number of factors that influence all the funds in the model. The idiosyncratic component is driven by fund-specific shocks.

As mentioned already, the advantage of factor analysis is the dimensionality reduction. Factor analysis condenses the information contained in a large number of original variables into a smaller set of factors with minimum loss of information. Say, for instance, that we are able to identify $K = 5$ factors that explain most of the behavior of our $N = 1000$ funds. In this case, we just need to estimate how our funds react to our five factors (i.e. 5000 coefficients) as well as what is the covariance structure of our factors (i.e. 10 coefficients). We have reduced the dimensionality of the problem from 499 500 estimates to 5010. Although the latter number is still large, it is much more reasonable than the former.

In practice, the use of factor analysis is supported by the observation that hedge fund returns tend to react together to some extent, particularly if we consider funds following the same type of strategy. This confirms the intuition that fund returns are likely to be affected by the same factors at the same time. Therefore, it is meaningful to attempt to capture the common behavior

---

[1] In econometric jargon, "factor exposures" are sometimes called "factor loadings".

of a series of funds by one or several factors. As we will see shortly, factor models lie at the heart of modern portfolio management and risk analysis, both for backward-looking portfolio evaluation and for forward-looking portfolio structuring and rebalancing. In particular:

- A factor model is useful in understanding why a portfolio had a certain return over a particular period of time. It throws light on the risks taken by an investment manager to achieve those returns and provides a decomposition of returns in terms of various bets made by the manager by over- or underweighting the exposure to certain risk factors.
- A factor model is essential for certain investment strategies that need to precisely attribute the risk to different sources. For instance, this is the case for indexing (where one tries to replicate some risk exposure) or market neutral portfolios (where zero exposure to specific sources of risk should be maintained continuously).
- A factor model is necessary to predict return, volatility and correlation figures in a consistent way. In particular, a factor model can capture time-varying features of volatility and achieve more accurate forward-looking risk forecasts.
- A factor model should help identify the value added by the manager over a passive portfolio.

However, to be effective, a factor model has to possess a minimum number of properties. First, it must be feasible to estimate its parameters in a reasonable amount of time. Second, it has to be intuitive to use. Third, it has to be parsimonious enough in terms of number of factors to avoid overfitting and guarantee adequate out-of-sample performance. And finally, it must reflect commonalities in fund returns in order to reduce noise and to achieve the decompositions desired in making investment decisions such as hedging, benchmarking, performance attribution and segmented analysis.

An important point to consider with factor models is whether we need a predictive model, an explanatory model, or both. The distinction is important, because explaining past covariance and forecasting future covariance are completely different activities. Using the same factor model for both predictive and explanatory purposes implicitly assumes that fund returns are influenced by factors that persist over time, and that there is some stability in factor exposures. So far, the vast majority of factor models suggested in the literature have employed *ex post* (observed) returns as a proxy for expected returns. In theory, this should not be a problem because the two series should converge. However, in practice, the rate of convergence critically depends on the assumption of rational agents' expectations, which itself is not necessarily guaranteed in environments in which investors have limited amounts of data and attempt to understand the complicated dynamics of the underlying economy. In the following discussion, we concentrate essentially on explanatory factors. We therefore express all our models in *ex post* form, i.e. we do not consider expectations. We revert later to the question of forecasting and predictability of hedge fund returns.

8.2   LINEAR SINGLE-FACTOR MODELS

Since the time of Newton, common scientific expertise has advanced by using linear equations to model most natural phenomena. It is therefore not surprising that the first asset pricing models we are going to consider are linear with respect to their factors. That is, they postulate that rates of return on all funds are related linearly to a set of K factors. This offers the advantage of being able to use linear regression analysis to estimate the parameters of the model.

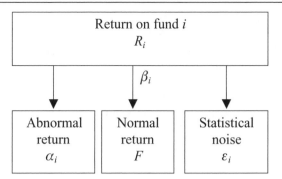

Figure 8.1   The three sources of return and risk in a single-factor model

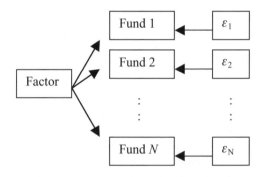

Figure 8.2   Fund returns are only related to each other through their common relationship with the factor

8.2.1   Single-factor asset pricing models

The simplest asset pricing model uses only one factor ($K = 1$) and expresses the return on each fund as a linear function of a factor F. Thus, fund returns are only related to each other through their common relationship with the factor F. In this case, we can write

$$R_i = \alpha_i + \beta_i \cdot F + \varepsilon_i \tag{8.1}$$

where α_i and β_i are parameters to be estimated, and ε_i denotes an idiosyncratic error term, which is assumed to be zero on average and uncorrelated with the common factor. Estimates of α_i and β_i are usually obtained by regression analysis, and usual statistical significance tests may be used to confirm that $\alpha_i \neq 0$ and $\beta_i \neq 0$, as well as to confirm the quality of the model fit. Such a single-factor model may easily be represented as a graph – see Figure 8.1. The "abnormal" return denotes the portion of the return not related to factor F, as opposed to the "normal" return.

Note that the model is silent about what factor F represents. Whatever the factor may be, it merely asserts that there exists an approximate linear relationship between factor F and the rate of return on *each* fund – see Figure 8.2. Stated differently, fund returns are only related to each other through their common relationship with the factor.

Single-factor models provide a simple but effective framework for understanding and predicting returns. Other things being equal, a 1% variation in the factor is expected to result in a $\beta_i\%$ variation in the return of fund i. Hence, beta is really a factor exposure indicator. A higher beta means more reaction to factor movements, while a lower beta means less reaction. Knowledge of the future value of F could be used to predict asset returns, albeit not perfectly given the presence of the random error term.

Single-factor models also provide a very simple framework for understanding and predicting risk. By construction, the three components of returns in Figure 8.1 are not correlated with each other. Calculating the variance of both sides of equation (8.1) and eliminating constant terms yields:

$$\sigma_i^2 = \beta_F^2 \sigma_F^2 + \sigma_{\varepsilon_i}^2 \tag{8.2}$$

which may be interpreted as:

Total fund variance = Factor-related variance + Specific variance

This risk decomposition is a very useful way of thinking about risk. However, it is entirely dependent on the assumption that $\mathrm{Corr}[\varepsilon_i; F] = 0$, which in turn depends very much on the validity of the model specification.

8.2.2 Example: the CAPM and the market model

The granddaddy of all single-factor models is the CAPM due to Sharpe (1964), for which he shared a Nobel Prize in 1990. It is by no means the only single-factor asset pricing model, nor is it necessarily the best, but it remains the most widely known and applied.

Rather than modeling rates of return, the CAPM considers *risk premium*, i.e. the expected excess return above the risk-free rate. Under a certain number of assumptions, the CAPM says that at equilibrium, the risk premium of fund i should be linearly related to the market risk premium. Algebraically:

$$R_i - R_F = \alpha_i + \beta_i \cdot (R_M - R_F) + \varepsilon_i \tag{8.3}$$

where R_i is the return on fund i, R_F is the risk-free rate and R_M is the return on the market portfolio.[2] This model is also called the market model, or the security market line. Intuitively, it simply says that the return on the ith fund is made up of three components (Figure 8.3):

- A "normal return", which corresponds to the fair reward for the market risk to which the portfolio is exposed. This risk premium of a fund depends on both the risk premium of the market itself (measured by $R_M - R_F$) and the sensitivity of the fund to the factor (measured by β_i).
- An "abnormal return", which is the value added by the manager, which can be positive, negative or nil. In practice, the abnormal return is often called the alpha (α_i) of the fund. According to the CAPM, alpha should be zero. Active managers attempt to seek incremental returns with a positive alpha, while passive managers will simply try to track the normal return and display an alpha equal to zero.
- Some statistical noise, which corresponds to the residual return (ε_i). The role of ε_i is to allow unexplained forces to affect randomly the rate of return.

---

[2] According to theory, the market portfolio should be the value-weighted portfolio of all available risky assets including financial assets, real assets and even human capital. However, since we cannot readily observe the returns on such a portfolio, a stock index (such as the S&P 500) is usually used in practice as a proxy measure of market return – in which case R_M denotes the return on the index portfolio used as a proxy.

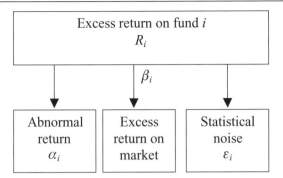

Figure 8.3   The three sources of return on a risky asset in the market model

8.2.3 Application: the market model and hedge funds

From a theoretical point of view, the CAPM represents an almost perfect blend of elegance and simplicity. Beta is an intuitively appealing measure of risk, whether one takes it as an asset's contribution to total societal risk or the part of risk that cannot be diversified away. From an empirical point of view, the model appears to be readily testable. Betas are easily estimated from standard time series regressions and a linear risk–return trade-off seems to be tailor-made for empirical testing.

Black *et al.* (1972), Blume and Friend (1973) and Fama and MacBeth (1973) produced the first extensive tests of the model and confirmed a remarkably linear relationship between beta and the monthly returns on US equities. This tended to support the CAPM, at least empirically. Later, however, Roll (1977) criticized empirical tests of the CAPM and made a number of relevant objections about its testability in general.[3] More recently, a number of researchers have evidenced the fact that multi-factor models perform better than single-factor models in explaining stock returns. We will focus on these models in the next section.

On the hedge fund side, the application of the market model has produced mixed results. Remember that one of the raisons d'être of alternative assets is to be non-correlated with traditional equity markets. Hence, when estimating the market model for a hedge fund, we often obtain regressions that have a low explanatory power, particularly when we consider funds outside the long/short equity category. As an illustration, we have estimated equation (8.3) for the five funds we considered in Chapter 4. The results are shown in Table 8.1. We see clearly that Funds 3 and 5, which hold essentially long and short positions in US equities, have the highest R^2 (0.54 and 0.42, respectively) of our sample, and display a statistically significant positive exposure to the US stock market. Fund 2, which is also invested in long and short positions in US equities, has a statistically significant positive exposure to the US stock market, but this exposure only captures a limited part of its behavior, as illustrated by the low R^2 (0.21). Fund 1, which is a fund of funds essentially invested in long/short

---

[3] Roll's objections can be summarized as follows:

- The *ex ante* linear relation of risk and return cannot be questioned by tests using *ex post* data. *Ex ante* and *ex post* returns are different quantities.
- The tests of the CAPM are tautological and follow from the mathematics of the efficient set of portfolios (i.e. the set of portfolios that provide the best possible return for a given level of volatility). In fact, there will always exist a linear relationship between the expected return of an asset and its beta with respect to an efficient portfolio.
- The total composition of the real market portfolio – and not of the market index used as a proxy – would have to be known for a test of the theoretical model that includes it as a variable.

Table 8.1   The market model applied to hedge funds (an asterisk indicates coefficients that are significantly different from zero at 95% confidence)

	α_i	β_i	R^2
Fund 1	0.36	0.19*	0.16
Fund 2	0.43	0.64*	0.21
Fund 3	0.54*	0.43*	0.54
Fund 4	0.59	0.06	0.02
Fund 5	4.09*	2.08*	0.42

Table 8.2   The market model applied to the CSFB/Tremont hedge fund indices, January 1994 to July 2002 (an asterisk indicates coefficients that are significantly different from zero at 95% confidence)

	α_i	β_i	R^2
Hedge fund index	0.36	0.25*	0.22
Global macro	0.69*	0.18*	0.05
Managed futures	0.31	−0.19*	0.06
Long/short equity	0.37	0.4*	0.33
Emerging markets	−0.06	0.54*	0.23
Dedicated short bias	0.01	−0.87*	0.59
Event-driven: distressed	0.51*	0.24*	0.29
Event-driven: risk arbitrage	0.2	0.12*	0.18
Event-driven: multi-strategy	0.31	0.19*	0.22
Convertible arbitrage	0.41*	0.04	0.01
Fixed income arbitrage	0.14	0.01	0.00
Equity market neutral	0.41*	0.08*	0.15

equity managers, presents the same type of results. Finally, Fund 4, which is an arbitrage fund, is almost unrelated to the market (R^2 equals 0.02) and has no statistically significant coefficient.

We repeated the same analysis on the CSFB/Tremont hedge fund indices. The results are summarized in Table 8.2. With the exception of dedicated short bias funds, all R^2 are lower than 0.50. Long/short equity, emerging market and event-driven are the only strategies where the market model still has a small explanatory power. For the arbitrage-type strategies, the market model seems irrelevant.

8.3   LINEAR MULTI-FACTOR MODELS

It is utopian to believe that rates of return on all available hedge funds (and hence, their covariance) can be satisfactorily explained by a single factor, whatever that factor may be. Hedge fund managers have different investment styles and opportunities, trade in multiple markets, take long and short positions, and use varying degrees of leverage. Hence, for most applications, a single-factor model will be too restrictive and will do a poor job at explaining hedge fund returns. Intuitively, there is more than one systematic risk factor in the picture. This is precisely where multi-factor models come in.

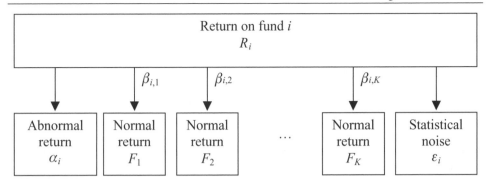

Figure 8.4   The sources of the return on a risky asset in a multi-factor model

8.3.1   Multi-factor models

Multi-factor models can be viewed as a natural extension of single-factor models. Simply stated, linear multi-factor models postulate that rates of return on all available funds (and hence, their covariance) are explained by a linear function of *several* variables, the so-called "factors". In its most generic form, a K-factor model can be written as:

$$R_i = \alpha_i + \beta_{i,1} \cdot F_1 + \beta_{i,2} \cdot F_2 + \cdots + \beta_{i,K} \cdot F_K + \varepsilon_i \tag{8.4}$$

or equivalently:

$$R_i = \alpha_i + \sum_{j=1}^{K} \beta_{i,j} \cdot F_j + \varepsilon_i \tag{8.5}$$

where R_i represents the return on the ith fund, $K > 0$ is the number of factors, $F_1, \ldots, F_K$ are the values of the factors, $\beta_{i,1}, \ldots, \beta_{i,K}$ are the corresponding sensitivities, and ε_i is a zero mean random variable (Figure 8.4). The particular case of $K = 1$ corresponds to the single-factor model we saw previously.

Moving from a single- to a multiple-factor asset pricing model is conceptually easy and intellectually appealing. Most of the results from the single-factor case carry over to multiple-factor models – only the notation becomes a little messier. However, the shift raises two important questions. First, how many factors are to be considered? Second, how should we determine these factors? The answers to these two questions are intimately linked and depend on the methodology used to build the factor model. In practice, there are essentially two main approaches used to identify factors, namely, principal component analysis (PCA) and common factor analysis (CFA).

8.3.2   Principal component analysis

Principal component analysis is a well-established statistical technique for exploring the (unknown) nature of the factor structure that is hidden behind some data set. It has applications in several fields such as data compression, visualization, exploratory data analysis, pattern recognition, time series prediction and of course finance. In this section, we do not examine in detail the computational aspects of PCA, but rather provide an intuitive introduction to this important technique.[4]

---

[4] See Kendall (1980).

8.3.2.1   A primer on PCA

From a mathematical standpoint, the goal of PCA is to explain the behavior of a number of correlated variables using a smaller number of uncorrelated and unobserved implied variables or implicit factors called *principal components*. Each implicit factor is defined as a linear combination of original variables, so that the set of principal components reproduces the original information present in the correlation structure. That is, the first principal component is the linear combination of the original variables that accounts for as much variation in the data as possible. Each succeeding principal component is the new linear combination of the original variables that accounts for as much of the remaining unexplained variation as possible, and is independent of the preceding principal components.

As an illustration, say we have a sample of N hedge funds and P measurable parameters for each of them. Examples of such parameters are the assets under management, the time since inception, the average return and the volatility over the last three years, the returns over a particular number of months, etc. Now, say N and P are so large that it is unwieldy and impractical to analyze how these P parameters are related to each other. We obviously cannot look at all the possible correlations and scatter plots, because of the excessive number of parameters and funds. We would therefore like some objective means of reducing the variables to a manageable number, while at the same time preserving as much of the variability in the data as possible. This is precisely where PCA comes into action. Basically, PCA looks for sets of parameters that are always highly correlated. Then PCA creates a new parameter by grouping (linear combination) these correlated parameters, therefore reducing the dimensionality of parameters without losing too much information. One drawback of the technique is that the new parameters do not have a direct economic interpretation.

One aspect that is often scrutinized is the *number of implied factors* that are relevant in PCA. At most, there can be as many possible principal components as there are variables. That is, to reproduce the total system variability of the original N variables, we need N principal components. However, we have to remember that principal components are extracted in decreasing order of importance. Consequently, the first few principal components usually account for a large proportion of the variance in the sample. In fact, since principal components are chosen solely for their ability to explain risk, a given number of implicit factors always capture a larger part of the asset return variance–covariance than the same number of explicit factors. Therefore, a standard approach to deciding when to stop extracting principal components is to generate a scree plot as suggested by Cattell (1966). The scree plot is a two-dimensional graph with all components on the x-axis and eigenvalues on the y-axis. Eigenvalues represent the variance accounted for by each principal component expressed as a score that totals the number of items.[5] The eigenvalues are typically arranged in a scree plot in descending order like in Figure 8.5.

From the scree plot you can see that the first couple of factors account for most of the variance, then the remaining factors all have small eigenvalues. You can thus choose the number of principal components to use depending on how much variance you want to explain. Therefore selecting the number of factors involves a certain amount of subjective judgment.[6]

---

[5] That is, the total of all the eigenvalues will be N if there are N items in the data sample, so some factors will have smaller eigenvalues. If the first factor has an eigenvalue of N_1, it accounts for $N_1/N\%$ of the variance of the data sample.

[6] Another approach is called the Kaiser–Guttman rule and simply states that the number of principal components is equal to the number of factors with eigenvalues greater than 1.0. An eigenvalue greater than 1.0 indicates that principal components account for more variance than accounted for by one of the original variables in standardized data. This is commonly used as a cut-off point for which principal components are retained.

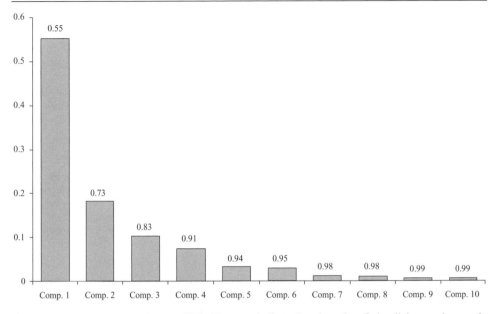

Figure 8.5   The scree plot for the CSFB/Tremont indices. For the sake of simplicity, we have only represented the first 10 components

Figure 8.5 shows the scree plot that we obtained when applying PCA to the time series of returns of the 12 CSFB/Tremont hedge fund indices since their creation. The scree plot indicates that the 12 indices (which cover all investment styles) share a common component, which explains 55% of the variance of the data sample. There is also a second common component that is orthogonal to the first component (by construction) and explains an additional 18% of the variance. Together, the first and second components explain 73% of what is happening. Adding a third component would raise the explanatory power to 83.2%, etc. In total, we could go up to 12 components and explain 100% of the variance.

Once the number of factors is chosen, the next step is the *extraction of the principal components* from the considered data sample. As mentioned already, these principal components are linear functions of the original variables.[7] In the CSFB/Tremont index, the first principal component is defined as

$$PCA_1 = (0.253 \times \text{Tremont general}) + (0.219 \times \text{Tremont global macro})$$

$$+ (0.347 \times \text{Tremont long/short equity}) + (0.584 \times \text{Tremont emerging markets})$$

$$- (0.571 \times \text{Tremont dedicated short}) + (0.197 \times \text{Tremont distressed})$$

$$+ (0.189 \times \text{Tremont multi-strategy})$$

Although it may seem hard to identify what PCA_1 effectively represents, a rapid correlation analysis evidences that it has a correlation of 0.71 with the MSCI World and 0.75 with the Nasdaq Composite. It is therefore likely to represent some sort of equity market indicator. A similar analysis can then be applied to the second component, the third, etc.

To understand what these components represent, it is useful to use a geometric representation. Consider again the sample of N hedge funds and P measurable characteristics. We can

---

[7] The weights to compute the uncorrelated principal components are called eigenvectors.

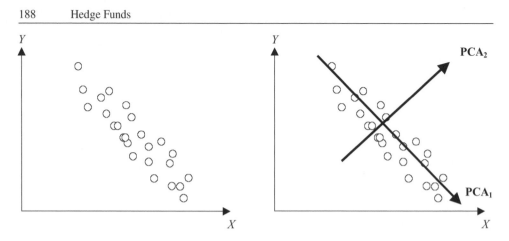

Figure 8.6 A geometric interpretation of what principal components represent in a two-dimensional space

represent the N funds by a large cloud in a P-dimensional space. If two or more character-istics are correlated, the cloud will be elongated along some direction in the P-dimensional hyperspace defined by their axes. PCA will identify this extended direction and form the first principal component. Next, we consider the $(P - 1)$-dimensional hyperplane orthogonal to the first component and search for the direction in the $(P - 1)$-space that represents the greatest variability. This defines the second principal component. The process is continued, defining a total of P orthogonal directions.

As an illustration, Figure 8.6 shows what happens with only two measurable characteristics ($N = 22$, $P = 2$). The first component (PCA$_1$) can be seen as a sort of regression line, which gives an optimal (in the mean square sense) linear reduction of dimension from two to one dimensions. The second component (PCA$_2$) is orthogonal to PCA$_1$. Note that this graph also illustrates the major drawback of PCA, i.e. the extreme difficulty in interpreting what the prin-cipal components (i.e. the new axes PCA$_1$ and PCA$_2$) effectively represent from an economic perspective.

The final step of PCA is usually the *rotation of the original axes*. For example, in our scatter plot we can think of the regression line as the original x-axis, rotated so that it approximates the regression line. This type of rotation is called variance maximizing because the criterion for (goal of) the rotation is to maximize the variance (variability) of the "new" variable (factor) while minimizing the variance around the new variable. In general, the idea is to rotate the axes in a more convenient direction without changing the relative locations of the points to each other.

The popularity of PCA comes essentially from two properties. First, PCA is the optimal (in terms of mean squared error) linear scheme for compressing a set of high-dimensional vari-ables into a set of lower-dimensional variables and then reconstructing. Second, the principal components can be constructed directly using either original multivariate data sets or using the covariance or the correlation matrix if the original data set is not available.[8]

---

[8] The correlation matrix is commonly used when different variables in the data set are measured using different units or if different variables have different variances. In a sense, it is equivalent to standardizing the variables to zero mean and unit standard deviation. This standardization is recommended for hedge funds because of their different degrees of leverage. After standardization, hedge fund returns can be compared irrespective of different degrees of leverage.

8.3.2.2   Application to hedge funds

Fung and Hsieh (1997a) were the first authors to use PCA to extract a set of implicit factors for hedge funds and to provide a quantitative classification scheme based on returns alone. Their idea is simply that if a group of managers follow the same strategy on the same markets, their returns should be correlated to each other, even though they may not be linearly correlated to the returns of asset markets. The advantage of using PCA in such a case is that it subsumes the inherent non-linearity of hedge fund returns and easily identifies the set of common factors.

Using a database provided by TASS Asset Management, AIG Global Investors and Paradigm LDC, Fung and Hsieh found that the first five principal components jointly explain about 43% of the cross-sectional variation in hedge fund returns. The good news is that by analyzing the qualitative self-description of the respective strategies of the funds that are correlated with the first five principal components, Fung and Hsieh were able to assign meaningful names to each of these principal components. The first component consists of funds applying a trend-following strategy on diversified markets, i.e. managed futures and commodity trading advisors. The second component represents global/macro funds. The third component is made up of long/short equity funds. The fourth component corresponds to funds that apply a trend-following style with an emphasis on major currencies. The fifth component is made up of distressed securities funds. Interestingly, the majority of market neutral and non-directional funds fall into the unexplained category in the principal component analysis.

More recently, Christiansen *et al.* (2003) applied a similar approach to the Zurich Alternative Investment Performance Database/CISDM (the former MAR database). They also identified five orthogonal components, but were able to explain more than 60% of the cross-sectional variation in hedge fund returns. The first component explains 24.92% of the variance (versus 11.87% in Fung and Hsieh) and essentially corresponds to long/short equity strategies. The remaining four components explain 12.65%, 10.80%, 7.04% and 4.65% of the variance versus 10.00%, 9.42%, 6.35% and 4.93%, respectively in the Fung and Hsieh analysis. The second component is identified as event-driven strategies, the third component is global macro and the fourth component is dominated by market neutral strategies mainly based on long/short US equity. Finally, the fifth component regroups funds active in the relative value arbitrage.

Amenc and Martellini (2001b, 2003a) suggested another extremely interesting application of passive hedge fund index or "index of the indexes indices". We already briefly introduced their methodology in Chapter 5. In fact, their approach is a natural generalization of the idea of taking an equally weighted portfolio of competing indices. Namely, they are looking for a portfolio of competing indices, where the portfolio weights make the combination of indices capture the largest possible fraction of the information contained in the data from the various competing indices. Technically speaking, this amounts to using the first component of a PCA of competing indices as a candidate for a pure style index. This first component typically captures a large proportion of cross-sectional variations because competing indices tend to be at least somewhat positively correlated. By construction, the resulting indices (one for each of the 13 strategies) have a higher degree of representation and stability of hedge fund performance than the individual indices already available on the market.

8.3.3   Common factor analysis

Common factor analysis is usually what people mean when they say factor analysis. The goal of common factor analysis is similar to PCA, that is, to transform a number of correlated variables into a smaller number of uncorrelated variables called *factors*. However, unlike PCA, the selected factors are observable and explicitly specified by a mix of explanatory and/or confirmatory analyses[9] rather than implied by the data. The number of factors, which should be kept as small as possible to maximize the benefits of dimensionality reduction, is often a trade-off between goodness-of-fit and overfitting. Most of the time, this crucial parameter is also assumed rather than being determined by the data.[10]

8.3.3.1 Examples of typical factors

Very often, with common factor analysis, the final choice of factors is done on an ad hoc basis. The standard criterion is to choose variables that are thought most likely to influence asset returns. Here again, quantitative analysts have a lot to gain by communicating with qualitative analysts, who talk to fund managers and may have relevant suggestions about which factors to use. Of course, quantitative analysts should also look at the empirical asset pricing literature. For many years, academics have been hunting for factors that would help explain the cross-section of expected returns. For instance, among the usual candidates for stock portfolios are the market value of equity or market capitalization (size) suggested by Banz (1981) and Reinganum (1981), the book-to-market ratio suggested by Stattman (1980), the leverage suggested by Bhandari (1988), the earnings-to-price ratio suggested by Basu (1983) and the stock liquidity suggested by Amihud (2002), among others. Recognizing that some of these factors are highly correlated (e.g. book-to-market ratio and leverage), several academics have suggested parsimonious extensions to the original market model. We will review two of them in greater detail, because they have shaped asset pricing research in recent years. One is Fama and French's (1992, 1996) research on the size and book-to-market factors, and the other is Jegadeesh and Titman's (1993) and Carhart's (1997) research on the momentum factor.

8.3.3.2 Size and book-to-market

Eugene Fama and Kenneth French, two professors at the University of Chicago, published a series of empirical studies that historically dealt the most damaging blow to both the CAPM and single-factor models. Fama and French monitored 9500 US stocks from 1963 to 1990, and observed that two classes of stocks tended to do better on average than the market as a whole: (i) small caps and (ii) stocks with a high book value-to-price ratio, customarily called "value stocks" in contrast to "growth stocks". Hence, Fama and French suggested including size and book-to-market ratio as remunerated risk factors to obtain a three-factor asset pricing model.

Their model is:

$$E(R_i) = R_F + \beta_{i,1}[E(R_M) - R_F] + \beta_{i,2} \cdot E(SMB) + \beta_{i,3} \cdot E(HML) \qquad (8.6)$$

or, in an *ex post* form:

$$R_i - R_F = \alpha_i + \beta_{i,1}[R_M - R_F] + \beta_{i,2} \cdot SMB + \beta_{i,3} \cdot HML + \varepsilon_i \qquad (8.7)$$

where R_i is the expected return on asset i, R_F is the return on the risk-free asset and R_M is the expected return on the market portfolio, SMB is the return on the size factor and HML

---

[9] In explanatory analysis, several factors are tested, with the hope that some of them will explain well the data being analyzed. A typical technique consists in screening hundreds of potential factors using stepwise regression. In confirmatory analysis, an economic model is formulated *a priori* (before seeing the data) and then tested on a given data set.

[10] Note that there exist econometric techniques to identify the optimal number of factors. See for instance Bai and Ng (2002).

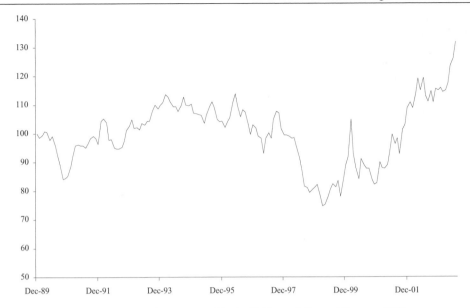

Figure 8.7   The performance of $100 invested in the SMB portfolio on 1 January 1990

is the return on the book-to-market factor. SMB is a zero-investment portfolio that is long small capitalization stocks and short big capitalization stocks (Figure 8.7).[11] HML is a zero-investment portfolio that is long high book-to-market stocks and short low book-to-market stocks (Figure 8.8). The parameter $\beta_{i,2}$ measures asset i's sensitivity to the size factor, and the parameter $\beta_{i,3}$ measures asset i's sensitivity to the book-to-market factor.

It is important to realize that the Fama and French model is not an equilibrium model. It is purely empirically motivated, and there is no theory telling us what gives rise to the SMB and HML factors.[12] In a sense, Fama and French looked at the data and chose factors based on what they found there. Nevertheless, several empirical tests evidenced that, when considering SMB and HML as additional factors, beta was no longer a reliable predictor of performance. This led Eugene Fama to declare that "beta as the sole variable in explaining returns on stocks . . . is dead".

Box 8.1   How to build the HML and SMB factors

In linear factor models, it is extremely convenient to use factors that correspond to the returns on a given observable portfolio. If the factor considered is an abstract concept that is not necessarily observable, we use a portfolio of assets whose returns are highly correlated with the (unobservable) factor values. The returns to the factor-mimicking portfolios mimic the factor values in a certain sense – remember that the factor values themselves

---

[11] The portfolio does not need any investment because the cash received from short selling stocks is used to finance the purchase of other stocks.

[12] The Fama and French findings imply that stocks with a high book-to-market ratio must be more risky than average – exactly the opposite of what a traditional business analyst would claim. However, there are several possible explanations for this phenomenon, e.g. a high book-to-price ratio could mean a stock is distressed, temporarily selling low because future earnings look doubtful. Or it could mean a stock is capital intensive, making it generally more vulnerable to low earnings during slow economic times. Black (1993) also pointed out that when markets are somewhat efficient, stock prices react to a firm's performance before accounting numbers. Thus it is not surprising that firms with a high book-to-market ratio show poor subsequent accounting performance.

are usually not directly observable. This is precisely the situation with the SMB and HML portfolios.

Fama and French's method for creating the HML and SMB portfolios is as follows. First, sort stocks simultaneously using two independent sorts, one on the market capitalization (small/big) and one on the book-to-market ratio (high/medium/low). Using the sorted universe, create six portfolios labeled small high (SH), small medium (SM), small low (SL), big high (BH), big medium (BM) and big low (BL). The size breakpoint that determines the buy range for the small and big portfolios is the median NYSE market equity. The book-to-market breakpoints that determine the buy range for the growth, neutral and value portfolios are the 30th and 70th NYSE percentiles.

Then, the HML and SMB portfolios are calculated as:

$$HML = (1/2*SH + 1/2*BH) - (1/2*SL + 1/2*BL) \tag{8.8}$$

and

$$SMB = (1/3*SH + 1/3*SM + 1/3*SL) - (1/3*BH + 1/3*BM + 1/3*BL) \tag{8.9}$$

Although SMB and HML are zero-investment portfolios, they earn positive returns, as illustrated in Figures 8.7 and 8.8. Fama and French argue that HML and SMB are state variables that describe changes in the investment opportunity set. The stocks considered each month to construct the HML and SMB factors include all NYSE, AMEX and NASDAQ stocks with prior return data. Note that the website of Kenneth French provides monthly updates on the value of these two factors.

8.3.3.3   Price momentum

Another essential piece of research suggesting the addition of new factors to the market model was that of Jegadeesh and Titman (1993). The two authors documented the existence of a

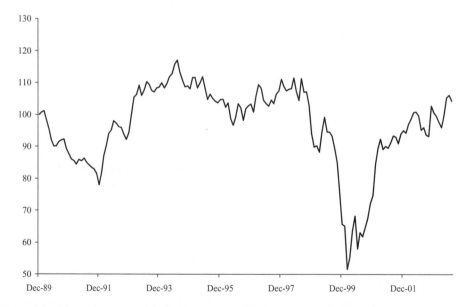

Figure 8.8   The performance of $100 invested in the HML portfolio on 1 January 1990

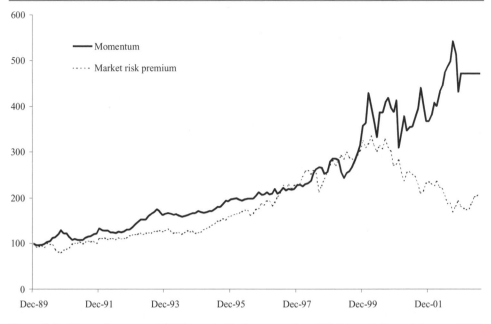

Figure 8.9   The performance of $100 invested in the momentum (WML) portfolio on 1 January 1990

momentum effect: strategies to buy stocks that have performed relatively well in the past and sell short stocks that have performed relatively poorly in the past generate significant positive returns over a 3–12-month horizon. These return continuation strategies have been tested extensively and confirmed on several markets.[13]

Following Carhart (1997), a large number of researchers have therefore suggested adding a momentum factor, WML (winners minus losers) to the Fama and French three-factor model. This gives a four-factor pricing model that explains the excess return of a security by the market portfolio and three factors designed to mimic risk variables related to size, book-to-market ratio and momentum:

$$R_i - R_F = \alpha_i + \beta_{i,1}[R_M - R_F] + \beta_{i,2} \cdot \text{SMB} + \beta_{i,3} \cdot \text{HML} + \beta_{i,4} \cdot \text{WML} + \varepsilon_i \quad (8.10)$$

where WML is the return on the momentum factor. WML is basically a zero-investment portfolio that is long past winners and short past losers (Figure 8.9).

The returns of the winner-minus-loser momentum portfolio are particularly impressive. However, we should note that they are mostly due to the poor performance of the losers. So, in order to capture the bulk of the momentum effect, short positions are necessary. In practice, holding the WML factor involves a very high turnover, and transaction costs and taxes may significantly erode momentum profits. Furthermore, the momentum effect is stronger among small cap stocks, which tend to be less liquid. Trying to implement a high-turnover strategy with small cap stocks is unrealistic. Hence the actual returns from a winner-minus-loser momentum portfolio are likely to be much lower in practice.

---

[13] See for instance Fama and French (1996), Chan *et al.* (1999) and Jegadeesh and Titman (1993) for the United States, Rouwenhorst (1998) for European markets, Chui *et al.* (2000) for Asian markets, or Rouwenhorst (1999) for emerging markets.

Box 8.2   How to build the momentum factor

The construction of the momentum factor parallels the calculation of Fama and French's SMB and HML factors.

For each month t from July of year $Y - 1$ to June of year Y, we rank the stocks based on their size in June $Y - 1$ and their performance between $t - 12$ and $t - 2$. We then use these two rankings to calculate 30% and 70% breakpoints for prior performance. The stocks are subsequently sorted into three prior performance groups based on these breakpoints. The stocks above the 70% prior performance breakpoint are designated W (for winner), the middle 40 are designated N (for neutral) and the firms below the 30% book-to-market breakpoint are designated L (for loser). The WML portfolio is the difference between the top 70% stocks and the bottom 30% – the neutrals are simply ignored. The stocks considered each month to construct the WML portfolio include NYSE, AMEX and NASDAQ stocks with prior return data. Note that the website of Kenneth French provides regular updates on the value of the WML factor.

8.3.3.4   Other market-based factors

The debate on whether the Fama and French three-factor model or the Carhart four-factor model explain well the economic risk of traditional assets is still ongoing, but it is not our primary concern here. In the domain of hedge funds, the challenge is still to identify a small number of economically interpretable factors that can capture the majority of the underlying risk for *all* the strategies.

There are many reasons to believe that the sources of risk in hedge funds should not be very different from the sources of risk in traditional assets. At the end of the day, both types of managers are actually investing in the same markets, probably even buying and selling the same stocks and bonds. The type of trades (buying versus selling) and the way these assets are managed, however, are different. Therefore, while many hedge fund investors believe that investing in hedge funds is all about the "search for alpha", a deeper analysis of hedge funds reveals that the "search for alpha" has to first start with an "understanding of beta".

Several factor models have been suggested in the literature over recent years – see for instance Schneeweis and Spurgin (1998), Schneeweis *et al.* (2001), Capocci (2001), Amenc *et al.* (2002a) or Amenc *et al.* (2002b), among others. Reading these studies provides a good overview of the potential return drivers, i.e. the factors that are likely to explain a significant proportion of the variation in hedge fund returns over time. Most of these return drivers are fundamentally associated with the underlying holdings of the strategy and the strategy itself. As an illustration, we have listed some of these factors, as well as the typical indicator/index associated with each of them. Note that for many of these factors, it is interesting to distinguish the absolute level of the factor from its percentage change.

Equity-related factors

- Market indices (S&P 500, MSCI World, etc.)
- Sectors (MSCI World sector indices)
- Traded volume (NYSE cumulated volume)

Equity trading styles

- Value versus growth (Fama and French factors)
- Small versus big capitalization (Fama and French factors)
- Momentum (Fama and French factors)

Interest rate factors

- T-bill rate (3-month Treasury rate)
- Slope of the yield curve (30-year Treasury yield minus three-month T-bill yield)
- Credit risk premium (difference between BBB and AAA yield)

Currencies and commodities

- Selected basket of exchange rates (USD/EUR, USD/JPY, etc.)
- Selected basket of commodities (gold, oil, etc.)

Stability-related factors

- Implied volatility index (VIX for options on S&P 100 index)
- Intra-month volatility of bond returns (intra-month standard deviation of the daily total rate of Lehman Brothers Aggregate Bond index)
- Intra-month volatility of equity returns (intra-month standard deviation of S&P 500 index)

Others

- Confidence index
- GDP growth
- etc.

In addition to these market-related factors, we may also include in our factor models some characteristics that are specific to a given fund rather than to a particular strategy or an investment style. For instance, fund size and fund age are likely to affect hedge fund performance in different ways, as illustrated in Figures 8.10 and 8.11. We see clearly that for bond arbitrage and market neutral, performance (i.e. Sharpe ratio) degrades rapidly as fund size is increased, while this effect is not as dramatic or reversed for other strategies. Convertible arbitrage and distressed securities fund performances even appear to improve with fund size. We also see that for most strategies, the younger funds have significantly better Sharpe ratios than the older funds, perhaps due to size and nimbleness. These results should be taken with caution, because younger funds are likely to be subject to the greatest reporting bias.

8.3.4   How useful are multi-factor models?

There are several domains of application for hedge fund multi-factor models. Among others, let us quote the following:

- The identification of the relevant drivers of performance of a portfolio of funds or a hedge fund index.

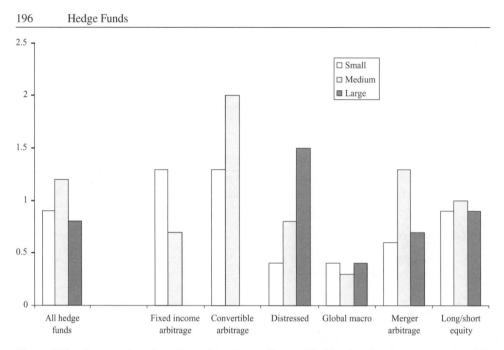

Figure 8.10   Sharpe ratios of equally weighted portfolios stratified by size. Small means less than $25 million of assets under management and large more than $200 million. Note that some categories are empty

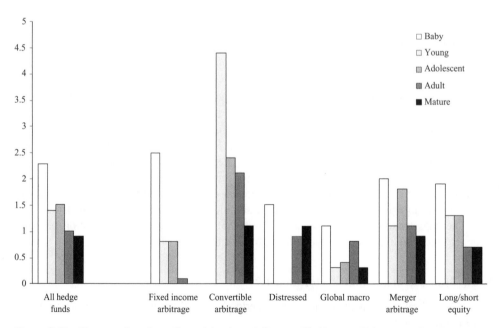

Figure 8.11   Sharpe ratios of equally weighted portfolios stratified by age. Baby means less than a year of existence, Young means 1 to 2 years, Adolescent means 2 to 3 years, Adult means 3 to 5 years and Mature means more than 5 years. Note that some categories are empty

- The understanding of the factors (sources of risk) that jointly explain the total risk of a portfolio of funds or a hedge fund index.
- The creation of a benchmark.
- The construction of index trackers or enhanced index portfolios.
- The construction of a portfolio of funds tilted toward specific risk factors of choice, for instance market neutral long–short portfolios meant to benefit from a specific view on macroeconomic factors.
- The determination of alpha.

Furthermore, factor models provide an interesting and natural explanation for the change in correlations observed between hedge funds. Correlation will be higher when systematic macroeconomic factors, which affect all assets in tandem, dominate fund-specific factors. If variations in asset returns are driven by both systematic factors and idiosyncratic (i.e. sector-specific) risks, then periods of high factor volatility will coincide with periods of high correlation. During these periods, the dominant source of variation will be due to the common factor. Unless idiosyncratic volatility is strongly correlated across sectors (which is not the case in our sample), periods of high cross-sector correlation will coincide with periods of high overall market volatility. Thus, correlation breakdown – the strong observed association between correlation and volatility – is not simply bad luck. It is to be expected. Moreover, it is not evidence that the structure of security returns periodically changes perversely; "breakdown" can be part and parcel of a stable factor model of returns.

Box 8.3   When lagged returns may help

As already mentioned in Chapter 5, hedge fund managers can smooth portfolio returns when marking illiquid securities using historical prices (e.g. last traded price, hence stale) or worse, a price that the manager thinks is reasonable. Pricing of these securities is thus stale or managed, and this potentially leads to understating volatility as well as betas and correlations with traditional indexes.

To take into account this phenomenon, Asness *et al.* (2001) suggest running a regression of returns on both contemporaneous and lagged market returns, and testing whether lagged betas are significant.

Using the CSFB/Tremont hedge fund index's monthly returns between January 1994 and September 2000, Asness *et al.* observe that (i) lagged betas are significant for every hedge fund style except managed futures and (ii) including lagged betas in the regression significantly reduces the alpha. Asness *et al.* also suspect some evidence of intentional stale prices, because the summed lagged beta in down markets is statistically significant only in down markets.

8.4   ACCOUNTING FOR NON-LINEARITY

Almost all the traditional asset pricing models, including the single-factor and multi-factor models that we have considered so far, are based on the assumption that the expected return on a hedge fund is a linear function of some common factors.

A first key assumption underlying such models is that volatility is the appropriate measure of risk to the investor. It is then a mathematical consequence of this that only systematic risk (i.e. the covariance[14]) is rewarded in financial markets. However, if this assumption seems quite reasonable for assets with returns that are symmetrically distributed, it does not seem so reasonable for hedge funds whose returns are asymmetrically distributed.[15] In such a case, investors will care about other aspects of the distribution, such as the skewness, kurtosis, etc.

A second key assumption underlying traditional asset pricing models is that risk exposures (i.e. beta coefficients) are constant through time. However, this is unlikely to be true for hedge funds, whose managers follow highly opportunistic strategies and have time-varying risk exposures. A large body of literature has recently documented that asset returns were to some extent predictable on the basis of proper instrument variables, and this modifies the constriction of portfolios in at least three ways. First, it introduces horizon effects, as mean and variance may no longer scale the same way with horizon – see Barberis (2000). Second, it allows market timing strategies. Portfolio managers use information about the current state of the economy to form return and risk expectations and adjust their portfolios accordingly. Third, it introduces multiple factors via hedging demands – if expected returns vary over time, investors will hold assets that protect them against this risk. Given all these changes, traditional static asset pricing models may be incorrectly specified if we do not allow for time variation in the risk exposures.

These new facts have attracted academic attention and led to a new series of asset pricing models. We briefly review them in this section and provide essential references for those readers who would like to investigate them in further detail.

8.4.1   Introducing higher moments: co-skewness and co-kurtosis

Investors are concerned about risk, and risk must be measured in terms of the entire probability distribution, which in turn can be measured with the moments of the distribution. Thus, several authors have posited that investors display a preference for positive skewness and prefer assets that are right-skewed to assets that are left-skewed – see for instance Rubinstein (1973), Kraus and Litzenberger (1976) or Harvey and Siddique (2000). If this is true, then investors should value the skewness contributions to their portfolios, or more precisely, the co-skewness of underlying assets. That is, assets that decrease a portfolio's skewness (i.e. that make the portfolio returns more left-skewed) are less desirable and should command higher expected returns. Similarly, assets that increase a portfolio's skewness should have lower expected returns. Note that it is only the co-skewness that should count, not the skewness alone.[16]

A similar case can be developed for kurtosis and co-kurtosis, and more generally, for any higher-order moment of the return distribution. In the general case, Scott and Horvath (1980) show that investors should have a negative preference for even moments and a positive preference for odd ones. Consequently, these moments should be considered in an asset pricing model. Only in very special and unlikely cases, such as quadratic utility or normality of returns, can we ignore the higher moments and focus on just mean and variance (or covariance).

Rubinstein (1973) derives an equation for the expected return in terms of an arbitrary number of co-moments. In his model, the expected return on an asset should be equal to the risk-free

---

[14] Remember that the variance of a portfolio is built from the covariance of its constituting assets.

[15] Consider, for instance, these two lotteries: the first costs one dollar, and there is one chance in 10 million of winning one million dollars; the second pays one dollar upfront, but there exists one chance in a million of having to pay one million dollars. Returns from both lotteries have the same mean, variance and even moments. Which one looks more attractive? Most people would prefer the first lottery.

[16] This is analogous to beta and variance. In the CAPM, it is only the beta that is rewarded, not the total volatility.

rate, plus a risk premium equal to a weighted sum of all co-moments of the return distribution. In particular, if investors only care about the first three moments, we obtain a three-moment CAPM:

$$E(R_i) - R_F = \beta_i \left[\frac{(E(R_i) - R_F)(E(R_M) - R_F)}{(E(R_M) - R_F)^2} \right] + \gamma_i \left[\frac{(E(R_i) - R_F)(E(R_M) - R_F)^2}{(E(R_M) - R_F)^3} \right] \quad (8.11)$$

$$\underbrace{\qquad\qquad\qquad\qquad}_{\text{Market volatility premium}} \qquad \underbrace{\qquad\qquad\qquad\qquad}_{\text{Market skewness premium}}$$

Kraus and Litzenberger (1976) derive an equation of the same form and evidence that this three-moment CAPM is consistent with a quadratic return generating process of the form

$$R_i - R_F = \alpha_i + \beta_{i,1}[R_M - R_F] + \beta_{i,2}[R_M - R_F]^2 + \varepsilon_i \quad (8.12)$$

This provides a convenient way to test for skewness preferences in asset pricing models, as we just need to test whether $\beta_{i,2}$ is statistically significant. Kraus and Litzenberger also state "it is trivial to extend the model to incorporate any number of higher moments". For example, if we assume identical investors, we can derive a four-moment CAPM where all four moments – mean, systematic variance, systematic skewness and systematic kurtosis – contribute to the risk premium of an asset. This corresponds to a cubic return generating process of the form

$$R_i - R_F = \alpha_i + \beta_{i,1}[R_M - R_F] + \beta_{i,2}[R_M - R_F]^2 + \beta_{i,3}[R_M - R_F]^3 + \varepsilon_i \quad (8.13)$$

As underlined by Barone-Adesi *et al.* (2002), the cubic model does not allow for a precise estimation of the co-skewness and co-kurtosis risk premiums, but it provides a powerful test of the relationship between risk and expected return implied by the asset pricing model.

Box 8.4   From market timing to co-skewness pricing

There is an interesting parallel between the quadratic asset pricing model and the Treynor and Mazuy (1966) approach to measure market timing. In its pure form, market timing involves shifting funds between a market index and a risk-free asset (cash), depending on whether the market as a whole is expected to outperform the risk-free asset. If a fund manager holds constant the relative proportion between cash and the market index, his fund's beta will be constant and his returns will plot along the security market line. But if he successfully engages in market timing activities, he will increase his market exposure on the upside and decrease it on the downside, thereby altering the linear security market line of the single-factor model. The new relationship should be curvilinear, portfolio return becoming a convex function of market return. Similarly, bad timing activities will result in a concave relationship. Therefore, to test for market timing, Treynor and Mazuy (1966) propose to add a quadratic term to CAPM, that is:

$$R_i - R_F = \alpha_i + \beta_{i,1}[R_M - R_F] + \beta_{i,2}[R_M - R_F]^2 + \varepsilon_i \quad (8.14)$$

where $\beta_{i,2} > 0$ indicates successful market timing ability.[17] This timing model is exactly the same as the quadratic asset pricing model used to include skewness preference.

---

[17] A formal treatment of this test can be found in Admati *et al.* (1986). Note that $\beta_{i,2}$ should not be used to rank market timers, since it combines both the quality of the manager's private information and his response to this information (his "aggressiveness").

Ranaldo and Favre (2003) have applied the quadratic and cubic asset pricing models. Their results are mixed. For eight out of 16 hedge fund strategies investigated, the coefficients of co-skewness and co-kurtosis are not significant. For the eight other strategies, the coefficients of co-skewness and co-kurtosis are significant, and therefore risk exposure should be compensated. Hence, the two-moment CAPM tends to underestimate the required rate of return for these hedge funds.

A very interesting observation by Chung *et al.* (2001) is that SMB and HML generally become insignificant or much less significant as systematic co-moments are added into the picture. This tends to suggest that Fama–French factors may simply be good proxies for higher co-moments of the return distribution. Given the econometric problems of estimating co-moments, SMB and HML could be superior in actual use.

8.4.2   Conditional approaches

Whatever their level of sophistication and number of factors, unconditional asset pricing models such as the ones we have investigated so far may provide incorrect conclusions when fund managers react to market information or engage in dynamic trading strategies – see Ferson and Schadt (1996) and Ferson and Warther (1996). For the sake of illustration, let us consider a one-factor model similar to the one introduced in equation (8.3). Let us assume that the manager of fund i engages in market timing activities, that is, the beta of his portfolio is β_{up} when the fund manager forecasts a positive performance and β_{down} otherwise.

The unconditional model is:

$$R_i - R_F = \alpha_i + \beta_i \cdot (R_M - R_F) + \varepsilon_i \qquad (8.15)$$

where R_i is the return on fund i, R_F is the risk-free rate and R_M is the return on the market portfolio. Equation (8.15) assumes that α_i and β_i are constant over time. Since this is not true, the regression corresponding to equation (8.15) may provide little or no useful information about the true values of α and β. As an illustration, Figure 8.12 illustrates the risk of using unconditional models when the returns (and thus the betas) are state dependent. The fund manager has no alpha ($\alpha = 0$) and clearly uses a bull market exposure (β_{up}) different from his down-market exposure (β_{down}). By contrast, an unconditional model would have concluded that the manager has an average beta and a positive alpha!

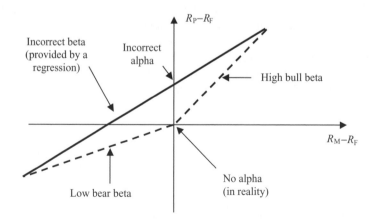

Figure 8.12   The mis-estimation of beta creates alpha when the manager does market timing

Several alternatives have been used in the financial literature to model time-varying returns and risk. The simplest assumption, of course, is that there is a linear relationship between the coefficients at time t and the coefficients at time $t - 1$. If we denote by Z_{t-1} the value at time $t - 1$ of the parameter that influences the alpha and beta coefficients of fund i at time t, we have:

$$\begin{cases} \alpha_{i,t} = \bar{\alpha}_i + a_i Z_{t-1} \\ \beta_{i,t} = \bar{\beta}_i + b_i Z_{t-1} \end{cases} \tag{8.16}$$

where $\bar{\alpha}_i$ is the average abnormal performance of the portfolio, $\bar{\beta}_i$ is the average risk exposure of the portfolio, and a_i and b_i need to be estimated. The idea is that at time $t - 1$, the hedge fund manager observes Z_{t-1} and adjusts his portfolio accordingly. Then, $a_i Z_{t-1}$ captures the time variation in the abnormal performance, i.e. the departure from the mean level of abnormal performance $\bar{\alpha}_i$. Similarly, $b_i Z_{t-1}$ captures the time variation in the risk exposure, i.e. the departure from the mean level of risk $\bar{\beta}_i$.

Then, applying the conditional model to equation (8.15), we arrive at

$$R_i - R_F = \alpha_i + \beta_i \cdot (R_M - R_F) + \beta_i \cdot (R_M - R_F)Z_{t-1} + \varepsilon_i \tag{8.17}$$

This new regression can be viewed as an unconditional multiple-factor model, with excess return as the first factor and the cross-product of excess market return with the lagged information variable as the additional factor. It is possible to interpret the additional factor as the return to a dynamic strategy, which holds Z_{t-1} units of the market index financed by borrowing Z_{t-1} at the risk-free rate.

Note that in the model we have just seen:

- Z_{t-1} denoted a single publicly available variable. In practice, several publicly available variables may influence the behavior of the alpha and beta coefficients. The conditional model will therefore express the excess return on the ith fund as a conditional linear function of the relevant lagged information variables at the beginning of the period.
- The model assumes a linear relationship between the regression parameters and a set of publicly available instruments. This idea was first introduced by Harvey (1989) and has been used extensively ever since – see for example Ferson and Harvey (1993).

Kat and Miffre (2002) provide an illustration of this technique for hedge funds using the Zurich Capital Markets database.[18] Kat and Miffre compare three conditional-based models, namely, the conditional market model, the conditional Fama–French three-factor model and an explicit conditional macrofactor model that considers the market factor and five macroeconomic factors (exchange rate risk, term structure of interest rates, international risk of default on short maturity securities, inflation risk and industrial risk). Their results reject the hypothesis of constant parameters for about 79% of the funds for the market model, and for all the funds for the two multi-factor models. When considering the conditional six-factor model, the best predictor of abnormal hedge fund performance is own return (39% of the time). Next come the default spread (22.1%), the dividend yield (16.9%), the term structure (13%) and the Treasury bills (11.7%). The impact of these variables is – of course – different in periods of expansion and recession.

---

[18] Kazemi and Schneeweis (2003) and Cerrahoglu et al. (2003) also use conditional approaches, but rely on a different technique called the stochastic discount factor.

8.5   HEDGE FUNDS AS OPTION PORTFOLIOS

For the public and the press, options and hedge funds share several anecdotal features. Both are perceived as complex, excessively leveraged and difficult to understand investments, except for specialists. Both were at the source of numerous media reports announcing spectacular gains and losses, which reinforced the view that all hedge fund managers and all derivative users were taking on risks that were far above average. Both have grown up outside of regular exchanges, in offshore countries for hedge funds and at over-the-counter desks for most active options. And both are easy to blame when there is a systemic market problem!

But the similarity between options and hedge funds is not just anecdotal. From an economic perspective, one can show that there exist several implicit option-related aspects in hedge funds. For instance:

- Hedge funds' special fee structures aim at aligning managers' incentives with fund performance. From a theoretical perspective, the incentive fee of hedge fund managers can be seen as a call option on their own fund performance. As explained by Anson (2001), this call option is granted for free by the investor to the fund manager. It has an exercise price of zero, a maturity of one year (usually) and volatility equal to the volatility of the hedge fund's before-fee returns.[19]
- Hedge funds are providing "real options" to non-hedge fund investors by allowing them to readily liquidate their illiquid investments when markets do not fulfill their demand and supply clearing function.
- By trading dynamically, hedge funds are tailoring their return-to-risk profiles to certain classes of investors, and this results in investments that have option-like payoff profiles. In fact, both options and hedge funds are securities with asymmetric non-linear payoffs.

The option-like return pattern of hedge funds obviously presents a challenge for investors. So far, all the models we have been considering (i) were only using factors that intuitively originated from the mix of assets in the funds' portfolios and (ii) were linear with respect to these factors. By contrast, options are sensitive in a non-linear way to several other risk sources (e.g. volatility, interest rates, convexity of the payoff, etc.). Given what precedes, a large body of the hedge fund literature has suggested adding some contingent claim factors, such as a number of ordinary put or call options into the return-generating process in order to capture the non-linearity with respect to risk factors. Let us now explain how these models work.

8.5.1   The early theoretical models

Henriksson and Merton (1981) were the first to suggest using options to explain the performance of managed portfolios. Their model is basically a simplified two-state framework for performance evaluation in which a fund manager attempts to forecast whether the market return will be higher or lower than the risk-free rate. The manager then adjusts his asset allocation according to his forecast by switching between two discrete levels of systematic risk: an up-market beta when he forecasts an up market and a down-market beta when he forecasts a down market.

---

[19] This perspective actually raises the issue of who is controlling the fund's volatility. Hedge fund investors should realize that they have provided hedge fund managers with a strong incentive to increase the volatility of the fund, and that this incentive to increase volatility is directly related to the magnitude of the incentive fee.

Henriksson and Merton show that in such a context, the fund's total return may be viewed as the sum of the return on the market and on a put option on the market. The exercise price of this put option equals the risk-free rate – as the option becomes valuable only if the market return is lower than the risk-free rate. Therefore, the following regression provides consistent estimates for timing and selectivity:

$$R_i - R_F = \alpha_i + \beta_{i,1} \cdot [R_M - R_F] + \beta_{i,2} \cdot \text{Max}[0, -R_M + R_F] + \varepsilon_i \qquad (8.18)$$

Henriksson and Merton show that $\beta_{i,2} > 0$ if and only if the fund manager has a superior market timing ability while $\alpha_i > 0$ still indicates selection ability. In fact, a positive parameter $\beta_{i,2}$ can be seen as the number of no-cost put options on the market portfolio provided by the market timing strategy. A negative $\beta_{i,2}$ and α_P equal to zero are equivalent to being short a number of put options on the market without receiving any cash.

Henriksson and Merton's approach has been extended in many directions over recent years.[20] In particular, Glosten and Jagannathan (1994) develop a theoretical framework to analyze the investment style of fund managers by including explicitly the returns on selected option-based strategies as risk factors. The new question is then to determine how many options and which strike prices should be considered.

8.5.2   Modeling hedge funds as option portfolios

8.5.2.1   The Fung and Hsieh (1997a) approach

Following the suggestions in Glosten and Jagannathan (1994), Fung and Hsieh (1997a) suggest that the return of hedge funds should be split in three types of components:

- Some *location factors* ("where does the manager trade?"), which tell us the asset classes the manager invests in. These location factors are typically approximated by the returns from a static buy-and-hold policy.
- Some *trading strategy factors* ("how does the manager trade?"), which give us insight on the type of dynamic strategy followed by a manager. These trading factors are typically approximated by the returns from option-based positions.[21]
- A *leverage factor*, which corresponds to a scaling of the two previous factors due to gearing.

To illustrate their claim and identify the location and trading strategy factors, Fung and Hsieh suggest a simple, but innovative, technique that is similar to non-parametric regression. Say we want to analyze the performance of a given hedge fund strategy with respect to a particular asset class. We divide the monthly returns of the asset class into five "states" or "environments" of the world, ranging from severe declines to sharp rallies. Then, the average returns of that asset class, as well as those of the hedge fund strategy, are computed in each state of the world. The final analysis is quite simple:

---

[20] For instance, Aragon (2002) analyzes the case of fund managers that are timing multiple markets, and Goetzmann *et al.* (2000), Bollen and Busse (2001) and Ferson and Khang (2001) focus on the biases that may arise when the econometrician observes return data at a frequency different from the frequency at which the manager times the market.

[21] Note that Schneeweis *et al.* (1996) study the ability of CTAs and managed futures to provide downside risk control when combined with an investment in equities. Their conclusion is that CTAs and managed futures may be used as a low-cost alternative to a put option for providing downside protection for an equity investment. However, the level of protection differs significantly. Protection from a put option is certain, but protection from managed futures is not. More recently, Cox and Leland (2000) provide an exhaustive analysis on dynamic investment strategies and their link to options. As an illustration, a fund manager who buys more assets as they rise and sells them progressively as they fall in value would have a payoff that is similar to a long call option. By contrast, a fund manager who short sells more assets as they fall and reduces his short position progressively as they rise in value would have a payoff that is similar to a long put option.

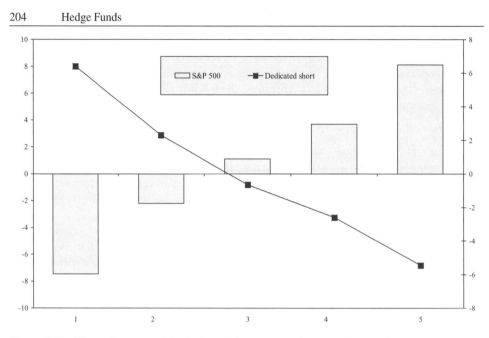

Figure 8.13 The performance of the dedicated short strategy (in % p.a., right scale) versus US equities (S&P 500, in % p.a., left scale)

- If the hedge fund strategy uses a buy-and-hold strategy in the given asset class, then its return in the five states of the world should align with those in the asset class in a straight line. This corresponds to the above-mentioned location factor.
- If the hedge fund strategy uses a dynamic trading strategy in the given asset class, then its return should be non-linearly related to the underlying asset class returns, particularly in the extreme cases (i.e. states 1 and 5).
- If the hedge fund strategy is non-related to the given asset class, then its return should be more or less even in the five states of the world.

The shape of the relationship between the returns of a given hedge fund strategy and a particular asset class is easy to represent as a graph. As an illustration, consider Figures 8.13–8.16, which present the most dramatic examples of location and trading strategy factors.

As expected, the dedicated short strategy has no option-like feature. It is negatively linearly related to the S&P 500. The CTA strategy has a return profile similar to a straddle (i.e. long a put and a call) on US equities. The global macro strategy behaves like a short put on the S&P 500 and has an almost linear profile with respect to the USD/JPY exchange rate.

Finally, distressed securities and risk arbitrage also behave like a short put on the S&P 500 (Figures 8.17 and 8.18).

8.5.2.2   The economic rationale

The approach suggested by Fung and Hsieh provides a useful insight on the type of option strategy one should expect when analyzing hedge fund returns. But does it correspond to any sort of economic intuition? Fortunately, the answer is positive. As an illustration, let us consider three strategies, namely, long/short equity, merger arbitrage and systematic traders (CTAs).

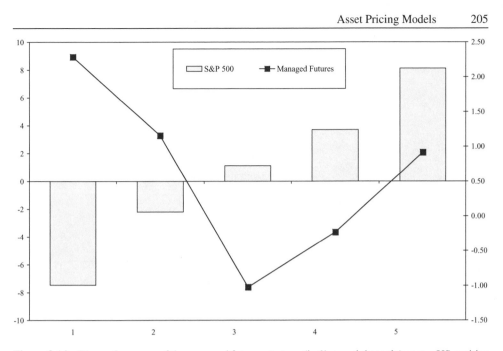

Figure 8.14   The performance of the managed futures strategy (in % p.a., right scale) versus US equities (S&P 500, in % p.a., left scale)

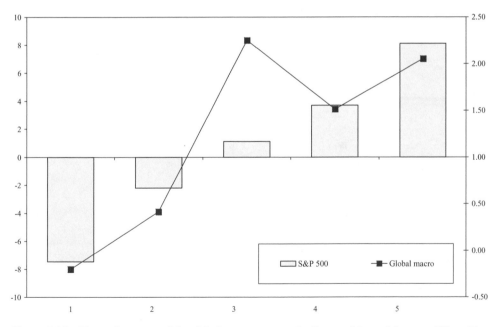

Figure 8.15   The performance of the global macro strategy (in % p.a., right scale) versus US equities (in % p.a., left scale)

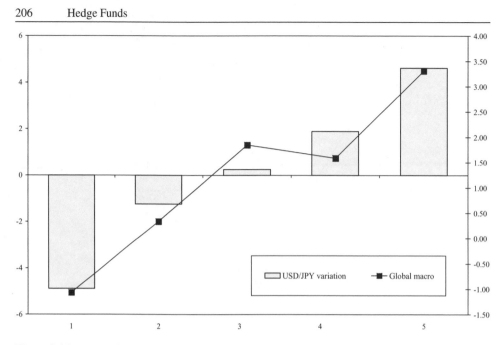

Figure 8.16   The performance of the global macro strategy (in % p.a., right scale) versus the USD/JPY exchange rate (in % p.a., left scale)

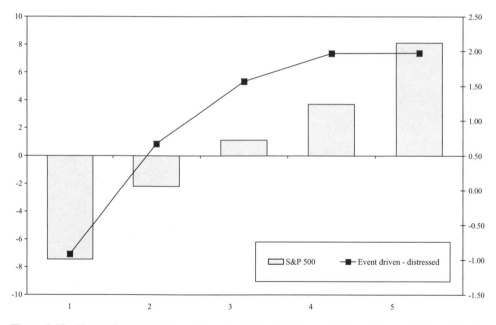

Figure 8.17   The performance of the distressed strategy (in % p.a., right scale) versus US equities (in % p.a., left scale)

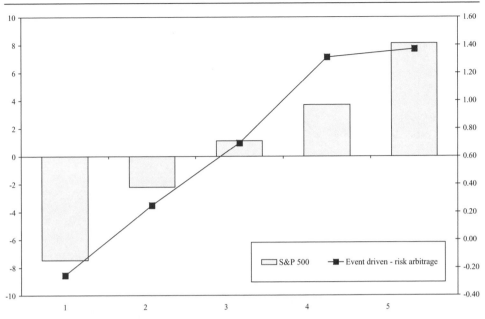

Figure 8.18   The performance of the risk arbitrage strategy (in % p.a., right scale) versus US equities (in % p.a., left scale)

Ideally, a long/short equity fund should participate in the upside performance of the market and limit its losses in the downside.[22] The fund will typically increase its market exposure (i.e. beta) when markets are expected to perform well, and reduce its market exposure (i.e. beta) when markets are expected to perform badly. The result is an asymmetric non-linear payoff. Now, consider a portfolio made of one at-the-money call option on a market index. Against the payment of a premium, this call option allows us to participate in the upside potential of the equity index. But if the index drops in value, the maximum loss is limited to the premium initially paid. Clearly, a successful long/short equity manager offers returns that are similar in nature to those of a call option.

Now, consider the case of merger arbitrage. Figure 8.19 shows a scatter plot of merger arbitrage returns versus those of the Russel 3000. A linear OLS regression does not fit the data very well. A local regression performs much better, but it has no economic interpretation. By contrast, an uncovered put option on the Russel 3000 seems to do almost as well as the local regression, and it has an economic interpretation.

Of course, one may wonder what the relationship is between merger arbitrage and selling puts. The answer is quite simple and is extensively developed in Mitchell and Pulvino (2001). Merger arbitrageurs assess the likely outcome of announced mergers and acquisitions, and bet that some merger spreads will converge to zero.[23] In a sense, they are short this spread by going long the target and short the acquirer. When the stock market performs well, mergers and takeovers are successful, and merger spreads converge to zero, which is good for merger

---

[22] As most long/short equity managers have a long bias, we simply ask for limiting the losses, not for offering a positive performance when markets are bearish. Note that this does not affect the generality of our approach.

[23] The merger spread is the difference between the offered price and the market price of securities whose issuers are involved in a merger or a takeover. Because the transaction may still fall through, be delayed or be renegotiated, the market price does not immediately climb to the announced deal price – see Lhabitant (2002c).

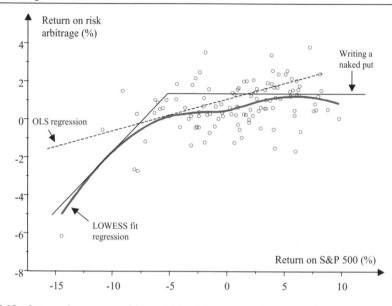

Figure 8.19   Interpreting merger arbitrage (risk arbitrage) as a short put option strategy

arbitrageurs. But, by construction, the merger spread is known and fixed at the initiation of the merger. Thus, the performance of the strategy does not depend on the performance of the market, but is capped at a maximum return. By contrast, when the stock market performs poorly, mergers and takeovers fail and merger spreads widen. This hurts merger arbitrageurs, who face very large potential losses. This clearly shows that merger arbitrageurs behave as if they were selling naked put options on the market. They have a limited upside profit when markets perform well and a large downside risk when markets perform poorly.

Finally, let us consider the case of systematic traders. The majority of them use automated trading systems that attempt to detect trends and profit from them. A typical (simplified) trading rule is to compare the level of a stock index with its moving average. For instance, if the price goes up and crosses the 30-day moving average, this is a buy signal. The long position is closed as soon as the price goes down and crosses the 5-day moving average. A similar rule can be implemented on the short side. That is, if the price goes down and crosses the 30-day moving average, this is a short-sell signal. The short position is closed as soon as the price goes up and crosses the 5-day moving average. At first glance, such a strategy will be profitable as soon as there is a trend and may lose money when the trend changes direction. It is not dependent on any subjective factor.[24]

At first glance, the payoffs from this type of strategy can easily be approximated by a straddle (i.e. a call plus a put option), as illustrated in Figure 8.13. A straddle is profitable as soon as there is a trend, but loses money if the market does not move much. It loses money if the market does not move much because of the two premiums paid to purchase the options. However, the exercise price of the straddle needs to be constantly rebalanced to take into account the myriad of possible entry and exit decisions of the trend-following strategy (e.g. the systematic exit rules linked to the 5-day moving average in our example).

---

[24] As an illustration, Jerry Parker from Chesapeake Capital (one of the largest systematic trading advisors in the industry) bought crude oil futures at $20 per barrel in 1990 and saw them rise to $40. When clients asked how he knew to buy crude, Parker replied that he bought oil . . . as it started to move up.

Now, given the prices of a market over any given period of time, the optimal payout of any trend-following system must be one that bought at the lowest price and sold at the highest price. Hence an alternative, suggested by Fung and Hsieh (2000a), is to use a lookback straddle (i.e. a lookback call plus a lookback put). A lookback call is an option that grants the owner the right to purchase an asset at its minimum price over a specified time period. A lookback put is an option that grants the owner the right to sell an asset at its maximum price over a specified time period. The lookback straddle, which is a combination of a lookback call and a lookback put, pays the owner the difference between the minimum and maximum price over a given time period and is identical to the payout. In a sense, it is a continuously rebalanced standard straddle that synthetically replicates the lookback strategy for investors – see Goldman *et al.* (1979).

Thus, although in practice hedge fund managers and commodity trading advisors may follow a myriad of complex dynamic trading strategies, a few simple option-based strategies capture a large proportion of the variation in their returns over time.[25]

8.5.2.3   Determining the option portfolio

Agarwal and Naik (2000c) generalize Fung and Hsieh's (1997a) approach and propose a general asset class factor model that characterizes the systematic risk exposures of hedge funds using both buy-and-hold and option-based strategies.

More specifically, the buy-and-hold risk factors consist of indexes representing:

- Equities, i.e. the Russell 3000 index, the lagged Russell 3000 index, the MSCI World excluding USA index and the MSCI Emerging Markets index.
- Bonds, i.e. the Salomon Brothers Government and Corporate Bond index, the Salomon Brothers World Government Bond index and the Lehman High Yield index.
- The Federal Reserve Bank Competitiveness-Weighted Dollar index and the Goldman Sachs Commodity index.
- Fama–French's small-minus-big (SMB) and book-to-market (HML) factors, as well as Carhart's momentum factor (winners-minus-losers).
- The change in the default spread (the difference between the yield on the BAA-rated corporate bonds and the 10-year Treasury bonds).

The option-based strategies originally consisted of an at-the-money option trading strategy (where the present value of the exercise price equals the current index value), an out-of-the-money option trading strategy (where the exercise price is half a standard deviation away from that of the at-the-money option) and a deep-out-of-the-money option trading strategy (where the exercise price is one standard deviation away from that of the at-the-money option) on the Russell 3000 index.[26]

Given the large number of possible market and trading strategy combinations that hedge funds can follow, Agarwal and Naik use a stepwise regression to ensure a parsimonious selection of factors. They obtain R^2 values that are dramatically higher than the ones obtained by Fung and Hsieh (2000b) using Sharpe's (1992) asset class factor model. Moreover, in the

---

[25] Note that this also explains why some hedge fund strategies are positively or negatively related to volatility, interest rates, etc. A long option (i.e. convex) payoff is always long volatility, while a short option (i.e. concave) payoff will always be short volatility.

[26] In a more recent paper, Agarwal and Naik (2003) implement their model using highly liquid at-the-money (ATM) and out-of-the-money (OTM) European call and put options on the S&P 500 Composite index trading on the Chicago Mercantile Exchange. To avoid collinearity, they do not consider in-the-money (ITM) options as their payoffs can be replicated by a combination of underlying asset and risk-free asset along with an OTM option. For example, the maturity payoff on an ITM call option can be replicated by a long position in the underlying asset, a long position in the risk-free asset and a long position in an OTM put with the same strike price.

case of the hedge funds that follow non-directional strategies, the proportion of observed R^2 attributable to trading strategies is, on average, 71% of the total R^2. In the case of the hedge funds that follow directional strategies, the average proportion of observed R^2 due to trading strategies is 51% of the total R^2. Last, but not least, their results show that a large number of equity-oriented hedge fund strategies exhibit payoffs resembling a short position in a put option on the market index, and therefore bear significant left-tail risk, risk that is ignored by the commonly used mean–variance framework.[27] By contrast, managed futures funds are generally "long options". Nonetheless, it is interesting to mention that Agarwal and Naik's analysis suggests that in a number of styles, excess return remained after adjustment for optionality, at least for the period they observed.

Box 8.5   Replication: the Amin and Kat (2001a) approach

Modeling hedge funds as option portfolios is an interesting intellectual exercise. However, there are three problems with this approach. First, it is not clear how many options (maturities, strike prices, underlying indices) should be included. Ideally, one would want to infer this from the available data, but in practice, the data sample will be too small to avoid ad hoc specification. Second, since only a small number of ordinary puts and calls can be included, there is a definite limit to the range and type of non-linearity that can be captured. Third, how do we value these options? Market quotes may not be arbitrage-free and suffer from a lack of liquidity, while theoretical prices are by definition suspect.

The approach suggested by Amin and Kat takes a completely different perspective – it actually focuses on performance evaluation rather than on explaining hedge fund returns. Instead of considering option portfolios, it concentrates on return distributions and is based on the following reasoning. When investing in a hedge fund, an investor acquires a claim to a certain payoff distribution. Now, can we create a dynamic trading strategy that offers exactly the same payoff distribution? Assuming we live in the world of Black and Scholes (1973), the answer is positive.

Using a continuous time version of the payoff distribution pricing model introduced by Dybvig (1988a,b), Amin and Kat determine the cost of the cheapest dynamic trading strategy, trading some reference index and cash, which generates the same payoff distribution as the hedge fund in question. They analyze the return distributions of 77 hedge funds and funds of funds in operation between May 1990 and April 2000 listed in the Zurich Capital Markets hedge fund database. Their conclusion is striking: investors could get the same risk-adjusted performance, on average 6.42%, more cheaply by using a dynamic trading strategy rather than by actually investing in the hedge funds in 72 out of the 77 cases . . .

8.6   DO HEDGE FUNDS REALLY PRODUCE ALPHA?

After having investigated all these asset pricing models, the question of whether hedge funds effectively produce alpha is open.

Let us recall that in practice, there are two ways of achieving superior returns in financial markets:

---

[27] This should be kept in mind when analyzing the impact of adding options in traditional portfolios. By definition, a short put option carries the risk of rare but large losses.

- The first approach consists of *increasing beta*, that is, accepting to take a particular risk for which the market compensates you. For instance, equities have a higher expected return than cash over time for the simple reason that they are a more risky investment than cash and that part of this risk is non-diversifiable (systematic). The same is true of long duration bonds versus cash, corporate bonds versus treasuries, etc.
- The second approach consists of *generating alpha*, i.e. outsmarting other market participants. Market timing, arbitrage and active security selection are examples of alpha strategies.

As we have seen, when we strip a hedge fund or a strategy and identify all the systematic risk it is exposed to, we often find that the fund manager is not doing anything particularly unique beyond taking in particular risk premiums.[28] These risk premiums cover beta exposures to liquidity risk, credit risk, volatility risk, currency risk, interest rate risk, etc. Thus, most hedge funds have a lot of betas embedded in their returns, and these beta sources are relatively easy to access and replicate.[29]

When a hedge fund's alpha is assessed using only the stock market as a risk factor, all these risk premiums appear as being alpha, because they are not correlated to stock market risk. But in fact, in a correctly specified model, this apparent alpha would largely be categorized as beta. Thus, it seems that the superiority of hedge funds therefore essentially relies on packaging up beta . . . and selling it at alpha prices.

---

[28] As an illustration of this lack of uniqueness, hedge funds in a given strategy are, for the most part, extremely correlated to one another.

[29] As an illustration, Fung and Hsieh (2002b) observe that fixed income hedge funds primarily have exposure to fixed income-related spreads, including the convertible bond/Treasury spread, the high yield/Treasury spread, the mortgage/Treasury spread and the emerging market bond/Treasury spread.

9

Styles, Clusters and Classification

If you call yourself Brad Pitt, it will not make you more attractive to women. But if you call your fund a hedge fund, it can get you into a very lucrative business and you will stay there masked because you do not have to disclose anything.

The group formed by hedge funds is anything but monolithic in the traditional sense of the word. The original long/short market neutral approach of Alfred Winslow Jones has progressively been replaced by a number of investment philosophies, strategies and specialties. Some managers claim to add value through knowledge of special asset markets, others through trading skills, and yet others through superior asset pricing models. This very variety is both a challenge and an opportunity, and any analysis that does not take such differences into account is likely to be flawed. Comprehending and benchmarking managers whose operations are essentially opaque, whose instruments vary widely, and who in many cases eschew predictable, passive factor exposures is not an easy task, but it is one of the keys to successful hedge fund investing.

When analyzing how well a hedge fund is performing as compared with its peers or with other managed or unmanaged portfolios having similar objectives, the concept of investment style is essential. In fact, it shapes the pattern of risk and returns more significantly than virtually any other element. It is therefore not surprising that style analysis has become an integral part of the investment process. In addition to fund classification, it is now commonly used in such areas as performance measurement and evaluation, exposure monitoring and risk management.

9.1 DEFINING INVESTMENT STYLES

The concept of investment style originates from the long-only side of the industry. There, traditional fund management companies tend to label their products using a few common categories based on asset classes, geographic focus, sectors, investment objectives, etc. As an illustration, observe for instance the unit trust section of the *Financial Times* or the mutual funds section in the *Wall Street Journal*. Hedge fund managers, in contrast, are not so detailed in their categorizations and tend to group themselves according to their strategy (convertible arbitrage, long/short equity, global macro manager, etc.). Beyond being merely labels, these categorizations implicitly assume that managers with similar investment styles are likely to perform more like each other than like the overall market or like managers with different styles. In fact, several studies have shown that the returns obtained by investors over a certain period of time were usually more dependent on their portfolio style than on their skills in picking individual funds.

Quality style information is essential to understand how well a fund is managed and to determine whether it would provide diversification benefits in a given portfolio. It is also necessary to monitor a manager for strategy shifts over time as well as to develop appropriate benchmarks and style peer groups with which a fund's returns should be compared. Moreover, given the obvious divergences in the performance of the different investment styles, style analysis may also help investors in switching actively between styles, or at least, in deciding which style is expected to be comparatively stronger for a specific time horizon.

Unfortunately, as stressed by Brown and Goetzmann (2003), diBartolomeo and Witkowski (1997) and Otten and Bams (2000), without some transparency, the self-reported investment style of fund managers does not always correspond to their actual investment behavior. In particular, when their performance is not too shining, some managers may be tempted to deviate from their originally stated objectives. They may take higher risks and/or follow different strategies to earn higher returns and consequently obtain a better performance rank in their self-stated objective group, even though they may still do poorly in the high-risk group to which they actually should belong based on their effective investment activities. For instance, a convertible arbitrage manager may start taking important bets on the credit risk of his portfolio and enter the arena of distressed securities; he may also stop hedging the equity portion of his convertibles and become directional on the underlying; alternatively, he may dramatically increase the leverage of his portfolio without necessarily disclosing it.

Surprisingly, investors and consultants seem to tolerate this game despite its foolishness. Consciously or not, they even encourage it by using the S&P 500 or the MSCI World as a benchmark. Unsurprisingly, hedge fund managers accept accolades and often more when their style is in favor relative to the benchmark's style,[1] but they cry foul when the reverse occurs. At the risk of spoiling the fun, we question the logic of benchmarking a fund to what its manager claims to be non-correlated with. Our prescription for sound performance evaluation and attribution is again common sense. Before making judgments about the quality of a track record, we should define a benchmark that captures the essence of the manager's true investment style. The benchmark should typically be a passive portfolio representative of the manager's investment style. By "passive", we mean that the benchmark should invest only in passively managed investment vehicles tracking an asset class (indices, index funds, etc.). The rebalancing of the portfolio, if any, should also be done according to an automated prespecified set of rules (e.g. rebalance to an equal weight every six months). By "representative", we mean that any systematic action taken by the manager should also be implemented in the benchmark. For instance, if a manager systematically buys growth stocks and sells short value stocks, his style benchmark should be long a growth stock index and short a value stock index. If a manager systematically buys stocks that have performed well, and sells short stocks that have performed badly, his benchmark portfolio should follow the same decision rule and exhibit this momentum bias. Once, and only once, the style benchmark has been identified, its return – and not the S&P 500 or the MSCI World return – should be deducted from the actual return of the fund. What is left is the value added or withdrawn by the fund manager with respect to its style benchmark. It is then the role of performance attribution to determine where this value comes from (e.g. timing, picking, luck), whether it is statistically significant, and whether it persists over time. But before getting there, we need to come back to the prerequisites, that is, identify the correct style benchmark.

9.2   STYLE ANALYSIS

As mentioned already, the self-classification of a hedge fund, its prospectus and its name are not very useful elements of information in identifying its true investment style.[2] Hence, qualitative

---

[1] As an illustration, a large number of long/short equity fund managers were unable to achieve decent absolute returns in 2001 and 2002. Nevertheless, they indulged in self-congratulation because they did much better than the S&P 500 during those two years and "preserved the capital invested".

[2] In the United States, the SEC requires that mutual funds invest at least 80% of their assets in the types of securities their name suggests. However, this regulation is not (yet?) applicable to hedge funds.

assessments of investment styles are likely to be biased, and we have to turn to quantitative techniques.

The two most common quantitative approaches to assessing a fund's investment style are fundamental style analysis and return-based style analysis. The former derives style information from portfolio holdings. The latter derives it from realized returns. Each method has its proponents and detractors, yet fundamental questions about the accuracy of each approach remain. Both share the same goal, i.e. to determine the combination of passive indices that would most closely replicate the performance of a given portfolio over a specific time period. The composition of this customized combination of passive indexes provides an implicit insight into the fund's investment strategy and may serve as a benchmark to measure the value added by the manager.

9.2.1 Fundamental style analysis

Fundamental style analysis (also called holding-based style analysis) is a common sense technique for determining the investment style of a fund by regularly examining its actual underlying holdings. No elaborate methodology is required to perform the analysis, only a consistent mapping framework that categorizes individual securities into predefined style groups, e.g. "large caps", "small caps", "US", "Europe". For example, if a portfolio contains a 5% long position in Microsoft, style analysis will map this position into a 5% allocation to "US large caps" shares, typically represented by the S&P 500 index. The choice of the predefined style groups depends, of course, on the purpose of the analysis.

The result of fundamental style analysis is a portfolio of passive indices that mimics the actual underlying asset allocation at a given point in time. Once a sufficient history of these holding-based snapshots is available, we can estimate the manager's average style profile. As an illustration, Brown and Goetzmann (2003) and Chan *et al.* (1999), among others, have successfully applied holding-based style analysis to mutual funds and illustrated how we can recover the investment style of their portfolio managers.

Suggested by Daniel *et al.* (1997), characteristic-based style analysis is a variant of fundamental style analysis. Rather than mapping assets by geographic or asset class membership, it considers the fundamental characteristics (size, book-to-market ratio, momentum, etc.) of these assets and creates a combination of passive indices that mimics the characteristics of the analyzed portfolio. As an illustration, aggressive growth portfolios tend to contain small-size stocks with lower book-to-market ratios and high momentum. Hence, the style benchmark chosen for this type of portfolio should mimic at least these three characteristics.

Unfortunately, the application of holding-based or characteristic-based style analysis to hedge fund portfolios is usually difficult, due to the lack of transparency. The most transparent funds may be willing to reveal the major characteristics of their holdings on an annual or quarterly basis, but the resulting reports are only snapshots taken at specific points in time. They are useful, but not sufficient to assess an effective investment style. Furthermore, they can easily be distorted by window-dressing,[3] and the cost of tracking holdings for a substantial assemblage of funds remains extremely high. Note that recently, some hedge fund managers have also started offering managed accounts with complete daily transparency at the positions level. This may be a solution to implement holding-based or characteristic-based style analysis.

---

[3] The term "window dressing" describes situations where a manager changes his fund's exposures just before and just after the quarterly or annual reporting. Hence, the reported exposures are correct, but unrepresentative of the average ones.

However, many experienced and successful managers are still reluctant to offer position transparency.

9.2.2   Return-based style analysis

Introduced by the Nobel laureate William F. Sharpe[4] (1988, 1992), return-based style analysis is a cheaper, more practical substitute for holding-based or characteristic-based style analysis. In contrast to the holding-based approach, return-based style analysis requires only the time series of returns of the fund under consideration. It is somewhat less precise than the holding-based technique, but it is easily applicable and, if done properly, reasonably accurate and objective. It has therefore gained popularity and has fundamentally changed the way many investment analysts assess the behavior of money managers.

9.2.3   The original model

The concept underlying return-based style analysis is extremely simple: whatever a manager claims, the only tangible element that we should trust is his fund's audited track record, which we can consider as tracks in the sand. By comparing these tracks with those left by a series of passive indices, style analysis figures out the combination of indices that would most closely replicate the actual performance of the fund over a specified time period.

From a modeling perspective, return-based style analysis can be seen as a particular extension of a multi-factor model. In fact, it is a factor model where (i) the factors are the returns on asset classes and (ii) we apply constraints to the coefficients in order to interpret them as portfolio weights. As seen already in Chapter 8, a typical factor model for a portfolio P can be written as:

$$R_t = \alpha + \sum_{i=1}^{k} \beta_i \cdot F_{i,t} + \varepsilon_t \tag{9.1}$$

where

R_t = the return on the portfolio at time t
α_i = the excess return (a constant) of the portfolio
$F_{i,t}$ = the value of factor i at time t
β_i = the change in the return on the asset per unit change in factor j
k = the number of factors
ε_t = the portion of the return on the portfolio not related to the N factors

The key ingredient for a successful factor model is the choice of appropriate factors. In style analysis, the N factors must be returns on representative asset classes, which are usually assimilated to market indices. These are sometimes called "style indices".

There are numerous sets of indices that may, for all practical purposes, be used in style analysis. However, to obtain reliable results, style indices should fulfill three minimal properties:

- They should be mutually exclusive, meaning that there should be no overlap between them. Simply stated, an asset belongs to one style index or another, but not to several indices simultaneously.

---

[4] William Sharpe originally used the expressions "effective asset mix" and "attribution analysis" to describe style analysis. The terms "correlational analysis" and "return pattern analysis" first put forward by consultants at Frank Russell have also been used in the literature.

- They should be exhaustive – they should collectively cover all market sectors and represent all possible return patterns. If the set of indices does not span the investment universe, the methodology may fail to identify a portfolio of indices that consistently explains the portfolio's behavior.[5]
- They should have returns that are sufficiently different. If the indices have too similar returns, the resulting collinearity may invalidate the analysis and produce spurious results such as highly unstable coefficients over time. If the correlation between specific indices is too high, we should consider dropping some of them to reduce collinearity.

In his 1992 paper, for example, Sharpe applied style analysis to the Trustees' Commingled US Portfolio (an open-end mutual fund offered by the Vanguard Group) and used 12 asset classes represented by the Salomon Brothers 90-day Treasury bill index, the Lehman Brothers intermediate-term Government bond index, the Lehman Brothers long-term Government bond index, the Lehman Brothers corporate bond index, the Lehman Brothers mortgage-backed securities index, the Sharpe/BARRA value stock index, the Sharpe/BARRA growth stock index, the Sharpe/BARRA medium capitalization stock index, the Sharpe/BARRA small capitalization stock index, the Salomon Brothers non-US Government bond index, the FTA Euro-Pacific ex Japan index and the FTA Japan index. More recently, Agarwal and Naik (2000d) applied style analysis to various hedge fund strategies, represented by the HFR indices from January 1994 to September 1998. Their style indices were the S&P 500 composite index, the MSCI World index excluding the US (developed markets other than the US), the MSCI emerging markets index, the Salomon Brothers Government and corporate bond index, the Salomon Brothers world Government bond index, the Lehman Brothers high yield index, the Federal Reserve trade-weighted dollar index and the UK gold price index.

If we employ equation (9.1) with some fund returns as the dependent variables and asset class returns as the independent variables, the beta coefficients can be estimated by most regression packages and may be interpreted as the fund's average historic exposures to the asset class returns over the estimation period. However, in the absence of constraints, some exposures could turn out to be negative. Furthermore, it is very likely that the exposures will not sum to 100%. This does not allow for easy interpretation of the coefficients as weights within a portfolio.

A first alternative consists in imposing a constraint requiring the beta coefficients to sum to 100%. When a portfolio uses leverage, some individual beta exposures may increase above 100%, but they should be compensated by negative beta exposures somewhere else (e.g. cash, if the fund borrows money, or another asset class, if the fund finances its long positions by selling short), so that the sum of exposures should still be 100%. Our model then becomes:

$$\begin{cases} R_t = \alpha + \sum_{i=1}^{k} \beta_i \cdot F_{i,t} + \varepsilon_t \\ \sum_{i=1}^{k} \beta_i = 100\% \end{cases} \qquad (9.2)$$

Do we want to allow negative exposures, which are equivalent to short sales? In some cases, we may allow them in style analysis because hedge funds use short selling. But in other cases, we will not allow short sales on some asset classes (e.g. real estate), or even on all asset classes, because we want to identify the combination of long-only positions in passive indices that

---

[5] The problem is similar to the omitted variable problem in regression analysis.

would most closely replicate the actual performance of a fund over a specified time period. Then, we may need to impose a constraint excluding the possibility of short positions. Our model then becomes:

$$
\begin{cases}
R_t = \alpha + \sum_{i=1}^{k} \beta_i \cdot F_{i,t} + \varepsilon_t \\
\beta_i \geq 0 \quad \text{for some } i
\end{cases}
\tag{9.3}
$$

The approach originally suggested by Sharpe (1992) constrained the beta coefficients to sum to 100% *and* required that each beta coefficient be greater than or equal to zero. The style analysis model then becomes:

$$
\begin{cases}
R_t = \alpha + \sum_{i=1}^{k} \beta_i \cdot F_{i,t} + \varepsilon_t \\
\beta_i \geq 0 \quad \text{for some } i \\
\sum_{i=1}^{k} \beta_i = 100\%
\end{cases}
\tag{9.4}
$$

De Roon *et al.* (2003) refer to this model as "strong style analysis". In the same vein, the case where only one portfolio constraint is imposed is referred to as "semi-strong style analysis" and the case where no constraint is imposed on the factor loadings is referred to as "weak style analysis". Note that we have included an intercept term in all our equations, while Sharpe's (1992) original model did not. However, this inclusion does not actually constitute a significant difference.[6]

We now have to estimate the coefficients of our model. Following what we did with regression analysis, we want to identify the series of beta coefficients that minimize the variance of the error term ε. Furthermore, these beta coefficients have to satisfy the constraints, if any:

Find $\beta_1, \ldots, \beta_k$

To minimize $\mathrm{Var}(\varepsilon)$

Subject to

$$\beta_1, \ldots, \beta_k \geq 0$$

$$\sum_{i=1}^{k} \beta_i = 100\%$$

where the error term ε is defined in equation (9.1), (9.2), (9.3) or (9.4), depending on which version of style analysis we want to implement.

Note that although the addition of constraints in our model seems natural and logical from an economic perspective, their presence means that we can no longer estimate the coefficients by running an OLS regression. Thus, we have to turn to quadratic programming techniques. These are relatively easy to implement, an example being Microsoft's Excel spreadsheet, which includes a basic optimizer called Solver. For more information on the details of these techniques, one can refer to Markowitz' (1959) critical line method or the simpler gradient method described in Sharpe (1987).

---

[6] As Becker (2003) explains in detail, because Sharpe's method is to minimize the variance of the error term, not the sum of squared errors, his model has an intercept term built in implicitly.

Box 9.1   Is the solution unique?

An interesting mathematical aspect is the question of the uniqueness of the style analysis solution. What if there were two entirely different sets of style coefficients, resulting in two entirely different style benchmarks, and the excess return of the manager over these two different style benchmarks were the same minimal value? Fortunately, if the style factors are not collinear, the answer is that such a situation can never occur. It can be proved mathematically that there always exists exactly one set of style coefficients such that the excess return of the manager over the corresponding style benchmark is minimal.[7]

Similarly to the traditional regression analysis case, it is possible to calculate an indicator of the quality of the fit provided by the constrained regression. This indicator is also called R-square (R^2), and is defined as the proportion of the variance explained by the style benchmark (i.e. the portfolio of k asset classes) compared with the total fund's variance. It is calculated as:

$$R^2 = 1 - \frac{\text{Var}(\varepsilon_P)}{\text{Var}(R_P)} \tag{9.5}$$

The maximum value is 1 and the minimum 0. A high R^2 implies that the style benchmark captures a large proportion of the fund variance. Note that while it is desirable from a statistical point of view to observe high R^2, it also raises an important question from an investment perspective. If most of a fund's performance can be replicated by investing in a passive portfolio of indices, why not invest in the passive portfolio right away, and save the expense of hiring an expensive manager? Hence, in practice, the likelihood of observing very large R^2 is usually low, as each hedge fund manager has his own specificities.

The application of return-based style analysis to analyze hedge funds has proved beneficial, but its results must be carefully interpreted. In particular, it is often stated that the beta coefficients provided by style analysis correspond to the actual hedge fund allocation among asset classes. This is clearly wrong. Return-based style analysis does not determine what was effectively in a fund in terms of asset classes, but rather the way the fund behaved on average over some period (the period used for estimating the coefficients). Thus, the most we can say is that the fund behaved on average "as if" it invested using these weights. A quote attributed to William Sharpe summarizes this as follows: "If it acts like a rabbit, treat it like a rabbit." After all, who cares if it really is a rabbit, provided it acts (and tastes) in exactly the same way?

9.2.4   Application to hedge funds

We now illustrate the power of style analysis and some of its limits by applying it to a sample of hedge funds. The first fund we consider is Bricoleur Partners LP. Created in November 1993 by Daniel Wimsatt and John Bloomberg, this long/short equity fund uses a research-intensive, fundamental, bottom-up, investment process. A contrarian, diversified approach leads to investments in out-of-favor and/or smaller capitalization securities having the potential to appreciate 50% within a year. Short sales of companies with diminished outlooks or valuations

---

[7] Minimizing the variance of excess return of the manager over the style benchmark amounts to finding the shortest distance between a point and a convex set in a certain Euclidean space; it is true in every Euclidean space that this distance is assumed at exactly one point on the convex set.

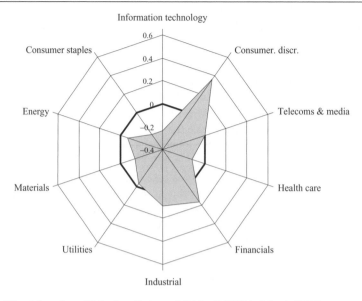

Figure 9.1   The style radar of Bricoleur Partners LP (April 2000 to March 2003)

over-extended by others' momentum investing techniques provide absolute profit opportunities and reduce market exposure. Opportunistic trading and technical analysis are also employed.

We first analyze the style exposures of Bricoleur Partners LP from April 2000 to March 2003 using MSCI sector indices as asset classes. We use the unconstrained version of style analysis, i.e. the model of equation (9.1). We plot the exposures as a radar graph in Figure 9.1. We find that only three sectors have positive style weights (consumer discretionary: +0.36, financials: +0.17, industrial: +0.10), one has a zero exposure (telecoms and media), and the rest have negative style weights (materials: −0.14, information technology: −0.24, health care: −0.12, energy: −0.17, utilities: −0.03). The tracking error between the fund and its style benchmark is 6.47% p.a. The R^2 of style analysis is equal to 0.40, which means that 40% of the fund variance is captured by a passive position in the above-mentioned style exposures. Hence, there is much that this analysis is not capturing – further investigation of the fund's characteristics is therefore recommended.[8]

Sectors are only one way to analyze the investment style of Bricoleur Partners LP; there are numerous other ways. For instance, Figure 9.2 shows the results of an alternative style analysis. We still focus on Bricoleur Partners LP from April 2000 to March 2003 and still use the unconstrained version of style analysis, i.e. the model of equation (9.1). But this time we take the Fama and French benchmark portfolios (BL, BM, BH, SL, SM, SH) plus T-bills as our asset classes. We find positive style weights for small growth (+0.22), big medium (+0.12), small medium (+0.07) and small value (+0.05), and negative style weights for big growth (−0.26) and big value (−0.11). The tracking error between the fund and its style benchmark is 6.47% p.a., and the R^2 is 0.55.

If we decide to constrain the weights to sum to 100%, we also need to consider cash as another asset class. In that case, our model becomes the model of equation (9.2). The new fund

---

[8] Note that a low R^2 does not mean a failure of the style analysis model. It simply means that the fund considered is not easily pigeonholed according to traditional sector benchmarks.

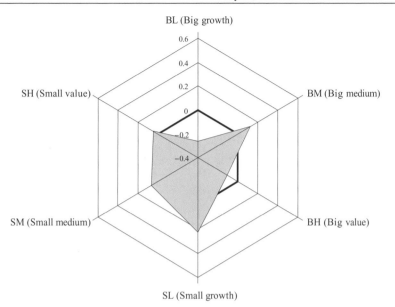

Figure 9.2 The style radar of Bricoleur Partners LP (April 2000 to March 2003) using Fama and French factors

radar (not displayed) is almost identical to that of Figure 9.2, with positive style weights for small growth (+0.22), big medium (+0.13), small medium (+0.05) and small value (+0.06), and negative style weights for big growth (−0.25) and big value (−0.13). The last position corresponds to cash (+0.91) and ensures that the total of the exposures is equal to 100%. The tracking error of the fund versus its style benchmark is 5.56% p.a. and the R^2 of style analysis is 0.56.

The advantage of forcing the coefficients to sum to 100% is that we can really interpret them as weights in a portfolio. Consequently, the performance of the style benchmark is directly comparable to the performance of the fund – see Figure 9.3. The divergences between the fund and its style benchmark are the result of the fund manager's specific investment decisions. In the case of Bricoleur Partners LP, these decisions had a positive impact, as the fund clearly outperformed its style benchmark.

The second fund to which we apply style analysis is Haussmann Holdings. Created in 1973, Haussmann Holdings is one of the oldest funds of hedge funds in the industry and also one of the largest. Managed by Permal Asset Management and advised by LCH Investments, a joint venture between LCF Rothschild Asset Management and MeesPierson, it invests money essentially with US long/short equity managers as well as with global macro managers who make bets on the direction of interest rates, bonds and currencies.

Figure 9.4 shows the style allocation of Haussmann Holdings as of June 2003 – in fact, the average style exposure from July 2000 to June 2003. Following the suggestion of Lhabitant (2001), we use the CSFB Tremont as style indices.[9] Based on the style radar, it is clear that the fund has a strong style exposure to long/short equity (+0.64), followed by emerging markets

---

[9] In this case, it makes sense to reject negative style exposures. For instance, how would we interpret a negative exposure to the dedicated short investment style?

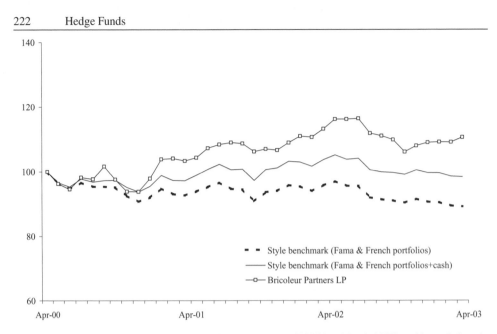

Figure 9.3 Comparison between Bricoleur Partners LP (April 2000 to March 2003) and its style benchmarks based on Fama and French portfolios (all investments are rescaled at 100 on April 2000)

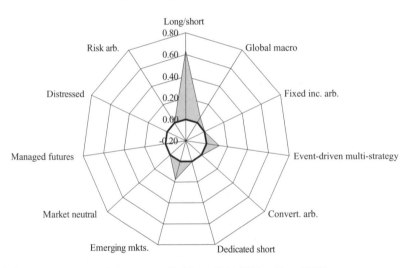

Figure 9.4 The style radar of Haussmann Holdings (July 2000 to June 2003)

(+0.17), event-driven multi-strategy (+0.12) and global macro (+0.06). All the other style exposures are nil, and the R^2 is remarkably high for a hedge fund (0.81).

Style radars provide a visually appealing way of presenting and comparing a fund's average style allocation at one point in time. This is specifically useful when analyzing funds of hedge funds and multi-manager portfolios, which offer investors an efficient way of diversifying risks across a number of managers and strategies. Are they truly diversified across styles? Fund radars help to provide a visual answer to this question. For those who prefer a quantitative indicator, style concentration may be measured by the Herfindahl–Hirschman concentration index, computed as the normalized sum of squared style exposures:

$$\text{HHI} = \sum_{i=1}^{k} \left(\frac{\beta_i}{\sum\limits_{j=1}^{k} \beta_j} \right)^2 \qquad (9.6)$$

Funds with a high Herfindahl–Hirschman concentration index are more concentrated than funds with a lower index. Adjusting by the sum of style exposures is necessary here because, depending on the version of style analysis employed, the sum of style exposures may differ significantly between funds, and this would bias the comparisons.

9.2.5 Rolling window analysis

The major drawback of style analysis is that it implicitly assumes that style exposures are constant over the period in question. However, in practice, assuming a fixed style allocation over a long time is hardly sustainable. It is therefore necessary to apply style analysis in a dynamic way, for instance using a rolling window analysis. The process is as follows. We divide the period under study into two segments. Returns in the first segment, the sample period, are used as a basis for constructing the style benchmark. The sample period is then rolled forward month by month and the process is repeated for each period, allowing the style benchmark weights to vary.

By using rolling windows, the fund's investment style is constantly monitored, making classification and style exposures readily identifiable. Such a rolling style benchmark tracks the manager's actual returns much more closely than static benchmarks. It determines how the fund's styles may have changed over time. It also allows faster reactions to changes in management style ("style drifts"), and so provides an early warning of potential changes in future performance. This is particularly useful for institutional investors, who want to know whether funds adhere to their stated investment styles over time.

As an illustration, Figure 9.5 shows the evolution of the style allocation for Haussman Holdings using the CSFB/Tremont as style indices and a 36-month rolling window. The style weights are constrained to be positive and sum to 100%, i.e. the model of equation (9.4). We can see that the fund's exposure to various styles has been fairly consistent. The apparent reallocation from global macro to emerging markets needs to be interpreted with caution, as a large number of global macro managers occasionally take bets in emerging markets. So the apparent drift may in fact be attributable to changes at the underlying macro funds level rather than to changes in the asset allocation of Haussman Holdings itself. Once again, collaboration between qualitative and quantitative analysts could easily check that point.

In contrast, the graph of Ocean Strategies Limited, another fund of hedge funds, indicates considerable fluctuations and variability in style exposures – see Figure 9.6. The R^2 is still high (0.61 in June 2003), but exposures to long/short equity and event-driven have widely fluctuated, and the fund has periodically shown exposure to almost all available styles. This instability in the exposure distribution may have four potential sources:

- The manager of Ocean Strategies Limited aggressively switches his allocations in and out of underlying managers or strategies in order to time the market. A high annual turnover in the fund of funds is a strong indicator of this type of situation.

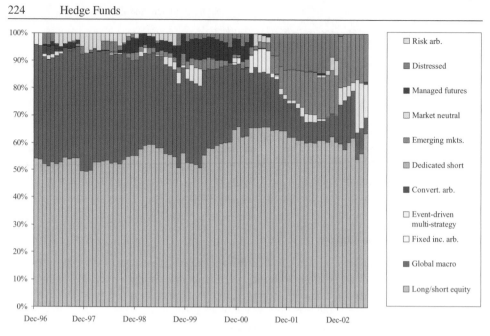

Figure 9.5   Evolution of style exposures of Haussmann Holdings

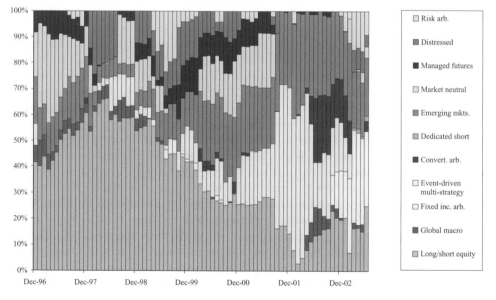

Figure 9.6   Evolution of style exposures of Ocean Strategies Limited

- Ocean Strategies Limited has a low turnover, but its underlying managers are changing the nature of their respective funds or their holdings. This typically happens if the underlying managers belong to the multi-strategy category, or have a discretionary mandate.
- The return data of Ocean Strategies Limited is noisy, due to errors in measurement, lack of synchronicity, etc.

- The benchmarks used for style analysis are poorly selected. For instance, if two benchmarks are too highly correlated (not mutually exclusive), the regression may fail to distinguish which of the two should be considered as relevant, and the weightings may oscillate from period to period. Likewise, if the set of benchmarks does not cover all the available styles, the regression will have trouble matching the fund's returns with the given benchmarks and will flip-flop between those that temporarily provide a best fit. This is unlikely to be the case here.

Fluctuating style exposures such as the ones of Figure 9.6 therefore call for more research to understand their origin. However, whatever the conclusion, we should not forget that these style exposures are simply estimates that might not be directly tied to the actual asset allocation of Ocean Strategies Limited. They simply correspond to the allocation of the portfolio of asset classes that best matched the behavior of the fund over the period in question. This is of course a strong paradigm shift for those who are accustomed to dealing with fundamental analysis and asset-based exposures, but it is a crucial element to keep in mind when gauging and using the results of style analysis.

9.2.6   Statistical significance

If you were hoping to avoid the now traditional discussion on statistical significance, you are in for a disappointment. So far, our presentation of style analysis has provided point estimates of the style exposures of a given portfolio, but has given no information on the uncertainty surrounding these estimates (confidence intervals, asymptotic distributions, etc.). This type of information would be helpful for at least three reasons: (1) to assess the accuracy of estimated style coefficients, (2) to test whether coefficients are significantly different from zero and (3) to determine whether style coefficients are significantly different from each other. Unfortunately, we are no longer using regression analysis, but constrained quadratic optimization. The presence of constraints considerably complicates the task of obtaining precise confidence intervals.

Lobosco and DiBartolomeo (1997) propose a convenient two-step procedure to approximate the confidence intervals for style weights. Their model can be summarized as follows. Say we want to conduct style analysis for a fund, using k style indices and N data points. First, we conduct a regular style analysis of the fund returns using the k indices. This provides the coefficient estimates β_i $(i = 1, \ldots, k)$, as well as the standard deviation of the residuals unexplained by the k indices, which we denote by σ_ε. Second, we conduct style analysis of each of the k style indices using the remaining $(k - 1)$ indices as explanatory variables. This provides the standard deviation of the residuals from style analysis of each index relative to the remaining $(k - 1)$ indices. We denote this standard deviation by σ_i for each index i.

Lobosco and DiBartolomeo show that the standard error of the style weight β_i $(i = 1, \ldots, k)$ is given by

$$\sigma_{\beta_i} = \frac{1}{\sqrt{N - k^* - 1}} \frac{\sigma_\varepsilon}{\sigma_i} \tag{9.7}$$

where k^* denotes the number of indices with non-zero style weights. Using this standard error, it is possible to build confidence intervals for the style parameters. For instance, the 95% confidence interval for the parameter β_i is $[\beta_i - 2\sigma_{\beta_i}; \beta_i + 2\sigma_{\beta_i}]$. If zero is included in this interval, then β_i is not statistically different from zero. Hence, all beta coefficients that are not statistically different from zero should be eliminated, and the two-step procedure repeated with the remaining indices until all coefficients are statistically different from zero.

Note that the approach of Lobosco and DiBartolomeo is valid only if none of the style weights is equal to zero or one.[10] If the latter condition is not satisfied, we need to turn to more complex techniques to build the confidence interval. For instance, Kim *et al.* (2000) develop a comparable Bayesian method to obtain statistically valid distributions and confidence intervals, regardless of the true values of style weights. More recently, Otten and Bams (2000) employed the estimation algorithm introduced by Kuhn–Tucker to obtain the asymptotic distribution function for the estimated style weights. They showed that the optimal parameter estimates for the model with constraints could be expressed in terms of the optimal parameter estimates for the model without the constraints (i.e. linear regression). Since the asymptotic distribution is well known for the unconstrained model, the asymptotic distribution for the constrained model follows through the relationship between the constrained and unconstrained parameter estimates.

9.2.7 The dangers of misusing style analysis

Experienced users of return-based style analysis know that despite the simplicity of the technique, applying it to hedge funds is something between an art and a science. In particular, return-based style analysis does not pretend to have all of the answers regarding hedge fund allocations: no analytical tool does. Return-based style analysis simply provides us with some useful information, and this information must be interpreted carefully. It can confirm what a fund manager is saying, or be used as an early warning tool, but it should not replace qualitative analysis and regular discussions with the fund manager.

In particular, it is important to understand that the time frame and the selection of adequate style benchmarks are crucial. On the one hand, the number of data points used to estimate all the coefficients should be sufficient, without overfitting or underfitting the data. But on the other hand, an overlap in the style indices results in noise as the model struggles to differentiate between the various returns. And if the style indices are not comprehensive, the resulting poor fit again creates noise. This is why, when it comes to interpretation, the difference between meaningful and misleading assessments of style exposures lies in whether the analyst has made use of the checks and balances inherent in the technique.

As mentioned already, when style analysis is used for exposure monitoring, the average exposure in the past is often confused with the current exposure, which is obviously wrong. This problem is well known to experienced users and is often referred to as a "rear-view mirror" perspective. In fact, style analysis works well for managers whose style exposure is relatively stable over time. This leads to a paradox – if we know that a technique is accurate only when the portfolio exposure does not change over time, how can it be used to monitor and evaluate the effects of changes in exposure? Difficult to answer.

Researchers have recently come up with several ways of alleviating the rear-view problem and improving the accuracy of style analysis. For instance, higher weighting may be given to more recent returns. This improves accuracy because it minimizes the delay between a change in a portfolio's exposure and the point in time when this change is sensed by style analysis.

---

[10] The reason is that Lobosco and DiBartolomeo use a Taylor series expansion to obtain their estimated variance. When some coefficients are equal to zero or one, they are on the boundary of the parameter space, which precisely prevents us from using a Taylor series expansion.

Alternatively, use may be made of a centered regression window, where the point of estimate is placed in the center rather than at the end of the window. The combination of these two methods is well known in statistics, where it is called locally weighted regression. Some commercial style analysis programs now offer it to improve the accuracy of style analysis results.

9.3   THE KALMAN FILTER

From a theoretical point of view, we have to admit that there is no argument to justify the use of rolling windows in style analysis. This even creates a contradiction between the estimation model (which assumes constant exposures) and the final output (which displays varying exposures). If style exposures change over time, their variations should be explicitly modeled rather than estimated by a rolling window assuming them to be constant. The Kalman filter is a tool that allows precisely this sort of modeling.

Named after Rudolph E. Kalman (1940), the Kalman filter is essentially a computational algorithm that makes optimal use of imprecise data on a linear (or nearly linear) system with Gaussian errors to continuously update the best estimate of the system's past, current and even future states. In a sense, the Kalman filter is similar to least squares fitting, but allows for real-time updates to the fit. Initially developed for signal processing and control applications, the Kalman filter had originally no particular link with finance. It is only recently that Swinkels and van der Sluis (2001) suggested applying it to a dynamic model of style analysis.

The Swinkels and van der Sluis model is formulated as follows:

$$\begin{cases} R_t = \alpha_t + \sum_{i=1}^{N} \beta_{i,t} \cdot F_{i,t} + \varepsilon_t \\ \alpha_{t+1} = \alpha_t + a_{t+1} \\ \beta_{i,t+1} = \beta_{i,t} + b_{i,t+1} \end{cases} \tag{9.8}$$

for $i = 1, \ldots, N$ and $t = 1, \ldots, T$. The error terms a_{t+1} and $b_{i,t+1}$ are assumed to be independently normally distributed with zero mean and constant variance, which implies that the coefficients α and β_i are allowed to evolve over time according to a random walk.[11]

In the Kalman filter terminology, the first equation of the system (9.8) is called the measurement equation, while the two other equations are called the transition equations, as they determine the way α and β_i are going to evolve over time. Note that the time-invariant version of this model (i.e. the traditional unconstrained style analysis) is obtained by setting both $a_t = 0$ and $b_{i,t} = 0$ for any time t and fund i. Of course, it is possible to add additional constraints (such as the non-negativity of the style exposures) or to hypothesize a different adjustment of the style exposures (mean reversion, etc.), sometimes at the cost of additional complexity in the estimation procedure – see Harvey (1989, 1993).

An interesting feature of the Kalman approach is that there are in fact two versions of the algorithm, which differ essentially in the set of information that they use. The Kalman filter uses all the past information to determine the current and future exposures. It is therefore very suitable for forecasting and predicting future exposures. The Kalman smoother, on the other hand, uses the entire sample of data to estimate all exposures in each period. Consequently, with the smoother, given a data set, the exposures in the middle of the sample will be influenced by the variation of exposures at the end of the sample. Therefore, the smoother is more

---

[11] See Harvey (1993). The random walk for α and β_i is in fact the most convenient model to start with if we have no particular idea as to how a fund manager increases or decreases his exposures. Of course, other models can also be specified.

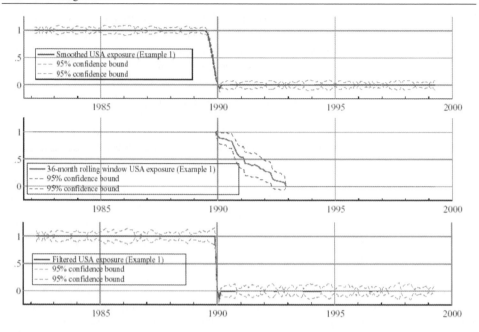

Figure 9.7 Estimating style exposures using the Kalman smoother, style analysis (rolling 36-month) and the Kalman filter. The model used by the Kalman filter and smoother assumes that the style coefficients evolve randomly
Source: Swinkels and van der Sluis (2001).

realistic for descriptive purposes, as well as for performance evaluation (where all the data is known).

As an illustration of the power of the Kalman filter and smoother, Swinkels and van der Sluis created a fictive fund that invested all its assets in the MSCI USA from May 1979 to December 1989 and switched to MSCI Europe from January 1989 to December 1999. Figure 9.7 shows the estimated style exposures using Kalman smoothing (top panel), style analysis (middle panel, 36-month rolling window) and Kalman filtering (bottom panel). Clearly, the Kalman filter reacts much faster than the smoother, which itself is faster than the rolling window regression. This is not really surprising, as the rolling regression takes time to accommodate such a sudden exposure change. In fact, it is only influenced by the new returns progressively as they enter the rolling window. After 18 months, style analysis has before it a sample of 18 USA returns and 18 European returns; it takes 36 months for the sample of returns to contain only European returns. The smoother, in contrast, starts its transition much earlier, because it is already taking into account future returns in its analysis. The filter only uses past information, but it reacts very quickly to a change in its environment. This confirms its usefulness and applicability to the changing nature of hedge fund portfolios.

Despite its apparent empirical superiority, the Kalman filter has admittedly not taken the lead over traditional style analysis. The reason is simply that the Kalman filter is quite complex to understand and implement. Its derivation, by whatever method, is bound to be lengthy and its equations are difficult to memorize. But it is precisely this complexity that gives the Kalman filter its enormous power. It represents an *omnium gatherum* for a wide range of linear problems in statistical inference.

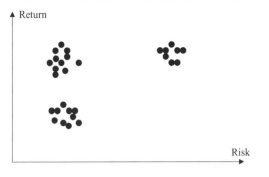

Figure 9.8   Risk and return characteristics for a sample of hedge funds

9.4   CLUSTER ANALYSIS

We now turn to a new set of techniques that aim at analyzing large universes of hedge funds. Cluster analysis[12] is a generic name given to a set of statistical techniques that attempt to aggregate similar objects – in our case, hedge funds – into groups or clusters that satisfy two main criteria. First, each cluster must be homogenous, in the sense that funds that belong to the same cluster should be similar to each other. Second, each cluster must be different from other clusters, that is, funds that belong to one cluster should be different from the funds of other clusters.

The beauty of clustering techniques is that clusters do not have to be prespecified, but can be identified automatically from the data. Indeed, the bases for cluster analysis are a multivariate set of funds, i.e. a series of funds characterized by more than one measurement and a measure of similarity between two funds, which is called a "distance". Its interpretation is straightforward: the smaller the distance is between two hedge funds, the more similar these funds are. By construction, the members of a cluster will be close (that is, similar) to each other and far (that is, different) from members of other clusters, still according to the distance (similarity) measure provided by the user.

Clustering has multiple applications, particularly for index construction, peer group selection, pattern recognition and fund classification purposes. Taxonomy is a typical example of an area where we want to distinguish between populations of funds, or we intend to classify them based on measured characteristics. We will come back to these applications later. For the moment, let us first have a look at how cluster analysis works.

9.4.1   Understanding cluster analysis

Consider, for instance, a sample of hedge funds for which two characteristics are available, namely, the return and volatility measured over a given period. Since we are only working with two characteristics, we are able to represent our data in a two-dimensional space, i.e. on a plane. Following the convention, we plot the realized return of each fund on the vertical axis and its volatility on the horizontal axis – see Figure 9.8.

How many clusters, that is, groups of similar funds, can we identify in this graph? In fact, the answer depends on what we are interested in. If we consider solely the return (i.e. if the distance between funds only considers returns), we will probably obtain two clusters, one with

---

[12] In the social sciences, cluster analysis is also sometimes called "unsupervised learning" or "learning by observation".

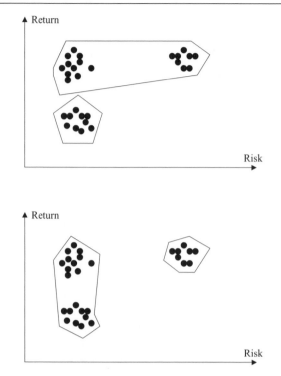

Figure 9.9   The return clusters (top) and the risk clusters (bottom)

high-return funds (top) and one with low-return funds (bottom). If we consider solely volatility (i.e. if the distance between funds only considers volatility), we will also obtain two clusters, one with high-risk funds (right) and one with low-risk funds (left). However, the two risk clusters will be different from the two return clusters, both in terms of number of points and constituent funds – see Figure 9.9. This clearly implies that the choice of a particular distance may influence the results significantly.

Now it is obvious that clustering only on the basis of risk or return is not a very good idea. Visually, we have three clusters of funds in our data set. To identify them, we need to use a distance measure that accounts simultaneously for risk and return. We will come back later to the question of how to build such a distance, but we know that if this distance makes sense, we should obtain three clusters as in Figure 9.10. These clusters minimize the intra-cluster distance (distance between points within a cluster) while at the same time maximizing the inter-cluster distance (distance between different clusters).

Visually identifying clusters is relatively easy as long as we are working in a two-dimensional space, that is, with only two characteristics. If we consider another characteristic in addition to risk and return, say for instance the assets under management of each fund, we can still represent our data graphically, but in a three-dimensional space. Clusters then become "bubbles" of points similar to each other and very different from points of other clusters. And it may be the case that new clusters emerge when assets under management are also taken into consideration – see Figure 9.11, where the low-risk, low-return group of funds is split between large funds and small funds.

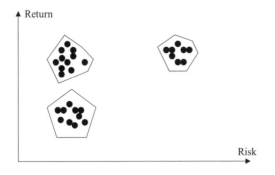

Figure 9.10   The clusters obtained when considering both risk and return

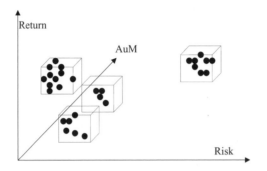

Figure 9.11   Three-dimensional clusters

With more than three characteristics, there is no simple graphical representation to help us. Identifying clusters then becomes extremely difficult, and is often highly subjective if done qualitatively. It is precisely for handling data sets with a large number of characteristics that cluster analysis has been developed. It identifies existing clusters in a systematic, non-biased, quantitative way and reveals associations and structure in data that, though not previously evident, are nevertheless significant and useful once found. Its approach consists in minimizing the intra-cluster distance while at the same time maximizing the inter-cluster distance. The only difference is that we are not working in one, two or three dimensions but in P dimensions, where P is the number of characteristics considered. The goal of cluster analysis can then be summarized as follows:

Given a data set of N hedge funds with P characteristics for each fund, determine a partition of the funds into K groups, or clusters, such that the funds in a cluster are more similar to each other than to patterns in different clusters. The value of K may or may not be specified.

9.4.2   Clustering methods

Typical clustering methods involve the following four steps: (1) define the funds' P measurable characteristics, (2) choose a distance to measure the similarity of funds, (3) choose and apply the clustering algorithm, (4) interpret and validate the clustering results.

9.4.2.1   Data representation and preparation

Clustering techniques can accept virtually any type of input. However, in practice, we are only interested in clustering a data set based on a series of well-known characteristics.[13] For hedge funds, these could be quantities such as the assets under management, the time since inception, the performance fees, the monthly returns or volatilities, or a mix of these as well as any other observable and measurable quantity. In the following, for the sake of illustration, we restrict ourselves to clustering hedge funds based on their respective track record (i.e. monthly returns).

The *data matrix* collects measurements about the monthly returns of each of the funds considered. Formally, if we have N hedge funds and P returns per fund, we can represent our data set as a matrix with N lines and P columns:

$$X = \begin{bmatrix} R_{1,1} & R_{1,2} & \cdots & R_{1,P} \\ R_{2,1} & R_{2,2} & \cdots & R_{2,P} \\ \vdots & \vdots & & \vdots \\ R_{N,1} & R_{N,2} & \cdots & R_{N,P} \end{bmatrix}$$

In this data matrix, each row contains the returns of a hedge fund. It is sometimes referred to as a "profile". Each month corresponds to a column. Hence, an element $R_{i,j}$ denotes the jth monthly return of the ith fund (with $i = 1, \ldots, N$, $j = 1, \ldots, P$).

Box 9.2   Standardizing the data

In some cases, it is desirable to standardize the data matrix. For instance, say we have two versions of the same fund, one with no leverage and one with a five-time leverage. The leveraged returns will be approximately five times larger than the non-leveraged returns. Do we want to consider the two funds as being identical or do we want to distinguish them? In the former case, we should normalize our data by withdrawing the mean return and dividing the result by the standard deviation. In the latter, we should leave the data as it is.

9.4.2.2   Definition of a distance function/similarity matrix

In order to find natural groupings in a set of data, we must now define the criteria that will be used to compare two funds. Instead of manipulating the data matrix directly, most techniques build up a proximity matrix (or similarity matrix) that contains the distance between any pair of funds. This distance should be a small value for very similar funds and a large value for very different funds. Naturally, there are several ways of defining such a distance.

In a one-dimensional space, we have only one return for each fund (e.g. one annual return). The data matrix is a one-column vector with N lines. It is then relatively easy to calculate a distance between two funds by simply taking the absolute difference between their returns. Such a distance between fund i and fund j can be written as:[14]

$$d(i, j) = |R_{i,1} - R_{j,1}| \tag{9.9}$$

---

[13] The literature also frequently contains the terms "variates", "variables", "responses", "attributes" or "features" instead of "characteristics".

[14] Note that this is only one possible way of calculating a distance. There exist several other less intuitive distance measures that we will not consider here.

In a two-dimensional space, we have two returns for each fund (e.g. two annual returns). The data matrix becomes a two-column vector with N lines, and the distance measure between two funds must consider both returns simultaneously. Once again, there may exist a large series of distance measures. For instance, we could extend our one-dimensional distance definition by using:

$$d(i, j) = |R_{i,1} - R_{j,1}| + |R_{i,2} - R_{j,2}| \tag{9.10}$$

But we could also use our knowledge of geometry and the Pythagorean theorem to calculate the distance between fund i and fund j as:

$$d(i, j) = \sqrt{(R_{i,1} - R_{j,1})^2 + (R_{i,2} - R_{j,2})^2} \tag{9.11}$$

The latter distance is intuitively appealing, as it is indeed the geometric distance between two objects in a two-dimensional variable space.

Box 9.3   Properties of a distance function

More generally, what are the properties that a distance function should fulfill? There are actually four.

- Identity: $d(i, i) = 0$ for all i
- Non-negativity: $d(i, j) \geq 0$ for all i and j
- Symmetry: $d(i, j) = d(j, i)$ for all i and j
- Triangle inequality: $d(i, j) \leq d(i, k) + d(k, j)$

One can show that a distance function that does not satisfy these properties may lead to inconsistencies.

Let us now extend our approach to the general case, that is, when N funds are each represented by P returns. Then, the data matrix is a matrix with N lines and P columns. There exists a large series of distances between two funds that one may use. The most common ones form the *Minkowski class of distances*. All members of this class have the following shape:

$$d(i, j) = \left(\sum_{k=1}^{p} |R_{i,k} - R_{j,k}|^q \right)^{1/q} \tag{9.12}$$

where q is a number to be specified by the user. When $q = 1$, the metric is a linear measure of distance known as the *Manhattan distance*, also called the *city-block distance*. It is simply calculated as the sum of the absolute differences between characteristics:

$$d(i, j) = \sum_{k=1}^{p} |R_{i,k} - R_{j,k}| \tag{9.13}$$

When $q = 2$, the distance metric is the standard *Euclidean distance*, that is, the square root of the sum of the square of the differences between each fund i and fund j characteristic:

$$d(i, j) = \sqrt{\sum_{k=1}^{p} (R_{i,k} - R_{j,k})^2} \tag{9.14}$$

As mentioned already, the Euclidean distance has an intuitive appeal as it is commonly used to evaluate the proximity of objects in two- or three-dimensional space. Note that although using values of q greater than 2 is theoretically possible, it has the drawback of giving a measure that is extremely sensitive to outliers. Thus, in practice, the Manhattan and Euclidian distances are the most widely used among the Minkowski class of distances.

In addition to the Manhattan and Euclidian distances, clustering sometimes relies on alternative distance measures on a case-by-case basis. For instance, in some applications, it is desirable to relate the distance between fund i and fund j to their *correlation coefficient* $\rho_{i,j}$. However, the correlation coefficient is not a distance measure – in particular, it can take negative values. A possible solution is therefore to use the following transformation:

$$d(i, j) = \frac{1 - \rho_{i,j}}{2} \tag{9.15}$$

which ensures that the distance is never negative.

It is also possible to use *binary distances*, where 1 indicates a match and 0 indicates no match between any pair of cases. Note that it is usual in binary matching to have several characteristics, because there is a risk that when the number of attributes is small, they may be orthogonal to (uncorrelated with) one another, and clustering will be indeterminate.

Finally, we should also mention the existence of another type of distance called the *Mahalanobis distance*. This distance is widely used when the characteristics used are correlated or have very different variances. In that case, the Euclidian distance may be biased, for at least two reasons:

- First, it weights equally each characteristic in the distance calculation, hence giving implicitly a larger weight to a characteristic having a large variance. We would prefer a distance that takes into account the variability of each characteristic when determining the distance of a fund from another fund. Characteristics with high variability should receive less weight than characteristics with low variability.
- Second, it assumes independence of the various characteristics, which is not always true in practice. Think, for instance, about the size of a fund versus its age. The two are likely to be very correlated, so that we are in fact comparing funds twice using the same type of characteristic. In a sense, we double-weight that feature compared to others. We would prefer a distance that takes into account the correlation between characteristics when determining the distance of a fund from another fund.

The Mahalanobis distance corrects these two biases by using both the standard deviations for each characteristic *and* the correlation between characteristics. It is effectively a weighted, normalized, Euclidean distance, where the weighting is determined by the sample variance–covariance matrix. In a sense, funds that have a Mahalanobis distance of less than 1 have a 68% chance of being classified as members of the same cluster, funds that have a Mahalanobis distance of less than 2 have a 95% chance of being classified as members of the same cluster, etc.

Graphically, with two characteristics (i.e. in a two-dimensional space), due to the rescaling, funds having the same Mahalanobis distance of a given point form an ellipsoid, while they would form a sphere using the Euclidean distance (Figure 9.12). The same idea can of course be extended to more than two dimensions – one can think of the characteristics as defining a multidimensional space in which each observation can be plotted.

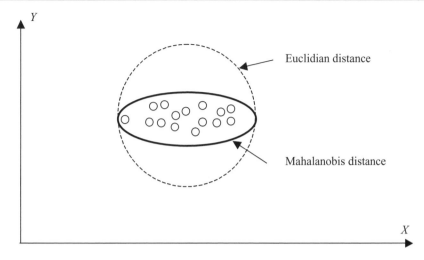

Figure 9.12 Euclidian distance versus Mahalanobis distance

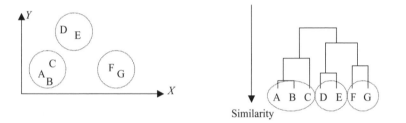

Figure 9.13 From data points (A, B, C, D, E) and clusters to a dendrogram

9.4.2.3   Clustering the data

Once the distance function has been selected, we need to determine the clustering algorithm, usually among the two main competing approaches, hierarchical clustering and partitional clustering.[15] Each approach encompasses a wealth of different algorithms for identifying the clusters, and the choice of a particular clustering method will often depend on the type of output desired.

Hierarchical clustering approaches proceed by stages and produce a sequence of partitions, each corresponding to a different number of clusters. The sequence of partitions is often represented as a tree of clusters (also called a dendrogram), in which every cluster node contains child clusters; sibling clusters partition the points covered by their common parent. Funds with high similarity are adjacent. Lines indicate the degree of similarity or dissimilarity between funds. In ultra-metric trees, line lengths indicate dissimilarities and by adding line lengths along the tree path connecting any two funds, the dissimilarity index for those two funds can be obtained. The dendrogram can be broken at different levels to yield a different number of clusters (Figure 9.13).

---

[15] See, for instance, Anderberg (1973), Hartigan (1975), Jain and Dubes (1988), Jardine and Sibson (1971), Sneath and Sokal (1973), Tryon and Bailey (1973).

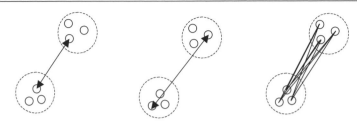

Figure 9.14   Single-link (left), complete-link (center) and average-link (right) clustering

Hierarchical clustering can adopt a top-down divisive or a bottom-up agglomerative algorithm. The divisive approach starts with all objects in a single, large cluster. This cluster is then gradually broken down into smaller and smaller clusters. Agglomerative techniques, on the other hand, start with usually single-member clusters, which are gradually merged until one large cluster is formed. In a few cases, the procedure is initiated from a coarser partition if some groupings are known.

Johnson (1967) suggested one of the simplest and easiest hierarchical clustering algorithms. Given a set of N funds to be clustered, and an $N \times N$ distance matrix, the basic process is as follows:

1. Start by assigning each fund to its own cluster, so that if you have N items, you now have N clusters, each containing just one fund. Let the distances between the clusters equal the distances between the funds they contain.
2. Find the closest pair of clusters and merge them into a single cluster, so that now you have one less cluster.
3. Compute distances between the new cluster and each of the old clusters (see below).
4. Repeat steps 2 and 3 until all items are clustered into a single cluster of size N.

Step 3 can be done in different ways, the most common being single-link, complete-link and average-link clustering (Figure 9.14):

- In single-link clustering (also called the nearest-neighbor technique, see Sneath and Sokal (1973)), the distance between one cluster and another is defined as being the *shortest* distance from any member of one cluster to any member of the other cluster. In other words, the distance between two clusters is given by the value of the shortest link between the clusters.
- In complete-link clustering (also called the diameter or maximum method), the distance between one cluster and another is defined as the *longest* distance from any member of one cluster to any member of the other cluster.
- In average-link clustering, the distance between one cluster and another is defined as the *average* distance from any member of one cluster to any member of the other cluster. A variation on average-link clustering is the method of D'Andrade (1978), which uses the *median* distance.

In addition to these three standard approaches, an alternative approach was suggested by Ward (1963). The rationale behind Ward's proposal is that grouping similar data into clusters implies somehow a loss of information, because we "forget" the individual data and only "remember" the cluster. Hence, we should form clusters in a manner that minimizes the loss associated with each grouping. In the agglomerative approach, this means that at each step in the analysis, the union of every possible cluster pair should be considered and the two clusters whose fusion results in a minimal amount of information loss should be combined. Ward suggests a sum-of-squares criterion to measure information loss. Merging two clusters then occurs only if this results in the smallest increase in the sum of squares.

Box 9.4   Example of Ward's approach

To illustrate Ward's approach, let us consider the case of univariate data. Say for instance that we have 10 funds whose performances last year were: 2%, 6%, 5%, 6%, 2%, 2%, 2%, 0%, 0%, 0%. The loss of information that would result from treating the 10 funds as one group with a mean return of 2.5% is represented by ESS, given by:

$$\text{ESS}_{\text{One group}} = (2 - 2.5)^2 + (6 - 2.5)^2 + \cdots + (0 - 2.5)^2 = 50.5$$

On the other hand, if the 10 funds are classified into four sets according to their returns:

$$\{0\%, 0\%, 0\%\}, \quad \{2\%, 2\%, 2\%, 2\%\}, \quad \{5\%\}, \quad \{6\%, 6\%\}$$

the ESS can be evaluated as the sum of squares of four separate error sums of squares:

$$\text{ESS}_{\text{One group}} = \text{ESS}_{\text{group1}} + \text{ESS}_{\text{group2}} + \text{ESS}_{\text{group3}} + \text{ESS}_{\text{group4}} = 0.0$$

Thus, clustering the 10 funds into four clusters results in no loss of information.

Unlike hierarchical clustering, *partitional clustering* does not proceed by steps but attempts to directly decompose the data set into a set of disjoint clusters. The criterion function that the clustering algorithm tries to minimize may emphasize the local or the global structure of the data. Typically the global criteria involve minimizing some measure of dissimilarity in the samples within each cluster, while maximizing the dissimilarity of different clusters.

Most partitional clustering algorithms represent each cluster by a centroid or a cluster representative; this is a somewhat summary description of all the objects contained in a cluster – we can think of it as being the average or median fund of the cluster. A very simple and efficient algorithm to generate clusters is the following:

1. Order all the objects according to a given criterion.
2. Make the first object the centroid for the first cluster.
3. For the next object, calculate the distance from each existing cluster centroid.
4. If the smallest calculated distance is smaller than some specified threshold value, add the object to the corresponding cluster and redetermine its centroid; otherwise, use the object to initiate a new cluster. If any objects remain to be clustered, return to the previous step.

The drawback of this algorithm, as can be shown, is that the resulting clusters depend on the order in which the objects were sorted at step 1.

The K-mean algorithm is by far the most popular partitional clustering tool used – see MacQueen (1967). It is a procedure that starts out with a set of K prespecified points and builds up the clusters around these points by moving funds iteratively from one group to another. Given a set of N funds to be clustered, and an $N \times N$ distance matrix, the basic process is as follows:

1. Choose K cluster centers to coincide with K arbitrarily chosen funds. Note that selecting a good initial partition will help speed up the process.

2. For each fund, compare the distance measured to each of the K cluster centers. Add the fund to the closest cluster.
3. Recalculate the cluster centroids using the new cluster memberships.
4. If a convergence criterion is not met, go to step 2.

Examples of typical convergence criteria are: no reassignment of funds to new cluster centers, cluster means do not shift more than a given cut-off value or maximum number of iterations reached. As a rule of thumb, the K-mean algorithm works well with clusters that are spherical in shape and have about the same variance,[16] but it is also very sensitive to initial starting values. When different starting values yield different classifications, one should choose the classification with the smallest mean square error, since this is often the objective function to be minimized. However, the differences with respect to the mean square error are often very small, even though the classifications might be very different. In addition, it is not always clear that the classification with the smaller mean square error is truly the better classification.

Box 9.5   Fuzzy clustering

The clustering approaches we have seen so far generate partitions; in a partition, each fund belongs to one and only one cluster, and clusters are disjoint. Fuzzy clustering extends this notion to associate each fund with every cluster using a membership function, which takes values in the [0,1] range. This membership function can be understood as the probability of belonging to a given cluster – see Zadeh (1965). This offers the advantage of handling in an elegant way the elements that have features belonging to more than one cluster.

The output of such algorithms is a clustering, but not a partition, in which each cluster is a fuzzy set of all the funds. Traditional clustering approaches are sometimes called "hard clustering", while fuzzy clustering is called "soft clustering". As an illustration, Figure 9.15 compares the results of hard clustering with soft clustering. The rectangles enclose two "hard" clusters in the data: $H_1 = 1, 2, 3, 4, 5$ and $H_2 = 6, 7, 8, 9$. A fuzzy clustering algorithm might produce the two fuzzy clusters $F_1 = 1, 2, 3, 4, 5, 7$ and $F_2 = 3, 6, 7, 8, 9$, depicted by ellipses.

9.4.2.4   Interpreting and validating the results

Clustering is broadly recognized as a useful tool for many applications. However, the results of clustering should be carefully evaluated before use.[17] Particularly for the techniques where there is no *a priori* indication of the actual number of clusters presented in a data set, there is a need for some kind of clustering results validation. As a first step, the stability of the clusters to different clustering techniques and distance measures should be tested, followed by a test of the stability according to population and characteristics.

A useful tool to compare two classifications CL_i and CL_j of N funds is the Rand (1971) index, which is defined as

$$\text{Rand}(CL_i, CL_j) = \frac{2}{N(N-1)} \sum_g \sum_{g^* > g} r_{g,g^*} \tag{9.16}$$

---

[16] From a statistical viewpoint, the clusters obtained by the K-mean can be interpreted as the maximum likelihood estimates (MLE) for the cluster means, if we assume that each cluster comes from a spherical normal distribution with different means but identical variance (and zero covariance).

[17] See for instance Halkidi *et al.* (2001) for cluster validation techniques.

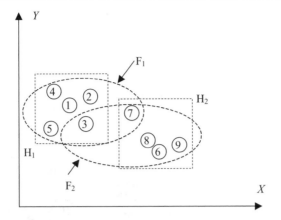

Figure 9.15   Fuzzy clusters versus hard clusters

where $r_{g,g*}$ is equal to 1 if two funds g and $g*$ belong in both classifications CL_i and CL_j of the same cluster, or in both classifications of different clusters. In a sense, the Rand index measures the proportion of consistent allocations. The Rand index is equal to $+1$ for a perfect fit, but values greater than 0.7 are usually considered sufficient – see Dreger (1986) and Fraboni and Salstone (1992).

9.4.3   Applications of clustering techniques

Let us now illustrate the use of clustering techniques with hedge fund data. We first consider the clustering of a sample from different strategies, and later illustrate the clustering of hedge funds based on their return histogram.

9.4.3.1   Managed futures versus convertible arbitrage

Our data set consists of the monthly returns from January 1999 to March 2003 from a series of 20 hedge funds following two investment styles, namely, managed futures (10 funds) and convertible arbitrage (10 funds). In addition, we use the CSFB Tremont indices that cover each of these two strategies. The annualized volatility, the annualized return and the maximum monthly loss of each fund/index is given in Table 9.1.

How many clusters do we have in our data set? Intuitively, from a strategy perspective, we should only observe two clusters, one for the convertible arbitrage and one for the managed futures funds. However, is this really the case in practice?

A two-dimensional graph representing the realized return of each fund on the horizontal axis and its volatility on the vertical axis (see Figure 9.16) seems to confirm that convertible arbitrage funds are in the northwest and that managed futures funds are in the southeast. However, there are a few exceptions such as Futures Select II, which falls right in the middle of the convertible arbitrage funds. Other funds such as Rivoli RIF or Exkhard are also quite close to the convertible arbitrage funds. We therefore need the help of clustering techniques to identify clusters in an impartial way.

Figures 9.17 to 9.21 show the dendrograms obtained with different clustering approaches. We clustered successively according to return (Figure 9.17), risk (Figure 9.18) and maximum monthly loss (Figure 9.19). We then clustered according to return, risk and maximum monthly

Table 9.1   Characteristics of a sample of convertible arbitrage and managed futures funds, January 1999 to March 2003

		Volatility (%)	Return (%)	Max. monthly loss (%)
	Convertible arbitrage funds			
C1	Advent	4.24	15.62	−2.57
C2	Alexandra	4.75	17.93	−1.79
C3	Alta Partners	8.05	26.69	−1.61
C4	Argent Classic (B)	12.96	20.67	−9.76
C5	Argent Classic (C)	0.68	10.03	0.48
C6	Argent Low Lev.	3.80	15.05	−1.91
C7	Clinton Riverside	4.85	18.15	−2.17
C8	GLG Mkt. Neutral	12.19	22.33	−3.61
C9	Helix Conv. Opp.	7.03	10.78	−4.78
C10	IIU Conv.	11.15	14.59	−1.96
	Managed futures funds			
F1	AIS Futures	40.56	8.70	−24.14
F2	AIS Futures II	23.35	8.49	−14.11
F3	Blue Danube	11.01	3.50	−8.29
F4	Exkhard	14.00	10.11	−5.76
F5	Future Select II	3.84	13.09	−0.65
F6	Graham Global	35.06	22.46	−18.10
F7	Legacy	43.92	9.05	−17.06
F8	Quadriga	31.74	26.03	−16.72
F9	Rivoli RIF	14.94	12.23	−7.30
F10	Salem	32.29	21.77	−13.68
	Indices			
IC	Tremont Conv. Arb.	4.11	15.32	−3.15
IF	Tremont Man. Futures	13.68	5.78	−8.62

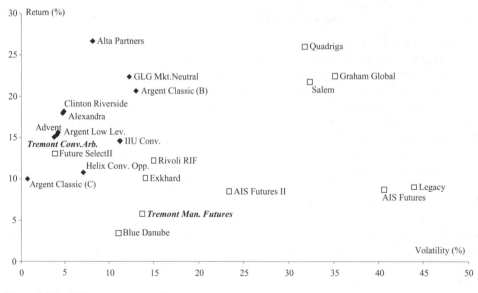

Figure 9.16   Risk–return perspective

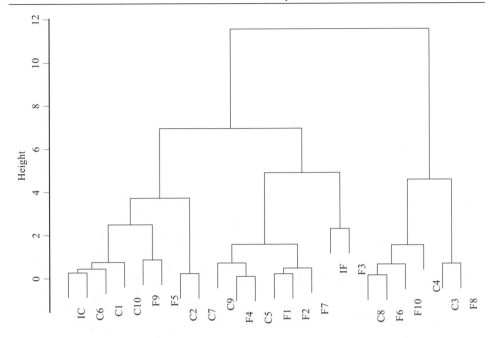

Figure 9.17   Clustering of selected funds according to return, using the Manhattan distance

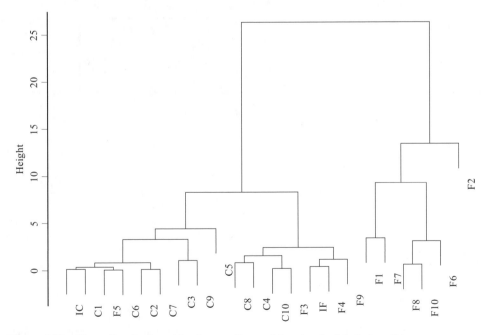

Figure 9.18   Clustering of selected funds according to risk, using the Manhattan distance

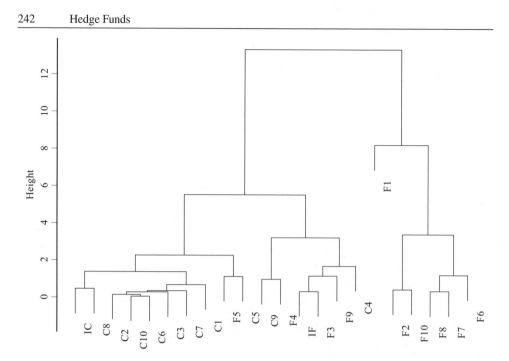

Figure 9.19 Clustering of selected funds according to maximum monthly loss, using the Manhattan distance

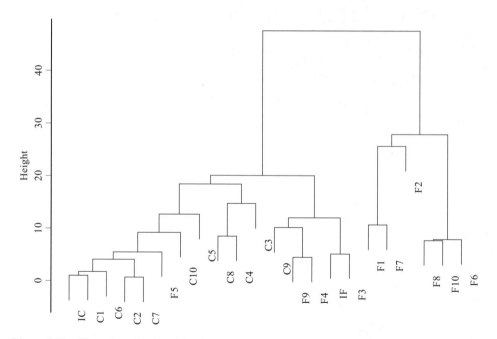

Figure 9.20 Clustering of selected funds according to risk, return and maximum monthly loss, using the Manhattan distance

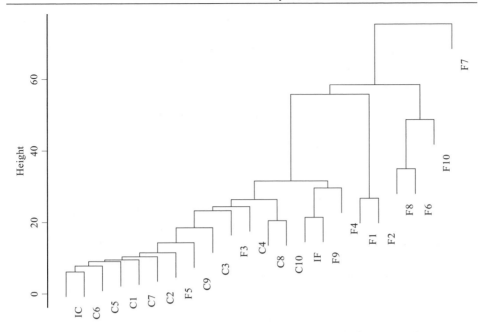

Figure 9.21   Clustering of selected funds according to 51 returns, using the Manhattan distance

loss simultaneously (Figure 9.20). Finally, we clustered with respect to the complete time series of monthly returns (Figure 9.21). Since we have 51 returns for each fund, this is equivalent to clustering on the basis of 51 different characteristics – or in a 51-dimensional space. The data was standardized in order to cancel out the impact of leverage. All analyses used the Manhattan distance, that is, the sum of the absolute differences between the characteristics considered. As one could expect, using different clustering criteria provides different dendograms.

9.4.3.2   Clustering of funds defined by histograms

Another application of clustering can be the grouping of funds based on their return histograms. Since the histograms are discrete distributions, they can be represented as feature vectors in a P-dimensional space, where P is the number of bins in the histogram.

9.4.3.3   Checking for heterogeneity of hedge fund returns: Martin (2001)

One of the earliest academic papers applying clustering techniques to analyze the investment style of hedge funds is Martin (2001). Based on the monthly data between January 1995 and June 1999 from the CISDM (formerly MAR) and HFR databases, Martin first uses cluster analysis to group funds so as to minimize intra-group variation while maximizing inter-group variation. The classification he derives corresponds to eight clusters, which approximately correspond to the following investment styles: managed futures, market arbitrage, event-driven, global established markets, emerging markets Latin America, emerging markets Asia, long-only equity and equity short.

To test for the stability of this classification, Martin uses a sample with August 1998 and a sample without August 1998, and compares the classifications obtained with both samples. He observes that managed futures, short sellers and long-only equity are among the most stable classifications, while event-driven and market arbitrage display significant equity-like exposure when August 1998 is included.

Next, Martin builds an equal-weighted index of the funds in each cluster, and compares each of the eight indices with its constituent funds. He observes significant heterogeneity in individual fund returns versus the index, and infers that conclusions derived from aggregate data are likely to be only weakly applicable to individual funds. In particular, the sensitivity of individual funds to economic variables such as spread levels, currencies and market indices varies widely across funds of the same cluster.

Brown and Goetzmann (2003) conduct a similar analysis confirming the heterogeneity of the hedge fund universe. They identify eight distinct styles or philosophies of asset management, and observe that risk exposure depends very much on style affiliation. Furthermore, they find that the persistence of fund returns from year to year has a lot to do with the particular style of fund management. In fact, 20% of the cross-sectional variability of fund returns can be explained solely by the fund's investment style.

9.4.3.4   Index and peer group construction

In addition to qualitative information such as manager self-classification and the manager's description of investment approaches, some hedge fund index providers also use clustering techniques to identify those funds that are most representative of a given style classification and include them in the corresponding index.

For instance, Zurich Capital Markets (ZCM) uses a K-partitioning approach that is very close to the K-mean algorithm. It also minimizes the average distance between all funds within a group and the fund that the algorithm chooses to represent the center of the cluster but, unlike the K-mean clustering, it ensures that cluster centers do correspond to an actual fund. The result is a set of five pure style indices, namely convertible arbitrage, merger arbitrage, distressed securities, event-driven multi-strategy and hedged equity.

Clustering approaches are also very useful in building coherent peer groups, to verify that a manager is classified correctly, to reclassify him if necessary and possibly to examine whether each manager's behavior and strategy are transparent enough and consistent over time. They also more objectively identify the degree to which hedge fund managers follow their stated strategies or deviate from them, as evidenced by Bares *et al.* (2001) on the Financial Risk Management[18] (FRM) database. The FRM database contained 2992 funds at the end of April 1999, managed by more than 1500 managers and divided into six distinct investment strategies, namely, trading, long/short market hedged, event-driven, relative value, market directional and multi-strategy. Unlike most other studies, Bares *et al.* focused on managers rather than on funds. They therefore created a unique track record for each manager by linking funds managed by the same manager with the same strategy. They imposed a track record of at least 36 months for each manager to enter the contest, and voluntarily excluded the market directional and multi-strategy styles. They were left with 629 managers following the trading, long/short market hedged, event-driven or relative value styles.

---

[18] Financial Risk Management is a London-based independent research and investment services company specialized in the construction of hedge fund portfolios.

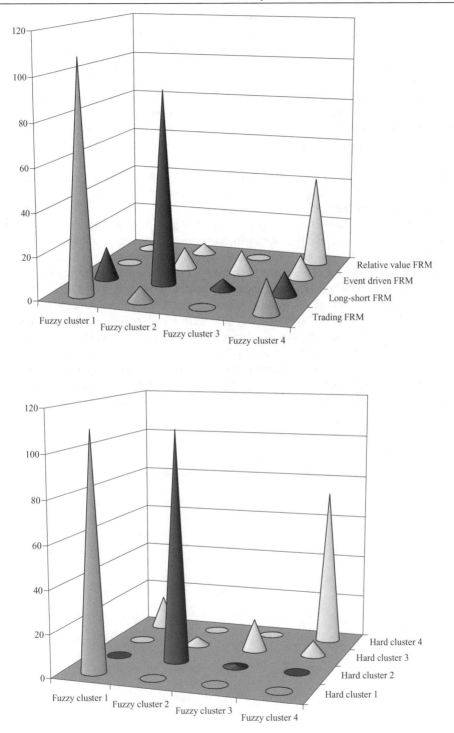

Figure 9.22 Correspondence between the managers in the FRM, the soft and the hard classifications

Bares *et al.* then used the K-mean algorithm with four distinct clusters and the Manhattan distance to partition the universe of managers. They observed a relatively good correspondence between the FRM classification and their cluster results, about 93% of the managers of cluster 1 being classified as trading, 71% of the managers of cluster 2 being classified as long/short, 40% of the managers of cluster 3 being classified as event-driven and 41% of the managers of cluster 4 being classified as relative value. To confirm this correspondence, Bares *et al.* built four equally weighted indices (one for each cluster) and regressed each index against the corresponding FRM style index. The R^2 of the regressions were 0.95, 0.94 and 0.84, respectively, for the first three clusters. The R^2 for the relative value cluster was only 0.17, but still significant.

Finally, Bares *et al.* also implemented fuzzy clustering, that is, constructed a probability $p_{i,j}(t)$ which measures manager i's inclination to follow style j at time t. Their results are summarized in Figure 9.22, where managers are taken into account only if their probability of belonging to a specific fuzzy cluster is greater than 0.5. We see that the majority of the managers are located on the diagonals of the table, which confirms the strong correspondence between the dominant fuzzy clusters, the hard clusters and the FRM investment style categories. As an illustration, 108 managers belong to both fuzzy cluster 1 and the FRM trading style, 91 managers belong to both fuzzy cluster 2 and the FRM long/short style, and 42 managers belong to both fuzzy cluster 3 and the FRM relative value style. The correspondence between fuzzy cluster 3 and the FRM event-driven category is less clear, with only 11 managers common to both groups. The correspondence between hard and fuzzy clusters provides a similar pattern.

To summarize, let us say that clustering techniques are a help to investors facing the flood of information and the multitude of dimensions that are typical of the hedge fund world. Given the absolute importance of classification in determining risk exposure and return outcome, appropriate style analysis and cluster construction are crucial to success.

Part III

Allocating Capital to Hedge Funds

10
Revisiting the Benefits and Risks of
Hedge Fund Investing

For most people, applying intellect to investment is like trying to cut your grass with a vacuum cleaner.

It may seem curious at this point to dwell on the benefits of hedge fund investing, as they are now well established and generally accepted by the vast majority of investors. Indeed, if you have managed to read up to this page, you are probably already convinced. But the important point with hedge funds is not simply to be convinced, it is to be convinced or unconvinced for the right reasons.

Hedge funds are entering the mainstream because they introduce a compelling new money management paradigm, which many investors are happy to embrace. Over the past few years, the difficult stock market conditions have made alternative assets in general and hedge funds in particular look like an El Dorado. Dazzled by the glitter of absolute performance, numerous investors have adopted hedge funds and included them in their portfolios, most of the time without really understanding what they were buying and with no clear understanding of the effective risk and return trade-off.[1]

There are anecdotes about extraordinary profits made by hedge funds as well as rumors about incredible failures due to fraud or excessive risk-taking. On the one hand, the legendary manager, George Soros, is credited with having compounded annual returns in excess of 30% after fees from 1969 to 2001. On the other hand, the over-leveraged Long Term Capital Management collapsed and was rescued only by the intervention of the Federal Reserve. Although representative of press coverage, these two funds are anything but representative of a rather large universe. Unfortunately, these outliers contribute significantly to the lack of public understanding of what hedge funds are in reality. Investing in hedge funds or rejecting them needs to be motivated by well-founded facts, not just by rumors or press coverage.

Before proceeding any further, let us clarify what we mean by "investing in hedge funds". Critically, we mean exposure to a broad and well-diversified portfolio of hedge funds. In practice, this typically implies investing in a fund of hedge funds. Indeed, most people do not have the time or the staff to deal with the complexity of reviewing, selecting and monitoring a dedicated, diversified portfolio of hedge funds. Moreover, the extra fees of funds of funds are significantly lower than the costs of hiring and supporting in-house staff. The other option, hiring consultants, is a lower cost alternative, but very few consultants are able to provide dynamic, strategy allocation recommendations, high-quality and independent research, and access to the best fund managers.

Whatever the choice of investment vehicle, it is essential to have a sufficiently diversified portfolio. Investing in only one or two hedge funds is extremely risky and entirely inappropriate

---

[1] The situation is reminiscent of a classic Woody Allen joke at the end of the film "Annie Hall". The character goes to a psychiatrist and says, "Doctor, my brother is crazy, he thinks he is a chicken". The doctor asks, "Well why don't you turn him in?" And the character answers, "I would, but I need the eggs". Needless to say, investors might end up being disappointed with their eggs!

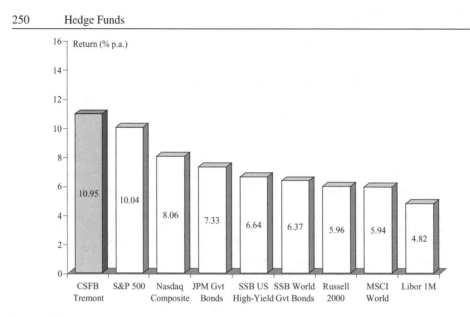

Figure 10.1   Annualized returns of several asset classes, January 1994 to June 2003

for the majority of investors. The best analogy is with equity portfolios. No rational investor would own only one or two stocks to gain equity exposure. The risk/reward trade-off is superior from holding a broad-based, diversified array of stocks. The same applies to hedge funds. Like equities, the specific risk associated with hedge funds is diversified away by holding a variety of investment styles.

So, assuming a well-diversified hedge fund investment, let us now highlight the benefits hedge funds offer investors as part of an overall traditional portfolio.

10.1   THE BENEFITS OF HEDGE FUNDS

While past performance does not necessarily help in predicting future performance, it still provides valuable insight into past hedge fund performance relative to traditional investments. In the following section, therefore, we examine hedge funds from a historical perspective. For the sake of simplicity, we use the CSFB/Tremont hedge fund index to represent hedge funds as a group, but all our discussions and conclusions are in fact independent of the choice of a particular index.[2]

10.1.1   Superior historical risk/reward trade-off

The first, and probably most important, reason for investing in hedge funds is simply superior performance. In sharp contrast to traditional buy-and-hold portfolios, hedge funds face few, if any, investment restrictions. Consequently, in the long run, hedge funds should be able to deliver returns that are better than those of bonds and equities. This is confirmed by Figure 10.1, which

---

[2] Chapter 5 contains an extensive discussion of the discrepancies between the different indices available in the industry. The CSFB/Tremont hedge fund index is capitalization weighted, and uses only funds that have at least $10 million of assets and can provide audited performance figures. We believe these criteria make it representative of the universe of funds in which an institutional investor may consider an investment.

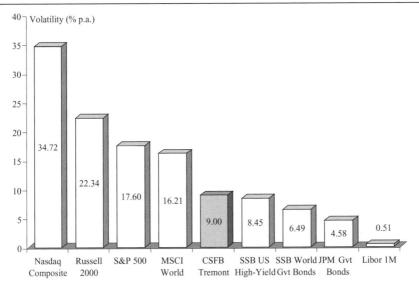

Figure 10.2   Annualized volatility of several asset classes, January 1994 to June 2003

shows the annualized rates of return produced by a buy-and-hold strategy in several asset classes from January 1994[3] to June 2003. The compound annual return of the CSFB/Tremont index was 10.95%, versus 10.04% for the S&P 500 and 6.37% for the Salomon Smith Barney World Government bond index. Although we cannot say if this order will be maintained in the future, it highlights at least the fact that hedge funds have, if recent history is anything to go by, provided better returns than long-only equities and bonds. This is not surprising, and there are many reasons. In particular, the most talented managers are attracted to set up or move into hedge funds because (i) they can thus obtain greater investment freedom; (ii) they can use their talents in a less constrained fashion; and (iii) they are rewarded more directly for their good performance.

To many, the fact that hedge funds as a group have outperformed traditional asset classes would not be particularly surprising if these superior returns had been achieved at the expense of greater risk. However, this does not seem to be borne out in practice – see Figure 10.2. The flexibility enjoyed by hedge funds in their investment strategy, and notably their ability to combine long and short positions and diversify across various financial instruments, enabled them to mitigate risk significantly. Consequently, hedge funds displayed an annualized volatility of 9%, which represents about half of the S&P 500 volatility (17.60%) and roughly a quarter of the Nasdaq volatility (34.72%). Only fixed income-related indices had a lower volatility than hedge funds over the period in question.

Some will argue – rightly – that standard deviation is not necessarily an appropriate risk measure, especially for hedge funds. Hedge funds' return objectives are absolute rather than relative, and the dispersion of returns below a prespecified target level is probably a more accurate measure of risk. But using alternative risk measures in this case provides a similar message: hedge funds carry less risk than equities. As an illustration, Figure 10.3 measures risk using the maximum drawdown, i.e. the largest amount of capital that would have been lost had an investor experienced the worst peak-to-trough decline in value. We can see that hedge

---

[3] January 1994 corresponds to the starting date of the CSFB/Tremont index.

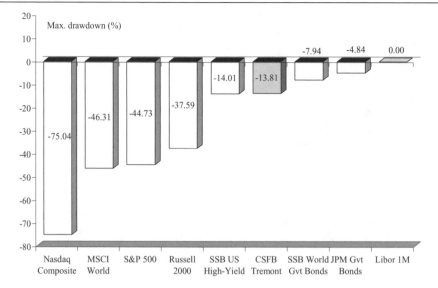

Figure 10.3   Maximum drawdown of several asset classes, January 1994 to June 2003

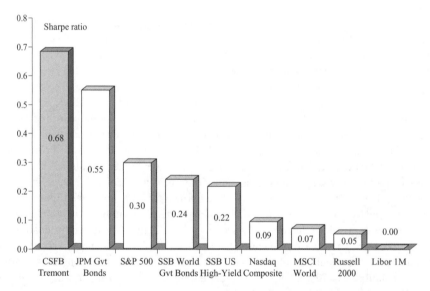

Figure 10.4   Sharpe ratios of several asset classes, January 1994 to June 2003

funds still maintain their advantage with respect to equities, and appear just a little bit riskier than government bonds.

Better returns and less risk should result in higher risk-adjusted performance. This is indeed the case – see for instance Figure 10.4 showing Sharpe ratios – and constitutes the major motive for hedge fund investing. Rather than accepting the conventional wisdom that investors need to accept greater risk in order to achieve greater returns, why not achieve greater returns while taking less risk by investing in a diversified portfolio of hedge funds? The argument seems tempting.

10.1.2   Low correlation to traditional assets

Allocating money to hedge funds because their managers achieve greater returns at lower risk would already seem like a sound investment decision. But the case for hedge funds becomes even more favorable when one considers correlation coefficients. Investors have historically taken comfort in the notion that a globally diversified portfolio of traditional assets (e.g. stocks and bonds) will provide good returns with only moderate risk, thanks to the important role that correlation between portfolio components plays in determining risk. The lower the correlation, the better, which was exactly what investors mixing stocks and bonds in their portfolios experienced. But the situation has changed dramatically in recent years.

On the equity side, the correlation between various markets now stands well above historical levels. For example, the correlation between the S&P 500 and the MSCI Europe, Australia and Far East (EAFE) index spiked from just above 0.2 in the early 1990s to nearly 0.8 in the early 2000s, not far from the 1.0 mark that represents perfect unison. Several arguments have been proffered to explain this evolution. The primary support for the continuance of high correlation was the globalization of the world's economy, with companies making and selling products throughout the world and currencies unifying. An alternative explanation lies in some herd behavior, with investors around the world pursuing internet-related stocks and abruptly moving out of their positions as the bubble began to deflate. In any case, the result is there: correlation may change again in the future, but in the meantime the geographic and sector diversification benefits of the long-only market have shrunk, sometimes to the point that much of the difference in equities' return and risk stems from currency fluctuations.

Furthermore, the United States has come to dominate the global equity market, accounting for over half of the total market capitalization, and this naturally encourages investors to pay closer attention to what is happening there. When Wall Street sneezes, the world catches a cold. As an illustration, Figure 10.5 shows the average monthly performance of several equity

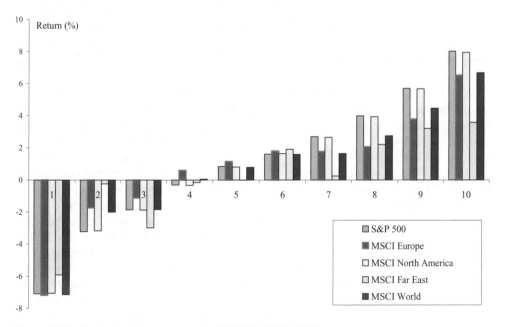

Figure 10.5   Ranked equity returns on the S&P 500 (1990–2002)

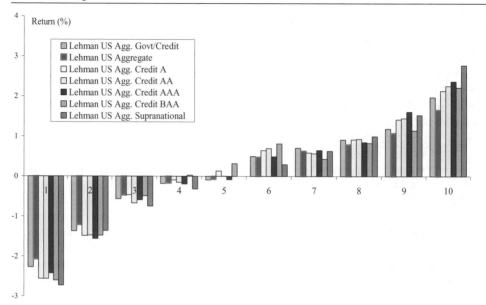

Figure 10.6   Ranked equity returns on the Merrill Lynch 10+ years US Treasury (1990–2002)

indices ranked according to the S&P 500 performance. That is, first, S&P 500 monthly returns are placed into performance deciles based on univariate sorting. The lowest 10% of S&P 500 returns are placed in the first decile, the second lowest 10% in the second decile, and so on until the tenth decile, which contains the months with the highest S&P 500 returns. Next, for the first decile, we calculate the average return of another index (say the MSCI Europe) for the same months. The process is then repeated for each remaining decile (i.e. each other index). The resulting series of averages is then plotted against the S&P averages. Clearly, we see that there is little evidence of diversification benefits across stock markets, at least over the period in question (1990 to 2002). Consequently, there is a need to find new diversification opportunities.

On the bond side, investors also observed an increase in correlation between various countries. In Europe in particular, adopting the euro eliminated currency risk and increased the degree of substitutability and the correlation between bonds of different governments. Consequently, investors started paying more attention to credit risk and liquidity issues as well as to doing some arbitrage along the yield curve. But the dominant driver across all types of bonds remains the overall level of interest rates, which is common to different bond markets and makes them move in unison. As an illustration, Figure 10.6 repeats our previous decile comparison, but this time with several fixed income indices. The index used as a reference for the construction of the deciles is the Merrill Lynch 10+ years US Treasury bonds. Not surprisingly, the overall pattern seems to confirm the existence of a high correlation between the different bond markets considered, and therefore signals the lack of diversification opportunities.

Finally, the question of the correlation between stock and bond markets is a trickier issue. Most investors are familiar with the idea that falling interest rates tend to go together with positive stock returns – the concept is usually encountered in introductory business textbooks. This should be statistically represented by a positive correlation coefficient between stock and bond returns, since bonds rise as interest rates fall. However, there are also times when the

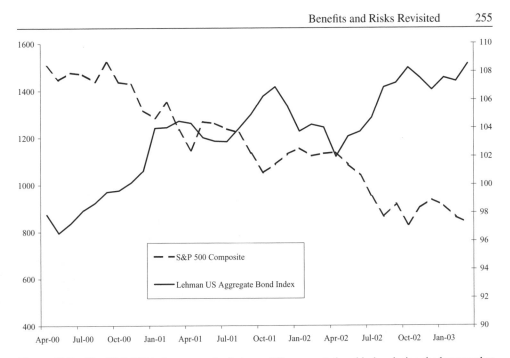

Figure 10.7   The S&P 500 index versus the Lehman US aggregate bond index during the bear market (March 2000 to March 2003)

correlation becomes negative. As an illustration, the 1950 version of Benjamin Graham's *The Intelligent Investor* claimed that the correlation between stock and bond returns was negative, and advised a 50–50 split. But the 1970 edition dropped the argument, because the correlation structure had changed and become positive. More recently, following the peak of the equity markets, the correlation between stock and bond returns changed again to negative – see Figure 10.7. It is likely to come back to its long-term average as soon as the global economic recovery is firmly established.

Overall, this lack of stability in the correlation coefficients makes it pretty clear that stocks and bonds are not always a good complement to one another in portfolios. Thus, we have to identify new directions if we want to diversify our traditional portfolios efficiently. This is precisely where hedge funds come into the picture. Driven by the skills of their portfolio managers, hedge funds aim at producing absolute returns, i.e. a positive return in both rising and falling markets. As a result, they tend to have a low to medium correlation with traditional asset class returns – see Figure 10.8. This is a clear sign that hedge funds can provide opportunities for diversification of traditional portfolios.

10.1.3   Negative versus positive market environments

All the statistics that we have presented so far capture essentially an average behavior. In practice, the actual behavior in up and down markets may diverge significantly. It is therefore worthwhile exploring separately the performance of hedge funds in negative versus positive market environments.

Figure 10.9 shows the annualized return of our various asset classes when we consider separately the months when the S&P 500 displays a positive performance and the months

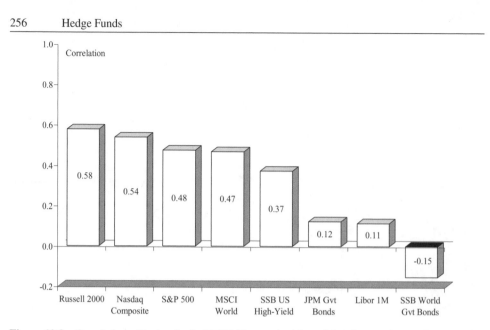

Figure 10.8 Correlation of hedge funds (CSFB/Tremont) with traditional asset classes, January 1994 to June 2003

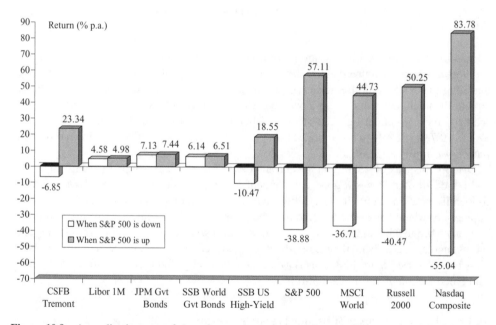

Figure 10.9 Annualized returns of several asset classes in bearish and bullish months of the S&P 500, January 1994 to June 2003

when the S&P 500 shows a negative performance. It is clear that fixed income asset classes offer stable returns whatever the equity market is doing. Equity-based asset classes, on the other hand, seem to follow the behavior of the S&P 500, and therefore do not offer much diversification potential when equity markets are falling. The same remark applies to the

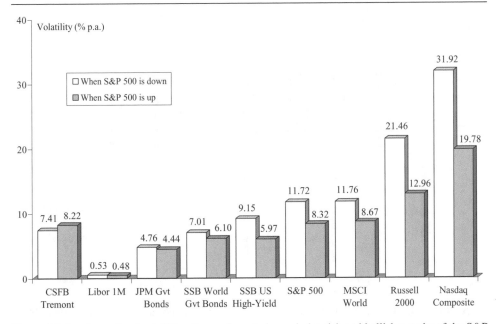

Figure 10.10 Annualized volatility of several asset classes in bearish and bullish months of the S&P 500, January 1994 to June 2003

high-yield market. The hedge fund index also seems to be correlated with the movements of the S&P 500, but with much less variation. In particular, we see that its downside risk is much smaller than that of the S&P 500. It is precisely this better downside risk management that creates the better overall performance. Indeed, the first thing to do in order to make money is to avoid losses in difficult market conditions. Hedge funds are designed to offer downside protection in falling markets (that is the origin of the term "hedge"), and the recent difficult environment for markets has allowed hedge funds to prove their value.

The volatility comparison of our asset classes during bearish and bullish months of the S&P 500 is also interesting – see Figure 10.10. While all asset classes have a lower volatility when equity markets display positive performance, the converse seems true for hedge funds (8.22% volatility when the S&P 500 is positive versus 7.41% when the S&P 500 is negative). This difference may be the consequence of a more aggressive behavior in up markets; it may also result from less stringent risk management constraints as well as from possible variations in leverage. At all events, it is not a concern, because it is only the "upside volatility" that is increased.

Figure 10.11 evidences that, in comparison with other asset classes, hedge funds were especially effective during the worst months of the equity markets, when capital preservation usually becomes a priority. Even in August 1998, at the time of the hedge fund crisis precipitated by the collapse of Long Term Capital Management, hedge funds as a group managed to display much better returns than equities (−7.55% for hedge funds versus −14.46% for the S&P 500).

With all these positive characteristics, it is not really surprising that the inclusion of hedge funds in traditional portfolios tends to have a favorable impact on both return and risk (see Figure 10.12). As an illustration, a portfolio made up of 60% equities (S&P 500) and 40% bonds (SSB Government bond index) would have had a performance of 8.69% p.a. and a

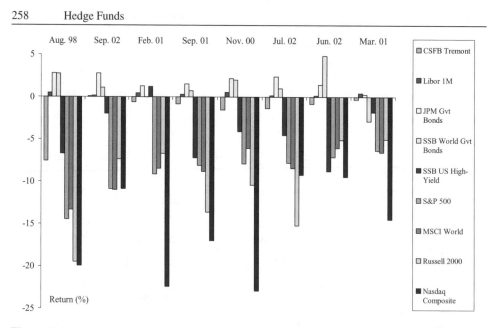

Figure 10.11   Monthly returns of several asset classes during the worst months of equity markets, 1994 onwards

volatility of 8.86% p.a. over the January 1994 to July 2003 period. If we substitute 10% hedge funds (CSFB Tremont) for 10% of the original equity allocation, we observe a modest increase in the return (8.80% p.a.), but a significant drop in volatility (7.67% versus 8.86% originally). If we substitute 20% hedge funds (CSFB Tremont) for 20% of the original equity allocation, we still observe a modest increase in the return (8.90% p.a.), but a larger reduction of volatility (6.77% versus 8.86% originally). And the risk reduction keeps going as the hedge fund weight increases.

Starting from the same portfolio made up of 60% equities (S&P 500) and 40% bonds (SSB Government bond index), we may rather decide to substitute 10% hedge funds (CSFB Tremont) for 10% of the original bond allocation. In this case, we observe an increase in risk as well as an increase in return. The goal is no longer to diversify, but rather to enhance the performance by taking additional risk. And the risk and return increases keep going as the hedge fund weight increases and the bond weight decreases.

Starting once again from the same portfolio made up of 60% equities (S&P 500) and 40% bonds (SSB Government bond index), we may finally decide to substitute 10% hedge funds (CSFB Tremont) for 5% of the original bond allocation and 5% of the original stock allocation. In this case, the risk decreases and the return increases! This lends weight to the idea that some allocation of hedge funds may be good for diversified traditional portfolios. The conclusion is generally valid, but with one important caveat. Comparisons of portfolio performance with and without hedge funds should take into account other features of their distribution of returns. For example, if the return distribution becomes more skewed in one direction (particularly in the negative direction), or it tends to bunch up at the extremes of the range of returns (i.e. have excessive kurtosis), the overall portfolio results may look improved in a mean–variance space, but are not improved in reality. It is simply that the use of standard deviation as the sole measure of risk for distributions that exhibit a relatively high probability of gain/loss is misleading.

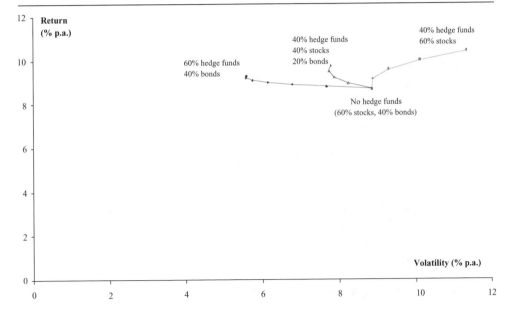

	Allocation to hedge funds (by reducing equities)						
Hedge fund weight	**0%**	**10%**	**20%**	**30%**	**40%**	**50%**	**60%**
Avg. return	8.69	8.80	8.90	9.00	9.10	9.21	9.31
Volatility	8.86	7.67	6.77	6.13	5.73	5.56	5.58
Skewness	−0.29	−0.46	−0.55	−0.51	−0.35	−0.16	−0.04
Kurtosis	1.17	1.14	1.13	1.13	1.09	0.98	0.84

	Allocation to hedge funds (by reducing bonds)				
Hedge fund weight	**0%**	**10%**	**20%**	**30%**	**40%**
Avg. return	8.69	9.14	9.58	10.00	10.41
Volatility	8.86	8.89	9.31	10.12	11.34
Skewness	−0.29	−0.63	−0.84	−0.89	−0.81
Kurtosis	1.17	1.68	2.14	2.24	1.94

	Allocation to hedge funds (by reducing stocks and bonds equally)				
Hedge fund weight	**0%**	**10%**	**20%**	**30%**	**40%**
Avg. return	8.69	8.97	9.24	9.51	9.77
Volatility	8.86	8.24	7.88	7.74	7.79
Skewness	−0.29	−0.55	−0.72	−0.78	−0.73
Kurtosis	1.17	1.44	1.81	2.12	2.29

Figure 10.12   The impact of including hedge funds in a diversified portfolio (initially, 60% equity and 40% bonds)

10.2   THE BENEFITS OF INDIVIDUAL HEDGE FUND STRATEGIES

Although the conclusions of the previous section seem to be quite general, hedge funds are not an "asset class" according to the standard meaning of the term. In particular, they are not homogenous but encompass a multitude of investment strategies whose return and risk

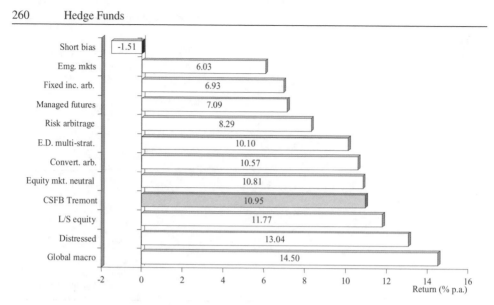

Figure 10.13   Annualized returns of several hedge fund strategies, January 1994 to June 2003

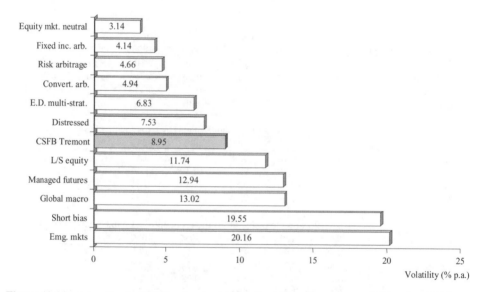

Figure 10.14   Annualized volatility of several hedge fund strategies, January 1994 to June 2003

characteristics differ widely. It is therefore interesting to analyze each of these strategies separately to verify whether they inherit the benefits of their ancestor, or whether their characteristics are significantly different. To maintain consistency with the previous section, we use the CSFB/Tremont 10-style classification standard and the CSFB/Tremont sub-index as a proxy for each strategy.

Figures 10.13–10.16 show the annualized returns, annualized volatilities, maximum drawdown and Sharpe ratio of several hedge fund strategies from January 1994 to June 2003. While the general hedge fund index displays an annualized return of 10.95%, the individual strategies'

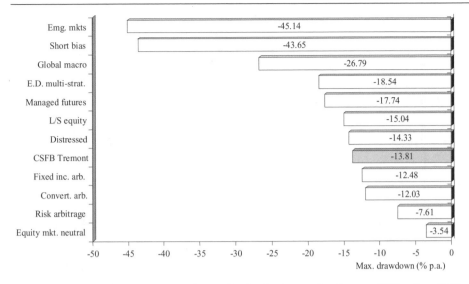

Figure 10.15   Maximum drawdown of several hedge fund strategies, January 1994 to June 2003

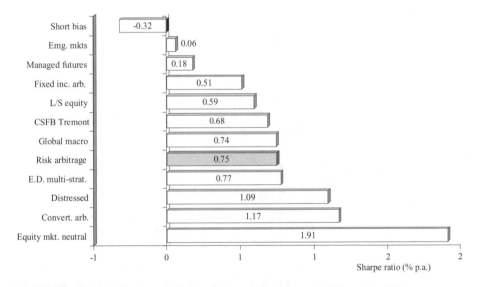

Figure 10.16   Sharpe ratio of several hedge fund strategies, January 1994 to June 2003

returns range from −1.51% (short bias) to +14.50% (global macro). The discrepancy seems even larger on the risk side, with a volatility ranging from 3.14% (equity market neutral) to 20.16% (emerging markets), versus 8.95% for the hedge fund index. The directional strategies (emerging markets, short bias, global macro and managed futures) as well as the long/short equity funds have the highest volatility. Not surprisingly, equity market neutral funds and arbitrage strategies were the most consistent among the group.

Figures 10.17 and 10.18 show the correlation of the various hedge fund strategies with equity markets (represented by the S&P 500) and with bond markets (represented by the SSB

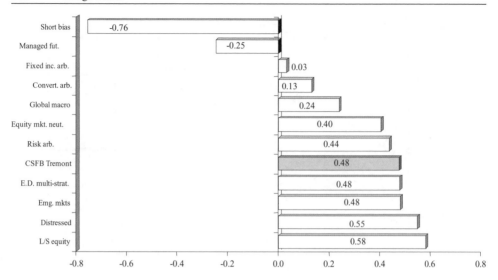

Figure 10.17   Correlation of hedge fund strategies with the S&P 500, January 1994 to June 2003

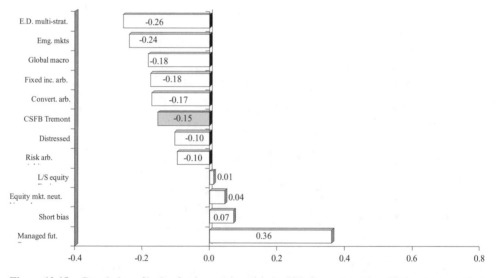

Figure 10.18   Correlation of hedge fund strategies with the SSB Government bond index, January 1994 to June 2003

Government bond index). The hedge fund strategies have very different correlation characteristics. Long/short equity funds are the most correlated to traditional equity markets, followed by distressed, emerging market and event-driven multi-strategy funds. These results are not really surprising as (i) most long/short equity managers have a net long investment style; (ii) distressed funds obviously come under pressure during periods of major financial stress, and most event-driven multi-strategy funds contain a substantial allocation of distressed securities; and (iii) most emerging market hedge fund managers are net long because of the inherent difficulties of borrowing stocks and selling short in emerging markets. However, even in these

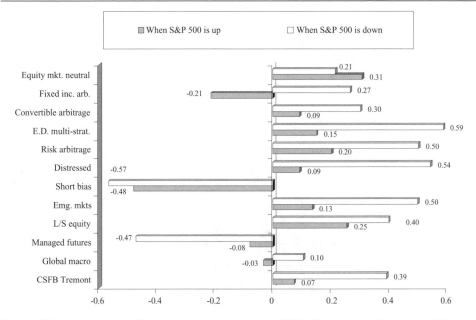

Figure 10.19 Correlation of hedge fund strategies with the S&P 500, January 1994 to June 2003

cases, the correlation remains between 0.48 and 0.58. In contrast, short sellers are consistently net short, and hence have a high negative correlation (−0.76) with equities. Managed futures also display a negative correlation (−0.25), while arbitrage strategies have generally low correlation figures with the S&P 500 returns, ranging from 0.03 for fixed income arbitrage to 0.44 for risk arbitrage. Finally, note the low level of correlation with the SSB Government bond index, which suggests that hedge funds could also be used to complement bond portfolios.

Although the correlation figures seem quite low, we have to remember that in terms of diversification, low correlation with equity markets is not in itself enough. What investors really need is low downside correlation, that is, investments that will perform well when the equity markets are not performing well. Figure 10.19 shows the downside correlation of our hedge fund strategies with the S&P 500, and reveals two interesting features. First, the correlation over the whole sample is not necessarily the average of the up-market and down-market correlation. As an illustration, consider the short bias funds. Their overall correlation with the S&P 500 is −0.76, while the upside correlation is −0.48 and the downside correlation is −0.57. Second, the majority of hedge fund strategies have a higher correlation with the S&P 500 when the latter is suffering from negative performance – the only exceptions are equity market neutral and short bias funds. This is not very good news, as it implies that many hedge fund strategies come under pressure during periods of major financial stress and partly lose their diversification properties precisely when we need them. However, the correlations remain at low levels for the majority of hedge funds, which implies that there are still some diversification benefits to capture. But an investor wanting to achieve low overall correlation might have to draw on the whole menu of hedge fund strategies, including short selling, in order to construct an intelligently diversified portfolio.

Investors tend to use hedge funds for one of two portfolio design purposes. Most high net worth individuals view them as return enhancers – aggressive investment options that

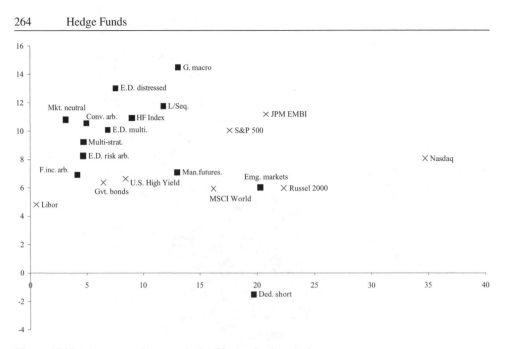

Figure 10.20   A mean–variance analysis of hedge fund strategies

generate above-market-level returns while taking greater-than-market levels of risk. Most institutional investors, however, view an allocation to absolute return strategies as a portfolio diversifier. If we divide the universe into four quadrants, with the CSFB Tremont hedge fund index at the center, we can clearly identify four groups of strategies – see Figure 10.20. A first group of strategies is clearly positioned as a low-risk, low-return universe with respect to the overall index. It encompasses all the relative value strategies, e.g. fixed income arbitrage, convertible arbitrage, risk arbitrage, market neutral and multi-strategy. These strategies are relatively unaffected by the market factors that drive traditional equity markets and therefore are considered as risk diversifiers for equity portfolios. However, while the volatility of these strategies is lower than that of government bonds, their return is higher, which suggests that they may also act as return enhancers when combined with bond portfolios.

A second group of strategies, comprising the global macro and long/short equity investment styles, is clearly positioned as a high-risk, high-return universe with respect to the overall index. The volatility of these strategies is lower than that of equities and their return is much higher, which suggests that they may act as return enhancers when combined with equity portfolios.

A third group of strategies, composed of the managed futures, emerging markets and dedicated short investment styles, is clearly positioned as a high-risk, low-return universe with respect to the overall index. These strategies may possibly be used as risk diversifiers for equity portfolios.

The last category contains only the distressed investment style, and is positioned as a low-risk, high-return strategy. However, we should be cautious in drawing any conclusions on this strategy, as (i) its low volatility is in fact essentially due to the lack of regular market pricing and natural tendency of managers to smooth the return on their portfolios, and (ii) its assets are highly illiquid, so that realizing gains or limiting losses is likely to be a problem.

10.3 CAVEATS OF HEDGE FUND INVESTING

To better interpret our previous findings, some caveats should be stated. First of all, we should recall that a bull market prevailed during a large part of the period examined (1994–2003). Hedge funds with a long bias benefited in a rising equity market, and their performance is upwardly biased. We recognize that a longer observation period would better represent strategy returns. Unfortunately, the hedge fund universe becomes very small for longer periods of analysis.

Next, we should also recall that our results were historical figures based on hedge fund indices, i.e. large diversified portfolios of hedge funds. But tracking exactly the performance of such indices is not easy, due to transaction costs and the large size of minimum investments. Furthermore, all indices are subject to biases that essentially result in overestimation of historical returns and underestimation of risk – see Chapter 5. Hence, in practice, the superiority of hedge fund investments over traditional assets relies heavily on the manager selection skill of the investor. The difference between a first and fourth quartile fund can often be the difference between success and disaster.

In addition to identifying the most talented managers, investors need to be able to invest in their funds. Unfortunately, the best managers tend to have enough capital and can do without additional investors. They close their funds to new investors, or at least they impose long lock-up periods of one to three years before investors can redeem. For this reason, it is often difficult for investors to gain exposure to certain hedge fund strategies without taking a chance on new managers who have no adequate track records. These neophytes may not produce the same results as their more experienced peers, and investors may be disappointed.

Looking forward, the massive amount of capital pouring into the hedge fund business is also worrying. Some strategies are capacity constrained by nature, e.g. merger arbitrage or

Table 10.1 Hedge fund returns, based on CSFB/Tremont indices, 1997 to 2003 (all returns are annualized, except for 2003; year-to-date until October)

	2003	2002	2001	2000	1999	1998	1997	1996	1995	1994
Hedge fund index	12.0	3.0	4.4	4.8	23.4	−0.4	25.9	22.2	21.7	−4.4
Convertible arbitrage	10.7	4.0	14.6	25.6	16.0	−4.4	14.5	17.9	16.6	−8.1
Dedicated short bias	−28.5	18.1	−3.6	15.8	−14.2	−6.0	0.4	−5.5	−7.4	14.9
Emerging markets	22.9	7.4	5.8	−5.5	44.8	−37.7	26.6	34.5	−16.9	12.5
Equity market neutral	5.7	7.4	9.3	15.0	15.3	13.3	14.8	16.6	11.0	−2.0
Event-driven	16.8	0.2	11.5	7.3	22.3	−4.9	20.0	23.1	18.3	0.7
Event-driven: distressed	21.5	−0.7	20.0	1.9	22.2	−1.7	20.7	25.5	26.1	0.7
Event-driven: multi-strategy	26.0	1.2	6.8	11.8	23.0	−9.0	20.5	22.7	12.9	0.6
Event-driven: risk arbitrage	7.4	−3.5	5.7	14.7	13.2	5.6	9.8	13.8	11.9	5.3
Fixed income arbitrage	6.6	5.8	8.0	6.3	12.1	−8.2	9.3	15.9	12.5	0.3
Global macro	15.2	14.7	18.4	11.7	5.8	−3.6	37.1	25.6	30.7	−5.7
Long/short equity	12.6	−1.6	−3.7	2.1	47.2	17.2	21.5	17.1	23.0	−8.1
Managed futures	7.7	18.3	1.9	4.2	−4.7	20.6	3.1	12.0	−7.1	12.0
Multi-strategy	20.6	6.3	5.5	11.2	9.4	7.7	18.3	14.1	11.9	−5.3
S&P 500	21.2	−22.1	−11.9	−9.1	21.0	28.6	33.4	23.0	37.6	1.3
SSB World Gvt bond index	8.7	19.5	−1.0	1.6	−4.3	15.3	0.2	3.6	19.0	2.3

convertible bond arbitrage, because the supply of investment opportunities is limited. Large money flows into such strategies may therefore challenge their performance by arbitraging away profit opportunities. Some analysts have argued that the capacity argument is not applicable to long/short equity managers and fixed income arbitrage managers, because they are playing in markets whose size is measured in trillions of dollars – see, for instance, McFall Lamm and Ghaleb-Harter (2001). However, all alpha-based strategies are inherently capacity constrained, either in terms of investment opportunities or in terms of talented managers. It is therefore not surprising that hedge fund returns appear to be in a long-term downward trend, with returns that fall far short of the stellar performance delivered in the 1980s and early 1990s (Table 10.1).

In conclusion, we will say that hedge fund investing offers several benefits, but it should not be considered as a "free lunch". It has its risks and its difficulties – the skewness and kurtosis evolution of Figure 10.12 should not be forgotten. Furthermore, most investors do not consider hedge funds as standalone assets, but combine several different alternative strategies that, in the aggregate, produce a desired return pattern. As we will see in the following chapters, including hedge funds in a portfolio may sometimes be quite complicated, and constructing allocations to these products requires an extensive understanding of their investment strategies and risks.

11

Strategic Asset Allocation – From
Portfolio Optimizing to Risk Budgeting

We can't control the market, but we can control our reaction to it.

Finally convinced of the apparent advantages of hedge funds as risk diversifiers or as absolute return generators, many investors and advisors are now contemplating their inclusion in traditional portfolios. Indeed, if there is superior skill, hedge funds should provide a better means of accessing it, due to their greater flexibility, ability to sell short, incentive structures, use of more esoteric instruments and more nimble management than on the long-only side. But the benefits of adding a fund of hedge funds to a traditional strategic portfolio are yesterday's news. The problem today is to reconcile the alternative and creative nature of hedge funds with the discipline required in an asset allocation process. This is a delicate task that raises several new questions. Should hedge funds be considered as a separate asset class or as a different way of managing traditional assets? What percentage should a rational investor allocate to them? How frequently should a hedge fund portfolio be rebalanced? All these issues should be clarified before any allocation is made. Unfortunately, as we shall see, analyzing hedge funds is not the same as analyzing traditional fund managers. The option-like payoffs and unusual correlation profiles of hedge funds open new avenues in portfolio construction. Consequently, hedge funds do not fit easily into traditional asset allocation processes, so extra attention is needed in order to make the best use of their valuable characteristics.

In this chapter, we discuss the different techniques for incorporating hedge funds in an asset allocation. We begin with an allocation involving only a simple mix of traditional asset classes, and then we introduce hedge funds as a separate asset class. Although this is the standard approach used to justify hedge fund allocations, we will see that it has several shortcomings, particularly when using a mean–variance framework. Hence, we will introduce other allocation techniques such as portable alpha construction, minimizing the correlation with the principal components of strategic portfolio risk, and risk budgeting. Although new in asset management, these quantitative techniques are borrowed from risk management, where optimizing risk by "spending" each unit of risk efficiently is a common objective.

11.1 STRATEGIC ASSET ALLOCATION WITHOUT HEDGE FUNDS

Strategic asset allocation consists of establishing a portfolio of asset classes that is consistent with an investor's long-term objectives and constraints. It is known to be one of the most important decisions, if not the most important, in any investment process, as it is the key to achieving the investor's financial goals and is the primary determinant of long-term investment results.[1]

---

[1] Brinson *et al.* (1986) found that strategic asset allocation explained nearly 93.6% of the variance in a sample of pension fund returns, versus only 6.4% for selectivity and timing. Brinson *et al.* (1991) reported similar results.

Nevertheless, most investors hate spending time on their strategic asset allocation. They prefer to identify great investments on instinct or to read about how famous investors pick stocks rather than to challenge the steps involved in creating their portfolio. As a consequence, their strategic asset allocation often gets insufficient attention or simply exists at best on paper. The whole game often seems to turn into picking the best stocks individually, with no consideration whatsoever for portfolio construction rules. This is a pity, because strategic asset allocation is obviously the only key to long-term investment success.

In fact, one of the major differences between institutional investment strategies and the approaches employed by most individual investors is the influence of emotions. Institutional investors generally adopt a disciplined approach to asset management. They follow a transparent and systematic investment process that both explicitly recognizes and manages risks in a portfolio. Furthermore, they review and rebalance their holdings to ensure that the latter remain consistent with their asset allocation policies. Individual investors, on the other hand, often react emotionally, buy overvalued assets in bull markets and sell them when they have plummeted in bear markets. Clearly, most individual investors would benefit from employing some of the highly disciplined investment habits of institutional money managers, and particularly from establishing a clear asset allocation policy.

11.1.1   Identifying the investor's financial profile: the concept of utility functions

First of all, it is important to realize that one best overall portfolio does not exist. There is at most an optimal portfolio for each investor, or each group of similar investors. To determine this portfolio, it is necessary to take into account the investor's time horizon, his risk appetite, his overall objectives, his age, his available income and the rest of the assets of his portfolio (including, if relevant, his liabilities), as well as any constraints, tax status, etc. A thorough review of all these elements is required before choosing any asset – the only way to be successful is to know what we want to achieve and what we want to avoid.

Academia and practice seem to have taken different paths to modeling investors' portfolio decisions. Academics rely on microeconomic theory and use utility functions to explain investors' decisions. To keep things simple, we will say that utility is a measure of the happiness or satisfaction an investor obtains from his portfolio – the higher an investor's utility, the happier the investor.[2] Thus, most theoretical portfolio selection models rest on the assumption that rational investors maximize their *expected utility* over a prespecified time horizon, and that they select their portfolios accordingly. Intuitively, expected utility should be positively related to the return of a portfolio (investors are greedy and prefer more return) but negatively related to the risk taken (investors are risk-averse and prefer less risk to more risk for a given level of return).

Box 11.1   Expected utility and the St. Petersburg Paradox

The notion of expected utility stems from Daniel Bernoulli's (1738) solution to the famous St. Petersburg Paradox posed in 1713 by his cousin, Nicholas Bernoulli. The paradox challenges the idea that people value a random payoff according to its expected size. The paradox posed the following situation: a coin is tossed until a head appears; if the first head appears on the nth toss, then the payoff is 2^n ducats. How much should one pay to play this

---

[2] For the foundations of utility functions, see von Neumann and Morgenstern (1947).

game? The paradox, of course, is that the expected payoff is infinite, namely:

$$E(\text{payoff}) = (1/2)2 + (1/4)2^2 + (1/8)2^3 + \cdots = 1 + 1 + 1 + \cdots = \infty$$

Yet while the expected payoff is infinite, one would suppose, at least intuitively, that real-world people would not be willing to pay an infinite amount of money to play the game. Daniel Bernoulli's solution involved two ideas that have since revolutionized economics. First, a person's valuation of a risky venture is not the expected size of that venture, but rather the expected utility from that venture. Second, a person's utility from wealth, $U(W)$, is not linearly related to wealth W, but rather increases at a decreasing rate – this is the famous idea of diminishing marginal utility. In the St. Petersburg case, the expected utility of the game to an agent is finite because of the principle of diminishing marginal utility. Consequently, the agent would only be willing to pay a finite amount of money to play the game, even though its expected payoff is infinite.

In microeconomic theory, utility is usually derived from wealth. In our case, rather than modeling the wealth of an investor, we focus on the return of his portfolio. Thus, we will consider the utility derived from the portfolio return. In theory, the utility function $U(R_P)$ of an investor could take any functional form. As an illustration, Bernoulli originally used a logarithmic function

$$U(R_P) = \ln(1 + R_P) \tag{11.1}$$

where R_P is the return achieved by the investor's portfolio, but we could also consider – for instance – a negative exponential utility function

$$U(R_P) = 1 - \exp(-\lambda \times R_P) \tag{11.2}$$

where $\lambda \geq 0$ is a risk-aversion parameter that is investor-specific. Figure 11.1 shows the negative exponential utility function for different values of λ (0.1, 1.0 and 10). In all cases, when the return increases, there is a corresponding increase in utility or satisfaction. However, we also see that once the investor has reached a certain return, there is almost no increase in utility for each unit of additional return. In a sense, the investor becomes risk-averse since he does not care much about the additional return.

Other functions may also be used to model an investor's utility. However, maximizing a complex utility function is difficult from a mathematical perspective and generally does not yield nice analytical solutions. Therefore, many academics conveniently accept the idea that utility functions should be simple trade-offs between risk and return, where risk is measured by variance. Mathematically, for a given investor owning a portfolio P with return R_P and variance σ_P^2, this type of utility function could easily be represented as

$$U(R_P) = R_P - \lambda \sigma_P^2 \tag{11.3}$$

where $\lambda \geq 0$ is a risk-aversion parameter that is investor-specific.[3] Such a utility function is called a quadratic utility function, because it is a quadratic function of the portfolio returns.

---

[3] A high value of λ signals a highly risk-averse investor, while a low value of λ signals a low level of risk aversion. As an illustration, consider an investor who has a a λ coefficient equal to 2, and who is currently invested in an asset that offers 5% return with 6% volatility. The current utility level of this investor is $5\% - 2(6\%)^2 = 0.0428$. If the volatility of the asset increases to 20%, its return should increase to 12.28% to maintain the same level of utility. In contrast, an investor with a λ coefficient equal to 1 would simply require a new return of 8.64% to maintain his utility level.

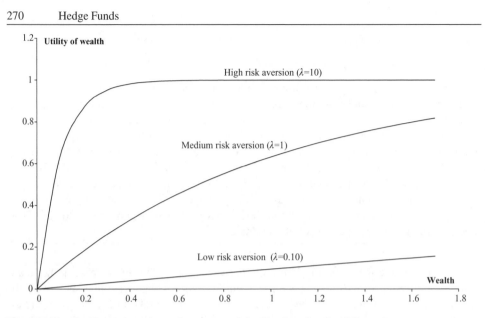

Figure 11.1   An illustration of negative exponential utility function for different λ parameters

Maximizing such a function is extremely simple and forms the basis of mean–variance analysis. For a given level of return, it is equivalent to minimizing the variance σ_P^2, which draws the bridge between utility maximization and asset allocation.

Most of the time, practitioners understand well the concept of utility function, the idea of trading off risk against return, and they generally spend a considerable amount of time assessing the particular characteristics and needs of each of their clients, usually through questionnaires and face-to-face interviews. However, they do not use utility functions explicitly, but rely on pre-optimized standard investment profiles (conservative, balanced, aggressive, etc.). Hence, they aim at determining which one best suits an investor's long-term goals and personality, or if there is indeed a need to create a new dedicated profile.

Although the practitioners' approach may appear unrelated to the academics' process, it is not. In fact, like Mr. Jourdain[4] who wrote prose without realizing it, practitioners are also assessing the utility function of investors. In fact, they are estimating the value of the above-mentioned risk-aversion parameter (λ) for each investor, even though they are sometimes not even aware of its existence. Then, they cluster investors in prespecified groups according to their risk aversion. The result of their work is some well-defined communities of investors, with similar utility functions. Then, they can start establishing the strategic asset allocation for each of these groups.

11.1.2   Establishing the strategic asset allocation

Strategic asset allocation is used to construct a portfolio of asset classes which meets an investor's long-term goals whilst matching his risk profile, rather than concentrating on

---

[4] In Molière's *The Bourgeois Gentleman*, Act II, Scene 4, Mr. Jourdain says, "For more than forty years I have been speaking prose without knowing anything about it, and I am much obliged to you for having taught me that".

the short-term performance of the varying asset classes. Strategic asset allocation usually remains in place over a long period of time and should enable the portfolio to meet its objective.[5]

Quantitative methods usually play an important role in strategic asset allocation. They bring a logical framework to the planning process, enhance discipline, transparency and risk control, and allow the creation of scenarios. Most of the time, strategic asset allocation relies on modern portfolio theory (MPT) as well as on portfolio optimization techniques.[6]

Portfolio optimization usually proceeds in a well-structured way, the sequence of steps being as follows:

1. Select the set of asset classes to be considered for the portfolio, as well as the level of granularity required. In the following, we restrict our analysis to equities, bonds and cash.
2. For each asset class, forecast the necessary statistics (return, volatility of return, correlation with other asset classes, etc.). Note the word "forecast", which means some sort of prediction and not just historical averages. Unfortunately, in some respects, traditional asset allocation is now guided by hope. Hope that equities will outperform other assets, hope that mainstream assets will return the same 10- to 25-year historical returns the industry has been showing clients for the last decade. But the key point for a forecast model used in an optimization procedure is to be forward looking.
3. Set appropriate constraints if necessary (e.g. minimum or maximum weights for some asset classes).
4. Run an optimizer, usually to create a portfolio of asset classes with the lowest possible risk for a target expected rate of return. That is, given N asset classes, the goal is to:

   o Choose the N asset class weights that
   o Minimize the risk of the portfolio
   o Subject to a target expected return for the portfolio.[7]

   Alternatively, optimizers can also create a portfolio of asset classes with the highest possible return for a target risk level. That is, given N asset classes, their goal is to:

   o Choose the N asset class weights that
   o Maximize the return of the portfolio
   o Subject to a target expected return for the portfolio.

5. Review the portfolios suggested by the optimizer, from both a quantitative and a qualitative perspective. It is important to take optimizers for what they are – powerful computing engines – rather than as producers of ideal solutions encompassing great quantities of wisdom and judgment.

---

[5] By contrast, tactical asset allocation focuses on moving the portfolio away from its long-term strategic benchmark to take advantage of short-term market opportunities.

[6] In recent years, portfolio optimizers have been increasingly applied to asset allocation, that is, at the asset class level rather than at the individual security level. This development is not really surprising. In many respects, asset allocation is a more suitable playing field for modern portfolio theory and its efficient frontiers than is portfolio selection. Whereas the stock selection problem usually involves a large universe of assets, an asset allocation problem typically involves a handful of asset classes and is therefore much easier to solve. Furthermore, the opportunity to reduce total portfolio risk comes from the lack of correlation across assets. Since stocks generally move together, the benefits of diversification within a stock portfolio are somewhat limited, while the correlation across asset classes is usually low and in some cases even negative.

[7] Note that such a model will provide a portfolio having the smallest risk for a specified minimum level of return. However, there may exist a portfolio having a greater return and an equivalent level of risk. In such a case, the portfolio returned by the optimizer would not be efficient.

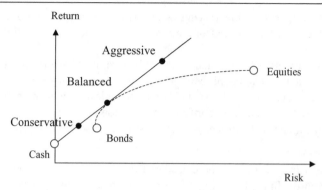

Figure 11.2   The traditional view of the efficient frontier

6. Finally, perform sensitivity analysis by adjusting the assumptions on returns, volatilities and correlations, as well as constraints. If necessary, run multiple scenarios and compare the results.

These six steps should be part of any asset allocation using an optimizer. But the fundamental and as yet unresolved question is how "risk" should be measured. The majority of optimizers follow Markowitz's (1952) original conjecture, that is, investors have quadratic utility functions and/or returns are normally distributed. In this case, the portfolio optimization problems described above can be reformulated in terms of expected returns and covariance between the different asset classes.

Mathematically, given N asset classes, we need to:

- Choose the weights $w_1, \ldots, w_N$ that
- Minimize $\sigma_P^2 = \sum_{i=1}^{N} \sum_{i=1}^{N} w_i w_j \sigma_{i,j}$
- Subject to $E(R_P) = \sum_{i=1}^{N} w_i E(R_i) = R^*$

where R^* is the target expected return and $\sigma_{i,j}$ is the covariance between the ith and the jth asset classes. Solving this problem involves minimizing a quadratic function (variance) subject to linear constraints. Under a few technical conditions, the problem is easy to solve by an algorithm that is much less computer-intensive than a general non-linear optimization code.[8] The set of all portfolios that solve this problem for different levels of expected returns is called the efficient frontier. Different investors will select their portfolios at different points along this efficient frontier, depending on their risk and/or return preferences.

An example of an efficient frontier is represented in Figure 11.2. The efficient frontier using only risky assets (stocks and bonds) is represented by a curve. If cash is added as a new asset class, the new efficient frontier becomes a straight line. Financial advisors now routinely use this type of optimization framework as a basis to build model portfolios and offer them to targeted groups of investors.

---

[8] The difficulty of solving the quadratic programming problem depends largely on the nature of the covariance matrix. If the latter is positive semi-definite, solving is relatively easy – the objective function is strictly convex and there is a sole local and global solution. Otherwise, if the covariance matrix is singular then the convex set of optimal solutions may contain more than one element, and the problem may be numerically more difficult to solve.

11.2   INTRODUCING HEDGE FUNDS IN THE ASSET ALLOCATION

11.2.1   Hedge funds as a separate asset class

The majority of investors who include hedge funds in their investment process treat them as a distinct asset class, alongside cash, bonds and equities. However, the jury is still out on whether hedge funds – and more generally, alternative investments – constitute a distinct asset class or not. Hedge funds' returns are different from those of traditional assets, but this does not necessarily mean they are a separate asset class. The reason is twofold.

First, just as primary colors cannot be obtained by mixing other colors, primary asset classes are those whose returns cannot be obtained by mixing other asset classes together. The majority of hedge fund managers trade assets that already belong to an existing asset class, e.g. equity and fixed income investments from the world's most liquid and highly regulated exchanges. In fact, most hedge funds involve all existing asset classes and are only alternative in the way they manage them. Rather than just holding assets and hoping that their price will go up, hedge fund managers use a variety of exposures (long, short, market neutral) and can therefore extract different returns at different times from familiar assets. But their returns are still functions of existing asset class returns.

Second, an asset class should normally comprise a set of assets that behave in some cohesive way. But hedge funds have no basic features that bind them together other than that they are different from traditional assets. In that sense, they would form an asset class made up of misfits unqualified for membership of any other club. This would be a rather bizarre asset class.

We therefore believe that, from a conceptual point of view, hedge funds are not really a new asset class and certainly not a cohesive asset class, but rather a collection of disparate and unconventional active management strategies. Nevertheless, for many investors, it is conceptually easier to consider hedge funds as a separate asset class, at least to begin with. This is particularly the case for institutional investors, both for regulatory and for reporting reasons. It is also convenient for investors who need to decide whether or not they want to capture an exposure to risks that are not correlated with the rest of their portfolio.

In this case, the term "asset class" should be considered not in its original sense, but rather as one of the key components of a diversified portfolio. For this purpose each asset class needs to have a specific risk–return function, and hedge funds fulfill that function.

11.2.2   Hedge funds versus traditional asset classes

However, treating hedge funds as a separate asset class is likely to result in the situation illustrated in Figure 11.3. On the left-hand side, we find traditional asset classes, e.g. stocks, bonds and cash.[9] They are relatively well known and their risk drivers are clearly identified. Stocks move in keeping with the markets, which in turn are reflected in either general or specialized indices (countries, sectors, value versus growth, small caps versus large caps, etc.); bonds are essentially driven by interest rates, as well as by some credit spreads in the case of corporate bonds; finally, cash is almost exclusively influenced by short-term interest rates. All these risk drivers are "market-based", and their influence is common to all traditional assets. Hence, by analogy with modern portfolio theory, we will say that most of the return of traditional asset classes is driven by "beta", that is, by exposure to these systematic market

---

[9] To keep things simple, we deliberately omit currencies from our discussion.

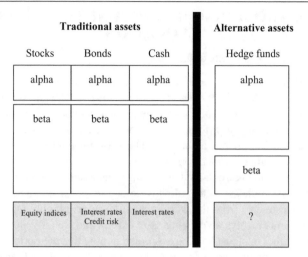

Figure 11.3   Hedge funds as a separate asset class

risks. The "alpha" part or value added, in contrast, is relatively small – if not negative after fees. There are two reasons. First, traditional money managers are so constrained by both regulations and benchmarks that it is difficult for them to generate a significant and consistent value added. Second, the benchmarks are clearly identified, so it is difficult to cheat and pretend that value has been added when it has not.[10]

On the right-hand side of Figure 11.3, we have hedge funds. In contrast to traditional assets, their managers emphasize their alpha advantage and claim to have very little beta embedded in their returns. Most investors blindly agree with this claim, which has been confirmed by numerous studies. Hedge funds in general are not strongly correlated with equity markets, and this is why we should include them in traditional portfolios.

However, this lack of correlation and low beta are precisely why most people feel uncomfortable with hedge funds. A low beta is a double-edged sword, because it also implies that we have not yet identified the return drivers of hedge funds. In this situation, how can we trust the alpha? Remember that a low beta often refers to equity and interest rate sensitivities, but there are numerous other types of risk that one can accept, e.g. liquidity risk, spread risk and commodity risk. The risk premiums associated with taking these risks would appear as alpha, while in fact they are just beta. Hence, the risk is high that many hedge funds are packaging some sort of beta and selling it at alpha prices.

Investors reluctant to go into complicated analyses are left with two extreme choices. The first is to consider hedge fund managers as people you would not want to associate with and to eschew hedge fund investments entirely. We disregard that option here. The second is to make a small fixed allocation (e.g. 5%) to hedge funds, while building a Great Wall between the universes of traditional and alternative investments. In a sense, what happens "behind the wall" is regarded as a lot of abracadabra.

---

[10] For instance, systematically extending bond duration or over-weighting corporate bonds in fixed income portfolios is likely to provide higher returns in the long run. This additional reward is simply a compensation for taking more interest rate risk and more credit risk. In any good performance attribution model, the source of this additional performance will be identified as a beta, not an alpha, increase.

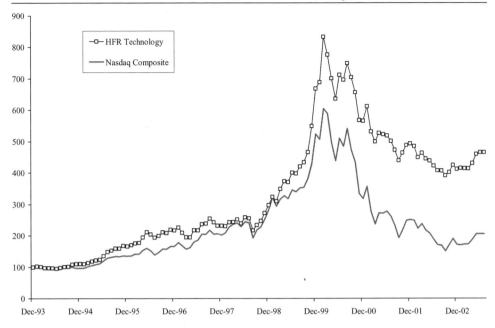

Figure 11.4 Comparison of the performance of the long/short technology strategy with that of the Nasdaq. The correlation between the two series in 0.90

Needless to say, we wholly disagree with this approach to hedge fund allocation.[11] We believe that, while hedge funds can be considered as a separate asset class for reporting or regulatory purposes, this is probably not the best way to approach them from an investment point of view. Our understanding is that there should not be any allocation in a portfolio – however small – if the risks, returns and interaction with other asset classes have not been carefully assessed.

11.2.3   Hedge funds as traditional asset class substitutes

An alternative way of looking at hedge funds is as substitutes (equivalent or superior in terms of risk and return) for traditional asset classes, such as equities and bonds. Indeed, some hedge fund strategies are conceptually close to their long-only equivalent. For instance, sector-specialized long/short equity funds tend to be quite well correlated with their long-only peers, because they tend to maintain an inherent strong net-long investment bias. This bias has even strengthened over recent years with the migration of a series of talented long-only asset managers to the long/short industry. The possibility of going short allows these hedge funds to better control their downside risk, so that ultimately their returns compound at a higher rate or better than those of traditional funds. As an illustration, Figure 11.4 compares the performance of the long/short technology sector with that of the Nasdaq. Although the two are obviously related, it is also clear that long/short managers managed their downside risk better. Hence, an idea

---

[11] I remember several conferences and meetings where I ironically challenged consultants and investors on their 5% allocation to hedge funds. "How did you arrive at this number?" The embarrassed explanations in fact hid the reality. A 5% allocation is perceived as sufficient to boost returns. It makes you appear as hedge fund aware even though you do not necessarily understand what is happening behind the wall. And if the whole thing blows up, you can still bear the loss.

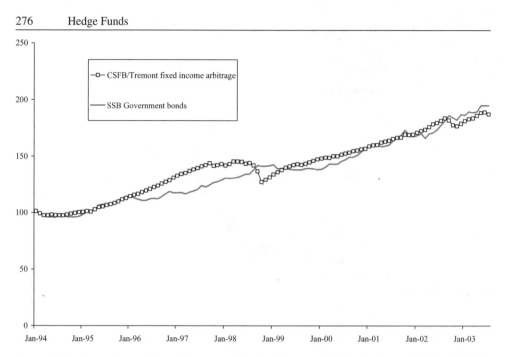

Figure 11.5 Comparison of the performance of the fixed income arbitrage strategy with that of the SSB Government bond index. Despite the similarity, the correlation between the two is less than 0.10

might be to substitute some long/short technology hedge funds for traditional technology stock allocations. Naturally, the same argument is applicable to other equity sectors, e.g. biotech, energy, financials, etc.

Over recent years, several marketers have reacted to the downtrend in equity markets by suggesting the replacement of traditional equity allocations by long/short equity portfolios. Important statistics to consider before following this suggestion are the correlation between hedge funds and the target sector, as well as the upside and downside capture.[12] Of course, investors should always prefer a high upside capture and a low downside capture relative to the target asset class.

More worrying is the fact that some marketers and even respected academics are now also presenting some hedge fund strategies as good substitutes for fixed income portfolios.[13] From a mean–variance point of view, this makes perfect sense. Many convertible arbitrage, fixed income arbitrage and market neutral funds have indeed a volatility that is close to that of bonds, but with a higher average return. Hence, replacing bonds by hedge funds in a portfolio will substantially boost the expected return without increasing the standard deviation. On the cash side, there has also been an explosion of "dynamic Treasury" products, whose objective is to beat the short-term Treasury by doing low-volatility interest rate arbitrages on the term structure of interest rates (Figure 11.5).

However, investors should be wary of considering hedge funds as enhanced bonds or cash equivalents. Low-volatility hedge funds are not exempt from risk, even if these risks did not

---

[12] Upside capture refers to the percentage of upside performance attained by a manager relative to an index in periods of positive index performance. Downside capture refers to the percentage of downside performance recorded by a manager in periods of negative index performance.

[13] See for instance McFall Lamm (1999) or Cvitanic *et al.* (2003).

materialize in the past. For instance, liquidity risk and credit risk are present in hedge funds, and might exhibit non-trivial correlation with market returns precisely when diversification is needed. Furthermore, the skewness and kurtosis of hedge fund distributions are often very different from those of fixed income portfolios. Even if volatility is low, event risk is still present. Thus, the case for hedge funds as a replacement for fixed income products is less straightforward than is often suggested, obliging investors to make a trade-off between profit and loss potentials.

11.3 HOW MUCH TO ALLOCATE TO HEDGE FUNDS?

"How much should we allocate to hedge funds?" Although investors ask us this question several times a day, we are still convinced that the problem itself is ill posed. As an illustration, consider the following two questions. First, what is the difference between having 10% of a portfolio in hedge funds with no leverage and 5% with a leverage of 2 (i.e. two dollars invested for one dollar of equity capital)? Second, what is the difference between having 5% of a portfolio in hedge funds with a net long bias and 5% in hedge funds with a net short bias? In the first case, the allocations in percentage terms are different, but the real exposures are identical. In the second case, the allocations in percentage terms are the same, but the real exposures are diametrically opposed. Clearly, by playing with the leverage and the direction of the net market exposure (long or short bias), it is possible to synthetically create any type of allocation, regardless of what the official allocation rule is. This is why the question of the exact percentage to be allocated to hedge funds does not make much sense. Nevertheless, it is still on most investors' lips, so let us try to provide some elements of a solution.

11.3.1 An informal approach

Most of the time, strategic asset allocation is extremely informal as far as hedge funds are concerned. In fact, for many investors, reviewing their hedge funds' asset allocation is like going for an annual health check-up. They know it's the right thing to do, yet it is time-consuming and potentially disruptive; as long as there are no outward symptoms, it often gets put off. Some even do not care about it. As an illustration, a survey by Arthur Andersen (2002) on the risk approach adopted by the Swiss intermediaries investing in hedge funds evidenced that many hedge fund service suppliers do not have a hedge fund asset allocation strategy, or claim to apply a "qualitative approach" – see Figure 11.6.

These results are not really surprising. As we will see shortly, hedge funds do not fit traditional asset allocation approaches very well. This misfit, combined with the conventional and incorrect wisdom that hedge fund manager selection is the primary driver of returns at the portfolio level, is the reason for the scant attention paid to the portfolio construction process. Furthermore, falling equity markets and large capital inflows into hedge funds have done little to enforce any sort of investment discipline or to justify the extraction of greater value at the portfolio level. Rather, they have allowed hedge fund allocations to develop in a rather unsophisticated way, compared with the risk management tools developed by investment banks and capital markets. In plain English, this is a shame. Hopefully, things are now changing. Cynics may argue that the sudden interest in quantitative asset allocation techniques is in large part a response to the marked underperformance of several funds of hedge funds since the Nasdaq crash in March 2000. Although that comment may not apply in all cases, there is probably some truth in it.

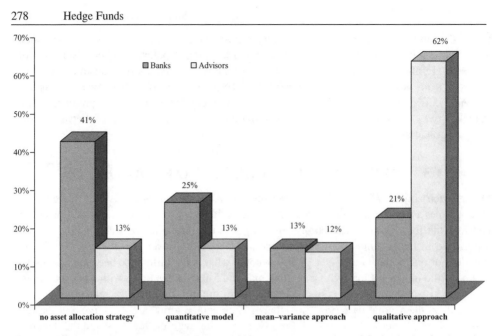

Figure 11.6 According to Arthur Andersen (2002), a large proportion of Swiss hedge fund service suppliers have no valid asset allocation strategy

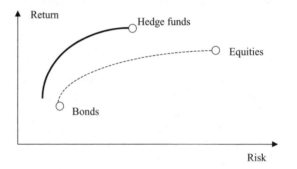

Figure 11.7 The traditional vision of the efficient frontier without hedge funds (dotted line) and with hedge funds (plain line)

11.3.2 The optimizers' answer: 100% in hedge funds

Marketers commonly use mean–variance optimizers to justify and encourage hedge fund allocations. Figure 11.7 illustrates the impact of adding hedge funds to a universe of traditional assets. It is undoubtedly the most frequently displayed graph in any alternative investment conference, article or marketing brochure. With their historical equity-like returns, bond-like volatility, and low correlation to both bonds and equities, hedge funds can boast of ideal positioning. Consequently, their inclusion in traditional portfolios significantly improves the efficient frontier, which shifts to the northwest direction (i.e. less risk and more return). While past performance is no guarantee of future results, this chart seems to say that hedge funds may offer something that traditional investments may not. Some advisors even use the term "free lunch", i.e. more return and less risk. But is all this really meaningful?

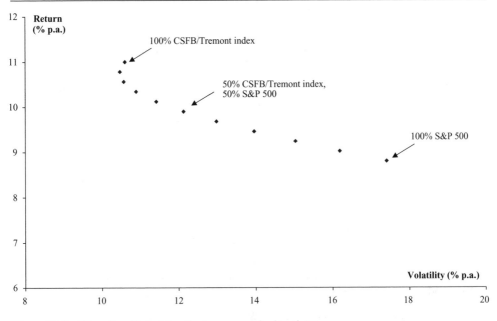

Figure 11.8   When the efficient frontier becomes a single point

The problem with mean–variance optimizers is that, when used without any control, they tend to suggest inappropriate optimal portfolios. As an illustration, Figure 11.8 shows the impact of adding hedge funds to a pure equity portfolio over the January 1994 to June 2003 period. More hedge funds means less risk and more return. Hence, the efficient frontier shrinks to a single portfolio, which is simply 100% in hedge funds. This seems to strengthen the argument for high net worth individuals and institutions to include hedge funds as part of their overall asset allocation. But in fact, it strengthens it too much to be accepted by the majority of investors!

Unfortunately, some financial advisors seem more interested in designing portfolios that are esthetically appealing to clients than they are in building investment strategies that actually have a higher probability of achieving their clients' objectives. Thus, their work consists in simply constraining the maximum weights for hedge funds in the optimization program. Although this usually results in more appealing weights, we believe the approach is intrinsically flawed. First, establishing additional constraints on how much (or little) of any investment can be included in a portfolio is strictly subjective and not a scientific or objective approach to portfolio management. Second, it is contradictory to seek to maximize an objective function only partially. This suggests that the objective function – a function of mean and variance – was badly chosen. The emphasis should therefore be on selecting the right objective function rather than on setting constraints.

11.3.3   How exact is mean–variance?

To understand why optimizers love hedge funds so much, it is necessary to go back to the roots of economic theory and, more precisely, to the notion of utility functions. An investor's utility $U(R_P)$ can be approximated by a polynomial function, for instance using a Taylor series expansion around the mean portfolio return $\bar{R}_P$. This gives

$$U(R) \approx U(\bar{R}_P) + \sum_{n=1}^{\infty} \frac{1}{n!} \frac{\partial^n U(\bar{R}_P)}{\partial R^n} (R - \bar{R}_P)^n \tag{11.4}$$

where $\partial^n U(\bar{R})/\partial R^n$ is the nth derivative of the utility function with respect to the return. Taking expectations on both sides of the equation and rearranging terms yields

$$E[U(R_P)] \approx U(\bar{R}_P) + \frac{1}{2} \frac{\partial^2 U(\bar{R}_P)}{\partial R^2} \underbrace{E[(R - \bar{R}_P)^2]}_{\text{variance}}$$

$$+ \frac{1}{3!} \frac{\partial^3 U(\bar{R}_P)}{\partial R^3} \underbrace{E[(R - \bar{R}_P)^3]}_{\text{skewness}} + \frac{1}{4!} \frac{\partial^4 U(\bar{R}_P)}{\partial R^4} \underbrace{E[(R - \bar{R}_P)^4]}_{\text{kurtosis}}$$

$$+ \sum_{n=5}^{\infty} \frac{1}{n!} \frac{\partial^n U(\bar{R}_P)}{\partial R^n} \underbrace{E[(R - \bar{R}_P)^n]}_{\text{higher order moments}} \tag{11.5}$$

As we are not interested here in the derivatives of the utility function, we can simplify the notation and express expected utility as:

$$E[U(R_P)] \approx U(\bar{R}_P) + a_1 \underbrace{E[(R - \bar{R}_P)^2]}_{\text{variance}} + a_2 \underbrace{E[(R - \bar{R}_P)^3]}_{\text{skewness}}$$

$$+ a_3 \underbrace{E[(R - \bar{R}_P)^4]}_{\text{kurtosis}} + \sum_{n=5}^{\infty} a_n \underbrace{E[(R - \bar{R}_P)^n]}_{\text{higher order moments}} \tag{11.6}$$

One of the more popular hypotheses used to explain choice under uncertainty is that investors' utility depends, positively, on the mean and, negatively, on the variance of returns. However, the Taylor approximation explicitly shows that higher order moments such as skewness and kurtosis, and more generally, any moment, also come into consideration.[14] According to Scott and Horvath (1980), under fairly weak assumptions concerning investors' utility functions, it can be shown that investors desire high odd moments (high mean return, positive skewness, etc.) and low even moments (low variance, low kurtosis, etc.). However, when working in the mean–variance framework, we implicitly assume that investors are myopic and only care about the first two terms of this Taylor series (i.e. the first two moments of the return distribution).

This simplifies the asset allocation problem tremendously, but the approximation is exact only if all the remaining terms of the Taylor series are equal to zero. That is, if either all the remaining derivatives of the utility function are equal to zero, in which case the utility was a quadratic function, or all the nth moments of the return distribution ($n > 2$) are equal to zero, in which case the return distribution is said to be elliptical.[15]

In reality, there is neither theoretical nor empirical support for these assumptions. First, quadratic utility unfortunately implies that the marginal utility becomes negative beyond a certain level, which is not descriptive of typical investors. Second, the normal distribution has

---

[14] As an illustration, consider a lottery ticket. The expected return is usually negative and the variance of returns is high, which makes it a particularly poor gamble. Nevertheless, some people still buy lottery tickets, probably because the skewness of the return distribution counteracts the unattractive mean and variance of returns.

[15] All elements of the class of elliptical distributions are symmetrical. The normal distribution is a special case of an elliptical distribution. Other special cases include distributions with finite support, e.g. the uniform distribution, which may also be characterized by mean and variance only.

infinite support and, for that reason, is not descriptive of reality because of limited liability. In addition, empirical distributions of hedge fund returns tend to display non-symmetry. Thus, it is difficult to conduct exact mean–variance analysis of portfolio choices under any of these assumptions.

Alternatively, we could accept mean–variance analysis and its results as a second-order approximation. For the majority of traditional assets, the approximation works well[16] and mean–variance analysis provides results that are consistent with the maximization of expected utility – see Levy and Markowitz (1979). However, hedge funds are peculiar animals because they offer relatively high means and low variances, but they also tend to give investors third- and fourth-moment attributes that are exactly the opposite of what investors desire, i.e. negative skewness and high kurtosis. This confirms that the relatively high mean and low standard deviation offered by hedge fund indices is no free lunch. Investors simply pay for it by accepting more negative skewness and higher kurtosis.

But any mean–variance analysis will simply ignore skewness and kurtosis, and therefore conclude that hedge funds are attractive. By using variance as a risk measure, we have conveniently avoided answering these questions, despite their importance.

11.3.4 Static versus dynamic allocations

Another problem with the majority of portfolio optimizers is that modern portfolio theory, which underlies the efficient frontier construction, assumes a single-period model of investment. That is, investors have to form a portfolio at time 0 and hold it until time T, which corresponds to their time horizon. During this period, each asset class generates a random rate of return so that at the end of the period (time T), the investor's wealth has changed by the weighted average of the returns. An optimizer will select the asset class weights at time 0 in order to maximize the expected return at time T for a given level of variance, or minimize variance for a given level of expected return from 0 to T. What happens in the middle of the period (between time 0 and time T) is irrelevant and does not influence the composition of optimal portfolios, because investors are not allowed to rebalance their portfolios.

The apparent superiority of hedge funds is therefore not surprising. The original asset classes, stocks and bonds, are static buy-and-hold portfolios, which are not revised during the period considered because the underlying managers must be invested at all times. An allocation which does not change through time is a myopic allocation, and in the microeconomic theory of saving and consumption, myopic solutions are rarely optimal. In contrast, hedge funds are dynamic portfolios. What we mean is that if we form a portfolio of hedge funds and hold it, our portfolio may appear to be static in terms of funds, but in reality, the underlying fund managers will react to new information or to the market conditions between time 0 and time T and adapt their portfolios accordingly. Comparing hedge funds with traditional asset classes is therefore the same thing as comparing a static investment policy with a dynamic one. Not surprisingly, the latter wins.

Some may wonder what happens if we modify our framework to allow traditional asset managers to also trade in the middle of the period, while keeping the objective of creating the best portfolio at the end of the period. The answer, provided by Robert Merton in the early 1970s and recently implemented by Detemple *et al.* (2003), is quite complex. To summarize, the resulting optimal portfolio contains three components:

---

[16] However, the approximation is only valid in a narrow interval around the mean return – see Lhabitant (1998).

- An allocation to a standard mean–variance portfolio.
- An allocation to a portfolio designed to hedge fluctuations in the expected risk-free rate of return by providing offsetting returns in environments when the risk-free rate of return is low.
- An allocation to a portfolio designed to hedge against changes in the expected market price of risk (Sharpe ratios) across assets.

Thus it is easy to understand why static mean–variance efficient portfolios are no longer efficient when multiple trading periods are considered: they are only a part of the optimal solution. Hedge funds, however, are allowed to trade dynamically and to invest in the two other hedge portfolios. Hence, comparing static mean–variance efficient portfolios with hedge funds is not very fair.

11.3.5   Dealing with valuation biases and autocorrelation

Finally, another advantage that hedge funds have over other asset classes lies in their valuation biases, which result in autocorrelation and overly smooth return series. This is particularly true for the merger arbitrage, distressed securities, convertible arbitrage and emerging market funds, and it leads to an underestimation of the volatility both of individual strategies and of managers, with obvious and severe consequences for asset allocation. In particular, hedge fund strategy indices that appear highly attractive when only reported returns and unadjusted volatility are considered become much less so when they are accounted for correctly.

A similar problem exists in real-estate indices, due to smoothing in appraisals and infrequent valuation of properties. Fortunately, with an understanding of the causes of smoothing, a model can be developed to undo the lags in, or "unsmooth", the data – see Geltner (1991, 1993). As a result we can infer a "true" time series of returns offering a more accurate picture of what is happening in the market today and what happened in the past.

In this approach, the observed (or smoothed) net asset value NAV_t^* of a hedge fund at time t is expressed as a weighted average of the true value at time t, NAV_t, and the smoothed value at time $t - 1$, NAV_{t-1}^*:

$$NAV_t^* = \alpha NAV_t + (1 - \alpha) NAV_{t-1}^* \qquad (11.7)$$

From there, it is possible to derive an unsmoothed series of returns with zero first-order autocorrelation:

$$R_t = \frac{R_t^* - \alpha R_{t-1}^*}{(1 - \alpha)} \qquad (11.8)$$

where R_t and R_t^* are the true underlying (unobservable) return and the observed return at time t, respectively. In the case of hedge funds, Kat and Lu (2002) suggest setting α equal to the autocorrelation coefficient at lag 1 to ensure that the newly constructed series R_t has the same (arithmetic) mean as R_t^* and no first-order autocorrelation.

As an illustration, Table 11.1 summarizes the results obtained using the CSFB Tremont indices for the convertible arbitrage, emerging markets and event-driven strategies. It is clear that the higher the first-order autocorrelation found in the raw data, the higher the rise of the standard deviation – and consequently, the less attractive the strategy from a risk-adjusted perspective. Of course, one may object that the notion of unsmoothing is far from rigorous.

Table 11.1 Statistics for original and unsmoothed returns of various CSFB/Tremont indices (1994–2003)

	Volatility	Skewness	Kurtosis	Autocorrelation
Original returns				
Convertible arbitrage	4.94	−1.67	4.39	0.56
Emerging markets	20.16	−0.96	5.00	0.30
Event-driven	6.50	−3.70	25.07	0.35
Event-driven: distressed	7.53	−3.00	18.16	0.29
Event-driven: multi-strategy	6.83	−2.92	18.59	0.35
Event-driven: risk arbitrage	4.66	−1.42	6.50	0.27
Unsmoothed returns				
Convertible arbitrage	9.52	−1.32	6.49	−0.09
Emerging markets	29.06	−1.45	7.11	0.03
Event-driven	9.64	−4.30	32.13	−0.01
Event-driven: distressed	10.40	−3.34	22.19	−0.01
Event-driven: multi-strategy	10.13	−3.27	23.04	−0.02
Event-driven: risk arbitrage	6.22	−1.35	6.83	0.03

It serves nonetheless to illustrate the possible impact of infrequent trading on hedge fund and hedge fund index returns.

11.3.6 Optimizer's inputs and the GIGO syndrome

In addition to the above-mentioned, optimizers need to be fed with a scarce hedge fund resource – data – to create successful portfolios. In the case of a mean–variance optimizer, the necessary risk and return parameters are primarily the variance–covariance matrix of future returns, as well as the expected value of these future returns for all the asset classes considered. But by definition, future returns cannot be directly observed, so the required parameters must be estimated. Although there is ample evidence that the risks and returns of major asset classes are to some extent predictable,[17] perfect forecasting is not here yet, so some simplifying assumptions are required.

Taking the easy way out, many investors use long-term historical statistics as estimates of future values. Unfortunately, this creates more problems than it solves. Implicitly, investors using long-term historical statistics are assuming (i) that returns in the different periods are independent and drawn from the same statistical distribution, and (ii) that the periods of available data provide a sample of this distribution. These hypotheses may simply be untrue, in which case the investment process will be comparable to driving a car forward while looking in the rear-view mirror. The result is that the optimizer provides the best historical efficient frontier, but not necessarily the best future one. This problem is particularly important with hedge funds, as their risk and return parameters change much more rapidly than those of traditional asset classes, so their behavior cannot be modeled with the same level of confidence.

Consider, for example, Figures 11.9–11.11, which show the 36-month rolling correlations of various CSFB Tremont indices with equity and bond markets. It is clear that these correlations

---

[17] See, for instance, Irwin *et al.* (1994), Barberis (2000) or Amenc and Martellini (2002).

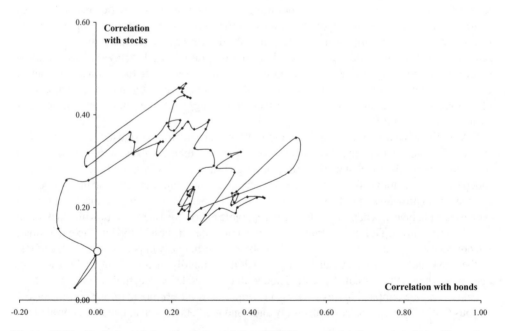

Figure 11.9 Evolution of the correlation of the CSFB/Tremont multi-strategy index with stocks (S&P 500) and bonds (SSB World Government bond). The most recent data point is indicated with a circle

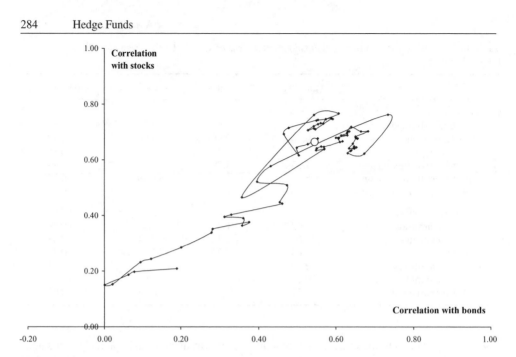

Figure 11.10 Evolution of the correlation of the CSFB/Tremont global macro index with stocks (S&P 500) and bonds (SSB World Government bond). The most recent data point is indicated with a circle

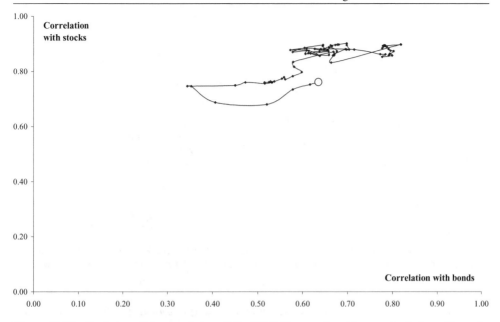

Figure 11.11 Evolution of the correlation of the CSFB/Tremont long/short equity index with stocks (S&P 500) and bonds (SSB World Government bond). The most recent data point is indicated with a circle

are anything but stable over time. Their variations are in fact normal and even expected, as hedge fund managers are paid hefty fees to adjust their portfolios to market conditions. As a consequence, correlation should decrease when managers expect a bear market, and should increase when they foresee a bull market. Investors relying on historical data to build their asset allocation will therefore face what statisticians call estimation risk, i.e. divergences between historical estimates and future reality.

The literature provides several methods for reducing the impact of estimation risk, but the least we can say is that they are not very user-friendly for non-statisticians. Let us mention some of them:

- The Black–Litterman (1990, 1991) approach provides the flexibility to combine long-term market equilibrium values with additional market views of the investor about the expected returns of arbitrary portfolios. This approach seems to be best suited to long-only asset classes, but it is usually not an ideal way of taking allocation decisions with regard to alternative asset classes.
- The statistical shrinkage approach adjusts expected returns to reflect the fact that they are indeed estimates and therefore subject to estimation risk. The Stein approach and other Bayesian-based approaches can be used here to adjust these parameter estimates over time.
- The bootstrap approach simulates historical returns thousands of times using a bootstrap method in order to obtain a range of optimal mixes, which will provide a range for optimal weights of various investments. The bootstrap method can also be used to perform various stress tests as well as to create a return/risk surface rather than a single efficient frontier estimate.

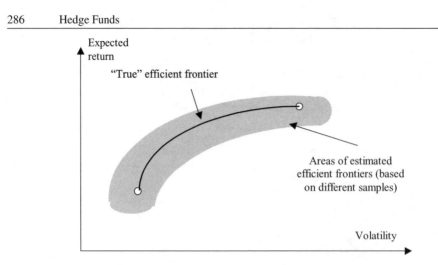

Figure 11.12   The impact of changing some inputs on the efficient frontier. Because of the instability of the optimization process, each estimated efficient frontier may be very different from others and from the original

Alternatively, many investors forecast simply by adjusting historical statistics on mean rates of return, standard deviation and covariance coefficients according to their beliefs. While this approach is better than the non-adjusted one, it introduces some subjectivity into the process, which may result in estimation risk, i.e. uncertainty about the parameters of the return process. As evidenced by Lewellen and Shanken (2000), the observable properties of prices and returns can differ significantly from the properties perceived by rational investors.

In all cases, the key problem is that the answers provided by optimizers are very sensitive to small changes in the value of estimated parameters submitted by investors, whatever their source – see for instance Perret-Gentil and Victoria-Feser (2003). In particular, a small change in a parameter works its way through the optimization process and may result in a large change in the final allocations of efficient and near-efficient portfolios[18] – see for instance Kallberg and Ziemba (1984) or Adler (1987). Some people call this the "butterfly effect", in reference to the complexity of the global weather system. The flapping of a butterfly's wings in Beijing may work its way through the system and result in a tornado in Oklahoma. See Figure 11.12.

Faced with this problem, investors often include many constraints in order to stabilize the optimization results. The end result, however, is that they constrain the problem to what they want, and it is unclear what, if anything, the optimizer contributes to portfolio investment value.

In order to limit the impact of estimation risk, the resampled efficiency algorithm invented and patented by Michaud (1998) provides an elegant solution to using uncertain information in portfolio optimization. The method is based on resampling optimization inputs, that is, it simulates a series of alternative optimization inputs that are consistent with the uncertainty in the investor's forecasts. For each series of inputs, it creates an efficient frontier. The "average" of all frontiers can then be used to select meaningful optimized portfolios.[19]

---

[18] Note that some loutish quantitative analysts have actually turned this feature to their advantage. As a judicious selection of inputs can justify almost any asset allocation policy, if at first the optimization model does not confirm the attractiveness of a favored asset allocation, they simply tweak the inputs in the right direction (for instance by changing the sampling period), or add a suitable constraint, and run the model again. *Et voilà* – the spectrum of efficient portfolios now includes the favored asset allocation policy.

[19] Because resampled efficiency is an averaging process, it is very stable. Small changes in the inputs are generally associated with only small changes in the optimized portfolios.

Another interesting approach, suggested by Chopra and Ziemba (1993), consists in analyzing the sensitivity of the final results to the optimization program's parameters. For instance, Chopra and Ziemba establish that estimation errors have a lower impact when they concern covariance as opposed to variance. In any case, the main source of instability lies in errors concerning expected returns, which explains why some authors only attempt to determine the minimum variance portfolio rather than the whole efficient frontier – as the minimum variance portfolio is independent of expected returns.

11.3.7 Non-standard efficient frontiers

In recent years, a number of authors have suggested keeping the portfolio optimization framework, but replacing variance by a number of alternative measures of risk.[20] In particular, downside risk measures such as semi-variance, value at risk or expected shortfall clearly answer some of the critics of standard deviation by focusing only on the undesirable returns.

An important issue is whether, in practice, non-variance risk measures lead to significantly different efficient portfolios. Several studies have shown that using semi-variance rather than variance does not drastically change the optimal asset allocation when traditional asset classes are considered. However, when asset classes with non-symmetric return distributions, as is the case with hedge funds, are part of the asset allocation program, the use of semi-variance or value at risk as risk measures may introduce significant changes in the optimal allocation. Therefore, these measures of risk may be more appropriate.

However, there are a number of problems with these new approaches. First and foremost, any measure of risk has to be predictable. It is one thing to use historical data to measure the past performance of a portfolio and it is another thing to forecast the risk of a portfolio. Statistical properties of semi-variance or value at risk are not well understood for non-normal distributions, and models for forecasting risk are not well developed yet. Second, the standard deviation of a portfolio is related to the standard deviations and correlations of the securities that comprise it, while the semi-variance or value at risk of a portfolio is not simply related to the semi-variances or value at risk and correlations of the underlying assets. And third, semi-variance and other measures of downside risk rely on about half the data points (i.e., only negative returns are used); much longer series of returns are therefore needed to obtain accurate estimates. The problem is even more acute with value at risk. So the question becomes one of a trade-off between simplicity and tractability on the one hand and realism on the other.

Thus any thorough analysis shows that the alternatives often have their own serious shortcomings, and that none of them address the basic limitations of mean–variance optimization. This explains why mean–variance efficiency is sometimes far more robust than is appreciated.

11.3.8 How much to allocate to hedge funds?

As the reader may have guessed, there is no standard answer regarding the weight that hedge funds should take in a portfolio. Most investors tend to forget it, and are convinced that they need hedge funds in their portfolios, even though they do not fully understand what they are. Not surprisingly, these investors face a high likelihood of disappointment, either because their expectations are too high, or because they are not fully aware of the new types of risk that hedge funds convey. Hedge funds are not the solution to all problems. When properly used, they are simply a solution to some problems.

---

[20] See for instance Favre and Galleano (2000), Rockafellar and Uryasev (2002) or Acerbi and Tasche (2002).

Our recommendations are once again based on common sense. First, investors should understand what they are investing in. They should go beyond the usual marketing pitch and study until they feel confident with the asset class. Second, investors should fix their investment targets (in terms of risk, return, liquidity, maximum loss, etc.) and be as precise as possible on anything that may be relevant, particularly regarding the constraints they want to impose on their portfolios. Third, investors should be consistent in their objectives and beliefs. For instance, hedge funds are not necessarily appropriate for investors who do not believe in active management, or are not convinced that some of the best active managers can only be accessed via hedge funds. Nor are they in principle necessary for pension funds, because there is no evidence or argument that they match pension fund liabilities. It is only after agreeing that they must either produce superior returns and/or provide diversification benefits whenever needed that an allocation might be considered. Finally, investors should control their risks: not only volatility, but anything that they consider as a risk source.

11.4   HEDGE FUNDS AS PORTABLE ALPHA OVERLAYS

Another way of looking at hedge funds is as portable alpha overlays. This approach, initially suggested by Robert C. Merton when developing his functional perspective of financial institutions, is relatively simple and can be summarized as follows: with the growing availability of derivatives, it is possible to extract an alpha earned by an active manager and transport it into another market, sector or even asset class with the same ease that "transporters" from the Star Trek science fiction series beamed individuals from one location to another. Consequently, there is no reason why an investor's choice of benchmark or asset class exposure needs to be tied to the source of alpha.[21]

The concept of portable alpha is best illustrated with equity market neutral hedge funds.[22] These funds normally hold a large number of long equity positions and an equal or close-to-equal dollar amount of offsetting short positions. Their total net exposure is close to zero, and their performance is derived from two sources, regardless of the direction of the overall market: the return of the stocks held long versus the return of the stocks sold short (long alpha plus short alpha), and the interest on the proceeds from the short sales – see Figure 11.13.

The portable alpha approach goes one step beyond the market neutral approach. Simply stated, it suggests combining the market neutral portfolio with a separate overlay account that holds futures positions[23] in the desired weighted asset class mix with a value equivalent to the market neutral portfolio. For instance, mixing the market neutral portfolio with S&P 500 futures will create a new portfolio whose return should exceed the S&P returns by the long/short alpha while preserving its overall market exposure. Hence, investors can easily use the alpha produced by a market neutral fund to augment the returns of other portfolios, passive or active, in their overall investment programs. The portable alpha portfolio can even be leveraged to match the risk and return preferences of the investor. The key to the process is of course to

---

[21] Note that Treynor and Black (1973) reached a similar conclusion and evidenced that the tools of risk management allowed asset allocation to be decoupled from active bets in the portfolio.

[22] By market neutral hedge funds, we mean funds that are effectively beta neutral with respect to equity markets. We have recently observed that a large number of self-called market neutral funds are in fact positively correlated to equity indices. Market neutrality is not a marketing argument, it has to be verified in performance.

[23] Alternatives to futures contracts are exchange traded funds, since (i) they can be bought and sold in much smaller amounts than futures and (ii) they exist for specific industry sectors, countries and risk factors (e.g. large caps versus small caps) that are not covered by futures contracts.

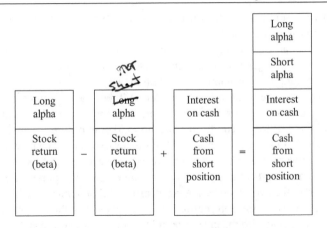

Figure 11.13 Creating a market neutral portfolio from beta exposures

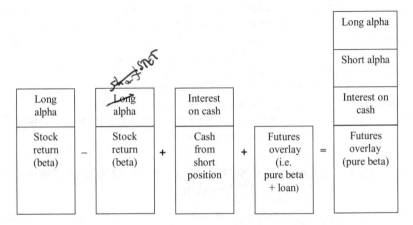

Figure 11.14 A market neutral portfolio can easily become a portable alpha overlay

identify a fund that delivers true alpha – or more precisely, true portable excess returns. See Figure 11.14.

The concept of portable alpha is also applicable to funds and strategies that are not necessarily market neutral. Consider for instance a hypothetical, non-market neutral portfolio. In general, its return can be written as

$$\text{Total return} = \text{Benchmark return} + \text{Alpha}$$

where the benchmark is chosen by the fund manager (it is generally a market index) and may differ from the investor's target benchmark (say another market index). We may rewrite this equation as

$$\text{Total return} = (\text{Benchmark return} - \text{Cash return}) + (\text{Alpha} + \text{Cash return})$$

The first part of the equation represents the excess return of the manager's benchmark over a risk-free investment. In a sense, it is the beta component of the non-market neutral portfolio. Most of the time, this component can be hedged by selling futures on the benchmark itself, which transforms the non-market neutral fund into a market neutral one. The second part of the equation represents the risk-free rate of return plus the manager's skill, i.e. the alpha component. It is this part that we need to transport to another asset class, usually by buying futures on the investor's target asset class. Of course, we are assuming that alpha is positive (at least on average) and that it is uncorrelated with the target asset class.

For example, suppose we want to hold the S&P 500, but the only managers whose skills we truly respect manage (1) an Australian market neutral (long/short) electric utilities strategy and (2) a Swiss bond portfolio. The former has no market exposure because the strategy is truly market neutral, but its fund has undesirable currency exposure. The latter has Swiss bond and Swiss franc exposure. If we hire both managers, we need to short the Australian dollar, Swiss franc and Swiss bond futures to an appropriate extent, and purchase S&P 500 stock index futures. Overall, the two superstar managers produce their alpha, which you have simply added on top of a passive S&P 500 return. The consequence is that in practical terms, the benchmarks chosen by portfolio managers should be more or less irrelevant to the investor as long as they can be hedged.

The concept of portable alpha – and the recognition that asset allocation and alpha generation are separable and independent decisions – is one of the most important developments of the 1990s. It applies also to traditional, actively managed portfolios, but hedge funds are a natural place to look for uncorrelated alpha. However, in practice, porting alpha is not without its costs and complications. In particular, it requires a fundamentally different mindset and structure for asset management. First, we need to find the managers that offer the most reliable prospective alphas, regardless of their strategy. Next, we combine these managers and port their overall alpha to the asset allocation that we want, and which is usually implemented using futures contracts and/or low-cost, indexed investment vehicles.

11.5   HEDGE FUNDS AS SOURCES OF ALTERNATIVE RISK EXPOSURE

Finally, the last way of considering hedge funds is as alternative risk sources, i.e. as investment vehicles that provide exposure to several types of risk – and therefore capture the associated risk premiums. Some of these risks are deemed traditional (equity markets, interest rates, credit), but the majority of them are still perceived as non-traditional (e.g. spreads, commodities, liquidity, volatility, correlation changes, market trends). This approach is conceptually very close to the multi-factor models we have been developing so far. It has the advantage of offering a consistent framework for both alternative assets and traditional assets, as illustrated by Figure 11.15.

In this approach, the sources of risk are common to all assets, which can capture the associated risk premiums. For instance, buying a US T-bond will expose you to interest rate risk (measured by an interest rate beta) and grant you the associated risk premium. Buying a corporate bond will essentially expose you to interest rate risk (measured by an interest rate beta) and slightly to credit risk (measured by a credit risk beta), and grant you a mix of the two associated risk premia. Buying a junk bond or, to be politically correct, a high-yield bond will expose you to the same risk sources, but will more heavily weight the credit. Finally, investing in a distressed securities hedge fund will expose you almost only to credit risk (measured by a credit risk beta), and perhaps slightly to interest rate risk, for instance if the hedge fund manager is using credit lines. What is important is that from the T-bond down to the distressed security, the risk sources are the same. It is only the exposures to these risks that change and, as a consequence,

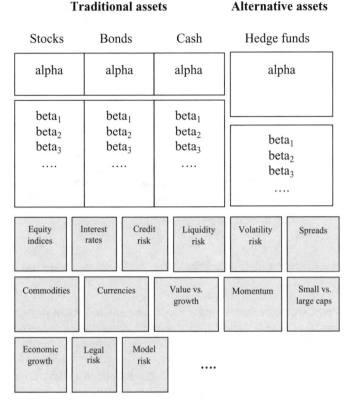

Figure 11.15   Hedge funds as risk providers

the quantity of risk premium that is collected. Hence, you should not manage the credit risk of a corporate bond differently from the credit risk of a distressed securities fund. And rather than thinking in terms of allocations, you should start thinking in terms of risk exposures and risk premia.

As an illustration, I must confess that I am often amused by the number of investors who adopt very conservative policies regarding the minimum rating and quality of the bonds in their traditional portfolios, but who are at the same time happy to enter funds of hedge funds where the distressed securities allocations represent up to 50%. Such behavior is inconsistent. If you are negative on credit risk, you should reduce your overall credit risk allocation. If you are positive on credit risk, you should be willing to increase it. The same applies to any other source of risk.

An alternative way of representing risk exposures is by means of the "risk cube" – see Figure 11.16. This three-dimensional figure shows that asset classes, geography and risk factors in fact all contribute to the risk and return of a given portfolio. It is therefore essential to have a unified framework for analyzing and managing risk.

Considering hedge funds as alternative risk sources opens the door to an increasingly popular activity in institutional asset management, which is termed risk budgeting. Simply stated, risk budgeting recognizes that the isolation of risk management from the investment process is less

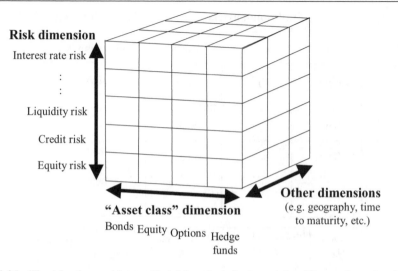

Figure 11.16   The risk cube provides a unified risk analysis framework for all "asset classes" and sources of risk

than optimal. Therefore, it attempts to make risk management a more proactive part of the investment process by allocating capital to assets on the basis of their expected contributions to overall return and risk in order to achieve superior returns while maintaining a desired level of aggregate risk.

How does risk budgeting work? Risk budgeting is essentially nothing more than good risk management that is firmly, systematically and proactively embedded in the investment process. After agreeing on the risk exposures that hedge funds may provide, the question is then to determine the type and amounts of risk an investor is willing to accept. This is the establishment of the risk budget. Once the risk budget has been agreed on, the task is then to allocate capital in the most efficient way in order to generate the best possible return while remaining within the risk budget.[24]

Risk budgeting emerged in the late 1990s in response to concerns about the level of risk being accepted in portfolios and as a consequence of the development of risk measurement and management tools. However, what is new in the risk budgeting formulation of asset allocation is the formalization of a risk lexicon and the application of new quantitative tools to improve portfolio performance. It is not the introduction of risk into the management process itself, as risk has long been an important element of portfolio management. In fact, most investment managers have engaged in some basic form of risk budgeting for many years, without really being aware that they were doing so. However, it is important to realize that risk budgeting is not just portfolio optimization, nor a guarantee against unforeseeable future mistakes. As stated by Rahl (2000), "Risk is not bad. What is bad is risk that is mispriced, mismanaged, misunderstood or unintended." Thus, the main aim of the risk budgeting process is improved consistency of performance by more systematically targeting desired risk levels and avoiding unacceptable or unwanted risks. In a sense, we may also call it risk targeting or risk allocation.

---

[24] The term risk budget here should cover the galaxy of risks that a portfolio faces. This implies that risk needs to be more broadly defined than by VaR and/or traditional risk measures.

Used appropriately, it can be a valuable complement to investment judgment, but it is not a substitute for that judgment.

Last but not least, it is worth noting that risk budgeting and the quest for portable alpha can be pursued independently, but they are interconnected and best seen as two sides of the same coin. They are bound together by the simple fact that, with hedge funds, asset allocation and the quest for alpha are separable.

12

Risk Measurement and Management

If you swallow a toad when the market opens, you will encounter nothing more disgusting the rest of the day.

Nicolas de Chamfort (1741–1794)

For many years, risk management was conspicuous by its absence in hedge fund investing. Risk was managed intuitively without any specific regulatory guidance. Diversification was considered as sufficient to avoid disasters, and risk management systems were perceived as avoidable costly investments that had not yet demonstrated their usefulness. Not surprisingly, budgets were preferably allocated to expertise and tools to make money rather than to measuring and managing risk on a formal basis.

It was only recently that the situation changed. The collapse of the fund Long Term Capital Management in August 1998, and more recently the Nasdaq crash in March 2000, made both hedge fund investors and managers conscious of the need for risk management. Multiple blowups and fraud cases (e.g. Manhattan Hedge Fund, Maricopa, HL Gestion or Lipper Convertible Arbitrage) helped convince the more reticent that risk management was no longer just an advantage or an esoteric subject, but a prerequisite for survival. Finally, the occurrence of events hitherto regarded as implausible strengthened the need to integrate stress testing formally into risk analysis.

Today, risk management has finally become a critical function in the hedge fund universe, both for managers and for investors. Some managers have adopted risk management as a tool to add value from a proprietary perspective. That is, they use advanced risk measurement techniques to both formulate quantitative strategies and manage their portfolios' liquidity and leverage. Other managers perceive risk management as a way to facilitate and improve communication with their clients and to give them greater confidence in what they are doing. And on the client side, the majority of investors want to understand risk management concepts as much as risk managers want to explain them.[1] The trend on the part of investors from accepting ("trust me") to requesting ("show me") is very clearly observable.

In practice, hedge fund investing implies taking two types of risk, namely, the pre- and the post-investment risks – see Jaeger (2002a). Pre-investment risk relates to the sound selection of managers using a thorough quantitative and qualitative evaluation and/or strategies that help meet fund objectives. Post-investment risk relates to the identification, measurement and management of risk exposures at both the manager and the investor's portfolio level. In this chapter, we essentially focus on post-investment risk. More specifically, we focus on how an investor or a fund of funds manager might measure and manage the risk of his portfolio. In that context, we believe that risk management should consist of the following activities:

---

[1] In reality, there are several investor segments, in which the requirements and the ability to understand and process risk information differ. For some client segments, using risk management as a basis for conversation may, in fact, be counterproductive; for others, it may mean the difference between securing a mandate or not.

- *Understanding the risk exposures of hedge funds.* In order to fully understand the behavior of a hedge fund, all its risk factors have to be identified. The combination of qualitative analysis and quantitative tools usually provides the best results here.
- *Measuring the exposures of hedge funds to each risk factor and aggregating these exposures at the fund level.* This can be done in two different ways. The simplest approach measures a fund's exposure to each risk factor in isolation while all other risk factors remain fixed. In mathematical terms, this is equivalent to taking a partial derivative of a fund's return with respect to the given risk factor. This is similar to the approach used when using duration and convexity for bonds, or delta, vega, gamma and rho for options. This is also the approach used when several simple regressions on different risk factors are run separately for the same fund. The aggregation of risk exposures at the fund level then involves the correlation matrix between risk factors, and the analysis of the diversification between the different risk factors. The alternative, which is usually more complex, involves analyzing the sensitivity of a fund to simultaneous changes in several risk factors. This is the approach used by multiple regression analysis.
- *Aggregating the risk of individual funds to obtain the risk of a portfolio of funds.* As the majority of investors do not invest in single hedge funds but rather in portfolios of hedge funds, this step is in fact the tip of the iceberg. Analyzing how the risks of different funds are diversified in a portfolio is a key to success.
- *Choosing which risks to bear and which ones to avoid.* This last step is of course dependent on the risk preferences of investors and the role that hedge funds play in their overall portfolios. However, some principles are common to the majority of investors, e.g. diversify unnecessary specific risks and/or avoid excessive leverage.

There are numerous excellent books on risk management techniques in general. Hence, in this chapter, we have chosen to focus essentially on four important aspects of risk management for hedge funds, namely, value at risk, Monte Carlo simulation, extreme value theory and diversification.

12.1   VALUE AT RISK

In the first chapters of this book, we saw how a large number of risk factor exposures, e.g. beta, delta, gamma, vega, rho, duration, convexity and sensitivity to various spreads, can be measured. These measures are extremely useful in understanding which risk factors really drive the returns of a hedge fund, but they should not be considered as risk measures. The reason is that we know nothing about the probability of a given adverse risk factor move. In the first chapters of this book, we also described a large number of risk measures, e.g. volatility, semi-variance and maximum drawdown. Most of these measures are statistical quantities that can easily be calculated for individual hedge funds, provided one has a sufficiently long time series of returns or net asset values. However, the difficulty with these risk measures lies less in measuring them at the individual hedge fund level than in aggregating them to estimate the total risk of a given portfolio. As soon as we stray from the ideal case of normally distributed returns and volatility as a risk measure, calculations become increasingly complicated. And in practice, as already mentioned, many low-volatility hedge funds depart from normality and exhibit negative skewness and positive kurtosis, especially in the case of funds investing in convertible arbitrage, risk arbitrage and distressed securities – see for instance Brooks and Kat (2001).

12.1.1   Value at risk (VaR) is the answer

Ideally, what we need in order to analyze risk is a measure that summarizes a portfolio's exposure to market risk as well as the probability of an adverse move. This measure should express risk using the same unit as the bottom line, i.e. dollars. Investors can then decide whether they feel comfortable with this level of risk or not. The question is: do we know such a risk measure? On the regulatory side, the answer seems to be positive. In the Basle Capital Accord, the Basle Committee on Banking Supervision (1988) recommended the adoption of a VaR-based approach to assessing risk and setting minimum capital requirements for banks and financial institutions. Hedge funds were not concerned by this measure. Nevertheless, 12 years later, a group comprising the largest hedge funds in the industry (Caxton Corporation, Kingdon Capital Management, LLC, Moore Capital Management, Inc., Soros Fund Management LLC and Tudor Investment Corporation) published the *Sound Practices for Hedge Fund Managers* report, which also recommended using VaR for measuring and communicating the risk of loss.

Today, VaR is one of the most widely used quantitative measurement tools for risk management. Although we already introduced it in Chapter 3, it is worth recalling that VaR is an estimate of the maximum loss from an adverse market move within a specified confidence level (e.g. 95% or 99%, which correspond to normal market conditions) over a specified trading horizon (e.g. one month). Mathematically speaking, VaR corresponds to a particular percentile of a return distribution.

The major advantage of VaR is the simplicity of its definition. VaR summarizes in a single number the worst potential loss which an investor risks incurring under normal conditions, whatever the risk sources and their complexity.[2] This allows decision-makers to decide whether they feel comfortable with the level of risk. If the answer is no, the process that led to the computation of the VaR can then be used to decide where and how to amend the risk. In addition, VaR provides investors with the standardized risk information they need without requiring the disclosure of proprietary data about underlying hedge fund positions. Thus, VaR facilitates risk transparency without necessarily opening the door to position transparency.

On the downside, one of the main disadvantages of VaR is that, although it is easy to define, it can be quite challenging to estimate in practice.

12.1.2   Traditional VaR approaches

To calculate the VaR of a portfolio of hedge funds, traditional approaches start by estimating the distribution of the portfolio profits and losses. They then disregard the tail events that are considered as abnormal (e.g. 1% or 5% of the cases) and only consider the worst remaining case. Though the methodology has become a *de facto* industry standard, there are several competing approaches to estimating the distribution of the portfolio profits and losses, with very different assumptions, limitations . . . and results – see Jorion (1997). Below, we briefly present some of these methods together with their limits. Without any loss of generality, let us assume that the portfolio we consider is made up of hedge funds whose performance is related (linearly or non-linearly) to a series of risk factors.[3]

The *parametric approach* (or *closed-form VaR* or *covariance VaR*) was introduced in October 1994 by J.P. Morgan's Riskmetrics.[4] It is fast and computationally simple because it relies on

---

[2] The confidence level is the degree of confidence that a loss will not exceed the VaR. For instance, at a 95% confidence level, a manager can expect (based on historical probabilities) to lose no more than the VaR measure 95% of the time over the risk horizon.

[3] The term "risk factor" should be taken here in its broadest sense.

[4] The methodology is available under www.riskmetric.com

several heavy assumptions. For instance, it assumes a normal probability distribution for all risk factors considered, as well as a linear relationship between changes in individual fund prices and changes in risk factors (options being simply approximated by their deltas, bonds by their durations, etc.). Consequently, the profits and losses on the portfolio in question are also normally distributed, with a variance that is determined by the covariance matrix and the exposures to the individual risk factors.

The *historical VaR* (or *non-parametric approach*) uses historical fluctuations in risk factors to simulate their impact on the valuation of the hedge funds that form the portfolio. Stated differently, it applies past asset returns to the present holdings. This provides a simulated return distribution of the portfolio, from which the VaR value can be determined. The advantage is that there are no normality or risk factor linearity requirements. However, the results may depend greatly on the historical period considered for the analysis. Implicitly, this approach assumes that the past is a fair representation of the future, and requires long time series, which are crucially lacking in the hedge fund industry.

Finally, the *Monte Carlo approach*[5] estimates VaR by simulating the random behavior of risk factors and estimating the impact of their changes on each fund's net asset value. To be effective, this approach usually requires complete transparency of the hedge funds' portfolios or a very good asset pricing model to understand the non-linear relationships between hedge fund returns and risk factor changes. Computationally intensive, Monte Carlo VaR is generally the slowest form of VaR to calculate.

As you have probably guessed, none of these three VaR methods is particularly well suited to hedge fund portfolios. The normality and linearity assumptions of the parametric VaR are at odds with the empirical behavior of hedge fund returns. The historical VaR requires long time series, which are a rare commodity in the hedge fund industry. And the Monte Carlo VaR requires precise, non-linear, hedge fund pricing models as well as the exact specification of the probability distribution of the risk factors.[6] This accounts for the fact that other forms of VaR have been developed and are commonly used for hedge funds.

12.1.3 The modified VaR approach

The chief criticism of the parametric VaR approach is that it assumes normally distributed returns. This obviously simplifies greatly the calculation of individual funds' VaR as well as the aggregation process to obtain the VaR of a portfolio. Remember that with normally distributed returns, the VaR of fund i is simply estimated as

$$\text{VaR}_i = \text{E}(R_i) + z_c \sigma_i \tag{12.1}$$

where z_c depends on the level of confidence ($z_c = -1.96$ with 95% probability, -2.33 with 99% probability, etc.), and $\text{E}(R_i)$ and σ_i are fund i's expected return and volatility, respectively. For instance, a fund with an expected return of $+5\%$ per month and a monthly volatility of 4% has a 95% one-month value at risk equal to -2.84% ($= 5\% - 1.96 \times 4\%$). That is, there is a 5% chance that the fund will lose more than 2.84% of its net asset value in a one-month interval.

---

[5] The name Monte Carlo was coined by physicist Nicholas Metropolis in the context of the Manhattan Project during World War II, because of the similarity of statistical simulation to games of chance, and because the capital of Monaco was a gambling center.

[6] Many implementations simply assume a normal distribution with a stationary covariance matrix for the risk factors, which is nonsense. It is precisely because things are not normal that we use Monte Carlo.

As suggested by Longin (2000), the VaR of a portfolio of N funds is easily obtained from the individual VaRs of the funds:

$$\text{VaR}_P = \sqrt{\sum_{i=1}^{N} \sum_{j=1}^{N} \rho_{i,j} w_i \, \text{VaR}_i \, w_j \, \text{VaR}_j} \tag{12.2}$$

where w_i is the weight of the ith fund and $\rho_{i,j}$ is the correlation between the ith and the jth fund.

The problem with parametric VaR is that it focuses only on the expected return and the volatility of the funds considered. Consequently, two funds having the same expected return and standard deviation are considered as equivalent – they have the same VaR. With strategies that have negatively skewed return distributions and fat tails, this can be seriously misleading. As an illustration, Favre and Galeano (2002) show that constructing a portfolio using the parametric approach without taking into consideration skewness and kurtosis could underestimate the portfolio risk by 12% to 40% p.a., depending on historical returns.

To adjust the parametric VaR and take into account skewness and kurtosis, Favre and Galeano suggest using a Cornish–Fisher approximation. The latter can be seen as an approximation that relies on moments of the distribution (e.g. skewness and kurtosis) rather than on the entire distribution. It is thus a further approximation to the already approximated distribution.[7]

The modified VaR is then calculated as:

$$\text{VaR}_i = E(R_i) + \left[z_c + \frac{z_c^2 - 1}{6} S_i + \frac{z_c^3 - 3z_c}{24} K_i - \frac{2z_c^3 - 5z_c}{36} S_i^2 \right] \sigma_i \tag{12.3}$$

where S_i and K_i are the skewness and kurtosis, respectively, of fund i. Note that if the distribution is normal, S and K are equal to zero, and we are back to equation (12.1).

As an illustration, Figure 12.1 compares the 95% one-month VaR and modified VaR in the case of several hedge fund indices. Naturally, the strategies that exhibit significant negative skewness and positive kurtosis see an increase in their VaR when these parameters are correctly accounted for.

The Cornish–Fisher modified VaR approach works remarkably well for distributions that have a small to moderate amount of skewness and kurtosis. However, it fails miserably when the distribution is too far from normality. The reason is that the modified VaR is based on an approximation of the return distribution around a normal distribution, and that any approximation fails if you depart too far from your starting point. In such cases, it is probably better to stop using distribution approximations and switch to extreme value theory (EVT).

12.1.4 Extreme values

Simply stated, EVT is an area of statistics exclusively devoted to the development of models and techniques for estimating the behavior of extreme events (maxima, minima, best and worst cases, etc.). In contrast to classical statistical inference that focuses on central measures of a distribution and where the normal curve is the norm, EVT focuses exclusively on modeling the tails of distributions.

Modeling the tail of a distribution is extremely useful as it allows us to estimate VaR beyond the range of observed data. For instance, the Basle Committee on Banking Supervision (1996)

---

[7] To our knowledge, the first to suggest using Cornish–Fisher in risk management was Zangari (1996) for portfolios containing options.

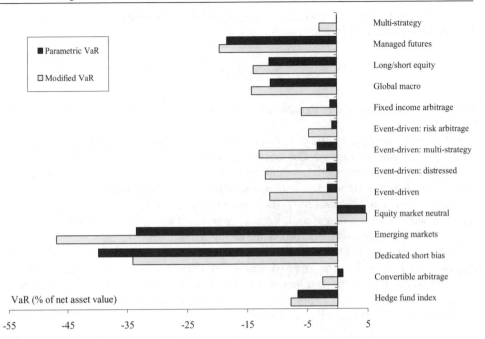

Figure 12.1   Parametric VaR versus modified VaR for CSFB/Tremont hedge fund indices

has set forth guidelines for commercial banks that stipulate a 10-day horizon and a 99% confidence level for VaR calculation. The 10-day horizon is obviously not applicable to hedge funds, as most of them only disclose monthly net asset values. But even over a monthly horizon, the 99% confidence level may create difficulties. For instance, with a hedge fund that has three years of existence (36 months), the VaR at 99% confidence is looking at a point in the tail of the return distribution that is likely to be far left of the worst observed historical loss. And even if it is not, traditional techniques only have very few extreme observations to estimate VaR with sufficient precision. This explains why EVT is a standard tool in the domains of radioactive emissions, flood analysis and climatological, hydraulic and seismic analysis, to mention but a few. These are fields where you do not often observe what you are modeling.

The justification for using EVT techniques is that the distributions of extreme returns differ significantly from normality. More specifically, the fundamental theorem of EVT shows that they converge toward a Gumbel, Fréchet or Weibull distribution[8] or, more generally, toward a subclass of the generalized extreme value distribution (GEV). Examples of such distributions are represented in Figure 12.2.

In practice, extreme value theory suggests two major related approaches to extreme returns. The first approach relies on the limit law for sample minima derived by Fisher and Tippett (1928). It consists of dividing the sample of available returns into consecutive blocks and focusing on the minimum return in each of these blocks. The second approach consists of looking only at those returns in the sample that are below a given threshold, and modeling these separately from the rest of the observations. All these EVT approaches are well described

---

[8] The Fréchet distribution is heavy-tailed (proportional to a power function), the Gumbel distribution is thin-tailed (proportional to an exponential), and the Weibull distribution is short-tailed (the tail is zero above some finite endpoint).

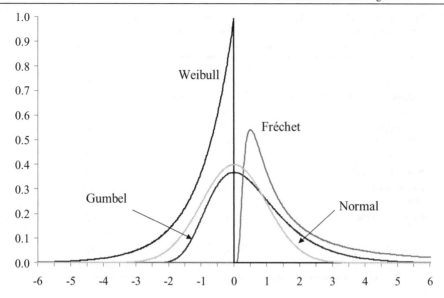

Figure 12.2   The Gumbel, Fréchet and Weibull densities compared to the normal

in Embrecht *et al.* (1997). A guide to their application to hedge funds can be found in Lhabitant (2004), particularly to calculate VaR and expected shortfall.

Let us illustrate the application of EVT to two funds of funds, Dinvest Total Return and Selectinvest Ltd. The former focuses exclusively on long/short equity and macro strategies, while the latter is dedicated to arbitrage strategies. Table 12.1 presents descriptive statistics for the two funds. The volatility of Selectinvest is extremely low (0.99% per month) compared to the volatility of Dinvest (3.32%), but the average return offered by Dinvest is higher (0.78% per month versus 0.59%). This confirms that the arbitrage and relative value strategies used in Selectinvest were able to deliver consistent returns with extremely low risk of loss, which makes the fund suitable for more risk-averse investors. In contrast, the long/short equity and global macro strategies used in Dinvest target higher returns, but are more volatile and also more correlated to the movements of equity markets.

Table 12.1 also signals that the risk profile of our hedge funds cannot be accurately described by the mean and standard deviation alone. The Jarque–Bera statistics indicate that returns are not normally distributed. Indeed, Dinvest and Selectinvest share the properties of hedge fund distributions, that is, low variances for the average returns achieved, negative skewness (returns below the mean are more likely than returns above the mean) and high kurtosis (fat tails). Hence, investors will also have to use these higher moments of the return distribution to assess the risk of their investments more accurately.

In Table 12.2, we can see that the fat-tailed return distributions of our two hedge funds lead the parametric VaR model to understate their true value at risk. At 95% confidence, the results provided by the parametric VaR and the EVT VaR methods are similar (−4.52% and −4.69% per month for Dinvest; −1.02% and −1.03% for Selectinvest). However, things deteriorate rapidly as we go deeper into the tails of the distribution. At 99% confidence, the parametric VaR of Dinvest is −6.95% versus −9.88% for the EVT VaR. For Selectinvest, the difference is even more striking, with −1.70% for the parametric VaR and −4.31% for the EVT VaR.

Table 12.1 Essential statistics for Dinvest and Selectinvest since inception. All figures are expressed on a monthly basis, except for the Sharpe ratio, which is annualized (note that the figures are calculated on different periods for each fund)

	Dinvest (since inception)	Selectinvest (since inception)
Number of observations	196	52
Mean return (%)	0.78	0.59
Volatility (%)	3.32	0.99
Sharpe ratio	0.66	0.39
Skewness	−1.28	−2.00
Kurtosis	7.27	5.65
Normality test (Jarque–Bera, 5%)	Rejected	Rejected
Best month (%)	+11.87	+2.42
	(Sep. 1992)	(Nov. 1998)
Worst month (%)	−17.56	−3.37
	(Nov. 1987)	(Aug. 1998)

Table 12.2 Comparing the empirical, parametric and EVT VaR for Dinvest and Selectinvest. All figures are expressed on a monthly basis

	Empirical VaR	Parametric VaR	EVT VaR	Exp. shortfall
Dinvest				
$VaR_{95\%}$	−3.84	−4.69	−4.52	−8.03
$VaR_{97.5\%}$	−7.03	−5.74	−6.63	−10.63
$VaR_{99\%}$	−8.38	−6.95	−9.88	−14.63
$VaR_{99.5\%}$	−10.23	−7.78	−12.74	−18.15
$VaR_{99.9\%}$	−17.40	−9.49	−20.99	−28.31
$VaR_{99.99\%}$	−19.01	−11.58	−38.11	−49.38
Selectinvest Ltd.				
$VaR_{95\%}$	−1.61	−1.03	−1.02	−3.78
$VaR_{97.5\%}$	−1.98	−1.34	−2.11	−6.08
$VaR_{99\%}$	−2.69	−1.70	−4.31	−10.76
$VaR_{99.5\%}$	−3.06	−1.95	−6.85	−16.17
$VaR_{99.9\%}$	−3.35	−2.45	−17.98	−39.83
$VaR_{99.99\%}$	−3.42	−3.07	−64.27	−138.24

This result is not surprising, given the level of skewness and kurtosis that we observed for the two funds.

However, an interesting result is obtained for a 99.99% confidence interval: the VaR of Selectinvest is larger than the VaR of Dinvest. In a sense, we could say that Dinvest is more risky "on average" than Selectinvest, but that Selectinvest has higher extreme risks. This is clearly representative of the risk inherent in arbitrage strategies versus the risk of long/short and global macro strategies. A confirmation of these higher extreme risks can be obtained by comparing expected shortfalls, i.e. the expected loss when the funds lose more money than their VaR.

12.1.5   Approaches based on style analysis

An alternative approach to measuring the VaR of hedge funds and hedge fund portfolios is suggested by Lhabitant (2001). Simply stated, it is a two-step procedure that combines style analysis with stress testing.

The first step is to compare hedge fund returns with a series of factors in order to derive the fund's sensitivity (the beta) to the factors, as well as the specific component of the fund's returns. Lhabitant suggests using as factors the CSFB/Tremont sub-indices and forcing the beta coefficients to be positive in order to maintain the economic intuition behind the model.[9] In this case, for a given hedge fund, his model can be written as:

$$R_t = \alpha + \sum_{i=1}^{9} \beta_i \cdot I_{i,t} + \varepsilon_t \tag{12.4}$$

where

$I_{1,t} = $ return on the CSFB Tremont convertible arbitrage index at time t

$I_{2,t} = $ return on the CSFB Tremont short bias index at time t

$I_{3,t} = $ return on the CSFB Tremont event-driven index at time t

$I_{4,t} = $ return on the CSFB Tremont global macro index at time t

$I_{5,t} = $ return on the CSFB Tremont long/short equity index at time t

$I_{6,t} = $ return on the CSFB Tremont emerging markets index at time t

$I_{7,t} = $ return on the CSFB Tremont fixed income arbitrage index at time t

$I_{8,t} = $ return on the CSFB Tremont market neutral index at time t

$I_{9,t} = $ return on the CSFB Tremont managed futures index at time t

As mentioned already in Chapter 8, equation (12.4) splits the return and risk of any hedge fund into two components: one explained jointly by the nine systematic factors[10] and the other that remains unexplained (Figure 12.3). The latter consists of a constant expected component (α), plus an unexpected one (ε_t) with a zero mean and a variance denoted σ_ε^2.

Secondly, knowing the style exposure of a hedge fund, one can easily obtain its VaR. Let us assume for instance that we want a confidence level of 99% for the one-month VaR.[11] Then, we "push" each individual risk factor in the most disadvantageous direction (at the one percentile value of its historical distribution) and estimate the overall impact on the fund, accounting for the correlation of risk factors. This gives us the VaR due to market moves (i.e. style index

---

[9] Having a negative exposure to a particular style could be hard to justify economically. For instance, what would a negative exposure to the short bias style mean?

[10] By systematic, we mean that the corresponding factors may influence the returns of all hedge funds.

[11] The choice of the holding period depends upon the time needed to liquidate a portfolio. It typically varies from one day for a trading portfolio to 30 days for a fund with a monthly redemption policy. The choice of the confidence interval is also relatively subjective. Banks typically use 95% to 99% as confidence intervals for measuring and reporting VaR.

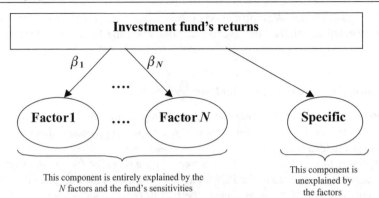

Figure 12.3   The style analysis of hedge fund returns

moves), which we call "value at market risk". Mathematically:

$$VaMR = \sqrt{\sum_{i=1}^{9}\sum_{j=1}^{9} \rho_{i,j} \cdot \beta_i \cdot F_i^* \cdot \beta_j \cdot F_j^*} \qquad (12.5)$$

where $\rho_{i,j}$ is the correlation between monthly returns of hedge fund indices i and j, and F_i^* is the one percentile extreme return of style index i returns over one month.

We now have to deal with specific risk (σ_ε^2), i.e. the difference between total risk (the observed fund variance σ_P^2) and systematic risk (the variance due to the market, i.e. the hedge fund style indices). We have:

$$\sigma_\varepsilon^2 = \sigma_P^2 - \sum_{i=1}^{9}\sum_{j=1}^{9} \rho_{i,j} \cdot \beta_i \cdot \sigma_i \cdot \beta_j \cdot \sigma_j \qquad (12.6)$$

By construction, the error terms ε_t of equation (12.4) are non-correlated and normally distributed with zero mean. Since we want a 99% confidence level, we can apply a factor push of 2.33 times σ_ε (corresponding to a 99% confidence level for a normal variable) to obtain the specific risk of a hedge fund. Mathematically, the value at specific risk (VaSR) is given by:

$$VaSR = 2.33 \times \sigma_\varepsilon \qquad (12.7)$$

if we assume normally distributed errors. Otherwise, it can be estimated empirically, as the error terms ε_t are observable.

To obtain the total VaR figure (Figure 12.4), we simply add market and specific risk figures, accounting for their zero correlation:[12]

$$VaR = \sqrt{(\text{Value at market risk})^2 + (\text{Value at specific risk})^2} \qquad (12.8)$$

How trustworthy is this approach? Lhabitant (2001) applied his VaR model to a sample of 2934 hedge funds from January 1994 to October 2000. Using a three-year observation period, he computed funds' exposures, the market parameters and the funds' VaRs (one month, 99% confidence level). Table 12.3 shows the different components of the VaR he obtained, expressed

---

[12] Note that, while the lower boundary constraint for betas is really binding, market risk and specific risk may not be absolutely orthogonal. In this case, a correlation term would be needed in equation (12.8) – see De Roon *et al.* (2003).

Table 12.3   Value at risk and its components. Each figure corresponds to a percentage loss with respect to net asset value

	Average VaMR					Volatility VaMR				
	1997	1998	1999	2000	Avg.	1997	1998	1999	2000	Avg.
Conv. arbitrage	5.88	5.95	9.04	8.44	7.57	5.16	6.32	8.00	7.40	7.04
Emerging	9.88	29.52	28.71	29.94	26.65	5.06	19.70	13.19	14.42	13.74
Event-driven	5.13	5.27	7.14	7.20	6.22	4.63	4.70	5.21	5.96	5.14
Long/short equ.	6.77	8.12	10.20	14.10	9.58	3.63	4.75	6.36	8.63	5.99
Managed futures	4.90	7.02	8.93	7.76	8.08	2.54	4.76	4.97	3.95	4.56
Market neutral	5.55	6.46	8.50	8.80	7.94	4.38	4.74	6.73	7.15	6.38
Multi-strategy	6.27	6.76	8.77	8.73	7.65	4.83	5.56	6.48	7.03	6.03
Fixed inc. arb.	5.79	7.77	10.72	11.98	8.90	5.30	7.24	7.78	8.00	7.11
Global macro	8.02	8.34	8.67	8.26	8.31	4.87	4.69	4.62	4.01	4.58
Dedicated short	11.95	10.62	10.79	7.71	10.60	5.60	4.76	4.94	5.14	5.11
All sample	6.10	6.83	9.15	9.55	8.07	4.70	5.75	6.68	7.18	6.25

	Average VaSR					Volatility VaSR				
	1997	1998	1999	2000	Avg.	1997	1998	1999	2000	Avg.
Conv. arbitrage	6.90	7.02	6.35	6.71	6.71	6.39	6.92	6.02	6.92	6.57
Emerging	5.13	9.76	11.58	12.74	10.90	2.05	6.87	5.14	6.61	5.63
Event-driven	5.93	5.69	4.63	5.17	5.31	5.60	5.11	4.44	5.89	5.21
Long/short equ.	5.79	5.80	6.77	8.63	6.65	3.67	3.57	4.58	5.64	4.38
Managed futures	11.22	7.75	7.09	6.98	7.33	8.46	4.21	4.04	4.15	4.35
Market neutral	6.46	6.62	7.60	7.85	7.40	4.88	5.00	5.35	5.14	5.17
Multi-strategy	7.03	6.84	7.22	7.67	7.17	5.18	5.04	5.75	6.12	5.53
Fixed inc. arb.	7.47	6.55	7.47	8.43	7.43	7.14	6.12	5.73	5.89	6.26
Global macro	7.52	6.29	4.93	5.03	5.99	4.55	4.20	2.90	2.98	3.74
Dedicated short	7.89	7.64	7.40	8.38	7.74	4.17	3.44	3.18	3.07	3.53
All sample	6.76	6.58	6.82	7.45	6.91	5.53	5.34	5.28	5.83	5.48

	Average VaR					Volatility VaR				
	1997	1998	1999	2000	Avg.	1997	1998	1999	2000	Avg.
Conv. arbitrage	9.29	9.60	11.33	11.04	10.48	7.96	8.97	9.69	9.85	9.31
Emerging	11.55	31.42	31.23	32.75	29.09	4.52	20.37	13.54	15.42	14.32
Event-driven	8.03	8.08	8.74	9.14	8.50	7.05	6.55	6.55	8.08	7.02
Long/short equ.	9.15	10.23	12.54	16.75	11.94	4.71	5.50	7.34	9.95	7.00
Managed futures	12.43	10.82	11.56	10.62	11.17	8.57	5.71	6.12	5.39	5.94
Market neutral	8.74	9.50	11.67	12.08	11.13	6.26	6.53	8.23	8.41	7.84
Multi-strategy	9.73	9.97	11.68	11.91	10.83	6.65	7.02	8.22	8.95	7.75
Fixed inc. arb.	9.75	10.54	13.34	14.93	11.98	8.56	9.06	9.29	9.51	9.09
Global macro	11.38	10.95	10.23	9.84	10.62	5.97	5.37	4.96	4.65	5.29
Dedicated short	15.25	13.61	13.65	12.07	13.84	4.58	4.53	4.41	4.44	4.49
All sample	9.42	9.87	11.72	12.42	10.97	6.89	7.41	8.13	8.89	7.93

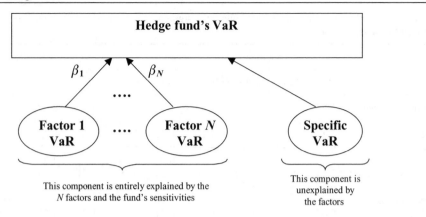

Figure 12.4   From style analysis to value at risk

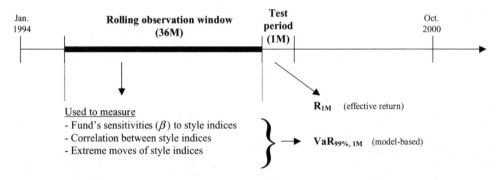

Figure 12.5   Validating the VaR model by comparing effective returns with model-based VaR

as a percentage of the net asset value. Overall, hedge funds have a monthly average VaR of 10.97%, which is split (on average) between a monthly VaMR of 8.07% and a monthly VaSR of 6.91%. However, these figures differ widely, both across investment styles and funds and across time. The less risky investment style appears to be event-driven (average VaR of 8.50%) and the riskier one is emerging markets (average VaR of 29.09%). Managed futures, global macro and dedicated short styles experienced an overall decrease of their VaR, while all other categories increased their risk figures. The larger increase is observed for emerging markets hedge funds, particularly after the Asian crisis of 1997. Note that the major source of risk remains the market risk rather than the specific risk component.

A key component to the implementation of model-based risk management is model validation, i.e. determining whether the model chosen is accurate and performing consistently. Hence, to confirm the validity of his VaR approach, Lhabitant also presented some back-testing results. Using a 36-month rolling window, he verified how often the actual losses at the end of a month have exceeded the level predicted by the model-generated VaR at the beginning of the month (Figure 12.5). If the portfolio movement undershoots the VaR number, this is recorded as an exception. Since the VaR is calculated at the 99% level, we can expect an exception every 100 months (Figure 12.6).

Out of a total of 96 549 three-year observation periods, Lhabitant observed 1026 exceptions. This gives an exception rate slightly higher than expected (1.06% versus 1%). However, some

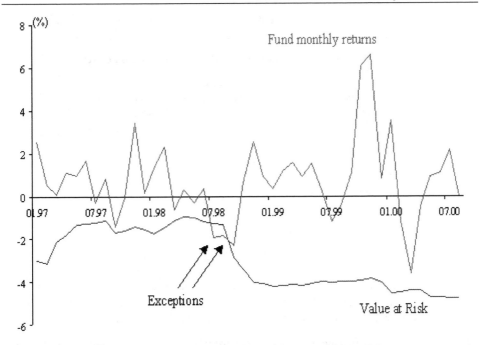

Figure 12.6   An exception occurs as soon as the monthly return is below the VaR

caution must be exercised, since 614 of these exceptions occurred in August 1998 immediately after the LTCM crisis, which can be regarded as an abnormal market situation. If this month is excluded from the sample, the exception rate falls to 0.43%, a rather conservative figure. Hence, the model seems to provide a pragmatic and effective approach to calculating VaR for hedge funds and hedge fund portfolios.

12.1.6   Extension for liquidity: L-VaR

Laporte (2003) recently suggested an interesting extension to the style-based value at risk model called L-VaR, which takes liquidity risk into consideration. By liquidity risk, we mean the loss that an investor may face when exiting from a hedge fund due to specific constraints (lock-up clauses, notification periods and/or a limited redemption schedule) that imply a waiting period before the effective sale of shares.

The approach suggested by Laporte starts by calculating a liquidity spread. If a waiting period of N months is necessary to exit from a hedge fund, the liquidity spread is calculated as:

$$\text{Spread}_t = \text{NAV}_{t+N} - \text{NAV}_t \tag{12.9}$$

Next, the liquidity spread of a hedge fund is compared with the liquidity spreads of the CSFB/Tremont hedge fund indices. The fund's liquidity spread can then be decomposed into a systematic part and a specific part. These two new components are then stressed and added to the traditional style-based value at risk model. The value at risk of a hedge fund is therefore split into five components, as illustrated in Figure 12.7.

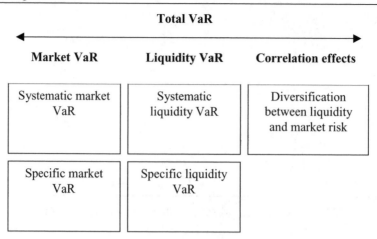

Figure 12.7   The decomposition of VaR in Laporte's model

The beauty of this model is that it is relatively easy to change the liquidity constraints set by a hedge fund and to analyze the impact on its VaR. Laporte, for example, considers three funds, namely the Maverick Fund, the Bayard Fund and the Ascot Fund:

- The Maverick Fund is managed as a traditional, truly hedge fund, taking both long and short positions primarily in US equities, with a bias toward large cap issues. The fund does not invest in bonds, currencies, commodities or derivatives, and only uses a moderate amount of leverage. Its strategy relies on a fundamental or bottom-up approach to security selection and analysis.
- The Bayard Fund's objective is to obtain 10–20% per annum return after fees over the long term, through investment in European equities long and short, managing company risk, and seeking to reduce exposure to market risk. The fund managers believe that they have superior experience and research skills within the European equity environment. Consequently, the long side of the Bayard Fund is exclusively focused on European growth companies. Short sales are used both to increase risk positions and to reduce market risk when appropriate.
- The Ascot Fund's objective is to achieve twice the long-term Treasury rate while maintaining a low volatility and smooth performance. Ascot engages primarily in the practice of index arbitrage and some convertible arbitrage. It may occasionally hold investments in private debt claims and publicly traded securities of bankrupt and distressed companies.

These three hedge funds have very different returns and, therefore, different liquidity profiles. Figures 12.8–12.10 show the VaR evolution as a function of the calendar time and of the selected period that we want to impose.

Most of the liquidity VaR of the Maverick Fund seems concentrated in 1997. In fact, the fund's performance in 1994 was poor, and it takes time for the model to forget it. In more recent years, the liquidity VaR was extremely low and seemed to decrease with longer waiting periods, because the fund recorded a very good performance – which implies that the waiting spread is actually positive and thus does not constitute a risk. The major source of VaR for Maverick is therefore market VaR rather than liquidity VaR. The Bayard Fund, in contrast, accumulated losses in 1999–2001 and thus has a very large liquidity VaR, while the Ascot Fund only experienced four negative months in the 1994–2002 period and thus has a null liquidity VaR.

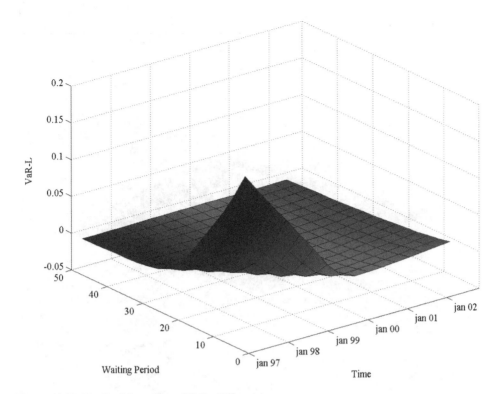

Figure 12.8 The liquidity-adjusted VaR of Maverick

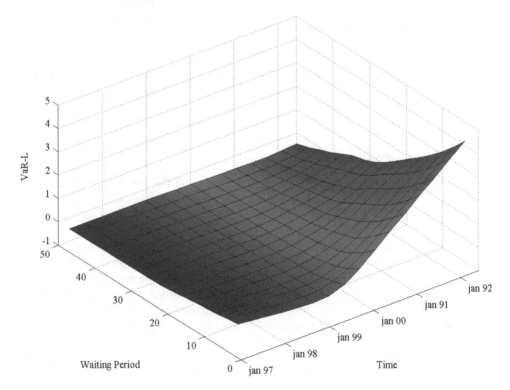

Figure 12.9 The liquidity-adjusted VaR of Bayard

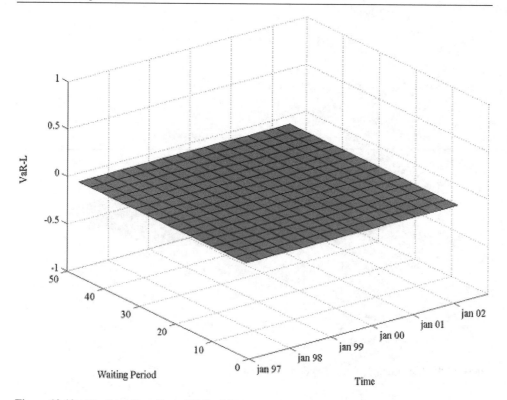

Figure 12.10   The liquidity-adjusted VaR of Ascot

Combining the three funds in an equally weighted portfolio allows us to observe simultaneously the beginning-of-period liquidity issues of Maverick and the end-of-period liquidity issues of the Bayard Fund – see Figure 12.11.

12.1.7   The limits of VaR and stress testing

Despite the promising results, it is necessary to bear in mind the definition of VaR and its limits. VaR should not create a false sense of security among fund managers and investors leading to higher leverage and larger exposure positions than would otherwise have occurred. This is definitely not the intended goal.

When correctly implemented, VaR models have proven to be very useful risk management tools. However, VaR is not perfect and has several limitations. It should therefore be used as a quantitative tool to complement, but not replace, human judgment and market experience. As an illustration, Long Term Capital Management itself had a fairly sophisticated VaR system, based on historical data, to try to limit potential losses. However, the combination of the exceptional market conditions at the end of 1998 (spreads moving many standard deviations), with excessive leverage, led to a disaster.

By definition, VaR only focuses on portfolio losses in "normal" market conditions. It ignores portfolio losses during rare or extreme market conditions, such as when risk factors take

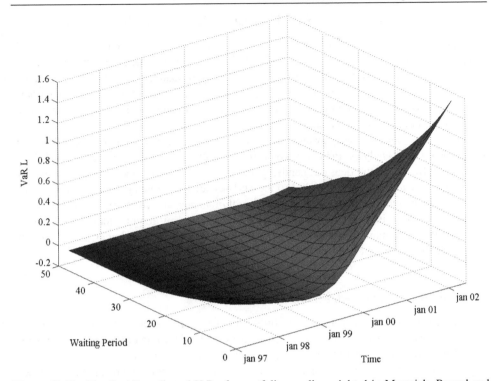

Figure 12.11 The liquidity-adjusted VaR of a portfolio equally weighted in Maverick, Bayard and Ascot

unprecedented values or values that occurred outside the historical period considered for the VaR model. Investigating what can happen during such circumstances is the role of stress tests.[13]

Generically speaking, stress tests involve specifying adverse market moves (scenarios) and revaluing the portfolio under these moves. The specification of the stress scenarios consists in selecting the market factors that are to be stressed and defining both the amount of stress and the time period over which the stress move will take place. These scenarios can be historical (e.g. the 1987 equity crash, the ERM crisis of 1992, the bond crash of 1994, the peso crash of 1994, the Asian crisis of 1997, the LTCM crash of 1998, the Nasdaq crash of 2000 and the credit spread crash of 2002) or fictive (e.g. a simple movement of x standard deviations on some risk factors).

Many of the models we have considered so far can easily perform stress tests if we feed them with stressed data (i.e. stress returns, volatility, skewness, kurtosis and correlations). Alternatively, another approach is to isolate the worst-case loss scenarios in a Monte Carlo simulation and examine which market data changes are associated with these results. This technique is reviewed in the next section.

---

[13] The Basle Committee on Banking Supervision (1996) requires banks that use a VaR model for determining their market risk capital requirements to implement a rigorous and comprehensive stress-testing framework. Further, the Bank for International Settlements and the Technical Committee of the International Organization of Securities Commissions oblige institutions with significant trading activities to execute stress tests on a regular basis, using a variety of assumptions which cover both hypothetical and historical events.

12.2   MONTE CARLO SIMULATION

The idea underlying Monte Carlo simulation is to approximate the behavior of a real-world system (say, a hedge fund) within an artificial simulated environment. Assuming that the evolution of the real-world system can be described by probability density functions, then the Monte Carlo simulation proceeds by sampling from these probability density functions. The outcomes of these random samplings, or trials, are accumulated or tallied in an appropriate manner to produce the desired result.

Let us say, for example, that we want to determine the probability of getting a three-of-a-kind using Monte Carlo analysis. First, we would program the computer to create a virtual deck of cards, shuffle them and deal out hands. With N cards left in the deck, the probability of obtaining a particular card would be $1/N$ if the card has not been drawn yet and zero otherwise. Then, we just instruct the computer to deal one million hands, and count the number of times a three-of-a-kind is obtained. The ratio of this number to one million provides an estimate of the probability of obtaining a three-of-a-kind at poker. Obviously, the larger the number of simulations, the better our estimate will be.

12.2.1   Monte Carlo for hedge funds

Monte Carlo simulation is particularly useful for predicting the overall outcome of a series of related events when we know only the statistical probability of the outcome of each component event. This is precisely what we are trying to do when we analyze the risk of a portfolio of hedge funds. To keep things simple, let us start by considering only one hedge fund. Say we have identified the fund's historical return distribution, either by using the fund's historical histogram or by smoothing the historical histogram into a probability distribution function. Then, using statistical software, we can easily draw one random number that follows the fund's return distribution. This random return can be considered as a possible scenario for the next month's return. By repeating the drawing say 10 000 times, we build a sample of 10 000 possible scenarios. The key thing here is that the distribution of the 10 000 simulated returns looks very similar to the "real-world" distribution they were drawn from. Consequently, the decisions taken by considering the statistics calculated from simulated returns should also be valid in the real world.

As an illustration, Figure 12.12 shows the historical return distributions of three hedge funds, namely, Arbitex Investors, Fairfield Sentry and Caxton Global Investments. Arbitex is a market neutral convertible arbitrage fund with an emphasis on volatility trading. Fairfield Sentry is an index arbitrage fund that delegates its management to B. Madoff. Caxton Global Investments is one of the largest global macro funds, with a broad mandate to trade worldwide.

We use the software @Risk^{TM} to obtain the probability density function that best fits each histogram, and obtain a logistic distribution for Arbitex, a log-logistic distribution for Fairfield and a general beta distribution for Caxton. These probability density functions are plotted as curves on the histograms.[14]

---

[14] In practice, we use @Risk^{TM}, and we have observed that most hedge funds have a good statistical fit using the lognormal, logistic, Weibull or generalized beta distributions. For funds that have a very strong option-like non-linear pattern, @Risk^{TM} sometimes suggests a triangular distribution fitted on the mode of the histogram. The three funds we are using as an example have been explicitly chosen for their specific fitted distributions.

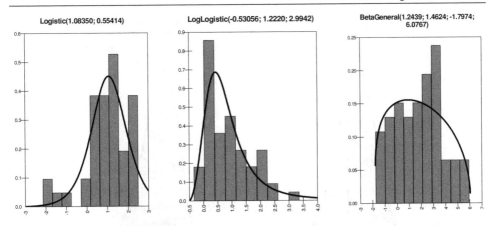

Figure 12.12 The historical return distributions of Arbitex Investors, Fairfield Sentry and Caxton Global Investments and their fitted distributions

Using fitted distributions, it is relatively easy to simulate a large number of returns for any application.[15] This suddenly solves the scarcity of data problem that most quants were facing when dealing with hedge funds. However, we should be cautious with the simulation results. In particular, we should remember that by definition, the majority of the observed data points are clustered around the mean. Hence, a distribution that fits the whole historical data set well will provide a good fit around the mean, but not necessarily in the tails of the distribution, particularly if these tails are "fat" or "thin". Thus, in some cases, it is preferable to use EVT to find the distribution that best matches the tail – and only the tail – of the fund return distribution.

Simulating the behavior of a hedge fund portfolio is also relatively easy. Say our portfolio contains N hedge funds. We could identify each fund's historical return distribution, and draw one random number per fund that follows the corresponding distribution. But doing so implicitly assumes that the N hedge fund returns can be drawn independently of each other, which is not true in practice. Thus, we have to draw our N returns simultaneously, *accounting for both the individual hedge fund's distribution and the correlation between funds*. The output of our simulation is then a series of N returns that correspond to one possible scenario. We therefore need to repeat the process say 10 000 times to have a sample of 10 000 possible scenarios for the joint behavior of our funds.

Armed with the results of the Monte Carlo simulation for all individual hedge funds, simulating the behavior of a portfolio is now straightforward. We simply need to weight the individual simulated returns and add them up to obtain the simulated portfolio return. Since we have 10 000 returns for each fund, we can obtain 10 000 possible scenarios for the portfolio return. The result is the left histogram of Figure 12.13, which corresponds to a gamma distribution. If required, we can also stress our model by forcing all the correlations between funds to equal one. This is particularly useful to see what happens if all funds start losing money together. The result is the right histogram of Figure 12.13, which corresponds – in our example – also to a gamma distribution.

---

[15] Note that random number generation is a complex subject in itself, and one that is far beyond the scope of this book. For our purposes, we will simply assume that some software has built-in routines that can produce series of pseudo-random numbers that are sufficient for making accurate simulations.

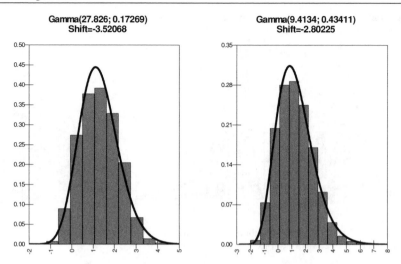

Figure 12.13 The simulated return distribution of the portfolio using historical correlations (left) and using a stressed correlation matrix, i.e. all correlations set equal to 1 (right)

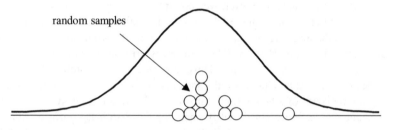

Figure 12.14 In usual sampling methods, most simulated samples are likely to cluster around the mean of the distribution

Note that this simulation approach can easily be applied in a multi-factor model. In this case, rather than simulating funds, we simulate risk factors (including specific risk). The weights in the portfolio become the betas or sensitivities of the fund returns to the factors considered.

12.2.2 Looking in the tails

Monte Carlo methods rely on averaging the results from a large number of samples to provide meaningful results. If, for example, we try to estimate the probability of getting a three-of-a-kind at poker with only one simulation, the conclusion is likely to be zero. It is only with several thousand trials that the three-of-a-kind percentage observed comes close to its theoretical probability.

A problem with simulation is that samples naturally cluster around the mean, while the outlying areas of the distribution – those areas to the far left or right – have not yet been sampled. Consequently, it usually takes quite a few samples before one appears in either of the two outlying areas. As an illustration, Figure 12.14 shows what typically happens if we simulate seven numbers from a normal distribution: they are all clustered around the mean.

Latin hypercube sampling provides an elegant solution to this problem. Simply stated, it divides the probability distribution into N areas of equal probability – each area has $1/N$

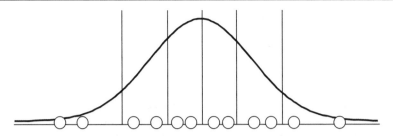

Figure 12.15   In Latin hypercube sampling, an equal number of samples is drawn from each area

of a chance of occurring. The procedure then samples each of these N areas as if they were different distributions. This ensures that we have sampled the area under the curve more fully with fewer trials.

Figure 12.15 shows an example of Latin hypercube sampling. The distribution has been divided into six areas of equal probability – the area under the curve between each bar is the same. Eight samples are then drawn, one from each of these six regions. The samples represent a random point within each region. This procedure generates outlying statistics faster than in normal sampling, as the sample technique guarantees points in the extreme regions for each eight-sample set.

Both traditional sampling and hypercube sampling "converge" on the same values when the sample size is large. However, the Latin hypercube is slightly more accurate for outlying statistics and perhaps slightly less accurate for mean statistics.

12.3   FROM MEASURING TO MANAGING RISK

Although a great deal of effort still goes into measuring adequately the risks of hedge fund portfolios, we have to admit that this is only the first part of the story. Measuring risk is a passive activity with little value added. It is only managing risk that adds value and enhances the long-term, risk-adjusted returns of a portfolio.

At the portfolio level, risk can be analyzed as a function of time. How high is the risk level today compared with last month? Has risk increased over time? Running rolling window analyses, a risk manager can easily answer that question, analyze the time-varying properties of a portfolio and draw graphs that show how stable any particular statistic has been. We will not expand on these techniques here. Of greater interest is the analysis of risk at different aggregation levels. Where does the risk come from? Where should we act to increase or reduce the risk of a portfolio? How do new weightings affect the portfolio total risk? To answer these questions, risk management requires information beyond the total VaR of a portfolio (denoted VaR$_P$).

The *marginal VaR* (MVaR) is the change in the portfolio VaR resulting from a marginal change in the relative position of fund i. Technically, it is equal to the first derivative of VaR with respect to the weight of the fund considered. For fund i, marginal VaR is defined as:

$$\text{MVaR}_i = \frac{\partial \text{VaR}_P}{\partial w_i} \tag{12.10}$$

A particular case is when $w_i = 0$, that is, the ith fund is not yet included in the portfolio. Then, the impact of including this fund with a target weight $w_i \neq 0$ can be approximated by the *incremental VaR* (IVaR), defined as:

$$\text{IVaR}_i \approx \left. \frac{\partial \text{VaR}_P}{\partial w_i} \right|_{w_i=0} \times w_i \tag{12.11}$$

Hence, the VaR of the augmented portfolio can be approximated by $\text{VaR}_P + \text{IVaR}_i$. Note that this is only an approximation, because IVaR_i is estimated without fund i in the portfolio.

Finally, the *component VaR* (CVaR) denotes the contribution of an individual fund to the VaR of the portfolio. It is different from the standalone VaR of the fund, because part of the fund's standalone risk will be diversified at the portfolio level. We thus require that component VaRs can solely be attributed to each of the individual instruments comprising that portfolio and aggregate linearly into the total diversified portfolio VaR:

$$\text{VaR}_P = \sum_i \text{CVaR}_i \tag{12.12}$$

Garman (1996a,b) derived analytical expressions for these marginal, component and incremental VaR metrics under the assumption that returns are drawn from a multivariate normal distribution. In the general case, however, there is no simple analytical procedure for estimating these metrics. Thus, for a slightly changed portfolio composition, the VaR has to be re-estimated.

Employing risk tools such as absolute, marginal and relative VaR, we can evaluate a given portfolio risk and determine the most efficient asset allocation and manager selection based on clearly defined risk and return parameters. As an illustration, consider a portfolio equally allocated (in dollar terms) in three funds, namely Arbitex Investors, Fairfield Sentry and Caxton Global Investments. We are interested in adding a fourth fund to this portfolio, and the choice is between the CTA Graham K4 and the long/short equity Maverick.

By decomposing the VaR of a portfolio into the effective CVaR contributions of each fund, a risk manager is able to identify the most significant sources of risk – what Litterman (1996) called the "hot spots". In our case, although the funds are equally allocated on a dollar basis, Figure 12.16 clearly shows that Caxton Global Investments contributes the majority (63.48%) of the risk in the portfolio, as well as the majority (51.51%) of the return, while Fairfield Sentry is a small risk contributor (7.41%).

Now, say that we want to reduce the overall VaR of the portfolio. What is the most effective way of doing so? Should we reallocate assets between our three existing funds, or should we include a new fund in a portfolio? Figure 12.17 shows the marginal VaR of our five funds in relation to our portfolio. Clearly, we should reduce the weight of the fund with the highest marginal VaR (Caxton Global Investments) and replace it by the fund with the lowest marginal VaR (Maverick, which even has a negative risk contribution – i.e. including it reduces the overall portfolio risk). From a risk management perspective, this makes sense. But is it also consistent from an expected return perspective? Is it compatible with the other requirements of the investor, such as the liquidity of the portfolio? And how do we handle the fact that Caxton is closed and only allows redemption once a year at calendar year end? This is precisely where the frontier between the science and the art of portfolio management lies.

And last, but not least, we should not forget that a small change in the allocation may significantly change the overall risk picture. As an illustration, Figure 12.18 shows the risk attribution obtained if we naively lower our Caxton allocation (-14%) to allow both Maverick (7%) and Graham K4 ($+7\%$) to enter in the portfolio. Clearly, a small dollar allocation does not necessarily imply a small risk allocation!

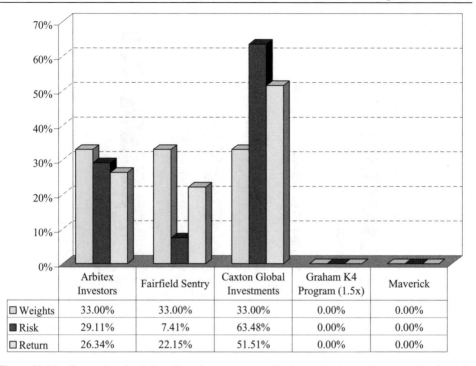

	Arbitex Investors	Fairfield Sentry	Caxton Global Investments	Graham K4 Program (1.5x)	Maverick
□ Weights	33.00%	33.00%	33.00%	0.00%	0.00%
■ Risk	29.11%	7.41%	63.48%	0.00%	0.00%
□ Return	26.34%	22.15%	51.51%	0.00%	0.00%

Figure 12.16 Comparing the dollar allocation, return contribution and risk contribution of the funds in a portfolio. All quantities are expressed on a relative basis (i.e. sum to 100%)

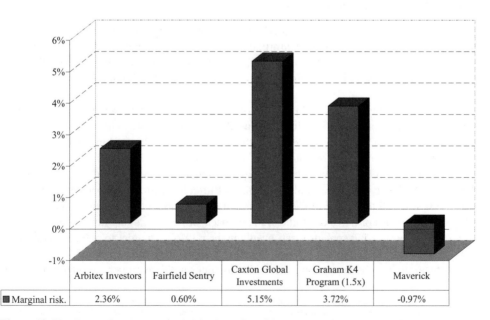

	Arbitex Investors	Fairfield Sentry	Caxton Global Investments	Graham K4 Program (1.5x)	Maverick
■ Marginal risk.	2.36%	0.60%	5.15%	3.72%	-0.97%

Figure 12.17 Comparing the marginal risk of a series of funds in relation to our portfolio

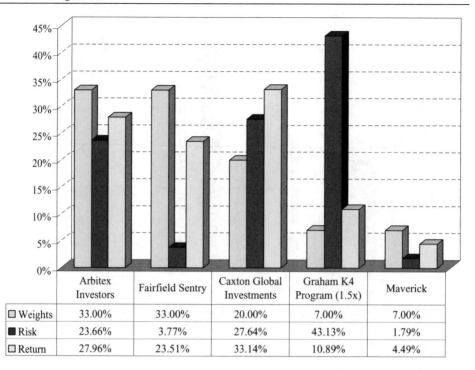

	Arbitex Investors	Fairfield Sentry	Caxton Global Investments	Graham K4 Program (1.5x)	Maverick
☐ Weights	33.00%	33.00%	20.00%	7.00%	7.00%
■ Risk	23.66%	3.77%	27.64%	43.13%	1.79%
☐ Return	27.96%	23.51%	33.14%	10.89%	4.49%

Figure 12.18 Comparing the dollar allocation, return contribution and risk contribution of the funds in a naively reallocated portfolio. All quantities are expressed on a relative basis (i.e. sum to 100%)

12.3.1 The benefits of diversification

As we have just illustrated, risk is a critical element that should be identified and controlled in the portfolio construction process. Unfortunately, investors often believe that diversification offers sufficient protection against risk. Their attitude is a common sense concept that has many parallels in popular language and culture, for example: "Don't put all your eggs in one basket".

However, choosing a diversified portfolio of hedge funds is not so easy and raises several problems. In particular, how many funds are needed to diversify away risk while maintaining the expected return? Obviously, more funds is better, but there are diminishing marginal returns and, eventually, diminishing absolute returns when portfolio size increases, since transaction costs remain relatively constant while incremental reductions in portfolio risk get smaller. Hence, the challenge is also to avoid what Warren Buffet has called "di-*worse*-ification".

The simplest tool to test the impact of increasing the number of hedge funds in a portfolio is the $1/N$ heuristics or naive diversification approach, which has a long history in asset allocation.[16] Simply stated, it spreads assets evenly in the portfolio in order to reduce overall risk, while at the same time ignoring the mathematical complexities underlying modern portfolio theory. According to the latter, naive diversification does not give proper consideration to the

---

[16] In fact, it was even recommended in the Talmud. Writing in about the 4th century, a certain Rabbi Isaac bar Aha gave the following asset allocation advice: "A man should always place his money, a third into land, a third into merchandise, and keep a third on hand". Harry Markowitz reported that he used this rule himself and justified his choice on psychological grounds: "My intention was to minimize my future regret. So I split my contributions fifty–fifty between bonds and equities".

correlations among the assets and should therefore result in sub-optimal portfolios. However, in practice, naive diversification usually results in reasonably diversified portfolios that are surprisingly close to the efficient frontier.

Extending the work of Amin and Kat (2002), Lhabitant and Learned (2003, 2004) extensively tested naive diversification strategies with hedge fund portfolios, both in mono-strategy and multi-strategy portfolios. The authors identified 10 hedge fund styles and determined the number of funds needed for a hedge fund portfolio to be well diversified with respect to various risk measures and over various periods.

Lhabitant and Learned observe that naive diversification is, as a general rule, a good protection against ignorance and can significantly decrease risk. Smart diversification – where the investor uses information about the investment style of the funds to allocate assets and avoid concentration in some strategies – provides even better results without requiring much more work. However, diversification within fund-of-hedge-fund portfolios should not be considered a free lunch. As evidenced above, naive diversification may, in some cases (fixed income arbitrage and event-driven strategies), result in a dramatic increase in risk, particularly in terms of skewness and kurtosis.

Lhabitant and Learned also observe that most of the diversification benefits are obtained with 5 to 10 funds, while funds of funds typically hold between 15 and 50 underlying funds. One may therefore wonder why funds of hedge funds are so diversified. Maybe they are simply afraid of blow-up risk? But shouldn't this risk be minimized by proper due diligence rather than by holding more funds in the portfolio? The question remains open for further research, but the two authors also evidence that the average correlation of a hedge fund portfolio with the S&P 500 index increases rapidly with the number of funds, which means that too much diversification in a fund of funds can reduce its value added as a traditional portfolio diversifier.

It is interesting to note that the hedge fund industry seems to be evolving towards more concentrated portfolios. New funds of hedge funds are now emerging as a way to achieve higher average returns. These newcomers typically run portfolios with less than a dozen underlying managers, and focus on smaller funds that can be more nimble and exploit opportunities that highly capitalized funds cannot. Not surprisingly, their managers generally want these portfolios to remain small, as too much asset growth would imply . . . more diversification.

13

Conclusions

Today's expert is a bloke who knows where yesterday's expert went wrong.

Finally! You have made it, as we have now reached the end of our quantitative journey. Our trip was obviously long, but we hope it was also instructive and, to some extent, pleasant. Together we have explored and surveyed a large number of tools and dispelled some inaccurate perceptions about quantitative techniques. Some of these techniques were relatively simple and probably well known. Others were less familiar or more complex. But all aim at the same goal, i.e. increasing the knowledge and understanding of what is really going on in the hedge fund industry.

As already mentioned, hedge fund investing has seen a long debate about the pros and cons of qualitative versus quantitative research. At times, competing and often polemical arguments for either one or the other approach seem to take more energy than the actual research does. On the one hand, the well-grounded, rich and concrete descriptions of qualitative analysis bring appealing explanations of how hedge funds operate and achieve their performance, whether positive or negative. Words, especially organized into stories, have a vivid, meaningful flavor that often proves far more convincing to the reader. On the other hand, advocates of quantitative methods contend that serious investing needs to rely more on solid scientific grounds, and defend the idea that in a complex world, hedge fund returns are complex functions of sets of variables. Both these functions and the relevant variables need to be objectively identified and quantified. Consequently, the simple functional relationship often assumed by qualitative empiricists often threatens its very validity.

Many investors believe that qualitative and quantitative research cannot be combined because the assumptions underlying each approach are so vastly different. Others think qualitative and quantitative research can be used in combination only by alternating between methods; qualitative research being appropriate to answer certain kinds of questions in certain conditions and quantitative research being right for others. Once again, we wish to emphasize our opinion. Despite the compelling illusion of precision that quantitative research can give, the reality is that we live in a qualitative world. Consequently, both qualitative and quantitative research should be used simultaneously to arrive at sound financial judgments. In fact, only the combination of both approaches can overcome the problems of each individual approach without becoming trapped in the problems of the other. Thus, qualitative and quantitative research should be seen as being complementary rather than substitutable. Rather than discounting either approach for its drawbacks, researchers should find the most effective way to incorporate elements of both to ensure that their studies are as accurate and thorough as possible. An ancient Chinese proverb claims that "Theory without Practice is Idle, Practice without Theory is Blind". This is perfectly applicable to hedge fund investing.

Until now, the integration of qualitative and quantitative research has been seriously curbed by the self-assumed quantitative illiteracy sentiment that affects the majority of the investment community. Only a minority had – or claimed to have – a functional working knowledge of quantitative techniques and tools. By using this book, we hope that a larger number of persons will be able to establish a first bridge towards quantitative research and to understand its results, its limits and its usefulness. Our premise is that many of the most popular quantitative techniques have certain elements in common, and that if these elements can be grasped, the reader can gain a working understanding of a wider variety of complex techniques and portfolio management tools.

Of course, we do not claim that this book is exhaustive, but we feel that it is a fairly comprehensive treatment of the major topics that are relevant for hedge fund investing as of today. We hope you will find it useful as a roadmap for your next journey, i.e. combining quantitative and qualitative methods in your search for positive and significant alpha. And in any case, please keep in mind that the capacity to generate pure alpha depends on skill, which is a scarce resource – unlike the number of hedge fund managers.

Online References

Many of the papers and references mentioned in this book are available on the following websites:

- Edhec Risk and Asset Management Research Center (http://www.edhec-risk.com).
- Center for International Securities and Derivatives Markets (http://cisdm.som.umass.edu).
- Centre for Hedge Fund Research and Education at London Business School (http://www.london.edu/hedgefunds/index.html).
- Alternative Investment Research Centre at the Cass Business School (http://www.cass.city.ac.uk/airc/index.html).
- Social Science Research Network (http://www.ssrn.com).
- *Journal of Alternative Investments* (http://www.iijai.com).

Bibliography

Abernathy, J.D. and A.B. Weisman (2002), "The dangers of historical hedge fund data", Working Paper, Stonebrook Structured Products LLC.

Acerbi, C. and D. Tasche (2002), "On the coherence of expected shortfall", *Journal of Banking and Finance*, **26**, 1491–1507.

Ackerman, C., R. McNally and D. Ravenscraft (1999), "The performance of hedge funds: risk, return, and incentive", *Journal of Finance*, **54**, 833–874.

Adler, M. (1987), "Global asset allocation: some uneasy questions", *Investment Management Review*, **Sept/Oct**, 13–18.

Admati, A.R., S. Bhattacharya, P.C. Pfleiderer and S.A. Ross (1986), "On timing and selectivity", *Journal of Finance*, **41**, 710–730.

Agarwal, V. and N.Y. Naik (2000a), "On taking the alternative route: risks, reward, style and performance persistence of hedge funds", *Journal of Alternative Investments*, **2**, 6–23.

Agarwal, V. and N.Y. Naik (2000b), "Multi-period performance persistence analysis of hedge funds", *Journal of Financial and Quantitative Analysis*, **35** (3), 327–342.

Agarwal, V. and N.Y. Naik (2000c), "Performance evaluation of hedge funds with option-based and buy-and-hold strategies", *Journal of Financial and Quantitative Analysis*, **Sept**, 1–52.

Agarwal, V. and N.Y. Naik (2000d), "Generalized style analysis of hedge funds", *Journal of Asset Management*, **1** (1), 93–109.

Agarwal, V. and N.Y. Naik (2003), "Risk and portfolio decisions involving hedge funds", *Review of Financial Studies*, **17**, 63–98 [published in 2004].

Amenc, N. and V. le Sourd (2003), *Portfolio Theory and Performance Analysis*, John Wiley & Sons.

Amenc, N. and L. Martellini (2001a), "It's time for asset allocation!", *Journal of Financial Transformation*, **3**, 77–88.

Amenc, N. and L. Martellini (2001b), "The brave new world of hedge fund indexes", Working Paper, EDHEC-MISYS Risk and Asset Management Research Center.

Amenc, N. and L. Martellini (2002), "Portfolio optimization and hedge fund style allocation decisions", *Journal of Alternative Investments*, **5** (2), 7–20.

Amenc, N. and L. Martellini (2003), "Desperately seeking pure style indices", Working Paper, EDHEC-MISYS Risk and Asset Management Research Center.

Amenc, N., S. Curtis and L. Martellini (2002a), "The alpha and omega of hedge fund performance measurement", Working Paper, EDHEC-MISYS Risk and Asset Management Research Center.

Amenc, N., S. El Bied and L. Martellini (2002b), "Evidence of predictability in hedge fund returns and multi-style multi-class tactical style allocation decisions", *Financial Analysts Journal*, **59** (5), 32–46 [published in 2003].

Amenc, N., L. Martellini and M. Vaissié (2002c), "Benefits and risks of alternative investment strategies", Working Paper, EDHEC-MISYS Risk and Asset Management Research Center.

Amihud, Y. (2002), "Illiquidity and stock returns", *Journal of Financial Markets*, **5**, 31–56.

Amin, G. and H. Kat (2001a), "Hedge fund performance 1990–2000: do the money machines really add value?", Working Paper, ISMA Centre.

Amin, G. and H. Kat (2001b), "Welcome to the dark side: hedge fund attrition and survivorship bias over the period 1994–2001", Working Paper, ISMA Centre.

Amin, G. and H. Kat (2002), "Portfolios of hedge funds", Working Paper, ISMA Centre.

Anderberg, M.R. (1973), *Cluster Analysis for Applications*, Academic Press, New York.

Anson, M. (2001), "Hedge fund incentive fees and the free option", *Journal of Alternative Investments*, **4** (2), 43–48.

Anson, M. (2002), "Funds of funds versus individual hedge funds", in Capital Market Risk Advisors (ed.) and AIMA Research, *A Guide to Fund of Hedge Funds Management and Investment*, October, pp. 10–15.

Aragon, G.O. (2002), "Timing multiple markets: theory and evidence", Working Paper, Boston College.

Artzner, P., F. Delbaen, J.-M. Eber and D. Heath (1997), "Thinking coherently", *Risk*, **10** (11), 68–71.

Artzner, P., F. Delbaen, J.-M. Eber and D. Heath (1999), "Coherent measures of risk", *Mathematical Finance*, **3** (9), 203–228.

Asness, C., R. Krail and J. Liew (2001), "Do hedge funds hedge?", *Journal of Portfolio Management*, **28** (1), 6–19.

Bai, J. and S. Ng (2002), "Determining the number of factors in approximate factor models", *Econometrica*, **70**, 191–221.

Bailey, J.V. (1992a), "Are manager universes acceptable benchmarks?", *Journal of Portfolio Management*, **18**, 9–13.

Bailey, J.V. (1992b), "Evaluating benchmark quality", *Financial Analysts Journal*, **48**, 33–39.

Bailey, J. and D. Tierney (1998), "Controlling misfit risk in multiple-manager investment programs", The Research Foundation of the Institute of Chartered Financial Analysts.

Banz, R.W. (1981), "The relationship between return and market value of common stocks", *Journal of Financial Economics*, **9**, 3–18.

Barberis, N. (2000), "Investing for the long run when returns are predictable", *Journal of Finance*, **55** (1), 225–264.

Bares, P.-A., R. Gibson and S. Gyger (2001), "Style consistency and survival probability in the hedge funds' industry", Working Paper, Swiss Federal Institute of Technology Lausanne, EPFL and University of Zurich, February.

Barnett, V. and T. Lewis (1994), *Outliers in Statistical Data*, John Wiley & Sons, New York.

Barone-Adesi, G., P. Gagliardini and G. Urga (2002), "Coskewness and its implication for testing asset pricing models", Working Paper.

Barry, R. (2003), "Hedge funds: a walk through the graveyard", Working Paper, Ross Barry Macquarie Applied Finance Centre.

Basle Committee on Banking Supervision (1988), "International convergence of capital measurement and capital standards", Working Paper.

Basle Committee on Banking Supervision (1996), "Amendment to the capital accord to incorporate market risks", Working Paper.

Basu, S. (1983), "The relationship between earnings yield, market value, and the return for NYSE common stocks: further evidence", *Journal of Financial Economics*, **12**, 129–156.

Becker, Th.R. (2003), "Exploring the mathematical basis of returns-based style analysis", in T.D. Coggin and F.J. Fabozzi (eds), *Handbook of Equity Style Management*, 3rd edn, John Wiley & Sons.

Bhandari, L.X. (1988), "Debt equity ratio and expected common stock returns: empirical evidence", *Journal of Finance*, **43**, 507–528.

Billingsley, R. and D. Chance (1996), "Benefits and limitations of diversification among commodity trading advisors", *Journal of Portfolio Management*, **23**, 65–80.

Black, F. (1993), "Beta and return", *Journal of Portfolio Management*, **20**, 8–18.

Black, F. and R. Litterman (1990), "Asset allocation: combining investor views with market equilibrium", Goldman, Sachs & Co., Fixed Income Research.

Black, F. and R. Litterman (1991), "Global asset allocation with equities, bonds, and currencies", Goldman, Sachs & Co., Fixed Income Research.

Black, F. and M. Scholes (1973), "The pricing of options and corporate liabilities", *Journal of Political Economy*, **81**, 1–26.

Black, F., M.C. Jensen and M. Scholes (1972), "The capital asset pricing model: some empirical tests", in M.C. Jensen (ed.), *Studies in the Theory of Capital Markets*, Praeger, Inc., New York.

Blume, M. and I. Friend (1973), "A new look at the capital asset pricing model", *Journal of Finance*, **28**, 19–33.

Bodie, Z., A. Kane and A.J. Marcus (1999), *Investments*, 4th edn, McGraw-Hill, New York.

Bollen, N.P.B. and J.A. Busse (2001), "On the timing ability of mutual fund managers", *Journal of Finance*, **56**, 1075–1094.

Booth, P.M., R.G. Chadburn, D.R. Cooper, S. Haberman and D. James (1999), *Modern Actuarial Theory and Practice*, CRC Press/Chapman and Hall, Boca Raton, FL.

Brealey, R.A. and E. Kaplanis (2000), "Changes in the factor exposures of hedge funds", Institute of Finance and Accounting (IFA) Working Paper No. 320, London Business School.

Breusch, T. and A. Pagan (1979), "A simple test for heteroscedasticity and random coefficient variation", *Econometrica*, **47**, 1287–1294.

Brinson, G.P., L.R. Hood and G.P. Beebower (1986), "Determinants of portfolio performance", *Financial Analysts Journal*, **July/Aug**, 39–44.

Brinson, G.P., B. Singer and G.P. Beebower (1991), "Determinants of portfolio preference II: an update", *Financial Analysts Journal*, **May/June**, 40–48.

Brittain, B. and Lyster Watson & Co. (2001), "Hedge funds and the institutional investor", *Journal of International Financial Management & Accounting*, **12** (2), 225–234.

Brooks, C. and H. Kat (2001), "The statistical properties of hedge fund index returns and their implications for investors", Working Paper, The University of Reading, ISMA Centre.

Brown, S. and W. Goetzmann (1995), "Performance persistence", *Journal of Finance*, **50**, 679–698.

Brown, S. and W. Goetzmann (2003), "Hedge funds with style", Yale International Center for Finance, *Journal of Portfolio Management*, **Winter**, 101–112.

Brown, S.J., W.N. Goetzmann and J.M. Park (1998), "Hedge funds and the Asian crisis of 1997", Working Paper, New York University.

Brown, S.J., W.N. Goetzmann and R.G. Ibbotson (1999), "Offshore hedge funds: survival and performance, 1989–1995", *Journal of Business*, **72**, 91–117.

Brown, S.J., W.N. Goetzmann and J. Park (2001), "Careers and survival: competition and risk in the hedge fund and CTA industry", *Journal of Finance*, **53** (5), 1869–1886.

Burke, G. (1994), "A sharper Sharpe ratio", *The Computerized Trader*, March.

Capocci, D.P.J. (2001), "An analysis of hedge fund performance", Working Paper, University of Liege.

Carhart, M. (1997), "On persistence in mutual fund performance", *Journal of Finance*, **52**, 57–82.

Cattell, R.B. (1966), "The scree test for the number of factors", *Multivariate Behavioral Research*, **1**, 245–276.

Cerrahoglu, B., A. Daglioglu and B. Gupta (2003), "Hedge fund strategy performance: using conditional approaches", Working Paper, Center for International Securities and Derivatives Markets.

Chan, L.K.C., H.-L. Chen and J. Lakonishok (1999), "On mutual fund investment styles", NBER Working Paper 7215.

Chande, T. (1999), "Controlling risk and managing investor expectations by modeling the dynamics of losses in hedge funds and alternative strategies", *Derivatives Quarterly*, **5** (3), 52–58.

Cheng, P. and Y. Liang (2000), "Optimal diversification: is it really worthwhile?", *Journal of Real Estate Portfolio Management*, **6**, 7–16.

Chopra, V. and W.T. Ziemba (1993), "The effect of errors in mean and co-variance estimates on optimal portfolio choice", *Journal of Portfolio Management*, **Winter**, 6–11.

Christiansen, C.B., P.B. Madsen and M. Christiansen (2003), "Further evidence on hedge funds performance", Working Paper, Aarhus School of Business.

Chui, A.C.W., S. Titman and K.C. Wei (2000), "Momentum, legal systems and ownership structure: an analysis of Asian stock markets", Working Paper.

Chung, Y.P., H. Johnson and M.J. Schill (2001), "Asset pricing when returns are nonnormal: Fama–French factors vs. higher-order systematic co-Moments", Working Paper.

Cleveland, W.S. (1979), "Robust locally weighted regression and smoothing scatterplots", *Journal of the American Statistical Association*, **74**, 829–836.

Cleveland, W.S. and S.J. Devlin (1988), "Locally weighted regression: an approach to regression analysis by local fitting", *Journal of the American Statistical Association*, **83**, 596–610.

Cox, J. and H. Leland (2000), "On dynamic investment strategies", *Journal of Economic Dynamics and Control*, **24**, 1859–1880.

Culp, C.L., R. Mensink and A.M.P. Neves (2000), "Value-at-risk for asset managers", in L. Rahl (ed.), *Risk Budgeting: A New Approach to Investing*, Risk Books, London, pp. 83–102.

Cvitanic, J., A. Lazrak, L. Martellini and F. Zapatero (2003), "Optimal allocation to hedge funds: an empirical analysis", *Quantitative Finance*, **3** (Feb), 28–39.

D'Andrade, R. (1978), "U-statistic hierarchical clustering", *Psychometrika*, **4**, 58–67.

Daniel, K., M. Grinblatt, S. Titman and R. Wermers (1997), "Measuring mutual fund performance with characteristic-based benchmarks", *Journal of Finance*, **52**, 1035–1058.

Danthine, J.P. and J.B. Donaldson (2001), *Intermediate Financial Theory*, Prentice Hall, Englewood Cliffs, NJ.

De Roon, F.A., Th.E. Nijman and J.E. ter Horst (2003), "Evaluating style analysis", CentER Discussion Paper 0064.

Detemple, J.B., R. Garcia and M. Rindisbacher (2003), "A Monte-Carlo method for optimal portfolios", *Journal of Finance*, **58** (1), 401–446.

DiBartolomeo, D. and E. Witkowski (1997), "Mutual fund misclassification: evidence based on style analysis", *Financial Analysts Journal*, **53**, 32–43.

Dreger, R.M. (1986), "Microcomputer programs for the Rand index of cluster similarity", *Educational and Psychological Measurement*, **46**, 655–661.

Dybvig, P. (1988a), "Distributional analysis of portfolio choice", *Journal of Business*, **61**, 369–393.

Dybvig, P. (1988b), "Inefficient dynamic portfolio strategies or how to throw away a million dollars in the stock market", *Review of Financial Studies*, **1**, 67–88.

Edwards, F.R. and M.O. Caglayan (2001), "Hedge fund performance and manager skill", Working Paper, Columbia University.

Elton, E.J. and M.J. Gruber (1995), *Modern Portfolio Theory and Investment Analysis*, 5th edn, John Wiley & Sons, New York.

Elton, E.J., M.J. Gruber and C. Blake (1995), "Fundamental economic variables, expected returns, and bond fund performance", *Journal of Finance*, **50** (4), 1229–1256.

Embrecht, P., C. Klüppelberg and T. Mikosch (1999), *Modelling Extremal Events*, Springer-Verlag, Berlin.

Fama, E.F. and K. French (1992), "The cross-section of expected stock returns", *Journal of Finance*, **67**, 427–465.

Fama, E.F. and K. French (1996), "Multifactor explanations of asset pricing anomalies", *Journal of Finance*, **51**, 55–84.

Fama, E.F. and J.D. MacBeth (1973), "Risk, return and equilibrium: empirical tests", *Journal of Political Economy*, **71**, 607–636.

Favre, L. and J.A. Galeano (2000), "Portfolio allocation with hedge funds: case study of a Swiss institutional investor".

Favre, L. and J.A. Galeano (2002), "Mean-modified value at risk optimization with hedge funds", *Journal of Alternative Investments*, **5** (2), 21–25.

Favre, L. and A. Signer (2002), "The difficulties of measuring the benefits of hedge funds", *Journal of Alternative Investments*, **5** (1), 31–41.

Feller, W. (1970), *An Introduction to Probability Theory and Its Applications*, Vol. 1, 3rd edn, John Wiley & Sons, New York.

Ferson, W. and C.R. Harvey (1993), "Explaining the predictability in asset returns", *Research in Finance*, **11**, 65–106.

Ferson, W. and K. Khang (2001), "Conditional performance measurement using portfolio weights: evidence for pension funds", *Journal of Financial Economics*, **65**, 249–282.

Ferson, W.E. and R.W. Schadt (1996), "Measuring fund strategy and performance in changing economic conditions", *Journal of Finance*, **51**, 425–462.

Ferson, W.E. and V.A. Warther (1996), "Evaluating fund performance in a dynamic market", *Financial Analysts Journal*, **52**, 20–28.

Fishburn, P.C. (1977), "Mean-risk analysis with risk associated with below target returns", *American Economic Review*, **67** (2), 116–126.

Fisher, R.A. and L.H.C. Tippett (1928), "Limiting forms of the frequency distribution of the largest or smallest member of a sample", *Proceedings of the Cambridge Philosophical Society*, **24**, 180–190.

Forbes, K.J. and R. Rigobon (2002), "No contagion, only interdependence: measuring stock market comovements", *Journal of Finance*, **57**, 2223–2261.

Foster, R. and S. Kaplan (2001), *Creative Destruction*, Doubleday/Currency, New York.

Fraboni, M. and R. Salstone (1992), "The WAIS-R number-of-factors quandary: a cluster analytic approach to construct validation", *Educational and Psychological Measurement*, **52**, 603–613.

Fung, W. and D.A. Hsieh (1996), "Performance attribution and style analysis: from mutual funds to hedge funds", Working Paper # 9609, Duke University.

Fung, W. and D.A. Hsieh (1997a), "Empirical characteristics of dynamic trading strategies: the case of hedge funds", *Review of Financial Studies*, **10** (2), 275–302.

Fung, W. and D.A. Hsieh (1997b), "Survivorship bias and investment style in the returns of CTAs", *Journal of Portfolio Management*, **24** (1), 30–41.

Fung, W. and D.A. Hsieh (1998), "Pricing trend following trading strategies: theory and empirical evidence", Final Report to The Foundation For Managed Derivatives Research, September.

Fung, W. and D.A. Hsieh (1999), "A primer on hedge funds", Working Paper, Fuqua School of Business, Duke University.

Fung, W. and D.A. Hsieh (2000a), "The risk in hedge fund strategies: theory and evidence from trend followers", *Review of Financial Studies*, **14** (2), 313–341 [published in 2001].

Fung, W. and D.A. Hsieh (2000b), "Performance characteristics of hedge funds and CTA funds: natural versus spurious biases", *Journal of Financial and Quantitative Analysis*, **35** (3), 291–307.

Fung, W. and D.A. Hsieh (2000c), "Measuring the market impact of hedge funds", *Journal of Empirical Finance*, **7** (1), 1–36.

Fung, W. and D.A. Hsieh (2001a), "Asset-based hedge fund styles and portfolio diversification", Working Paper, Fuqua School of Business, Duke University.

Fung, W. and D.A. Hsieh (2001b), "Benchmark of hedge fund performance, information content and measurement biases", Working Paper [published in 2002 as Fung and Hsieh (2002a)].

Fung, W. and D.A. Hsieh (2002a), "Hedge fund benchmarks: information content and biases", *Financial Analysts Journal*, **58** (1), 22–34.

Fung, W. and D.A. Hsieh (2002b), "Risk in fixed income hedge fund styles", *Journal of Fixed Income*, **12**, 6–27.

Garman, M. (1996a), "Improving on VaR", *Risk*, **9** (5), 61–63.

Garman, M. (1996b), "Taking VaR to pieces", *Risk*, **10** (10), 70–71.

Gatev, E.G., W.N. Goetzmann and K.G. Rouwenhorst (1999), "Pairs trading: performance of a relative value arbitrage rule", Working Paper, Yale School of Management.

Geltner, D. (1991), "Smoothing in appraisal-based returns", *Journal of Real Estate Finance and Economics*, **4** (3), 327–345.

Geltner, D. (1993) "Temporal aggregation in real estate return indices", *Journal of Real Estate Research*, **21** (2), 141–166.

Gibbons, M., S. Ross and J. Shanken (1989), "A test of the efficiency of a given portfolio", *Econometrica*, **57**, 1121–1152.

Glosten, L.R. and R. Jagannathan (1994), "A contingent claim approach to performance evaluation", *Journal of Empirical Finance*, **1** (2), 133–160.

Goetzmann, W., J. Ingersoll Jr. and Z. Ivkovich (2000), "Monthly measurement of daily timers", *Journal of Financial and Quantitative Analysis*, **35**, 257–290.

Goldman, Sachs & Co. and Financial Risk Management Ltd. (1998), "Hedge funds demystified – their potential risk in institutional portfolios", July.

Goldman, Sachs & Co. and Financial Risk Management Ltd. (2000), "Hedge funds revisited", Pension & Endowment Forum.

Goldman, M.B., H.B. Sosin and M.A. Gatto (1979), "Path-dependent options: buy at the low, sell at the high", *Journal of Finance*, **34**, 1111–1127.

Greene, W.H. (2000), *Econometric Analysis*, 4th edn, Prentice Hall, Upper Saddle River, NJ.

Gregoriou, G. (2002), "Hedge fund survival lifetimes", *Journal of Asset Management*, **3** (3), 237–252.

Guthoff, A., A. Pfingsten and J. Wolf (1998), "Der Einfluß einer Begrenzung des Value at Risk oder des Lower Partial Moment One auf die Risikoübernahme", in A. Oehler (Hrsg.), *Credit Risk und Value-at-Risk Alternativen*, Schaffer-Poeschel Verlag, Stuttgart, S. 111–153.

Halkidi, M., Y. Batistakis and M. Vazirgiannis (2001), "On clustering validation techniques", Working Paper, University of Athens.

Hartigan, J. (1975), *Clustering Algorithms*, John Wiley & Sons, New York.

Harvey, A.C. (1989), *Forecasting Structural Time Series Models and the Kalman Filter*, Cambridge University Press, Cambridge.

Harvey, A.C. (1993), *Time Series Models*, 2nd edn, Prentice Hall/Harvester Wheatsheaf, London.

Harvey, C. and A. Siddique (2000), "Conditional skewness in asset pricing tests", *Journal of Finance*, **55**, 1263–1295.

Henriksson, R.D. and R.C. Merton (1981), "On market timing and investment performance II: statistical procedures for evaluating forecasting skills", *Journal of Business*, **54** (4), 513–533.

Huber, P.J. (1981), *Robust Statistics*, John Wiley & Sons, New York.

Hübner, G. (2003), "The generalized Treynor ratio: a note", Working Paper, University of Liège and Maastricht University.

Hwang, S. and S.E. Satchell (2001), "Tracking error: ex-ante versus ex-post measures", Working Paper, City University Business School.

Irwin, S., C. Zulauf and B. Ward (1994), "The predictability of managed futures returns", *Journal of Derivatives*, **Winter**, 20–27.

Jacobs, B.I. and K.N. Levy (1999), "Alpha transport with derivatives", *Journal of Portfolio Management*, **25** (5), 55–60.

Jaeger, L. (2002a), *Managing Risk in Alternative Investment Strategies: Investing in Hedge Funds and Managed Futures*, Financial Times/Prentice Hall, New York.

Jaeger, L. (2002b), "The significance of liquidity and transparency for multi-manager hedge fund portfolios", in Capital Market Risk Advisors (ed.) and AIMA Research, *A Guide to Fund of Hedge Funds Management and Investment*, October, pp. 44–47.

Jain, A.K. and R.C. Dubes (1988), *Algorithms for Clustering Data*, Prentice Hall, Englewood Cliffs, NJ.

Jardine, N. and R. Sibson (1971), *Mathematical Taxonomy*, John Wiley & Sons, London.

Jarque, C.M. and A.K. Bera (1987), "A test for normality of observations and regression residuals", *International Statistical Review*, **55**, 163–172.

Jegadeesh, N. and S. Titman (1993), "Returns to buying winners and selling losers: implications for stock market efficiency", *Journal of Finance*, **48**, 65–91.

Jensen, M.C. (1968), "The performance of mutual funds in the period 1945–1964", *Journal of Finance*, **23**, 389–416.

Jobson, J.D. and B. Korkie (1981), "Performance hypothesis testing with the Sharpe and Treynor measures", *Journal of Finance*, **36**, 888–908.

Johnson, S.C. (1967), "Hierarchical clustering schemes", *Psychometrika*, **2**, 241–254.

Jorion, Ph. (1985), "International portfolio diversification with estimation risk", *Journal of Business*, **58**, 59–78.

Jorion, Ph. (1997), "Value at Risk: the new benchmark for controlling market risk", University of California, Irvine, CA.

Kahneman, D. and A. Tversky (1979), "Prospect theory: an analysis of choice under risk", *Econometrica*, **47**, 263–291.

Kallberg, J.G. and W.T. Ziemba (1984), "Mis-specification in portfolio selection problems", in G. Bamberg and A. Spremann (eds), *Risk and Capital*, Springer-Verlag, New York, pp. 74–87.

Kalman, H.E. (1940), "Transversal filters", *Proceedings of the IRE*, **28**, 302–310.

Kat, H. (2003), "10 Things that investors should know about hedge funds", *Journal of Wealth Management*, **5** (4), 72–81.

Kat, H. and S. Lu (2002), "An excursion into the statistical properties of hedge fund returns", Working Paper, City University.

Kat, H. and J. Miffre (2002), "Performance evaluation and conditioning information: the case of hedge funds", Working Paper, University of Reading.

Kaufman, L. and P. Rousseuw (1990), *Finding Groups in Data*, John Wiley & Sons, New York.

Kazemi, H. and G. Martin (2000), "Issues in asset allocation", Working Paper, Schneeweis Partners, LLC.

Kazemi, H. and Th. Schneeweis (2003), "Conditional performance of hedge funds", Working Paper, Center for International Securities and Derivatives Markets.

Keating, C. and W.F. Shadwick (2002), "A universal performance measure", Finance Development Centre, London, January.

Kendall, M.G. (1980), *Multivariate Analysis*, 2nd edn, Griffin, London.

Kim, T.H., D. Stone and A. White (2000), "Asymptotic and Bayesian confidence intervals for Sharpe style weights", Working Paper, University of California, San Diego, CA.

Kraus, A. and R. Litzenberger (1976), "Skewness preference and the valuation of risk assets", *Journal of Finance*, **Sept**, 1085–1100.

Laporte, N. (2003), "Modeling liquidity risk in a VaR model", MSCI Working Paper.

Levy, H. and H.M. Markowitz (1979), "Approximating expected utility by a function of mean and variance", *American Economic Review*, **69**, 308–317.

Lewellen, J. and J. Shanken (2000), "Estimation risk, market efficiency, and the predictability of returns", NBER Working Paper 7699.

Lhabitant, F.S. (1998), "On the (ab)use of expected utility approximations for portfolio selection, portfolio performance and risk management", Working Paper, HEC University of Lausanne.

Lhabitant, F.S. (2000), "Derivatives in portfolio management: why beating the market is easy", *Derivatives Quartely*, **7** (2), 37–46.

Lhabitant, F.S. (2001), "Assessing market risk for hedge funds and hedge funds portfolios", *Journal of Risk Finance*, **Spring**, 1–17.

Lhabitant, F.S. (2002a), "Risk management with style", *European Investment Review*, **1**, 65–71.

Lhabitant, F.S. (2002b), "Anatomie einer long/short transaction", in *Die hedge funds verstehen*, Coninco Verlag, Montreux, pp. 223–226.

Lhabitant, F.S. (2002c), *Hedge Funds: Myths and Limits*, John Wiley & Sons, London.

Lhabitant, F.S. (2003), "Investir dans les hedge funds: un regard quantitatif dans la boîte noire", *Banque & Marchés*, **63**, 40–47.

Lhabitant, F.S. (2004), "Hedge funds: a look beyond the sample", in G. Gregoriou and F. Rouah (eds), *Readings in Hedge Funds*.

Lhabitant, F.S. and M. Learned (2003), "Hedge fund diversification: how much is enough?", *Journal of Alternative Investments*, **5** (3), 23–49.

Lhabitant, F.S. and M. Learned (2004), "Hedge fund diversification: not a free lunch", in G. Gregoriou and F. Rouah (eds), *Readings in Hedge Funds*.

Liang, B. (1999), "On the performance of hedge funds", *Financial Analysts Journal*, **55** (4), 72–85.

Liang, B. (2000), "Hedge funds: the living and the dead", *Journal of Financial and Quantitative Analysis*, **35** (3), 309–326.

Liang, B. (2001), "Hedge fund performance: 1990–1999", *Financial Analysts Journal*, **Jan/Feb**, 11–18.

Liang, B. (2002), "On the performance of alternative investments: CTAs, hedge funds and funds-of-funds", SSRN Working Paper.

Litterman, R. (1996), "Hot spots and hedge", *Journal of Portfolio Management* (Special Issue), 52–75.

Lo, A. (2002), "The statistics of Sharpe ratios", *Financial Analysts Journal*, **58**, 36–52.

Lo, A.W. and C.A. MacKinlay (2002), *A Non-random Walk Down Wall Street*, Princeton University Press, Princeton, NJ.

Lobosco, A. and D. DiBartolomeo (1997), "Approximating the confidence intervals for Sharpe style weights", *Financial Analysts Journal*, **53** (4), 80–85.

Longin, F.M. (2000), "From value at risk to stress testing: the extreme value approach", *Journal of Banking and Finance*, **24**, 1097–1130.

Loretan, M. and W.B. English (2000), "Evaluating 'correlation breakdowns' during periods of market volatility", in *Bank for International Settlements: International Financial Markets and the Implications for Monetary and Financial Stability*, Bank for International Settlements, Switzerland, pp. 214–231.

MacQueen, J. (1967), "Some methods for classification and analysis of multivariate observations", in L.M. Le Cam and J. Neyman (eds), *Proceedings of the Fifth Berkeley Symposium on Mathematical Statistics and Probability*, Vol. I, *Statistics*, University of California Press, Berkeley, CA, pp. 281–297.

Malkiel, B.G. (1995), "Returns from investing in equity mutual funds, 1971 to 1991", *Journal of Finance*, **50** (2), 549–572.

Markowitz, H. (1952), "Portfolio selection", *Journal of Finance*, **7**, 77–91.

Markowitz, H.M. (1959), *Portfolio Selection: Efficient Diversification of Investments*, John Wiley & Sons, New York.

Marmer, H.S. and F.K. Ng (1993), "Mean–semivariance analysis of option-based strategies: a total mix perspective", *Financial Analysts Journal*, **May/June**, 47–54.

Martin, G. (2001), "Making sense of hedge fund returns: a new approach", in E. Acar (ed.), *Added Value in Financial Institutions: Risk or Return*, FT Publishing, London, pp. 165–182.

McFall Lamm, R. (1999), "Why not 100% hedge fund?", *The Journal of Investing*, **Winter**, 87–97.

McFall Lamm Jr., R. and T.E. Ghaleb-Harter (2001), "An update on hedge fund performance: is a bubble developing?", Deutsche Asset Management Research Monograph.

Merriken, H.E. (1994), "Analytical approaches to limit downside risk: semivariance and the need for liquidity", *Journal of Investing*, **3** (3), 65–72.

Michaud, R.O. (1989), "The Markowitz optimization enigma: is 'optimized' optimal?", *Financial Analysts Journal*, **Jan/Feb**, 31–42.

Michaud, R. (1998), *Efficient Asset Management: A Practical Guide to Stock Portfolio Optimization and Asset Allocation*, Harvard Business School Publishing, Boston.

Mitchell, M. and T. Pulvino (2001), "Characteristics of risk in risk arbitrage", *Journal of Finance*, **56** (6), 2135–2176.

Mitev, T. (1995), "Classification of commodity trading advisors using maximum likelihood factor analysis", Working Paper, University of Massachusetts.

Modigliani, L. (1997), "Are hedge funds worth the risk?", *U.S. Investment Perspectives*, Morgan Stanley Dean Witter, December.

Modigliani, F. and L. Modigliani (1997), "Risk-adjusted performance", *Journal of Portfolio Management*, **23**, 45–54.

Morrison, D.F. (1976), *Multivariate Statistical Methods*, 2nd edn, McGraw-Hill, New York.

Newman, P., M. Milgate and J. Eatwell (eds) (1992), *The New Palgrave Dictionary of Money and Finance*, Macmillan, London (three volumes).

Otten, R. and D. Bams (2000), "Statistical test for return-based style analysis", Working Paper, Maastricht University.

Perret-Gentil, C. and M.P. Victoria-Feser (2003), "Robust mean–variance portfolio selection", Working Paper, University of Geneva, April.

President's Working Group on Financial Markets (1999), "Hedge funds, leverage and the lessons of long-term capital management", Working Paper.

President's Working Group on Financial Markets (2000), "Sound practices for hedge fund managers", Working Paper.

Putnam Lovell (2002), "Institutional or institutionalized: are hedge funds crazy", Discussion Paper, December.

Rahl, L. (2000), *Risk Budgeting: A New Approach to Investing*, Risk Books, London.

Rahl, L. (2001), "NAV/fair value practices survey results", *Journal of Alternative Investments*, **Winter**, 55–58.

Ramsey, J.B. (1969), "Tests for specification errors in classical linear least-squares regression analysis", *Journal of the Royal Statisitical Society, Series B*, **31**, 350–371.

Ranaldo, A. and L. Favre (2003), "How to price hedge funds: from two- to four-moment CAPM", UBS Research Paper.

Rand, W.M. (1971), "Objective criteria for the evaluation of clustering methods", *Journal of the American Statistical Association*, **66**, 846–850.

Rathjens, P. (2001), "Sources of returns and risk in hedge funds", Arrowstreet Capital, L.P.

Reinganum, M.R. (1981), "Misspecification of capital asset pricing: empirical anomalies based on earnings yield and market values", *Journal of Financial Economics*, **9**, 19–46.

Reynolds Parker, V. (1996), "International investing coupled with enhanced currency overlay: an opportunity for perfectly portable alpha".

Reynolds Parker, V. (2001), *Managing Hedge Fund Risk*, Risk Books, London.

Rockafellar, R.T. and S. Uryasev (2002), "Optimization of conditional value at risk", *Journal of Risk*, **2**, 21–41.

Roll, R. (1977), "A critique of the asset pricing theory's tests – Part I: On past and potential testability of the theory", *Journal of Financial Economics*, **4**, 129–176.

Ronn, E.I., A. Sayrak and S. Tompaidis (2000), "The impact of large changes in asset prices on intra-market correlations in the domestic and international markets", Manuscript.

Rousseuw, P.J. and A.M. Leroy (1987), *Robust Regression and Outlier Detection*, John Wiley & Sons, New York.

Rouwenhorst, K.G. (1998), "International momentum strategies", *Journal of Finance*, **53**, 267–284.

Rouwenhorst, K.G. (1999), "Local return factors and turnover in emerging stock markets", *Journal of Finance*, **54**, 1439–1464.

Rubens, J.H., D.A. Louton and E.J. Yobaccio (1998), "Measuring the significance of diversification gains", *Journal of Real Estate Research*, **16**, 73–86.

Rubinstein, M. (1973), "The fundamental theorem of parameter preference security valuation", *Journal of Financial and Quantitative Analysis*, **8** (1), 61–69.

Rudolf, M., H. Wolter and H. Zimmermann (1999), "A linear model for tracking error minimization", *Journal of Banking and Finance*, **23**, 85–103.

Schneeweis, T. (1998a), "Dealing with myths of managed futures", *Journal of Alternative Investments*, **Summer**, 9–17.

Schneeweis, T. (1998b), "Dealing with myths of hedge funds", *Journal of Alternative Investments*, **Winter**, 11–15.

Schneeweis, T. (1999), "Alpha, alpha, who's got the alpha?", *Journal of Alternative Investments*, **2** (3), 83–97.

Schneeweis, T. and S. Chung (2000), "Overview of commodity investment", Working Paper, March (www.aima.org).

Schneeweis, T. and G. Martin (2001), "The benefits of hedge funds: asset allocation for the institutional investor", *Journal of Alternative Investments*, **4** (3), 27–37.

Schneeweis, T. and J.F. Pescatore (1999), *The Handbook of Alternative Investment Strategies*, Institutional Investor, London.

Schneeweis, T. and R. Spurgin (1996), "Comparisons of commodity and managed futures benchmark indices", CISDM Working Paper Series, August.

Schneeweis, Th. and R. Spurgin (1997), "Comparisons of commodity and managed futures benchmark benchmarks", *Journal of Derivatives*, **Summer**, 33–50.

Schneeweis, Th. and R. Spurgin (1998), "Multifactor analysis of hedge funds, managed futures and mutual fund return and risk characteristics", *Journal of Alternative Investments*, **1**, 1–24.

Schneeweis, T. and R. Spurgin (1999), "Quantitative analysis of hedge fund and managed futures return and risk characteristics", in P. Lake (ed.), *Evaluating and Implementing Hedge Fund Strategies*, 2nd edn, Euromoney Books, London.

Schneeweis, T. and R. Spurgin (2000a), "Dealing with myths of traditional stock and bond performance", *AIMA Newsletter*, February.

Schneeweis, T. and R. Spurgin (2000b), "Hedge funds: portfolio risk diversifiers, return enhancers or both?", *AIMA Newsletter*, July.

Schneeweis, T. and R. Spurgin (2000c), "The benefits of index option-based strategies for institutional portfolios", *AIMA Newsletter*, June.

Schneeweis, Th. and R. Spurgin (2000d), "The benefits of index option-based strategies for institutional portfolios: summary version", Working Paper, CISDM, University of Massachusetts.

Schneeweis, T. and R. Spurgin (2001), "Alternative investments: what drives the returns?", *AIMA Newsletter*, June.

Schneeweis, Th., R. Spurgin and D. McCarthy (1996a), "Survivor bias in commodity trading advisor performance", *Journal of Alternative Investments*, **1**, 1–24.

Schneeweis, Th., R. Spurgin and M. Potter (1996b), "Managed futures and hedge fund investment for downside equity risk management", *Derivatives Quarterly*, **Fall**, 62–72.

Schneeweis, T., R. Spurgin and V.N. Karavas (2000), "Alternative investments in the institutional portfolio", AIMA Research.

Schneeweis, T., H. Kazemi and G. Martin (2001), "Understanding hedge fund performance: research results and rules of thumb for the institutional investor", Research Paper, Lehman Brothers, November.

Scott, R. and P. Horvath (1980), "On the direction of preference for moments of higher order than the variance", *Journal of Finance*, **35**, 910–919.

Sharpe, W.F. (1964), "Capital asset prices: a theory of capital market equilibrium under conditions of risk", *Journal of Finance*, **19**, 425–442.

Sharpe, W.F. (1966), "Mutual fund performance", *Journal of Business*, **39**, 119–138.

Sharpe, W.F. (1987), *Asset Allocation Tools*, 2nd edn, The Scientific Press, New York.

Sharpe, W.F. (1988), "Determining a fund's effective asset mix", *Investment Management Review*, **Dec**, 59–69.

Sharpe, W.F. (1992), "Asset allocation: management style and performance measurement", *Journal of Portfolio Management*, **18** (2), 7–19.

Sharpe, W.F. (1994), "The Sharpe ratio", *Journal of Portfolio Management*, **Fall**, 49–58.

Sharpe, W.F., G.J. Alexander and J.V. Bailey (1998), *Investments*, 6th edn, Prentice Hall, Englewood Cliffs, NJ.

Siegmann, A. and A. Lucas (2002), "Explaining hedge fund investment styles by loss aversion: a rational alternative", Tinbergen Institute Discussion Paper, May.

Sneath, P.H.A. and R.R. Sokal (1973), *Numerical Taxonomy*, Freeman, San Francisco, CA.

Sortino, F. and R.A.H. van der Meer (1991), "Downside risk", *Journal of Portfolio Management*, **Summer**, 27–31.

Sortino, F. and L. Price (1994), "Performance measurement in a downside risk-framework", *Journal of Investing*, **Fall**, 59–65.

Sortino, F., R. van der Meer and A. Plantinga (1999a), "The Dutch triangle: a framework to measure upside potential relative to downside risk", *Journal of Portfolio Management*, **Fall**, 50–58.

Sortino, F., R. van der Meer and A. Plantinga (1999b), "The upside potential ratio", *Journal of Performance Measurement*, **4** (1), 10–15.

Stattman, D. (1980), "Book values and expected stock returns", unpublished MBA Honors paper, University of Chicago.

Summers, L.H. (1985), "On economics and finance", *Journal of Finance*, **40**, 633–635.

Swinkels, L.A.P. and P.J. van der Sluis (2001), "Return-based style analysis with time-varying exposures", Working Paper, Tilburg University.

Tamarout, Z.B. (2001a), "Credit in convertible bonds: a critical view (Part I)", *AIMA Newsletter*, February.

Tamarout, Z.B. (2001b), "Credit in convertible bonds: a critical view (Part II)", *AIMA Newsletter*, December.

Till, H. (2002a), "Measuring risk-adjusted returns in alternative investments", *Quantitative Finance*, **2**, 237–238.

Till, H. (2002b), "Risk considerations unique to hedge funds", *Quantitative Finance*, **2**, 409–411.

Till, H. and J. Eagleeye (2002), "Traditional investment versus absolute return programs", *Quantitative Finance*, **3**, 42–47.

Treynor, J.L. (1966), "How to rate management of investment funds", *Harvard Business Review*, **43**, 63–75.

Treynor, J.L. and F. Black (1973), "Portfolio selection using special information, under the assumptions of the diagonal model, with mean–variance portfolio objectives, and without constraints", in G.P. Szego and K. Shell (eds), *Mathematical Methods in Investment and Finance*, North-Holland, Amsterdam, pp. 367–384.

Treynor, J.L. and K. Mazuy (1966), "Can mutual funds outguess the market?", *Harvard Business Review*, **44**, 131–136.

Tryon, R.C. and D.E. Bailey (1973), *Cluster Analysis*, McGraw-Hill, New York.

Von Neumann, J. and O. Morgenstern (1947), *Theory of Games and Economic Behavior*, 2nd edn, Princeton University Press, Princeton, NJ.

Ward, J.H. (1963), "Hierarchical grouping to optimize an objective function", *Journal of the American Statistical Association*, **58**, 236–244.

White, H. (1980), "A heteroscedasticity-consistent covariance matrix estimator and a direct test for heteroscedasticity", *Econometrica*, **48**, 812–838.

Yoon, G. (2003), "Correlation coefficients, heteroskedasticity, and contagion of financial crisis", Working Paper, Pusan National University and University of York.

Zadeh, L. (1965), "Fuzzy sets", *Information Control*, **8**, 338–353.

Zangari, P. (1996), "A VaR methodology for portfolios that include options", *Risk Metrics*[TM] *– Monitor*, **Q1**, 4–12.

Ziemba, W.T. (2003), "The stochastic programming approach to asset, liability and wealth management", Monograph, The Research Foundation of The Association for Investment Management and Research.

Index